Atlas of NATIONAL PARKS *and* RESERVES *of* South Africa

Atlas of NATIONAL PARKS *and* RESERVES *of* South Africa

with text by
Mariëlle Renssen

MapStudio

Contents

Quickfinder

Alphabetical list of content

Overview: Southern Africa

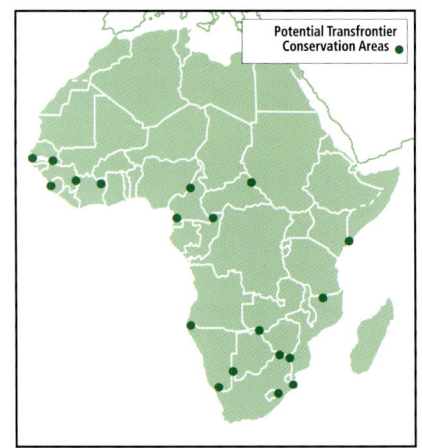

Peace Parks

The concept of Peace Parks is slowly gaining momentum, with many proposals in place for the next few years.

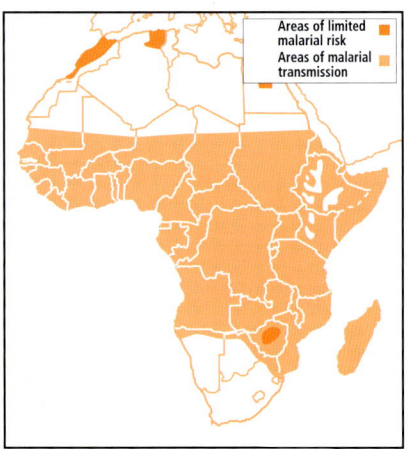

Areas of limited malarial risk
Areas of malarial transmission

Malaria Areas

Malaria is a major problem in Africa for locals as well as tourists. It is always advisable to take the necessary medication and injections prior to departure, as prevention is better than cure.

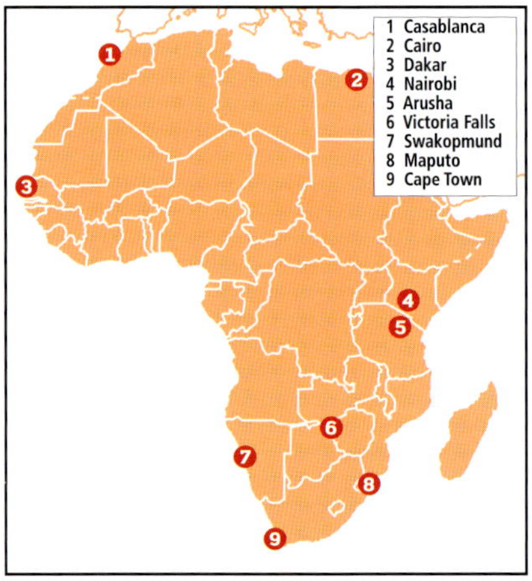

African Adventure Capitals

It is a misconception that locals walk barefoot and communication is restricted to antiquated telephone systems. Africa's capitals are remarkably developed and boast a surprisingly sophisticated infrastructure. Adventurers should enjoy success with most of their information needs, particularly in the more popular travel destinations, as indicated on the map. These destinations are the main adventure activity hotspots or serve as the best point of entry to specific adventure regions.

Km 500
Mi 300

N

Luau●

Lobito ●

●Huambo

A N G O L A

Cuito
●Cuanavale

Kavango

Kunene

Mau

World's largest inland delta: Okavango Delta (covers approximately 15,000km²/5790 sq. miles)

N A M I B I A

Swakopmund ●
Walvis Bay ●

■Windhoek

B O T S W A N A

The small town of Kolmanskop was once heralded as a valuable centre for the region's fledgling diamond industry. In its heyday it was alive with starry-eyed prospectors delving the desert sands for precious stones during the boom times. Its attraction now is as a tourist stop to explore the sand-ravaged ghost town.

Lüderitz ●

Keetmanshoop
●

The Orange River (also known as the Gariep River) forms a natural border between South Africa and Namibia. Originating in the high mountain slopes of the Drakensberg on the eastern coast of southern Africa, the Orange empties into the Atlantic, stretching some 2,200km (1367mi) across what is mostly dry, arid and inhospitable terrain.

Orange/Gariep

●Upington

Springbok
●

S O U T H
A F R I C A

Beaufort West ●

Knysna

1 Casablanca
2 Cairo
3 Dakar
4 Nairobi
5 Arusha
6 Victoria Falls
7 Swakopmund
8 Maputo
9 Cape Town

Cape Town, with its moderate climate, scenic splendour and a high profile as one of the world's top tourist destinations, currently enjoys ever-growing acclaim in the international holiday and hospitality industry and, especially after September 11, has a newfound status as one of the safest destinations in the world. According to the World Trade Organisation, South Africa has moved up from the 52nd most popular destination in the early 1990s to 25th in 2002.

Map labels

DEMOCRATIC REPUBLIC OF THE CONGO

T A N Z A N I A

Lake Malawi

Kitwe•

Z A M B I A

M A L A W I

Lilongwe ■

Lusaka ■

Cahora Bassa Dam

Zambezi

Lake Kariba

Z I M B A B W E

M O Z A M B I Q U E

Mutare•

•**Beira**

The capital of Zimbabwe was known as Salisbury until President Robert Mugabe adopted the city's traditional name in 1982, the change being an attempt to rid the African nation of its colonial past. It had previously been known as Southern Rhodesia (until 1964) and then as Rhodesia ('Northern Rhodesia' was renamed Zambia).

•**Inhambane**

Gaborone

Nelspruit

World's shortest border: Botswana's border with Zambia (70m/765yd)

Pretoria ■

World's largest salt pans: Makgadikgadi pans complex (covers approximately 12,000km²/4632 sq. miles)

Mbabane ■

S W A Z I L A N D

Bloemfontein ■

Maseru ■ **L E S O T H O**

•**Durban**

•**Port Edward**

Known as Lourenço Marques in its colonial heyday as a popular resort town famed for relaxed hospitality, Maputo is one of the most important port and harbour towns on Africa's southeast coast. Maputo acts as the departure point for much of southern Africa's gold bullion destined for the rest of the world.

•**East London**

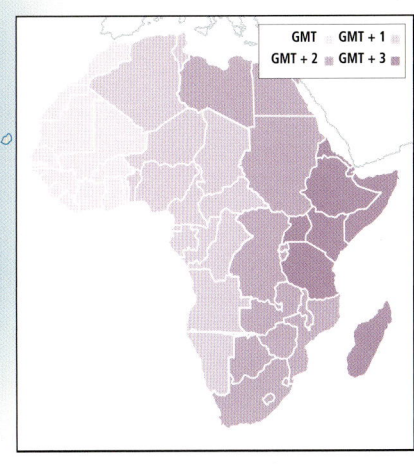

GMT | GMT + 1 | GMT + 2 | GMT + 3

Time zones

Africa is fairly conveniently broken-up into appropriate time zones based on the geological positioning. The Democratic of the Congo is split up into two time zones due to its width and position in Africa.

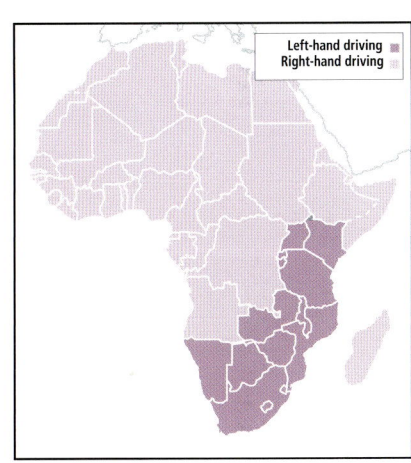

Left-hand driving
Right-hand driving

Left or Right?

In many parts of Africa, drivers are required to drive on the left-hand side of the road, which requires an unusual 'acclimatisation' period for many foreign travellers. It is important to ascertain the rules of the road for your destination prior to departure.

BE SAFE

Most of the capital cities in Africa are generally as safe as anywhere in the world, but nonetheless the issue of personal safety and security remains an area of some concern in many parts of the continent. Generally, throngs of people - both locals and visitors - tend to discourage serious crime, but they may also attract chancers, with pickpockets, muggers and other petty criminals taking advantage of unsuspecting Westerners porting cameras and other sophisticated equipment.

Where such incidents – have been reported (as opposed to being brushed off due to the travellers' time constraints or fear of reprisal), these tend to be restricted to more secluded or out-of-the-way places, and in general to the hours after darkness has fallen. This is particularly true of the seedier areas, such as cities' unofficial drug enclaves and red-light districts catering for a sex industry which, more often than not, caters almost exclusively for the tourism market. Be warned.

CANNED HUNTING

An alarming number of unscrupulous 'safari operators' offer the 'thrill of the hunt' to equally conscience-deficient travellers determined to leave Africa with a trophy of a lion skin or zebra pelt. While there are a number of officially sanctioned and approved hunting operations scattered throughout Africa – the merits of which are best determined by undividuals – there are increasing reports of 'canned hunting'. Here lions are enclosed in restricted areas with little chance of escape, and are easily trapped in the sites of a firearm. Even pro-hunting organisations such as Safari Hunters International have condemned canned hunts as barbaric.

Parks covered in this atlas

KEY

1 **East London Coast Conservation Area:**
   Cape Henderson NR
   Fort Pato NR
   Gulu NR
   Kwelera NR
   Umtiza NR

2 **Great Fish River Reserve Complex:**
   Andries Vosloo Kudu NR
   Sam Knott NR
   Doubledrift GR

3 **uKhahlamba-Drakensberg Park:**
North:
   iNjasuti
   Rugged Glen
   Cathedral Peak
   Monk's Cowl
Central:
   Kamberg
   Lotheni
   Giant's Castle
   Highmoor
   Mkhomazi
South:
   Bushman's Nek Valley
   Cobham NR
   Garden Castle
   Vergelegen

4 **Greater St Lucia Wetland Park:**
   Cape Vidal
   Sodwana Bay NP
   St Lucia Marine Reserve
   St Lucia Marine Sanctuary
   Mfabeni/Mission Rocks
   Charters Creek
   False Bay Park
   Fanie's Island
   Lake eTeza
   Mapelane NR

5 **Maputaland:**
   Lake Sibaya
   Kosi Bay NR

6 **Kruger NP**
Mpumalanga:
   Londolozi GR
   Sabi Sand GR
   Mthethomusha GR
Limpopo:
   Andover GR
   Manyeleti GR
   Timbavati GR
   Klaserie NR
   Umbabat NR
   Thornybush GR
   Kapama GR
   Makuya GR
   Letaba Ranch GR

7 **Cradle of Humankind:**
   Heia Safari GR
   Rhino and Lion Reserve
   The Cradle NR
   Hartbeeshoek GR

8 **Magaliesberg Nature Area:**
   Kgaswane Mountain Reserve
   Mountain Sanctuary Park
   Hartbeespoort Dam NR

LEGEND FOR INFO PANELS

🛏	Accommodation
🛏	Self catering
🏕	Campsite
🚐	Caravan park
🥾	Trails

LEGEND FOR PARK MAPS
See page 142

NAMIBIA

Kgalagadi Transfrontier Park

Molopo NR

Ai-Ais/Richtersveld Transfrontier Park

Augrabies Falls NP

Spitskop NR

Goegap NR

Namaqua NP

Northern Cape

Akkerendam NR

Oorlogskloof NR

Bird Island

Cederberg Wilderness Area

Tankwa Karoo NP

Karoo NP

Verlorenvlei

Rocherpan NR

Matjiesrivier NR

Western Cape

Columbine NR

Groot Winterhoek Wilderness Area

West Coast NP

Anysberg NR

Swartberg NR

Tienie Versfeld Wildflower Reserve

Gamkaberg NR

Kammanassie NR

Jonkershoek NR

Limietberg NR

Marloth NR

Boosmansbos Wilderness Area

Assegaaibosch NR

Hawekwas Cons. Area

Outeniqua NR

Table Mountain NP

Hottentots Holland NR

Vrolijkheid NR

Bontebok NP

Grootvadersbosch NR

Gouritz Wilderness

Kogelberg Biosphere Reserve

Harold Porter National Botanical Garden

Fernkloof NR

Riviersonderend NR

De Hoop NR

Walker Bay NR

Salmonsdam NR

Waenhuiskrans NR

Agulhas NP

De Mond NR

ZIMBABWE

MOZAMBIQUE

BOTSWANA

Musina NR
Mapungubwe NP
Nwanedi GR
Makuya GR
Honnet GR
Langjan NR
Blouberg NR
Ben Lavin NR
Maleboch NR
Wonderkop NR
Hans Merensky NR
Lapalala Wilderness GR
Limpopo
Polokwane GR
Wolkberg
Ndzalama Wildlife Reserve
Selati GR
Makalali Private Reserve
Balule NR
Kruger NP
D'Nyala NR
Percy Fyfe NR
Wilderness GR
Mokolo Dam NR
Waterberg Biosphere
Doorndraai Dam NR
Blyde Olifants Conservancy
Marakele NP
Mabula GR
Nylsvlei NR
Legalameetse NR
Blyde River Canyon NR
Ben Alberts NR
Ohrigstad Dam NR
Mt Sheba NR
Madikwe GR
Borakalalo NP
Rust de Winter NR
Mabalingwe GR
Lydenburg NR
Gustav Klingbiel NR
Vaalkop Dam NR
Rhenosterspruit NR
Diepsloot NR
Verloren Vallei NR
Sterkspruit
Pilanesberg NP
Tswaing NR
Loskop Dam NR
Ligwalagwala Community Conservation Area
Marico Bosveld NR
Metani GR
Roodeplaat Dam NR
Dullstroom NR
Botsalano GR
Magaliesberg Nature Area
Leeuwkloof Valley Conservancy
Nooitgedacht Dam NR
Songimvelo GR
Lichtenburg Game Breeding Centre
Nooitgedacht GR
Plumari Africa Reserve
Cradle of Humankind
Rietvlei NR
Bronkhorst-spruit Dam NR
Mpumalanga
SWAZILAND
North West
Krugersdorp GR
Klipriviersberg NR,
Marievale Bird Sanctuary
Jericho Dam NR
Tembe Elephant GR
Barberspan Bird Sanctuary
Rondebult Bird Sanctuary
Suikerbos-rand NR
Gauteng
Morgenstond Dam NR
Ndumo GR
Faan Meintjies NR
Pongola Bush NR
Ntendeka Wilderness Area
Pongolapoort NR
Kosi Bay NR
Maputaland
SA Lombard NR
Bloemhof Dam NR
Vryheid Hill NR
Ithala GR
Mkhuze GR
Phinda Resource Reserve
Sandveld NR
Klipfontein NR
Ncandu NR
Greater St Lucia Wetland Park
Mt Everest GR
Chelmsford NR
Thakazulu GR
Hluhluwe-iMfolozi Park
Vaalbos NP
Willem Pretorius NR
Golden Gate Highlands NP
Sterkfontein Dam NR
eMakhosini-Opathe Heritage Park
Erfenis Dam NR
Royal Natal NP
Spioenkop Dam NR
KwaZulu-Natal
Soetdoring NR
Free State
Weenen GR
Wagendrift NR
Richards Bay GR
SOUTH AFRICA
Naval Hill, Signal Hill, Grant's Hill
Moor Park
Blinkwater NR
Craigie Burn NR
uMlalazi NR
aMatikulu NR
Karkloof NR
Rustfontein Dam NR
uKhahlamba-Drakensberg Park
Albert Falls NR
Kalkfontein Dam NR
Midmar Dam NR
uMhlanga Lagoon NR
LESOTHO
Himeville NR
Queen Elizabeth Park
Bluff NR, Kenneth Stainbank NR, Beachwood Mangroves, North Park
Rolfontein NR
Coleford NR
Vernon Crookes NR
Doornkloof NR
Gariep Dam NR
Tussen-die-Riviere GR
Mount Currie NR
uVongo River NR
Oviston NR
Oribi Gorge NR
uMtamvuna NR
Luchaba GR
Mkambati NR
Silaka NR
Hluleka NR
Eastern Cape
Mountain Zebra NP
Tsolwana GR
Cwebe NR
Dwesa NR
Camdeboo NR
Fort Fordyce NR
Mpofu GR
East London Coast Conservation Area
Bosberg NR
Thomas Baines NR
Great Fish River Reserve Complex
Shamwari GR
Addo Elephant NP
Waters Meeting NR
Kariega GR
Lalibela GR
Amakhala GR
Baviaanskloof Wilderness Area
Groendal Wilderness Area
Formosa NR
Woody Cape NR
Tsitsikamma NP
Keurbooms River NR
Robberg NR
National Lake Area
Kidd's Beach NR
Kayser's Beach NR

Cape Town/
Kaapstad

Table Mountain National Park

TABLE MOUNTAIN NP
NEAREST TOWN
Cape Town

NEAREST AIRPORT
Cape Town International

SIZE
29 000ha

FAUNA/FLORA
1 Bontebok
2 Grysbok
3 Caracal
4 Mongoose sp.
5 Cape Clawless Otter
6 Chacma Baboon
7 Sugarbird
8 Ground Woodpecker
9 Rare White Peripatus
10 Table Mountain Ghost Frog
11 Mountain *Fynbos*

MAIN CONTACT DETAILS
021 701 8692
tablemountain@sanparks.org
www.tmnp.co.za

ACCOMMODATION INSIDE PARK
Olifantsbos Cottage
021 701 8692
tablemountain@sanparks.org
www.tmnp.co.za

Eland and Duiker Cottages
021 422 2816

Hoerikwaggo Cottages
021 465 8515

ACCOMMODATION OUTSIDE PARK
021 426 4267
www.tourismcapetown.co.za

Table Mountain's erosion-resistant hulk of sandstone, Cape Town's best-loved, top-rated and most visible landmark, rates equally with the Cape Peninsula as the double "must-see" attraction for visitors to the city. The mountain's fickle tablecloth – now cottony, billowing, tumultuous; now ephemeral, wispy, dissolving – starts off as warm, moisture-laden sea air driven over the craggy buttresses by the "Cape doctor", a demon Southeaster blowing November to March. Sometimes barrelling over at 120km per hour, the moist air cools and condenses into the mutable cloud Capetonians know so well. Visitors of a fit and active persuasion have over 350 routes by which to summit Table Mountain, although they range from easy to very difficult. Any route, simple or tricky, must be planned in detail; the weather is highly capricious and some paths steep, slippery and narrow. Otherwise, in the time it takes to turn 360°, visitors can be zipped up some 1000m in a hi-tech bubble cablecar. The views from the top of Lion's Head are not too shabby either – but, please, no hiking alone. A brand-new 3-day Hoerikwaggo (Khoisan for "sea mountain") trail up and over the famous tabletop dishes up a full-flavoured feast of Table Mountain's spoils. Starting with a harbour boat trip, visitors are whisked through historic parts of the city, then dine on fragrantly spiced Malay dishes and sleep in restored washhouses where slavewomen scrubbed their Dutch masters' clothes. Hitching a ride via the cableway, they explore the length of the *fynbos*-strewn mountaintop, focusing on Nature's finer details with the help of Xhosa-clicking guides, ending up at the stone Overseers Cottage with the city's myriad pinpricks of lights like a sequinned apron below. The trail ends at the foot of Nursery Ravine in Kirstenbosch Gardens, the first botanical garden in the world to be named a UNESCO World Heritage Site.

SEASONAL INFORMATION

Gate opening times
08:00 – 17:00
Day visitors allowed

Thermopylae 1899
Table Bay
SA Seafarer 1966
Lighthouse
Three Anchor Bay 11
Sea Point
Bantry Bay
Clifton Bay
Camps Bay
Camps Bay
Theatre on the Bay
Het Huis te
Kraaiestein 1698
Antipolis 1977
Oudekraal
Llandudno Bay
Romelia 1977
Sandy Bay
Oude Schip
Maori 1909
Boss 400
Hout Bay
Karbonkelberg
Sanctuary Zone
Duiker Island West Fort
Vulcan Rock 1781
Astor
Katzmaru 1970
Die Josie
Chapman's Point
Noordhoek
Toll Booth
Chapman's Bay
Kakapo 1900
Klein Slangkop Point
Kommetjie Bay
Slangkop Point
Clan Munroe 1905
The Anchor
Slangkop
174m
Die Eiland
Witsand Bay
Schuster's Bay
Schusterskraal
Bonteberg
227m
Lookout
Post
Menskop Point
Olifantsbos Bay
Nolloth
1965
Phyllisia 1968
Hoek van
Bobbejaan
Bloubergstrand
Platboom Bay
Cape of Good Hope
Shir-Yib
1970

Athens 1865
Victoria & Alfred
Waterfront
Cape Town
Convention
Centre
Noon
Gun
Castle of
Good Hope
Lion's
Head
670m
Rhodes
Memorial
Devil's Peak 1001m
Orion's Cave
Kirstenbosch
National Botanical
Garden
Boshof
Gateway
**Table Mountain
National Park**
Van Riebeeck's
Hedge
Alphen 1714
Maynardville
Open Air
Theatre
Constantia
Kenilworth
Race Course
Little
Lion's
Head
436m
World of
Birds
7
Groot
Constantia
1685
The
Leopard
Mariner's
Wharf
Constantiaberg
928m
Elephant's Eye
Cave
The Lonely
Bridge
Spotty
Dog
Rondevlei
Zeekeuwlei
Rondevlei
Bird Sanctuary
Hout
Bay
11
Tokai
Forest
Higher
Steenberg Peak
537m Muizenberg
Cave
Muizenberg
Chapman's Peak
592m
Silvermine
1687
10
Neptune's Corner
Rhodes Cottage
Tunnel
Cave
Silvermine
Nature Reserve
Peer's
Cave
Kalk Bay Cave
5.5
Trappies Caves
*False
Bay*
Kakapo 1900
*Tidal
Lagoon*
1
Fish Hoek
Fish Hoek Bay
Rooikrans
364m
Else Peak
303m
Skeleton Rock
Hartenberg
Circa 1730
Else Bay
**Table Mountain
National Park**
**Simon's
Town**
Clan Stuart 1914
*Simon's
Bay*
Lighthouse
Phoenix 1829
Just Nuisance
Statue
Red Hill
256m
Simonsberg
548m
*SWARTKOP
MOUNTAINS*
Miller's Point
Camel
Rock
7.5
Dassiekop
314m
8 M4
M65
Smitswinkel Bay
Thomas T Tucker 1942
Olifantsbos
Cottage
Judas Peak
319m
Blaasbalk Cave
**Cape of Good Hope
Nature Reserve**
Old
Cannon
Dias
Monument
1488
Da Gama
Monument 1497
Bordjiesrif
114m
Kommetjieberg
107m Tania 1972
Matrooskop
GROOT-BLOUBERG
Rooikrans
Lighthouse
Cape Point
Canal Walk
M5
N1
N1
R102
N2
SA Astronomical
Observatory
N2
M5
M17
M9
M6
M63
M41
M42
M5
M41
M5
M4
M5
R310
M6
M65
M4
M65
M4
M65
M6

ATLANTIC OCEAN

TWELVE APOSTLES
CONSTANTIABERG

**Kirstenbosch
National Botanical
Garden**

To Skeleton Gorge
Yellowwood Trail
Skeleton Stream
Stinkwood Trail
Reservoirs
(No Access)
Fynbos Walk
Proteas
Nursery Stream
Buchus
Ericas
Braille Trail
Smuts Track
Education
Centre
Garden
Centre
Gate 2 Garden
Centre Entrance
The Koppie
Proteas
Cycads
Toilets
Xhosa Hut
Toilets
Lecture Hall
Silver Tree
Tea Room
Lawn
Water-wise
Garden
Parking
Pearson
House
NBI
Admin
Office
Fynbos
Lodge
To Cape Town
Irrigation Dam
(No Entry)
Toilets
*Colonel
Bird's
Bath*
Pearson's
Grave
Useful Plants
Garden
Mathew's
Rockery
Vygies
Fragrance
Garden
Medicinal
Plants
Peninsula
Garden
Vlei
Garden
Pond
Nedbank
Lodge
Pearson
House
To Hout Bay
Seed
Orchard
Toilets
Restios
Concert
Stage
Annuals
Sculpture
Garden
Wooden Gates
Parking
Church of the
Good Shepherd
Van Riebeeck's Hedge
Gate 3
Rycroft Entrance
Gate 1 Visitor's
Centre Entrance
Conservatory
Info & tickets
Visitor's Centre
Bookshop
Gift Shop
Coffee Shop
Toilets
Liesbeek River
Rhodes Drive
Nursery
(no entry)
Garden
Office
Klaassen's Road
Parking
Toilets
M63

The Garden is open all year
08:00 – 19:00 (Sept to Mar)
08:00 – 18:00 (Apr to Aug)

13

Cape Town/Kaapstad

Hottentots Holland Nature Reserve,
Jonkershoek & Assegaaibosch Nature Reserves

These three valley-and-mountain realms form a contiguous expanse of natural wild territory that begs to be explored in hiking boots, on the saddle of a mountainbike or from the vantage point of a 4x4. The smaller Assegaaibosch nestles within the Jonkershoek reserve, whose high-thrusting Jonkershoek mountains strangely enough fall under the greater Hottentots Holland Nature Reserve. And all around the protected *fynbos* wilderness are forestry plantations, offering shady pine-fragrant paths.

The **Hottentots Holland reserve** is best for its two heart-racing kloofing excursions following the Riviersonderend River. If you're reasonably fit, love getting – and staying – wet and have a sense of derring-do, you can choose between the 7m jump of Riviersonderend Canyon or the three waterfalls of Suicide Gorge. Okay, so the 14m gravity-defying leap here gave this last route its name. Your day will be filled with rock scrambling, swimming between towering narrow walls and plummeting into pools – and once in, there's no way out. . .

Sections of the Boland Hiking Trail cross this reserve and you have walk options as varied as 3hrs to 3 days. Or choose from two mountainbiking trails, one 4x4 drive (another on its way) and the first Cape hiking route for the blind, the Palmiet Trail. Plates in Braille emphasise nuggets of interest.

In the **Jonkershoek reserve**, five day-hikes of varying length and difficulty trace their way along the Eerste River, up steep mountain slopes, across scraggy sandstone and quartzite escarpments and through parcels of relic forest. Clear tea-coloured waters splashing over stones and pebbles in the valley contrast with the high wraparound views onto jagged mountain skylines.

If sweat and hot tired feet aren't for you, one of the three short walks in **Assegaaibosch**, to a wild-flower garden, takes just half an hour. Alternatively, find a shady oak, kick back, relax and have a picnic.

HOTTENTOTS HOLLAND NR
NEAREST TOWN
Elgin/Grabouw/Villiersdorp
NEAREST AIRPORT (ALL PARKS)
Cape Town International
SIZE
42 000ha
FAUNA/FLORA
1 Cape Mountain Zebra
2 Eland
3 Bontebok
4 Red Hartebeest
5 Leopard
6 Grey Rhebok
7 Klipspringer
8 Duiker
9 Grysbok
10 Mountain *Fynbos*
MAIN CONTACT DETAILS
028 841 4301/2
lourensl@hottentotsholland.co.za
www.capenature.org.za
ACCOMMODATION INSIDE PARK
Huts for hikers only
Tents by request for hikers
Overberg Tourism
028 214 1466
info@overberg.org
www.tourismcapeoverberg.co.za
ACCOMMODATION OUTSIDE PARK
(ALL PARKS))
info@overberg.org
www.tourismcapeoverberg.co.za

JONKERSHOEK NR
NEAREST TOWN
Stellenbosch
SIZE
9800ha
FAUNA
1 Leopard
2 Honey Badger
3 Chacma Baboon
4 Mongoose sp.
5 Rock Agama Lizard
MAIN CONTACT DETAILS
021 866 1560
jonkerhk@cncjnk.wcape.gov.za

ASSEGAAIBOSCH NR
NEAREST TOWN
Stellenbosch
SIZE
204ha
FLORA/FAUNA
1 Frog sp.
2 Red-sided Skink
3 Striped Mouse
4 Mountain *Fynbos*
ACCOMMODATION INSIDE PARK
Assegaaibosch Manor House
021 659 3500/3409
hcassels@capenature.co.za
www.capenature.org.za

Kierie Kwaak
021 883 3163

SEASONAL INFORMATION

Gate opening times
Hottentots Holland:
06:00 – 19:00
Open throughout the year
Jonkershoek/Assegaaibosch:
07:30 – 18:00
Day visitors allowed

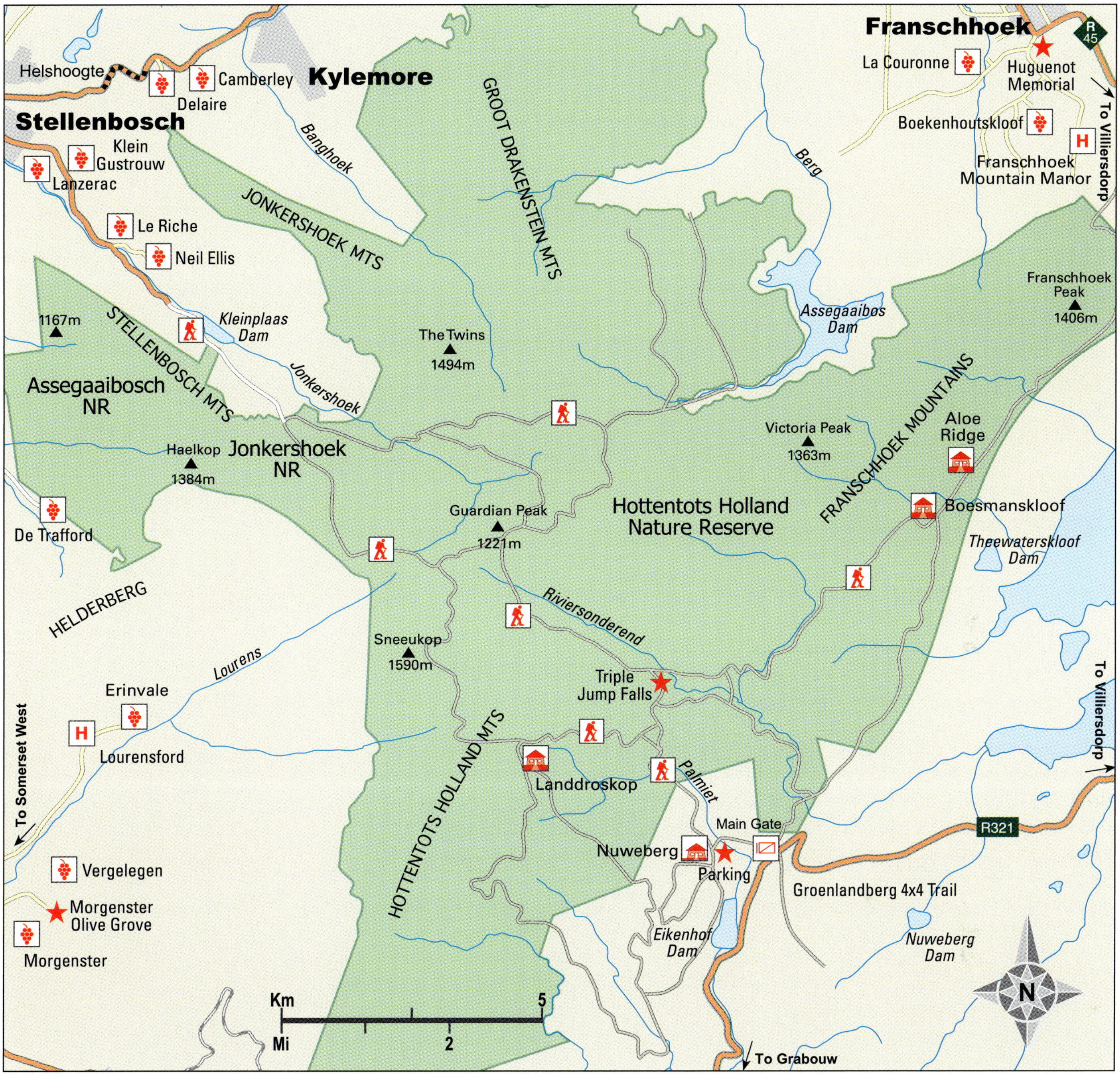

Upper map

Stellenbosch

Helshoogte
Camberley
Delaire
Kylemore

Franschhoek
La Couronne
Huguenot Memorial
Boekenhoutskloof
Franschhoek Mountain Manor
To Villiersdorp

Klein Gustrouw
Lanzerac
Le Riche
Neil Ellis

Banghoek
JONKERSHOEK MTS
GROOT DRAKENSTEIN MTS
Berg
Assegaaibos Dam
Franschhoek Peak
1406m

1167m
Kleinplaas Dam
STELLENBOSCH MTS
Jonkershoek
Assegaaibosch NR
Haelkop 1384m
Jonkershoek NR
De Trafford

The Twins
1494m

Victoria Peak
1363m
Aloe Ridge
FRANSCHHOEK MOUNTAINS
Boesmanskloof
Theewaterskloof Dam

HELDERBERG
Guardian Peak
1221m
Hottentots Holland Nature Reserve
Riviersonderend

Erinvale
H
Lourensford
Lourens
Sneeukop
1590m
HOTTENTOTS HOLLAND MTS
Triple Jump Falls
Landdroskop
Palmiet
Nuweberg
Main Gate
Parking
To Villiersdorp
R321
Groenlandberg 4x4 Trail
To Somerset West

Vergelegen
Morgenster Olive Grove
Morgenster
Eikenhof Dam
Nuweberg Dam

Km 5
Mi 2

N

To Grabouw

Lower map

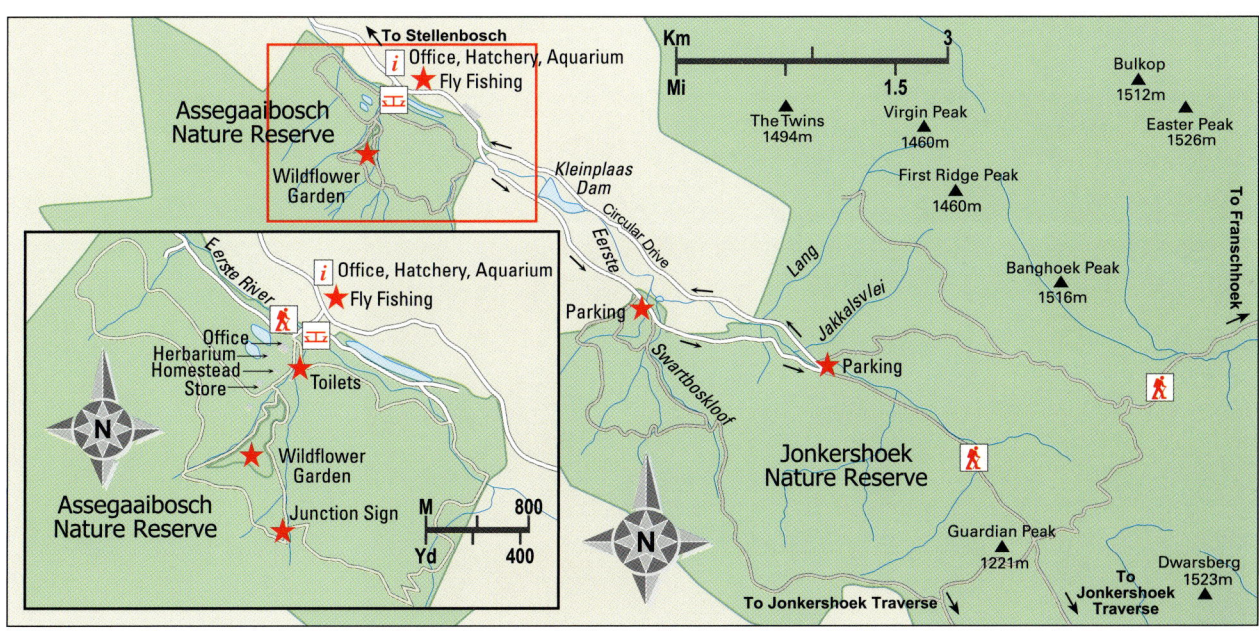

To Stellenbosch
Office, Hatchery, Aquarium
Fly Fishing
i
Assegaaibosch Nature Reserve
Wildflower Garden
Kleinplaas Dam
Circular Drive
Eerste

Km 3
Mi 1.5

The Twins
1494m
Virgin Peak
1460m
Bulkop
1512m
Easter Peak
1526m
First Ridge Peak
1460m

To Franschhoek

Eerste River
Office
Herbarium
Homestead
Store
i Office, Hatchery, Aquarium
Fly Fishing
Toilets
Wildflower Garden
Junction Sign

N

Assegaaibosch Nature Reserve

M 800
Yd 400

Parking
Swartboskloof
Lang
Jakkalsvlei
Banghoek Peak
1516m
Parking

Jonkershoek Nature Reserve

Guardian Peak
1221m
Dwarsberg
1523m
To Jonkershoek Traverse
To Jonkershoek Traverse

N

15

Cape Town/
Kaapstad

Cederberg Wilderness Area,
Matjiesrivier Nature Reserve

The great wild territory of the **Cederberg Wilderness Area**, stretching to infinity under a wheeling sky, is peopled by grotesque human- and animal-like beings transformed into rock. A mountainous area of ancient sandstone, the abrasive powers of wind-blown sand, dissolving rain and biting snow have produced in the Cederberg a landscape of surreal sculptures, balancing boulders and shattered rocks. This is hiking paradise. The less visited northern section, cradled by Thomas Bain's Pakhuis Pass to the north and the characterful old Moravian mission settlement of Wuppertal to the east, has as its centrepiece three pinnacles, the Little, Middle and (regular) Krakadouw peaks. Hikes in the central zone, accessed from Algeria forest station, hint at inherent challenges with intriguing names that can be translated as "Great and Little Heartache" and "Hellish Kloof". No translation needed in the Crystal Pool or Machine Gun Ridge. Most famous is the much-photographed 30m Wolfberg Arch.

Visitors staying at Sanddrif on the Dwarsrivier farm and, further on, Kromrivier, focus on the southern part of the Cederberg – to the east the Wolfberg Cracks and Wolfberg Arch, to the west Maltese Cross and Sneeuberg – the region's highest mountain. Memorable is the seemingly vertical climb up to the Cracks, some nimble slithering and sliding to get to the main aperture, and the scariest moment – worming under an enormous boulder wedged just tens of centimetres above the ground.

The **Matjiesrivier Nature Reserve**, made up of eight farms, is riddled with caves and rocky overhangs displaying precious – and often well-preserved – San rock art that at times dates back 6000 years. Six elephants accompanied by rows of animal-skin-clad figures, believed to be *shamans* in trance ceremonies, give Elephant Cave its name while Stadsaal Caves presents sculpted overhangs, wind-buffeted rock pillars and interconnected caverns. Easy access from Dwarsrivier and Kromrivier.

Cape Town/
Kaapstad

Knysna National Lake Area

KNYSNA NATIONAL LAKE AREA
NEAREST TOWN
Knysna

NEAREST AIRPORT
George

SIZE
1827ha

FAUNA/AVIFAUNA
1 Knysna Seahorse
2 Pied Kingfisher
3 Grey Heron
4 Little Egret
5 Whitebreasted Cormorant
6 Yellowbilled Duck
7 Greater Flamingo
8 Egyptian Goose
9 African Fish Eagle
10 Blue Crane
11 Kelp Gull
12 Knysna Lourie
13 African Black Oystercatcher

MAIN CONTACT DETAILS
044 382 2095
peetj@sanparks.org
www.knysna-info.co.za
www.explore-southafrica.co.za
021 975 4472
reservations@saparks.com
www.saparks.com

ACCOMMODATION INSIDE PARK
None

ACCOMMODATION OUTSIDE PARK
Diepwalle Campsite
044 382 2095
peetj@sanparks.org
www.knysna-info.co.za

Oyster Creek Lodge
The Point
044 382 0808
oystercreek@sainet.co.za
www.oystercreeklodge.co.za

The St James of Knysna
044 382 6750
stjames.knysna@pixie.co.za
www.stjames.co.za

Waterfront Lodge
The Point
044 382 1696
waterfr@mweb.co.za
www.waterfront-lodge.co.za

T
ens of thousands of visitors can't be wrong, and to prove it, Knysna has a couple of times been voted South Africa's most popular town of the year. This holiday hot-spot has more character than most overrun leisure destinations, partly due to its position on the 20km-or-so Knysna lagoon, partly due to its pretty Georgian and Victorian building façades. Just be prepared in peak season to sit in miles of bumper-to-bumper traffic along Knysna's main street. . .

In terms of what to do? If the cold wet feel of an oyster sliding down your throat does it for you, stop by the lagoonside Knysna Oyster Co. on Thesen Islands. For oyster aficionados, this is the Pacific Oyster (*Crassostrea gigas*). If it's the beer you like cold and wet (and flavourful), try Mitchells Brewery for naturally brewed Foresters Draught or Bosun's Bitter. For great views, visit the eastern Knysna Head via George Rex Drive; a footpath to the shoreline, over a bridge to a rock outcrop provides a great vantage point. There is also a viewsite.

If you want to be waterbound, enjoy a *John Benn* cruise on the lagoon, or hire a houseboat of your own. Naturalists can be dropped off at the Western Head's Featherbed Nature Reserve to walk the Bushbuck Trail.

If the natural outdoors is your great escape, go no further than the Harkerville and Diepwalle state forests. Towering yellowwoods with robust girths, a glimpse of the Knysna Lourie's crimson wings in flight, sighing wind and dappled sunlight are all yours on foot or mountainbike. There's a whole bunch of trails to choose from, snaking through remnant indigenous hardwoods and pine and eucalypt plantations. Don't expect to bump into any of the three or so grey pachyderms recently spotted in Diepwalle – Knysna's remaining elephants are secretive, silent and terribly shy!

SEASONAL INFORMATION

Gate opening times
24 hours
Day visitors allowed

Goudveld

Forest Massage

Armitage Bowls

Lelievlei
Nature
Reserve

Rondebosse

Rooiels

Jonkersberg
884m

Grootdraai

Gouna

Gouna

Portland Manor

Portland Mini
Market

Heatherhill Herbs

Bushpig Fabric

Fairie Glen
Berry Farm

Forest Children

Gouna

Steenbras

Phantom Pass

Knysna

To Uniondale

Grootkops

George Rex
Slipway

Knysna National
Lake Area

R339

Concordia

Akkerkloof
Dam

To Sedgefield

Lightleys
Houseboats

Local Crafters

Sout

Pledge
Nature
Reserve

i

Cycads

N2

Belvidere
Church

Lagoon Side Traders

Knysna

George Rex Grave

Kruisfontein

N2

Mitchells Brewery

Renette's
Candles

Knysna
Lagoon

John Benn
Jetty

Knysna Oyster Co.

Birds of Africa

Hornlee

To Plettenberg Bay

Lake Brenton

Thesen's
Island

Knysna National
Lake Area

Leisure
Island

Steenbok
Nature
Reserve

Brenton-on-
Sea

Butterfly
Reserve

Phantom

Woodbourne

Buffels
Bay

Castle Rock

Featherbed
Nature Reserve

Paquita

The Fairholme

Eastern
Head

Western Head

Duikerrots

East Cape

Walker
Bay

Buffalo Bay

Walker Point

INDIAN OCEAN

N

Km   2,5

Mi   1.25

19

Cape Town/
Kaapstad

West Coast National Park,
Columbine & Tienie Versfeld Reserves

The West Coast is for those who want to get away from trafficked highways, city lights and electronic information overload. Cold Benguela Current-washed shores are stark, rocky and windswept, the coastline is hugged by rudimentary villages of whitewashed fishermen's cottages, and visitor accommodation is rustic and unpretentious. Which is just the way anglers, 4x4 enthusiasts, naturalists and hikers like it. Each spring, though, the West Coast's stern countenance puts on a pretty party face. Colourful petals unfurl in the boldest of hues, often blanketing the landscape, depending on the season. The Postberg Nature Reserve on the northwestern shore of Langebaan Lagoon, all part of the **West Coast National Park**, is often the furthest you need go to experience this phenomenon, although the **Tienie Versfeld Wildflower Reserve** in Darling (self-appointed springflower centre) puts on an impressive display too. The turquoise waters of the lagoon lure tens of thousands of migratory birds, which can be observed from several bird hides positioned along its shores. Sometimes, the waters take on a salmon-pink hue as flamingos congregate here; look out too for the threatened African Black Oystercatcher's pillarbox-red beak and legs ("Polly red-stocking" to some).

Expansive beaches, rocky coves and bulky grey granite outcrops characterise Tieties Bay and the shoreline of the **Columbine Nature Reserve**. Anglers and campers love its ruggedness and the sandveld vegetation here also has its day in spring, prettifying the coast with mesembryanthemums and daisies. For something quite different, you can do a tour of, and then stay the night in, the Cape Columbine lighthouse, one of only 15 manually controlled lighthouses (of a total of 45) in the country. It looms 80m above the sea, and its single 400-watt light is magnified by a lens weighing nearly two tons to throw a beam visible for 80km out to sea!

WEST COAST NP
NEAREST TOWN
Langebaan

NEAREST AIRPORT (ALL PARKS)
Cape Town International

SIZE
20 000ha

FAUNA
1 Cape Mountain Zebra
2 Springbok
3 Kudu
4 Southern Right & Humpback Whale
5 Heaviside's & Bottlenosed Dolphin
6 Cape Gannet
7 Lesser & Greater Flamingo
8 African (Jackass) Penguin
9 Cape (Kelp) Gull

MAIN CONTACT DETAILS
022 772 2144
reservations@parks-sa.co.za
www.parks-sa.co.za

ACCOMMODATION INSIDE PARK
Kraalbaai Houseboat, Joanne's Beach
Cottage, Abrahamskraal White House,
Van Breda Cottage
022 772 2144

ACCOMMODATION OUTSIDE PARK
(ALL PARKS)
Langebaan
022 772 1515
lbninfo@mweb.co.za
www.langebaaninfo.com

**TIENIE VERSFELD WILDFLOWER
RESERVE**
NEAREST TOWN
Darling

SIZE
20ha

FAUNA/FLORA
1 Geometric Tortoise
2 Renosterveld
3 *Sambreeltjie*

MAIN CONTACT DETAILS
Darling Tourism
022 492 3361
www.darlingtourism.co.za

COLUMBINE NR
NEAREST TOWN
Paternoster

SIZE
263ha

FAUNA
1 Heaviside's & Bottlenosed Dolphin
2 Humpback & Southern Right Whale
3 Cape Fox

MAIN CONTACT DETAILS
022 752 2718

ACCOMMODATION INSIDE PARK
The Beach Camp
082 926 2267
info@ratrace.co.za

Municipal Campsite
022 752 2718

SEASONAL INFORMATION

Gate opening times
07:00 –19:30 (1 Apr to 30 Sept)
06:00 – 20:00 (1 Oct to 31 Mar)
Postberg section: 09:00 – 17:00
(open Aug to Sept only)
Day visitors allowed
Columbine section: 07:00 – 19:00

Shell Bay Point
Stompneuspunt
Britannia Bay
Cape St Martin
Vasco da Gama Nautical Museum
Groot-Paternosterpunt
Stompneusbaai
Vasco da Gama Monument
Sandy Point
Sandy Bay
St Helena
St Helena Bay
Steenberg's Cove
Rondekop
Steenberg's Bay
West Point
Slippers Bay
Seal Island
Paternoster Bay
Skuitjiesklip
Soutpan
Paternoster
Paternoster
Fisherman's Cottages
Kasteelberg 185m
Klipheuwel
Droëdasvlei
Columbine NR
Oep se Koep
Besterskraal
Katzenberg 107m
Nooitgedacht
Tieties Bay
Varswater Bay
Koeltebaai
Hol Bay
North West Bay
13
Voël Island
Trekoskraal
Duminy Point
Groot Kreefgat
Swartriet to Tieties Bay
Prosesfontein Monument
Vredenburg
Witpilaar
Salcor
West Bay
Hospitaalpunt
Flowers (Aug/Sept)
Jacobsbaai
Mauritz Bay
Jacobsbaai
Halt
Saldanha Holiday Resorts
Saldanha Steel
Tabakbaai Holiday Resorts
Morrison's Point
Danger Bay or Tabak Bay
Diazville
Long Point
87m Môreson
Saldanha Yacht Club
NSRI
Jakkalskloof
Small Craft Harbour
Mussel Rafts
North Bay
Marcus Island
Saldanha Bay
Lynch Point
Club Mykonos
Oliphantskop Farm Inn
North Head
Malgas Island
Salamander Bay
Leentjiesklip
Elandspunt
Seebries
Jutten Island
Schaapen Island
Langebaan Country Club
Military Area
Oosterwal
Langebaan Park Headquarters
South Head
193m Postberg
Postberg NR
131m Seeberg
Bird Hide
Plankies Bay
Stoney Head
Plankiesbaai
83m
Tzaarsbank
Preekstoel
Langebaan Lagoon
Bird Hide
Vondeling Island
Kraalbaai Houseboat
Churchhaven
Fisherman's Village
Bird Hide
Joanne's Beach Cottage
Bird Hide
Geelbek Environmental Centre
VOC Beacon
ATLANTIC OCEAN
Abrahamskraal
Geelbek Trails
Sixteen Mile Beach
N
Km 8
Mi 4

Dwarskersbos Resort
Dwarskersbos
Sandboskraal
St Helena Bay
Soverby
13
Pelican
Stywelyne
Perdedam Wild Flowers
Weglopersheuwel
Berg River Mouth
Laaiplek
Noordhoek
Doctor Reef
Port Owen
Velddrif
Nuweplaas
Salt Factory
Bird Watching
R399
To Piketberg
17
Laingville
Patrysberg
10
Die Plaat
Prosesfontein Monument
R399
11
Sisher-Saldanha Railway
20
R27
Great Berg
Cloeteskraal
24
Langrietvlei Wetlands
Kerseontein
R45
9
Langeenheid
7
Kotze
Bergrivier
West Coast Fossil Park
Langebaanweg
Spanjaard
21
11
Driehoeksfontein
R45
7
Ysterfontein
21
Swartfontein
9
Hopefield
R27
Groenheuwel
West Coast National Park
Fossil Deposits
Massenberg 160m
38
Swartberg 286m
Baarhuis
Suurfontein
Zwartwater
R27
Blombos
Yzerfontein Salt Pan
To Moorreesburg
Meeurots
Yzerfontein
Yzerfonteinpunt
Yzerfontein Holiday Resort
7
Yzerfontein Hill 83m
R315
Tienie Versfeld Wildflower Reserve
To Darling
To Cape Town
Uitkoms

21

Cape Town/
Kaapstad

Robberg Nature Reserve,
Keurbooms River Nature Reserve & Monkeyland

The magic of the **Robberg Nature Reserve** is that this high rocky peninsula juts out into the ocean, giving you a seagull's perspective of foamy waves breaking far below and secret lonely beaches accessed only by hikers and fishermen. Three routes of half an hour to four hours encompass, variously, rocky paths, dunes, a boardwalk and the wave-washed shoreline, where your footprints are possibly the only ones. You may encounter seals, Cape (Kelp) Gulls and other waterbirds, or even a Cretaceous mudstone cleft that is visible proof of the break-up of Gondwana. Sunsets from your elevated eyrie here are quite memorable.

Pristine is a word one can use with absolute confidence to describe the thickly forested, serpentine curve of the river gorge in the **Keurbooms River Nature Reserve**. Best explored via the two-day Keurbooms canoe trail, your reward is a rustic log cabin on stilts, embraced by riverine forest and accessible only from the water. If you're up early enough, this is where you could easily spot Malachite and Giant Kingfishers, hear the soul-expanding call of the African Fish Eagle, catch a Knysna Lourie in flight, or even glimpse the rare Narina Trogon. Paradise indeed.

It may sound like a zoo, but that's exactly what it's not. The **Monkeyland** sanctuary is set within tangled afromontane forest where canopy trees rise to 30 or 40m – a perfect habitat for hundreds of different species of primates to freely roam. And that's exactly what they do, foraging, chattering, and nimbly gliding and swinging through the treetops. Visitors joining a highly educational guided eco-tour emerge wised-up and fascinated. So would you after spying the white fur halo of a Cottontop Tamarin, the intellectual gaze of a Spectacled Langur or the quizzical heart-shaped face of an Owl Monkey. Gibbons, capuchins, howlers, ring-tailed lemurs – you can't be anything but absolutely sold.

ROBBERG NR
NEAREST TOWN
Plettenberg Bay

NEAREST AIRPORT (ALL PARKS)
George

SIZE
174ha

FAUNA/FLORA
1 Blue Duiker
2 Southern Right Whale
3 Common & Bottlenosed Dolphin
4 Cape Fur Seal
5 Albatross sp.
6 Broadbilled Prion
7 Whitechinned Petrel
8 Cape Gannet
9 Cape Cormorant
10 Cape (Kelp) Gull
11 Montane *Fynbos*
12 Candelabra flower

MAIN CONTACT DETAILS
044 533 2125/85
robkeur@mweb.co.za

ACCOMMODATION INSIDE PARK
None

ACCOMMODATION OUTSIDE PARK
(ALL PARKS)
044 533 4065
info@plettenbergbay.co.za
www.plettenbergbay.co.za

KEURBOOMS RIVER NR
NEAREST TOWN
Plettenberg Bay

SIZE
740ha

FAUNA/FLORA
1 Bushpig
2 Caracal
3 Genet
4 Chacma Baboon
5 Blue Duiker
6 Bushbuck
7 Rock Dassie
8 Vervet Monkey
9 Cape Beech
10 Giant Stinkwood
11 Yellowwood sp.
12 Western Keurboom

MAIN CONTACT DETAILS
044 802 5310
george@cnc.org.za

ACCOMMODATION INSIDE PARK
Whiskey Creek Cabin
044 802 5310/11
goukamma@cnc.org.za

MONKEYLAND
NEAREST TOWN
Plettenberg Bay

MAIN CONTACT DETAILS
044 534 8906
info@monkeyland.co.za
www.monkeyland.co.za

SEASONAL INFORMATION

Gate opening times
Robberg NR:
07:00 – 20:00 (summer)
07:00 – 17:00 (winter)
Keurbooms River NR:
08:00 – 17:00

Keurboomsrivier State Forest

To Stormsrivier

Kurland

R102

Kurland

To Kruisville

Keurbooms

R340

N2

The Crags

Monkeyland

Keurbooms River
Nature Reserve

Matjiesrivier
Cave

Forest
Hall

Bietou

Plettenberg   Aventura Eco

Keurboomstrand

Arch Rock

Arch Rock

Wittedrif

Mallard
River Lodge

Dune Park
Holiday Resort

H

Keurbooms
Beach

Keurbooms Hotel
and Chalets

Plettenberg
Bay

Keurboomsrivier

Keurbooms
Lagoon

To Knysna

N2

Piesang

Golf
Course

H Plettenberg
Lookout Beach

Deep Blinders

H Beacon Isle

Beacon Island

INDIAN
OCEAN

Plettenberg
Bay

i

Beach Walks

Robberg Lodge

Athina 1967

H

Robberg

Plettenberg Park

i

Robberg NR

Nelson Bay
Cave

Nelson's Bay

Die Eiland   *Sandbaai*

Whale Rock

Cape Seal

Jack's Point

N

Km   4

Mi   2

Marloth, Grootvadersbosch
& Anysberg Nature Reserves

CAPE NATURE CONSERVATION AND MUSEUMS   KAAPLANDSE NATUURBEWARING EN MUSEUMS

MARLOTH
NATURE RESERVE / NATUURRESERVAAT

On the lower slopes of the Langeberg, a constant imposing presence, the **Marloth Nature Reserve** is guaranteed to reward you with layers of misty mountains all around. In spring and summer, the Marloth flower route presents 2.5km of proteas and ericas in full bloom, with stands of indigenous forest (yellowwood, stinkwood and ironwood) thrown in as a treat. The six-day Swellendam hiking trail, for fit experienced walkers only, skirts multiple mountain peaks, the most intriguing four of which are named Tien-, Elf-, Twaalf- and Eenuurkop (ten, eleven, twelve and one o'clock peak).

Still in the protective folds of the Langeberg, another nature reserve, **Grootvadersbosch**, and the adjoining **Boosmansbos Wilderness Area** have earned themselves the rating of World Heritage Site. No wonder, with their treasure of close to 35 tree species characterising indigenous forest, surrounded by *fynbos*. Paths in Boosmansbos (named after a hermit who lived his secluded life here in the 19th century) are unmarked, in keeping with the spirit of true wilderness. A cycle trail explores part of the Grootvadersbosch reserve.

Change of scenery when you get to the Little Karoo's **Anysberg Nature Reserve**. Here, the terrain serves up Bokkeveld shale mountains, round Karoo koppies, shady kloofs and sparsely vegetated plains. Exercise your imaginative powers by putting faces to weird and wonderful eroded formations of sandstone. Expansive views even allow you to make out the undulating Klein Swartberg in the far distance. There are no formal hiking trails – although walkers should not be deterred! – but the best way to experience these wide open spaces is the 3-day guided horse trail, spotting Gemsbok with rapier horns and painted faces, pausing before ancient San rock art, eating *roosterkoek* and *potjie* round a crackling wood fire and sleeping under a star-studded canopy. It doesn't get better than this.

MARLOTH NR
NEAREST TOWN
Swellendam

NEAREST AIRPORT (ALL PARKS)
Cape Town International

SIZE
14 123ha

FAUNA
1   Leopard
2   Baboon
3   Porcupine
4   Wood Owl
5   Tambourine Dove

MAIN CONTACT DETAILS
028 514 1410
marlothnr@telkomsa.net

ACCOMMODATION INSIDE PARK
Bushbuck and Suikerbekkie Cottages
Glenstream, Wolfkloof, Protea Valley,
Goedgeloof, Boskloof Huts
028 425 5020
bredasdorp@capenature.co.za

ACCOMMODATION OUTSIDE PARK
028 514 2770
infoswd@sdm.dorea.co.za
www.swellendamtourism.co.za

GROOTVADERSBOSCH NR AND
BOOSMANSBOS WILDERNESS
AREA
NEAREST TOWN
Heidelberg

SIZE
250ha

MAIN CONTACT DETAILS
028 722 2412
gvbosch@telkomsa.net
www.capenature.org.za

ACCOMMODATION INSIDE PARK
Podocarpus Cabin, Scolopia,
Apodytes Forest Cabin, campsite
028 425 5020
bredasdorp@capenature.co.za

ACCOMMODATION OUTSIDE PARK
028 722 2700
heidelinfo@telkomsa.net
www.heidelberginfo.co.za

ANYSBERG NR
NEAREST TOWN
Ladismith/Laingsburg

SIZE
62 500ha

MAIN CONTACT DETAILS
See Grootvadersbosch NR

ACCOMMODATION INSIDE PARK
Agama, Seps, Leguaan, Chameleon,
Gecko Cottages, campsite
028 425 5020

ACCOMMODATION OUTSIDE PARK
Tourist Info, Laingsburg
023 551 1019

SEASONAL INFORMATION

Gate opening times
Marloth NR:
08:00 – 16:00
Grootvadersbosch NR:
08:00 – 16:00 (Mon to Fri)
08:00 – 18:00 (Sat to Sun)
Day visitors allowed
Anysberg NR:
07:00 – 18:00

Km 30
Mi 15

To Beaufort West

Hilandale

To Touws River

20

18

R354

15

13

Laingsburg

N1

Baviaan

N1

54

Matjiesfontein

Floriskraal
Dam

Historic Village

Pieter
Meintjies

19

Bushman Cave

Rooinek

39

11

WITTEBERGE

1332m

Avondrust

Anysberg
Nature Reserve

To Ladismith

Touws

Anysberg

Plathuis

Kareevlakte

R
62

Brak

Radioactive
Springs

Doring

Boerboonfontein

Bellair
Dam

N

Montagu

To Matroosberg

Lemoenshoek

16

Poortjieskloof
Dam

Boosmansbos
Wilderness Area

Nooitgedacht

66

R
62

Grootberg
1638m

To Ashton

Proteavallei

Barrydale

Goedgeloof

R324

40

Grootvadersbosch
Nature Reserve

Marloth
Nature Reserve

Boskloof

Tradouws
Pass

13

R400

Ten O'Clock
1195m

R322

Forest
Station

14

Rheenendal
Mill

11

Suurbraak

LANGEBERG

Swellendam

Heidelberg
Wildflower Garden

Riviersonderend

Buffeljagsrivier

To Stormsvlei

24

N2

Bontebok
National Park

N2

42

Heidelberg

To Riversdale

25

R319

Askraal

Duiwenhoks

R324

R322

Breë

35

To Bredasdorp

Malgas

Slang

To Witsand

25

Cape Town/
Kaapstad

Limietberg Nature Reserve,
Hawekwas Conservation Area

The **Limietberg Nature Reserve** has its green tentacles snaking through low river-cut valleys and up over multiple rocky mountain ranges – both the Du Toitskloof and the Bain's Kloof passes which ambitiously climb high over the landscape are testament to this. Whether it's the Wemmershoek, Dutoits, Hawekwas, Limiet or Slanghoek mountain uplands, there can be no doubt that any of the diverse hiking trails established here offer walkers great scenery and views. A special feature of these walks is that most are crossed by rivers, streams, waterfalls or rock pools – the best place to be on a hot Cape summer's day. In January and February, look hard for the brightly coloured Red Disa Lilies in stream-fed, shaded kloofs. The Miaspoort trail, which crests Huguenot Peak (a two-hour climb), is initially strenuous but rewards tired hikers with bird's-eye views of the encircling mountains.

Abutting onto the Limietberg reserve and sprawled along the foothills of the Limietberg uplands, the **Hawekwas Conservation Area** is also intersected by rivers and streams, guaranteeing shady river routes. Although sometimes spelled Hawequas (which conjures up images of North American Indian reservations rather than the southern tip of Africa), the alternative, Hawekwas, is more fitting to its Khoi-Khoi origins; the Hawekwa people once lived in the Dutoits mountains. Also the headquarters of a scout adventure society (though not always occupied), hikers and campers are welcomed here to share the 10km of mountain trails, the granite pools along the Spruit River and to splash about in the manmade cement dam.

LIMIETBERG NR
NEAREST TOWN (BOTH PARKS)
Paarl

NEAREST AIRPORT (BOTH PARKS)
Cape Town International

SIZE
117 000ha

FAUNA/FLORA
1 Leopard
2 Caracal
3 Klipspringer
4 Chacma Baboon
5 Rock Dassie
6 Cape Sugerbird
7 Seedeater (Protea) Canary
8 Verreaux's (Black) Eagle
9 Trout sp.
10 Mountain *Fynbos*
11 Red Disa Lily
12 Giant Protea

MAIN CONTACT DETAILS
021 659 3500
hcassels@capenature.co.za
www.capenature.org.za

ACCOMMODATION INSIDE PARK
(BOTH PARKS)
Limietberg Hut, Tweede Tol
021 659 3500
hcassels@capenature.co.za
www.capenature.org.za

ACCOMMODATION OUTSIDE PARK
(BOTH PARKS)
021 872 3829
paarl@cis.co.za
www.paarlonline.com

HAWEKWAS CONSERVATION AREA
SIZE
1200ha

FAUNA
1 Leopard
2 Klipspringer
3 Duiker
4 Cape Clawless Otter
5 African Fish Eagle

MAIN CONTACT DETAILS
021 659 3603
ross@kingsley.co.za

SEASONAL INFORMATION

Gate opening times
08:00 – 18:00
08:00 – 20:00 (Fri)
Campsite check in/out 10:00
Day visitors allowed
Tweede Tol:
06:00 – 19:00 (summer)
07:00 – 18:00 (winter)

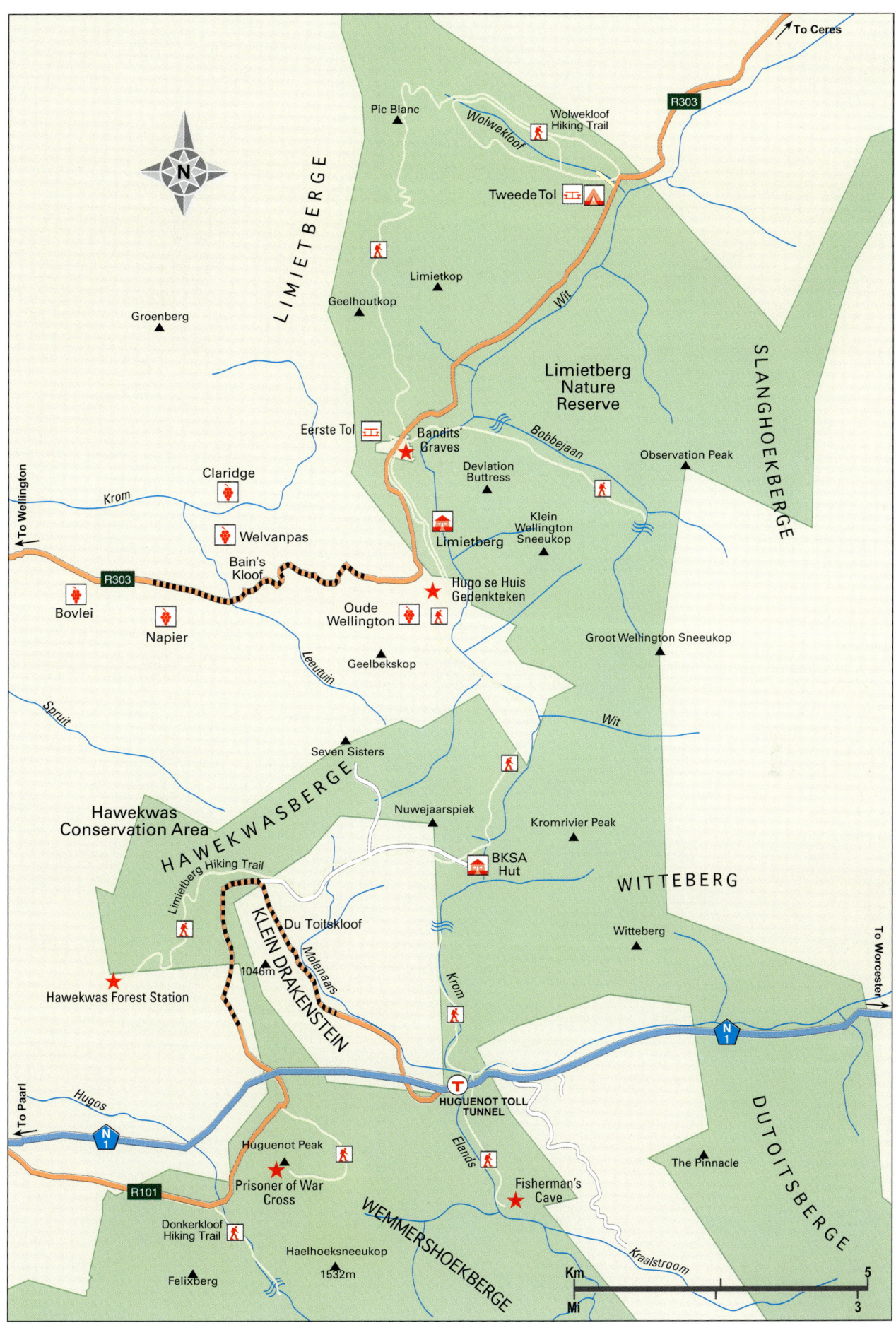

To Ceres

R303

Pic Blanc

Wolwekloof
Hiking Trail

Wolwekloof

Tweede Tol

LIMIETBERGE

Limietkop

Geelhoutkop

Groenberg

SLANGHOEKBERGE

Limietberg
Nature
Reserve

Wit

Eerste Tol

Bandits'
Graves

Bobbejaan

Observation Peak

To Wellington

Krom

Claridge

Deviation
Buttress

Klein
Wellington
Sneeukop

Welvanpas

Limietberg

Bain's
Kloof

R303

Hugo se Huis
Gedenkteken

Bovlei

Oude
Wellington

Groot Wellington Sneeukop

Napier

Leeutuin

Geelbekskop

Wit

Spruit

Seven Sisters

HAWEKWASBERGE

Nuwejaarspiek

Kromrivier Peak

Hawekwas
Conservation Area

Limietberg Hiking Trail

BKSA
Hut

WITTEBERG

Du Toitskloof

KLEIN DRAKENSTEIN

Witteberg

1046m

Molenaars

Hawekwas Forest Station

Krom

N1

To Worcester

To Paarl

Hugos

N1

HUGUENOT TOLL
TUNNEL

DUTOITSBERGE

Huguenot Peak

Elands

R101

The Pinnacle

Prisoner of War
Cross

Fisherman's
Cave

Donkerkloof
Hiking Trail

WEMMERSHOEKBERGE

Haelhoeksneeukop

Kraalstroom

Felixberg

1532m

Km

Mi

5

3

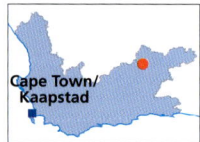

Karoo National Park

Stark denuded landscapes punctuated by dolerite koppies rearing out of sweeping flat plains – and miles and miles of wide open spaces – get under your skin in this national park with a difference. Wheeling Black Eagles – the country's highest numbers congregate here – nest in the rugged cliffs of the Nuweveld mountain plateau, and the park's scrubby vegetation makes wildlife viewing a pleasure, especially along the 13km Lammertjiesleegte Route across the plains. Take the time to appreciate the smaller reptilian creatures (among them a Terrapin, Monitor and an Agama) – they are, after all, modern evolutionary representatives of ancient giants that roamed here some 240 million years ago. Dinosaur fossil remains and those of other mammal-like reptiles can be inspected on the Fossil Braille Trail, which allows visually-impaired visitors to share this ancient heritage. The 4x4 trail climbs precarious mountain passes with spectacular open-sky views, and a restored shepherd's cottage offers night shelter.

KAROO NP
NEAREST TOWN
Beaufort West
NEAREST AIRPORT
Cape Town International
SIZE
75 000ha
FAUNA
1   Black Rhino
2   Cape Mountain Zebra
3   Springbok
4   Kudu
5   Aardwolf
6   Aardvark
7   Chacma Baboon
8   Bat-eared Fox
9   Riverine Rabbit
10 Terrapin
11 Tortoise sp.
12 Agama
13 Rock Monitor
14 Horned Adder
15 Cape Eagle Owl
16 Heron sp.
17 Verreaux's (Black) Eagle
MAIN CONTACT DETAILS
023 415 2828
wendyj@parks-sa.co.za

ACCOMMODATION INSIDE PARK
Main Restcamp, Mountain View Restcamp
023 415 2828
wendyj@parks-sa.co.za

ACCOMMODATION OUTSIDE PARK
023 415 1488
bwtbinfo@xsinet.co.za
www.beaufortwestsa.co.za

SEASONAL INFORMATION

Gate opening times
05:00 – 22:00
Day visitors allowed

De Hoop Nature Reserve

This reserve of exquisite natural beauty feels remote and undiscovered. Bird lovers will want to spend much of their time at De Hoop Vlei, particularly in summer when thousands of waterbird species swell in number with the arrival of Palaearctic waders escaping colder climes. In the Potberg section of the reserve is the Western Cape's only remaining breeding colony – 25 breeding pairs and counting – of rare Cape Vultures. Hikers could spot dolphins and seals, and between May and December, the reserve is a perfect vantage point for the giant Southern Right Whales that calve and mate in De Hoop's sheltered bays. Cherry on the top is the newish five-day Whale Trail, whose overnight stops are in charming thatched A-frame and Arniston-style cottages. Hiking luxury's the word. The scenery is astounding – craggy limestone cliffs, eroded rocky outcrops, pristine wind-swept dunes, distilled-water rock pools, and 360° views from here to an emerald Breede River valley.

DE HOOP NR
NEAREST TOWN
Bredasdorp
NEAREST AIRPORT
Cape Town International
SIZE
34 000ha
FAUNA/FLORA
1   Leopard
2   Cape Mountain Zebra
3   Bontebok
4   Eland
5   Grey Rhebok
6   Chacma Baboon
7   Caracal
8   Yellow Mongoose
9   Southern Right Whale
10 Common & Bottlenosed Dolphin
11 Cape Fur Seal
12 Cape Vulture
13 Waterbird sp.
14 Lowland *Fynbos*
MAIN CONTACT DETAILS
028 425 5020
bredasdorp@capenature.co.za

ACCOMMODATION INSIDE PARK
Lekkerwater, Ouhuis, fully-equipped cottages, basic cottages, rondawels, De Hoop Campsite
028 425 5020
bredasdorp@capenature.co.za

Potberg Environmental Education Centre
028 542 1114
potberg@telkomsa.net

ACCOMMODATION OUTSIDE PARK
Tourist Info, Bredasdorp
028 424 2584

SEASONAL INFORMATION

Gate opening times
07:00 – 18:00
07:00 – 21:00 (Fri)
Day visitors allowed

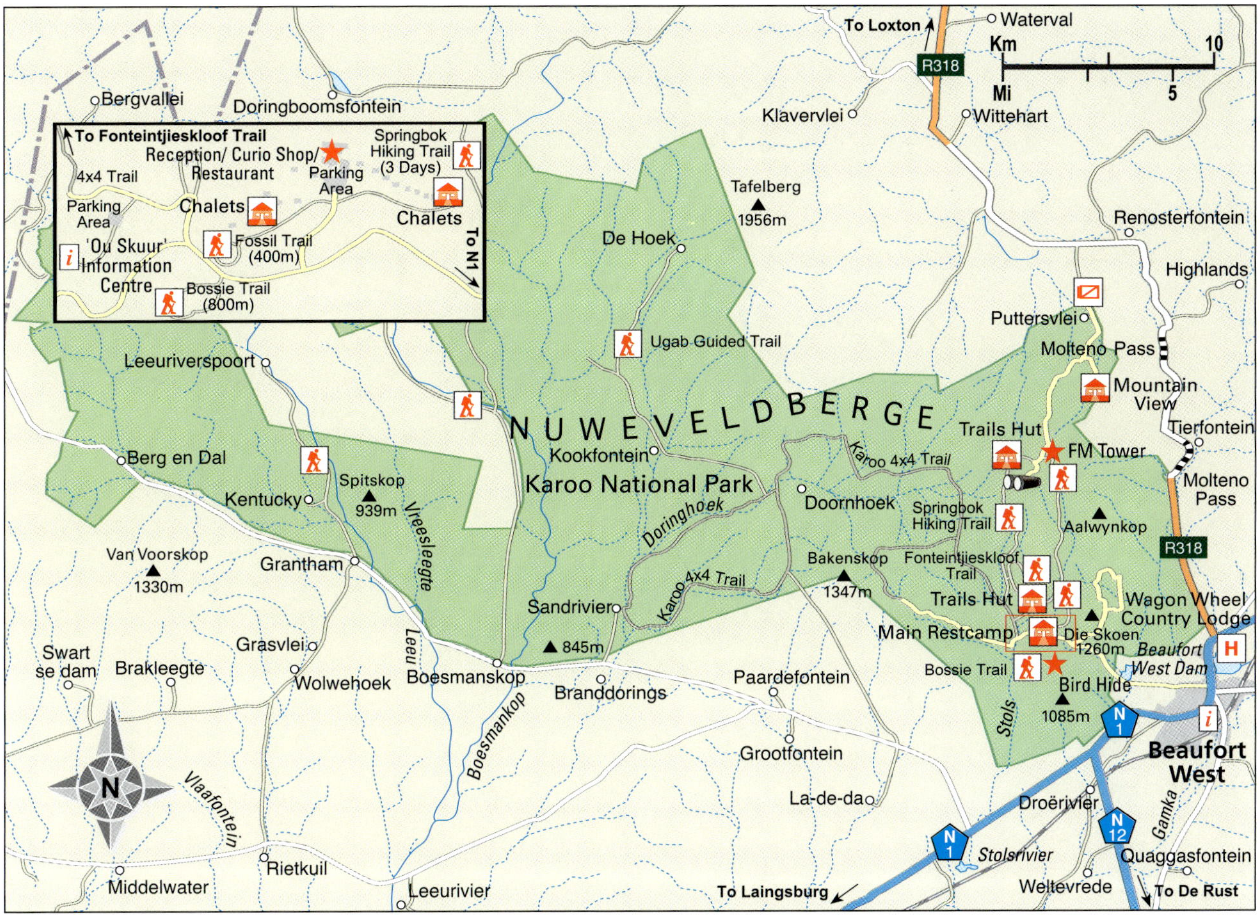

Map 1 — Karoo National Park / Nuweveldberge

To Loxton

Waterval

R318

Km 10
Mi 5

Bergvallei
Doringboomsfontein

Klavervlei
Wittehart

To Fonteintjieskloof Trail
Reception/ Curio Shop/ Restaurant
Springbok Hiking Trail (3 Days)
4x4 Trail
Parking Area
Parking Area
Chalets
Chalets
Fossil Trail (400m)
'Ou Skuur' Information Centre
Bossie Trail (800m)
To N1

Tafelberg 1956m

Renosterfontein

Highlands

De Hoek

Puttersvlei

Molteno Pass

Mountain View

Leeuriverspoort

Ugab Guided Trail

N U W E V E L D B E R G E

Trails Hut

Tierfontein

FM Tower

Molteno Pass

Berg en Dal

Spitskop 939m

Kentucky

Kookfontein

Karoo National Park

Doringhoek

Karoo 4x4 Trail

Doornhoek

Springbok Hiking Trail

Aalwynkop

R318

Van Voorskop 1330m

Grantham

Vreesleegte

Leeu

Sandrivier

Karoo 4x4 Trail

Bakenskop 1347m

Fonteintjieskloof Trail

Trails Hut

Wagon Wheel Country Lodge

Swart se dam

Brakleegte

Grasvlei

Wolwehoek

Boesmanskop

Boesmankop

Branddorings

845m

Main Restcamp

Die Skoen 1260m

Beaufort West Dam

H

Paardefontein

Bossie Trail

Stols

Bird Hide 1085m

i

Grootfontein

La-de-da

Beaufort West

N1

Vlaafontein

Rietkuil

Leeurivier

Droërivier

N12

Quaggasfontein

N1

Stolsrivier

Weltevrede

Gamka

To De Rust

Middelwater

To Laingsburg

N

Map 2 — De Hoop Nature Reserve

To Swellendam/N2

To Swellendam/N2

Swellendam

N2

R324

R319

Malgas

R317

Wydgeleë

De Hoop NR

Witsand

Infanta

To Swellendam/N2

Bredasdorp

To Bredasdorp

Malgas

Wydgeleë
10

Potberg Trail

i

Potberg 611m

Potberg Environmental Education Centre

Klipspringer Trail

Vulture Colony

Breë

Witsand

Port Beaufort

Infanta

Tierhoek Picnic Site
10

i

De Hoop Nature Reserve

De Hoop Mountain Bike Trail

Kabiekop 242m

De Hoop Vlei

De Hoop
10

Hamerkop

Noetzie

Cape Infanta

Koppie Alleen

Vaalkrans

i

Die Mond

No Access to Reserve

To Arniston

Skipskop

INDIAN OCEAN

Km 6
Mi 3

N

Agulhas National Park,
Waenhuiskrans & De Mond Nature Reserves

Agulhas National Park, proclaimed in 1999, seeks to protect a wealth of indigenous coastal and limestone *fynbos* species and a rich local and migrant birdlife. This southernmost tip of Africa is most famous, though, for its treacherous seas which have battered so many ancient sea vessels it has become known as the graveyard of ships. Don't miss the Agulhas lighthouse museum and the shipwreck museum in the sleepy town of Bredasdorp.

A broad, turquoise-watered river mouth, dune milkwood forests and limestone *fynbos* heathland give **De Mond** its character, attracting beach anglers and walkers to its unspoilt shores. You share the territory with the Damara and Caspian Terns and threatened African Black Oystercatchers. Do look out for puff adders in spring!

Also newly protected is Arniston's coastline from the **Waenhuiskrans Cave** to the beacon on its wildly beautiful rocky promontory. Open only to walkers and 4x4s, the aim is to preserve old fish traps, ancient middens and dune-sensitive vegetation.

AGULHAS NP
NEAREST TOWN
L'Agulhas/Struisbaai

NEAREST AIRPORT (ALL PARKS)
Cape Town International

SIZE
20 000ha

FAUNA (ALL PARKS)
1 Southern Right Whale
2 Grysbok
3 African Black Oystercatcher
4 Damara Tern

MAIN CONTACT DETAILS
028 435 6222/6078
www.sanparks.org

ACCOMMODATION INSIDE PARK
None

ACCOMMODATION OUTSIDE PARK
L'Agulhas Caravan Park
021 458 2258/8/9

WAENHUISKRANS NR
NEAREST TOWN
Arniston/Waenhuiskrans

SIZE
267ha

MAIN CONTACT DETAILS
028 314 0062
www.capenature.org.za

ACCOMMODATION INSIDE PARK
None

DE MOND NR
NEAREST TOWN
Arniston, Waenhuiskrans

SIZE
954ha

MAIN CONTACT DETAILS
028 424 2170
demond@isat.co.za

ACCOMMODATION INSIDE PARK
De Mond Cottage
028 425 5020
bredasdorp@capenature.co.za

ACCOMMODATION OUTSIDE PARK
028 424 2584
suidpunt@brd.dorea.co.za
www.capeagulhas.info

SEASONAL INFORMATION

Gate opening times
Agulhas NP:
09:00 – 16:30
De Mond NR:
07:00 – 16:00
Day visitors allowed

Groot Winterhoek Wilderness Area

Age-old weathering of these mountains of Table Mountain sandstone has resulted in jagged peaks that at times tower over 2000m. Within their folds are eroded rock features and ancient Bushman paintings, a magical playpen for intrepid hikers. Because of their height, winter sees the upper slopes blanketed in snow with plummeting night temperatures and frost-covered landscapes – so hikers should always come prepared for all types of weather conditions. This mountain territory is unpredictable at the best of times. What's appealing in this wild domain is that walkers are invited to ramble randomly, not necessarily sticking to the marked day trails.

GROOT WINTERHOEK WILDERNESS AREA
NEAREST TOWN
Porterville

NEAREST AIRPORT
Cape Town International

SIZE
19 200ha

FAUNA/FLORA
1 Leopard
2 Klipspringer
3 Grey Rhebok
4 Grysbok
5 Caracal
6 Genet
7 African Wild Cat
8 Mongoose sp.
9 Cape Rockjumper
10 Verreaux's (Black) Eagle
11 Pale Chanting Goshawk
12 Jackal Buzzard
13 Southern Rock Lizard
14 Sandsnake
15 Boomslang
16 Mountain *Fynbos*

MAIN CONTACT DETAILS
022 931 2900
porterville@cnc.org.za
www.capenature.org.za

ACCOMMODATION INSIDE PARK
Veepos Guest House, De Tronk Cottage,
Huts at Perdevlei
022 931 2088
cederberg@cnc.org.za

ACCOMMODATION OUTSIDE PARK
022 931 3732
pvilletourism@mbury.new.co.za

SEASONAL INFORMATION

Day visitors allowed
Permit required

Map 1 (Agulhas / De Mond)

To Bredasdorp
To Bredasdorp

Kosiers Kraal Game Farm

Grashoek

Mierkraal

Nachtwacht

Bontebok Fence Monument

13

8

R316

5

To Skipskop

6

Kassiesbaai Fishing Village

Nuwejaars

3

Voëlvlei

To Elim

13

9

Voëlvlei

8

6

Arniston

Waenhuiskrans

Waenhuiskrans NR

9

Heuningnes

Waenhuiskrans Cave

De Mond

Struispunt

Arniston 1815

R319

Soetendalsvlei

Soutpan

14

12

Forest Station

Sterna Trail

Die Maggie

De Mond Nature Reserve

Soetanysberg
249m

Struis Bay

Hoëkrans

Agulhas National Park

INDIAN OCEAN

5

Molshoop

Fishermen's Cottages

Sandberg
156m

Hotagterklip

Thatch Roof Church

Struis Bay

Oriental Pioneer 1974

Die Walle

L'Agulhas Caravan Park

Harbour Lights
Struisbaai Caravan Park

Mango Point

Rasperpunt

L'Agulhas

Lighthouse Museum

Cape Agulhas

N

Km   10
Mi   5

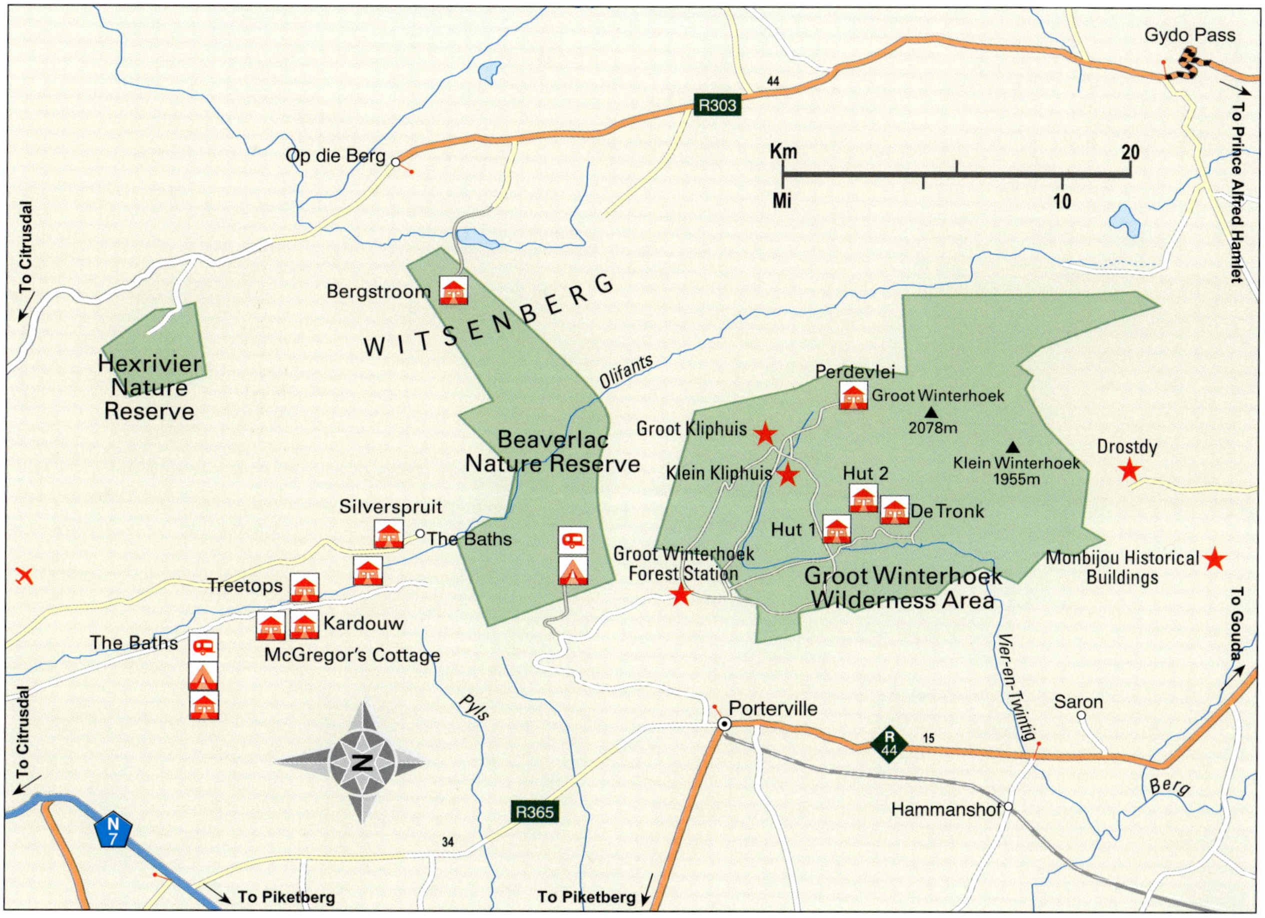

Map 2 (Witsenberg / Groot Winterhoek)

Gydo Pass

44

R303

To Prince Alfred Hamlet

Op die Berg

Km   20
Mi   10

To Citrusdal

Bergstroom

W I T S E N B E R G

Olifants

Perdevlei

Groot Winterhoek
2078m

Hexrivier Nature Reserve

Beaverlac Nature Reserve

Groot Kliphuis

Klein Kliphuis

Hut 2

Klein Winterhoek
1955m

Drostdy

Silverspruit

The Baths

Hut 1

De Tronk

Treetops

Groot Winterhoek Forest Station

Groot Winterhoek Wilderness Area

Monbijou Historical Buildings

The Baths

Kardouw

McGregor's Cottage

To Gouda

Pyls

Vier-en-Twintig

Saron

To Citrusdal

N7

Porterville

R44

15

Berg

Hammanshof

R365

34

To Piketberg

To Piketberg

Kogelberg Biosphere Reserve,
Harold Porter National Botanical Garden

The **Kogelberg Biosphere Reserve** in the southern reaches of the Hottentots Holland mountains remains true to biosphere principles of unspoilt, untouched wilderness embracing a high diversity of plantlife and natural features. Because early 18th-century farmers found this zone of steep kloofs and rugged mountain slopes too inaccessible, it has escaped human intervention over the years. An array of hiking trails explores the rough mountain terrain and the Palmiet River. Between August and October, the flowering *fynbos* is especially pretty. The Oudebosch–Leopard's Gorge day trail ends in the **Harold Porter National Botanical Garden**.

Sandwiched between stony mountains and a cold crashing sea, this botanic garden's speciality is the 10ha cultivated fynbos tract and the 190ha of untamed natural *fynbos*. If you've never seen a Red Disa for real, this is the place to find one growing naturally, between mid-December and end January. The tranquil waterfalls and amber-hued pools are a favourite among visitors.

KOGELBERG BIOSPHERE RESERVE
NEAREST TOWN
Kleinmond
NEAREST AIRPORT (BOTH PARKS)
Cape Town International
SIZE
18 000ha
FAUNA/FLORA
1 Leopard
2 Cape Clawless Otter
3 Klipspringer
4 Freshwater Crab
5 Micro-frog
6 Peregrine Falcon
7 Mountain *Fynbos*
MAIN CONTACT DETAILS
028 271 5138
kogelbrg@cyberhost.co.za
www.capenature.org.za
ACCOMMODATION INSIDE PARK
Kogelberg-Oudebosch
021 659 3500
hcassels@capenature.co.za
🛏 ☒
ACCOMMODATION OUTSIDE PARK
(BOTH PARKS)
028 271 5657
info@ecoscape.org.za
www.ecoscape.org.za

HAROLD PORTER NBG
NEAREST TOWN
Betty's Bay
SIZE
200.5ha
FAUNA/FLORA
1 Protea Seedeater (Canary)
2 Orangebreasted Sunbird
3 Cape Sugarbird
4 *Disa uniflora*
5 Guernsey Lily
MAIN CONTACT DETAILS
028 272 9311
haroldporter@sanbi.org
www.sanbi.org
☒
ACCOMMODATION INSIDE PARK
None

SEASONAL INFORMATION
Gate opening times
Kogelberg:
07:00 – 16:00
No day visitors allowed, only hikers
Harold Porter:
08:00 – 16:30 (weekdays)
08:00 – 17:00 (weekends, public holidays)

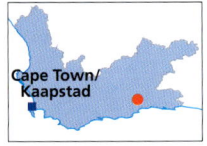

Outeniqua Nature Reserve
& Gamkaberg Nature Reserve

The dramatic **Outeniqua** mountain range, thrust up and pummelled into shape aeons ago at a time of massive upheaval in the earth's crust, makes for challenging hiking terrain. Trails are generally tough, steep and out of bounds to the unfit. Crossing treacherous passes, tracing tracks scoured into the rocks by the ox-wagon wheels of early settlers, and drinking in mountaintop views of the staggering Swartberg, Little Karoo and Indian Ocean all leave the hiker fully satiated with the spendours of nature. Be prepared for fickle weather conditions, even on a perfect day.

The **Gamkaberg Nature Reserve** virtually covers the entire isolated mountain range of Gamkaberg, lying between the Swartberg and Outeniqua mountains in the Little Karoo. As a result, the Oukraal hiking trail, which overnights at a primitive stone shelter on a plateau (can't get closer to nature than this!), gives onto unrivalled views of the Swartberg and Outeniqua mountains.

OUTENIQUA NR
NEAREST TOWN
George
NEAREST AIRPORT (BOTH PARKS)
George
SIZE
38 000ha
FAUNA/FLORA
1 Leopard
2 Klipspringer
3 Verreaux's (Black) Eagle
4 Cape Sugarbird
5 Mountain *Fynbos*
MAIN CONTACT DETAILS
044 870 8323/5
outenr@mweb.co.za
www.capenature.org.za
ACCOMMODATION INSIDE PARK
None
ACCOMMODATION OUTSIDE PARK
044 801 9295
info@georgetourism.co.za
www.georgetourism.co.za

GAMKABERG NR
NEAREST TOWN
Calitzdorp
SIZE
9428ha

FAUNA/FLORA
1 Leopard
2 Cape Mountain Zebra
3 Honey Badger
4 Eland
5 Golden Mimetes
MAIN CONTACT DETAILS
044 213 3367
gamkanr@mweb.co.za
www.capenature.org.za
ACCOMMODATION INSIDE PARK
Tierkloof Bushcamp, Oukraal, Ou Stal,
Groenefontein's, Batis Campsites
044 802 5310
george@cnc.org.za
🛏 🅰 ☒
ACCOMMODATION OUTSIDE PARK
044 213 3775
calitzdorpinfo@kannaland.co.za

SEASONAL INFORMATION
Gate opening times
Outeniqua NR:
08:00 – 17:00
Gamkaberg NR:
Open daily from sunrise to sunset
Day visitors allowed

Top Map (Kogelberg / Atlantic Ocean region)

To Gordon's Bay

To Grabouw
Patryslaagte

N2
Houhoek Inn
Houhoek
Houhoek Trail
Houhoek 890m

Steenbras Dam

Steenbras Catchment Area

Rock View Dam

Kogelberg Dam

Palmiet

Lebanon State Forest

To Caledon

R44
Koeël Bay

Spark's Bay

Arrieskraal Dam

Kogelberg Biosphere Reserve

Km 5
Mi 2.5

10
R43

Whale Lookout

Dwarsrivier Peak 700m

Dwars
Louws

Palmiet River Walk

HighlandsTrail

Kogelberg Trail

Perdeberg Trail

13
R44

Bot

Rooiels
Rooiels

Kogelberg Trail

Perdeberg Peak 650m

Office & Oudebosch Cabins

Three Sisters Peak 360m

Jeans Hill Hut

Wild Horses

11
Afdaks

R43

Buffelsrivier Dam

Leopard's Kloof Walk

Platberg 910m

Disa

Buffelsriver

Kleinmond

Rooisand NR
Fisherhaven

Drostersgat

Pringle Bay
Pringle Bay

Marie Vogts' Rondawel

Harold Porter National Botanical Garden

Beach House on Sandown Bay

Die Mond

Kleinmond Lagoon

Meerensee

R44
Silversands
Betty's Bay
Betty's Bay

Jackass Penguin Colony
Stoney Point

The Meridian 1821

Hawston
To Hermanus

Cape Hangklip

ATLANTIC OCEAN

Bottom Map (Oudtshoorn / George region)

To Calitzdorp

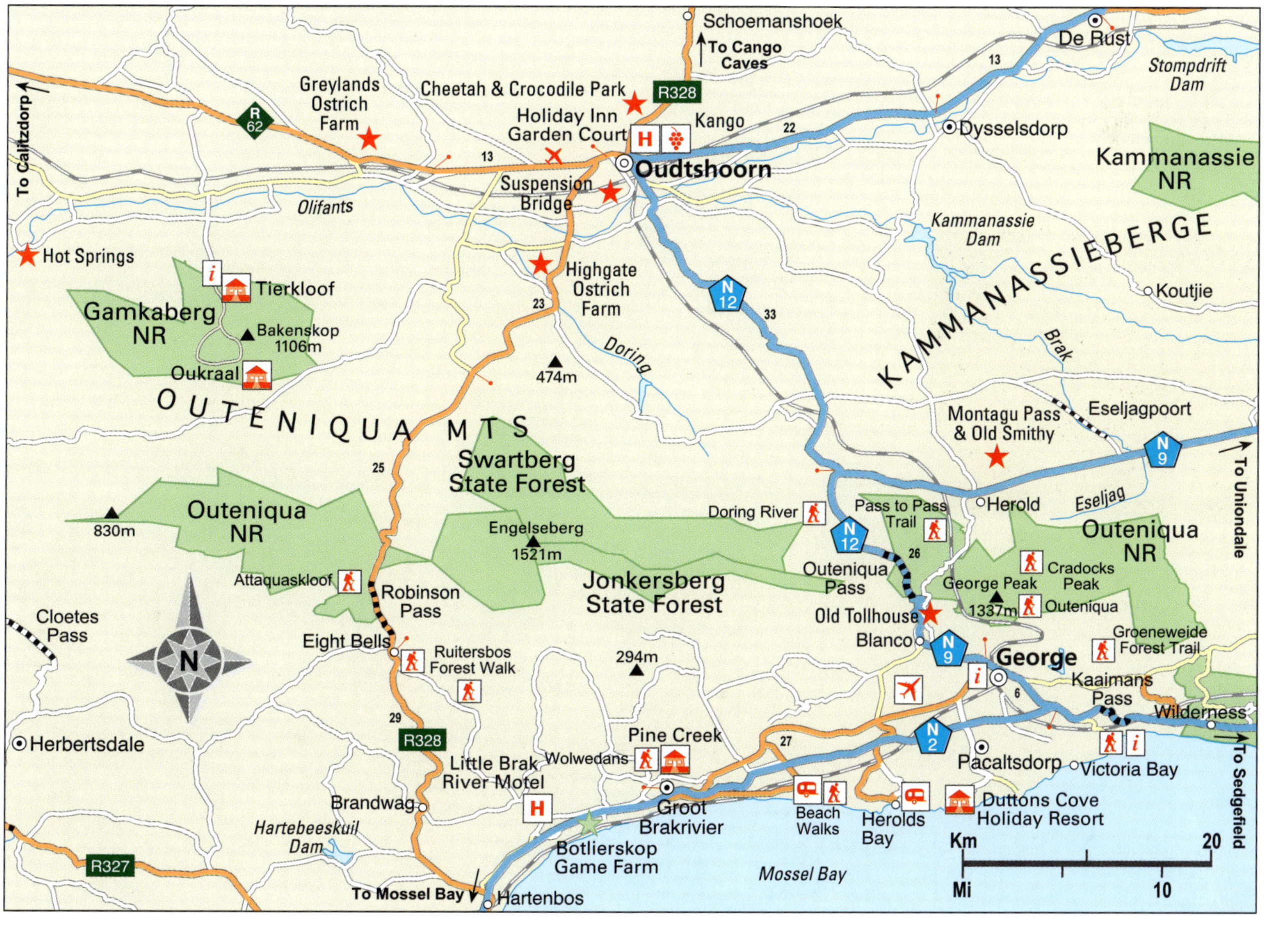

Schoemanshoek
To Cango Caves

De Rust

Stompdrift Dam

R62
Greylands Ostrich Farm

Cheetah & Crocodile Park

R328
Kango

13

Kammanassie NR

Holiday Inn Garden Court

Oudtshoorn

22
Dysselsdorp

Suspension Bridge

Olifants

Kammanassie Dam

KAMMANASSIEBERGE

Hot Springs

Tierkloof

Highgate Ostrich Farm

N12

Koutjie

Gamkaberg NR

Bakenskop 1106m

23

Doring

33

Brak

Oukraal

OUTENIQUA MTS

474m

Montagu Pass & Old Smithy

Eseljagpoort

N9
To Uniondale

Swartberg State Forest

Doring River

Pass to Pass Trail

Herold

Eseljag

25

Outeniqua NR

830m

Engelseberg 1521m

Jonkersberg State Forest

N12

Outeniqua Pass

Old Tollhouse

George Peak 1337m

Cradocks Peak

Outeniqua NR

Outeniqua

Cloetes Pass

Attaquaskloof

Robinson Pass

Blanco

N9

Groeneweide Forest Trail

N
Eight Bells

Ruitersbos Forest Walk

294m

George

Kaaimans Pass

Wilderness

29
R328

Pine Creek
Wolwedans

27

N2
Pacaltsdorp

Victoria Bay

To Sedgefield

Herbertsdale

Little Brak River Motel

Brandwag

Hartebeeskuil Dam

Groot Brakrivier

Beach Walks

Herolds Bay

Duttons Cove Holiday Resort

Km 20
Mi 10

R327

Botlierskop Game Farm

Mossel Bay

To Mossel Bay
Hartenbos

33

Swartberg Nature Reserve,
Kammanassie Nature Reserve

Truly spectacular mountain-scapes win hands-down here in terms of luring 4x4s, hikers and campers to the **Swartberg**'s dramatic soaring heights. At the highest points, views unfold in almost every direction for hundreds of kilometres, from the Great to the Little Karoo, from the Outeniqua to the Nuweveld mountains. All overnight accommodation is in the Gamkaskloof valley, aka Die Hel – or simply, Hell. For 130 years, only pack-donkeys could penetrate this isolated valley in the Swartberg mountains. Solar panels and candles provide light in restored traditional cottages that, for over a century, were lived in by hardy, self-sufficient farmer-settlers.

The river- and stream-riven inselberg that is **Kammanassie** mountain was compressed and folded into the long, oval dome shape it takes on today. Its well-watered deep, narrow kloofs are presided over by powerful-winged Black Eagles and Jackal Buzzards. Despite its upland terrain, Cape Mountain Zebra nimbly negotiate the nature reserve together with small antelope.

SWARTBERG NR
NEAREST TOWN
De Rust/Prince Albert
NEAREST AIRPORT (BOTH PARKS)
George
SIZE
121 000ha
FAUNA/FLORA
1 Leopard
2 Klipspringer
3 Springbok
4 Verreaux's (Black) Eagle
5 Pied Kingfisher
6 Protea sp.
MAIN CONTACT DETAILS
044 802 5310/11
george@cnc.org.za
www.capenature.org.za
ACCOMMODATION INSIDE PARK
Gamkaskloof, Bush Camp, campsite
044 279 1739
sberg.cnc.karoo@pixie.co.za
www.capenaturew.org.za
ACCOMMODATION OUTSIDE PARK
(BOTH PARKS)
023 541 1366
princealberttourism@intekom.co.za
www.patourism.co.za

KAMMANASSIE NR
NEAREST TOWN
De Rust
SIZE
49 430ha
FAUNA/FLORA
1 Cape Mountain Zebra
2 Grey rhebok
3 Kudu
4 Kammanassie Blue Butterfly
5 Jackal Buzzard
6 Cape Sugarbird
7 *Fynbos* sp.
8 Kammanassie Conebush
MAIN CONTACT DETAILS
044 752 1110
kammanas@mweb.co.za
www.capenature.org.za
ACCOMMODATION INSIDE PARK
None

SEASONAL INFORMATION
Gate opening times
Swartberg NR:
08:00 – 18:00
Kammanassie NR:
Closed to the public

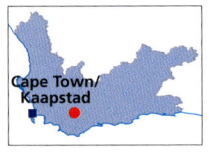

Vrolijkheid Nature Reserve,
Riviersonderend Nature Reserve

Common to these two nature areas are the eternal stretch of the Langeberg and the Riviersonderend mountains, the latter cut by the long, winding river "with no end". They share blazing hot summers, rockscapes and mountain and valley views. Trails in **Vrolijkheid** cross distinctive sandstone and shale terrain, which supports arid Robertson Karoo vegetation – dwarf trees, succulents and thorny shrubs – while views overlook both mountain ranges and the hamlets of Robertson and McGregor.

The nature reserve in the **Riviersonderend** mountains, whose river is a tributary of the Breede, features similar mountain *fynbos* that puts on glorious displays of everlastings, ericas and giant proteas. Sharply carved gorges, soaring peaks and forested kloofs make this an adventurous hikers' playground.

VROLIJKHEID NR
NEAREST TOWN
Robertson
NEAREST AIRPORT (BOTH PARKS)
Cape Town International
SIZE
1900ha
FAUNA/FLORA
1 Springbok
2 Klipspringer
3 African Goshawk
4 Jackal Buzzard
5 Verreaux's (Black) Eagle
6 Robertson Dwarf Chameleon
7 Mountain Renosterveld
8 *Botterblom* Daisy
MAIN CONTACT DETAILS
023 625 1621
vrolijkheidnr@lando.co.za
www.capenature.org.za
ACCOMMODATION INSIDE PARK
Guesthouse, rondavels (available Feb only)
028 425 5020
bredasdorp@capenature.co.za
www.capenature.org.za
ACCOMMODATION OUTSIDE PARK
023 626 4437
info@robertson.org

RIVIERSONDEREND NR
NEAREST TOWN
Riviersonderend
SIZE
2500ha
FAUNA
1 Blue Crane
2 Chacma Baboon
3 Puff Adder
MAIN CONTACT DETAILS
028 261 1511, 028 261 1365/409
ACCOMMODATION INSIDE PARK
None
ACCOMMODATION OUTSIDE PARK
Riviersonderend Tourism
028 261 1511

SEASONAL INFORMATION
Gate opening times
Vrolijkheid NR:
07:00 – 16:00
Riviersonderend Nature Reserve:
Sunrise to sunset
Day visitors allowed

Map 1 (Top – Oudtshoorn / Swartberge)

To Beaufort West
Kommandokraal
Old Water Mill
54
Sand
Kleinwater
N12 32
Prince Albert
Tierberg 1921m
Western Cape
To Prince Albert Road
Oukloof Dam
Kareedouwberg
R407
4
Swartberg Pass
53
Gouekrans
19
Klaarstroom
9
Bothashoek
Swartberg Nature Reserve
Eastern Cape
Ou Tol
11
Meiringspoort
G R O O T   S W A R T B E R G E
To Uniondale
13
Cango Caves
Matjiesrivier
22
Grootkraal
33
To Calitzdorp
Schoemanspoort
26
Olifants
Schoemanshoek
Cango Ostrich Farm
Buffelsklip
R328
De Rust
38
R341
Greylands Ostrich Farm
Cheetah & Crocodile Park
13
Stompdrift Dam
Kammanassie Nature Reserve
Holiday Inn Garden Court
Kango
22
Dysselsdorp
R62 13
H
Oudtshoorn
KAMMANASSIEBERGE
Suspension Bridge
Kammanassie Dam
Bergplaas
Buffelsdrif
To Uniondale
Gamkaberg NR
23
Highgate Ostrich Farm
Koutjie
Daskop
Molenrivier
474m
Brak
30
N9
R328
N12 33
Montagu Pass & Old Smithy
Eseljagpoort
Speelmanskraal
Outeniqua Nature Reserve
Perdepoort
20
To Mossel Bay
9
Herold
To George

Map 2 (Bottom – Robertson / Riviersonderend)

Buitenstekloof
To Koo
Boschrivier
Arangieskop
Circular Route
Riverside
Breë
Kenmoor
Noree
Dassieshoek NR
Pat Bush Private NR
R43
R60
Voorspoed
Tierberg 950m
Triangle
Berg-en-dal
Kwaggaskloof Dam
5
Cilmor
Kniepdiep
Rooiberg
Dassieshoek
Grand
Doornrivier
8
Alfalfa
Eilandia
Vinkrivier
5
H
Robertson
Spes Bona
14
Brandvlei
Dublin
12
Clairvaux
Roodezandt
5
Welverdiend
Gemsbokkop 850m
Graham Beck
Robertson
Ashton
Jonkersrivier
Moddergat
Middeldoornrivier
Oorskot
Clariswold
Elnor
Springfield
R60 12
Ashton
Stettyn
14
Clariswold
Bon Courage
14
Excelsior
Van den Berg's
Hammanshof
Bosfontein
De Knop
Liqueur
Viljoensdrift
Van Loveren
R43
10
Wansbek
Suurberg 706m
18
De Wetshof
To Bonnievale
18
Highlands
Perdekop 692m
12
Vrolijkheid
Rooiberg 706m
R317
Dasbos
Vrolijkheid NR
Goedverwacht
Riviersonderend State Forest
Keerweder
Boerbok
Konings
Wolwedrif
12
Mooiuitsig
Wolfieskop 1262m
Kasra
McGregor
McGregor
Rooikat
To Villiersdorp
Olifantsberg 1600m
Ionaskop 1646m
Die Hoek
Weltevrede
De Hoek
Steenboksvlakte
R I V I E R S O N D E R E N D   M T S
Poesjenels
Greyton-McGregor Boesmanskloof
Whipstock Farm
Viljoenshoogte Pass
Olifantsdoorns
Moravian Mission
1466m Kanonberg
Riviersonderend Nature Reserve
Boesmansrivier
Bainbrecht Bridge
Genadendal
Bell Tower
Greyton
Zeekoeijacht
Oubos
Boskloof
Nooitgedacht
12
Fonteinskloof
Happy Valley
Jongenskloof
Lindeshof
Riviersonderend
Middelplaas
Serjeantsrivier
Dwarskloof
R406
Twistwyk
Ongegund
Km
10
Tierkloof
Môrelig
Springfontein
Kwartelrivier
N2
Mi
5
R406
To Caledon
To Caledon
To Stormsvlei

Wilderness National Park,
Goukamma Nature Reserve

Ebb & Flow is absolutely apt in describing the restcamp of wooden cottages perched on stilts in the **Wilderness National Park**. Raised decks at the edge of a reeded vlei witness the tidal rising and falling of the Touws River as a multitude of birds flits past – some brazenly checking out the humans as they perch on the deck rails. Eilandvlei, Langvlei and Rondevlei, strung together by the Touws River, ensure a healthy showing of aquatic birds.

In the **Goukamma Nature Reserve**, head over the high dunes for a taste of wild sea spray and perhaps catch the Bottlenose and Common Dolphins playfully surfing the waves. If the time of year is right, Southern Right Whales loll and spurt close to shore. For a dose of tranquillity, swim, sail or canoe on the Goukamma River. Mvubu Bushcamp is excellent as night rental – wood, reed and thatch buildings nestle in the treetops of a milkwood forest, on Groenvlei's shores.

WILDERNESS NP
NEAREST TOWN
Wilderness

NEAREST AIRPORT (BOTH PARKS)
George

SIZE
250 000ha

FAUNA
1 Knysna Turaco (Lourie)
2 Kingfisher sp.
3 Grey Heron
4 Little Egret
5 Common & Bottlenosed Dolphin
6 Southern Right Whale

MAIN CONTACT DETAILS
044 877 1197
gardenroute@sanparks.org
www.sanparks.org

ACCOMMODATION INSIDE PARK
Ebb & Flow Restcamp
See Main Contact Details

ACCOMMODATION OUTSIDE PARK
044 877 0045
weta@wildernessinfo.co.za
www.wildernessinfo.co.za

GOUKAMMA NR
NEAREST TOWN
Knysna

SIZE
2500ha

FAUNA/FLORA
1 Southern Right Whale
2 Common & Bottlenosed Dolphin
3 African (Jackass) Penguin
4 Cape Clawless Otter
5 Knysna Turaco (Lourie)
6 African Black Oystercatcher

MAIN CONTACT DETAILS
044 383 0042
goukamma@mweb.co.za
www.capenature.org.za

ACCOMMODATION INSIDE PARK
Mvubu & Groenvlei Bushcamps,
Musselcracker House, Steenbras Flat,
3 rondawels, 2 river lodges
044 802 5310
george@cnc.org.za

ACCOMMODATION OUTSIDE PARK
044 382 5510
knysna.tourism@pixie.co.za

SEASONAL INFORMATION

Gate opening times
Wilderness NP:
Open 24 hours
Goukamma NR:
08:00 – 18:00
Day visitors allowed

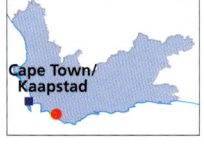

Walker Bay Nature Reserve
& Fernkloof Nature Reserve

The reserve is an amalgam of five coastal areas, the main one being **Walker Bay**. Its famous long length of beach, Die Plaat, has been trawled by countless walkers who revel in the thunderous crashing waves which, at times, can be rough and dangerous. Appealing white sands and rocky limestone outcrops share the limelight with the scenic Klein River lagoon, which at times pummels its way through dune sands to the sea. Walker Bay is most famous for its Southern Right Whales – watched by countless visitors – when they breed here between June and November. Bryde's and Humpback Whales are also known to pass this way.

Trails in the **Fernkloof Nature reserve** in the Kleinrivier mountains thread through *fynbos* and mountain scrub. It's a territory of solid mountain buttresses sliced by small riverine kloofs, so walkers should train their binoculars on the giant wingspans of, potentially, Black Eagles and Black Harriers. A greater and more thrilling challenge for dedicated twitchers is to stealthily track Spotted Eagle Owls and possibly, even, the Cape Eagle Owl under cover of night.

WALKER BAY NR
NEAREST TOWN (BOTH PARKS)
Hermanus

NEAREST AIRPORT (BOTH PARKS)
Cape Town International

SIZE
1000ha

FAUNA
1 Southern Right Whale (Aug–Nov)
2 Bryde's & Humpback Whale
3 Cape Clawless Otter
4 Bushbuck
5 Duiker
6 Grysbok
7 Steenbok
8 African Black Oystercatcher

MAIN CONTACT DETAILS
028 314 0062
cncdeon@maxitec.co.za
www.capenature.co.za

ACCOMMODATION INSIDE PARK
None

ACCOMMODATION OUTSIDE PARK
(BOTH PARKS)
028 312 2629
infoburo@hermanus.co.za

FERNKLOOF NR
SIZE
1800ha

AVIFAUNA
1 Cape Eagle Owl
2 Verreaux's (Black) Eagle
3 Spotted Eagle Owl
4 Jackal Buzzard
5 Black Harrier
6 Cape Sugarbird
7 Flycatcher sp.
8 African Olive Pigeon

MAIN CONTACT DETAILS
028 312 2629
infobu007@hermanus.co.za
www.hermanus.co.za

ACCOMMODATION INSIDE PARK
Galpin Hut (hikers only)
028 314 1562

SEASONAL INFORMATION

Gate opening times
Walker Bay NR:
Sunrise to sunset
Permit required
Fernkloof NR:
07:00 – 19:00
No entrance fee

Map 1 — Wilderness National Park / Goukamma area

To George

Touws

Bergplaas
State Forest

Bergplaas

Woodville

Diep

Perdekop
932m

Fairleigh
514m

Karatara

Old Millwood Village

Jubilee Creek
NR

721m

Millwood
Gold Mine
Trail

Barrington

5

Big Tree

Woodville

7

11

Karatara

14

Goudveld

Homtini
Pass

Rheenendal

Die Hoek

8

Rooiels

Giant Kingfisher Trail

Ebb & Flow

Hoekwil

Wilderness
Resort

Outeniqua
Choo-Tjoe

Duiwerivier

Wilderness
National Park

18

Elandskraal

Spioenkop
340m

Goukamma

Phantom
Pass

George Rex Slipway

The Phantom
Forest

Phantom
Pass

Eilandvlei

Langvlei

Rondevlei

Swartvlei

N2

Belvidere
Church

H

Wilderness

15

Kleinkrantz

7

4

Goukamma

3

N2

Keytersnek

Belvidere

To Knysna

Holiday Inn
Garden Court
Wilderness

To George

H

Sedgefield

Swartvlei
Beach

Lake
Pleasant

Groenvlei

Goukamma
Groenvlei
Trail

8

9

Gerick's
Point

Sedgefield
Beach

Rushmere
Farm
Cottages

Goukamma
NR

Deep Reefs

Platbank

Buffelskop

Buffelsbaai

Km
Mi

8
4

N

INDIAN
OCEAN

Map 2 — Walker Bay / Hermanus area

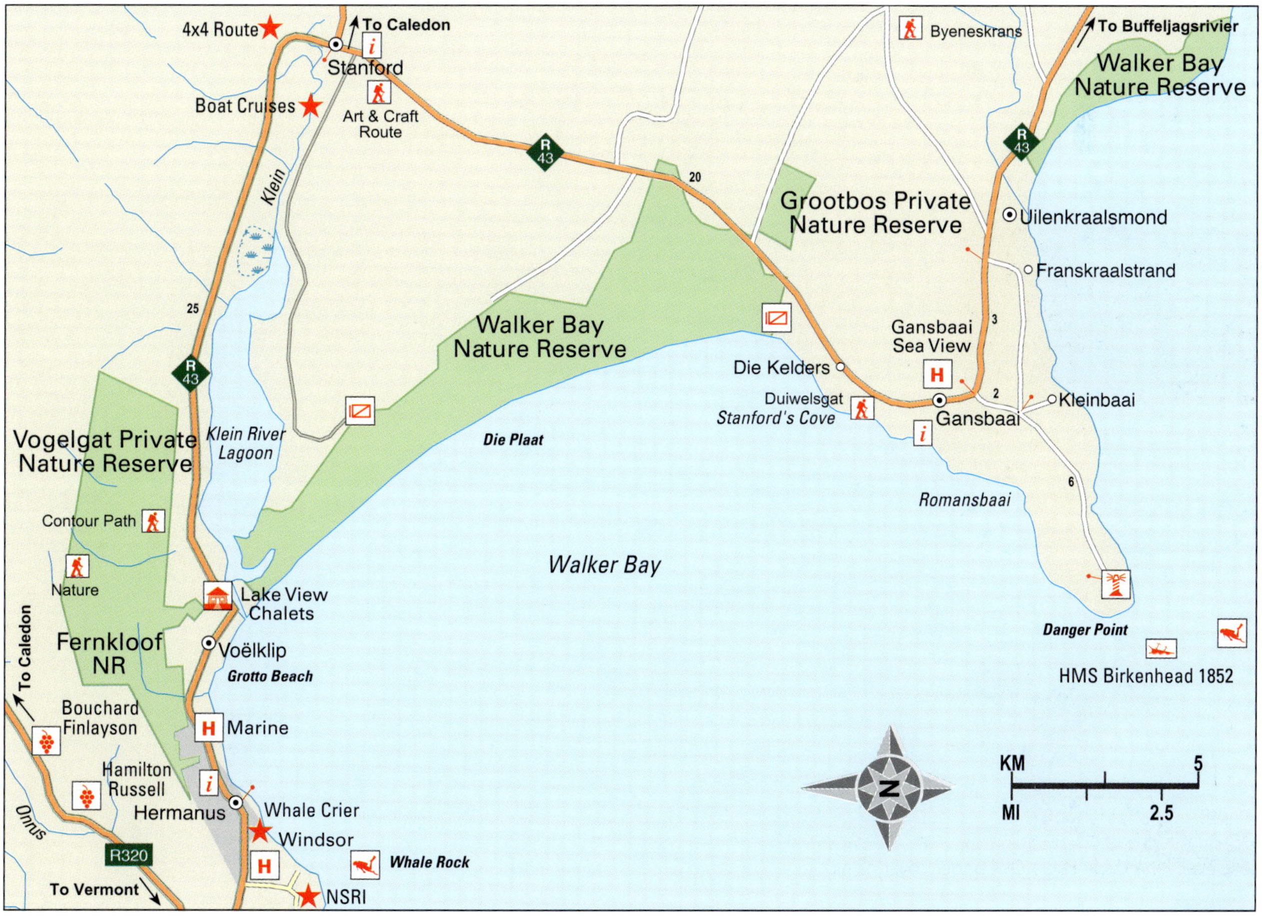

4x4 Route

To Caledon

Stanford

Byeneskrans

To Buffeljagsrivier

Walker Bay
Nature Reserve

Boat Cruises

Art & Craft
Route

R 43

R 43

Klein

20

Grootbos Private
Nature Reserve

Uilenkraalsmond

Franskraalstrand

25

R 43

Walker Bay
Nature Reserve

Klein River
Lagoon

Die Plaat

Die Kelders

Duiwelsgat
Stanford's Cove

Gansbaai
Sea View

H

Gansbaai

3

2

Kleinbaai

Vogelgat Private
Nature Reserve

Contour Path

Nature

Fernkloof
NR

To Caledon

Lake View
Chalets

Voëlklip

Grotto Beach

Walker Bay

Romansbaai

6

Danger Point

HMS Birkenhead 1852

Bouchard
Finlayson

Hamilton
Russell

H

Marine

Hermanus

Whale Crier

Onrus

Windsor

Whale Rock

R320

H

To Vermont

NSRI

KM
MI

5
2.5

Z

37

Bird Island, Verlorenvlei, Rocherpan Nature Reserve

These three nature zones are positively "for the birds". On **Bird Island** the gorgeously made-up Cape Gannets, blue eyes enhanced by fine liquid eyeliner, steal the show. Visitors can take a closer peek from the gannet lookout, sometimes witnessing their unique mating dances. Bird Island is one of only six sites worldwide where Cape Gannets breed, and also the only breeding site easily accessible to the public.

Verlorenvlei, at Elands Bay, an impressive 13.5km in length, can be canoed, allowing birdwatchers to stealthily mingle with the birdlife. Malachite Kingfisher and Purple Heron count among the showier species, and recent visits by rarities like Black Egret, Goliath Heron and Palmnut Vulture spice up the birdwatching stakes. The vlei at **Rocherpan Nature Reserve** dries up between March and June, so when it does fill again, birds flock to its reviving waters. The clownlike White Pelicans and pink-accessorised Greater and Lesser Flamingos are the most entertaining.

BIRD ISLAND
NEAREST TOWN
Lambert's Bay

NEAREST AIRPORT (ALL PARKS)
Cape Town International

SIZE
3ha

FAUNA
1   Cape Gannet
2   Cormorant
3   African (Jackass) Penguin
4   Cape Fur Seal

MAIN CONTACT DETAILS
022 931 2900
porterville@cnc.org.za

ACCOMMODATION INSIDE PARK
(ALL PARKS)
None

ACCOMMODATION OUTSIDE PARK
027 432 1000
lambertsinfo@mweb.co.za

VERLORENVLEI
NEAREST TOWN
Elands Bay

SIZE
13.5km long, 1.4km wide

AVIFAUNA
(VERLORENVLEI, ROCHERPAN)
1   Glossy Ibis
2   Minnow

3   Whitebacked Duck
4   Great Creasted Grebe
5   Cape Shoveller

MAIN CONTACT DETAILS
027 432 1000

ACCOMMODATION OUTSIDE PARK
022 972 1640
info@elandsbay.co.za

ROCHERPAN NR
NEAREST TOWN
Velddrif

SIZE
914ha

MAIN CONTACT DETAILS
022 952 1727

ACCOMMODATION OUTSIDE PARK
Tourist Info, Velddrif
022 783 1820

SEASONAL INFORMATION
Gate opening times
Bird Island:
07:00 – 19:00 (summer)
07:00 – 17:00 (winter)
Rocherpan:
08:00 – 17:00 (May to Aug)
07:00 – 18:00 (Sept to Apr)

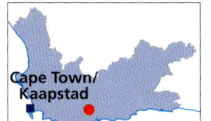

Bontebok National Park

Cradled on one side by the imposing bastion of the Langeberg and the Breede River to the other, this national park was established to save the last few remaining Bontebok from following in the wake of today's extinct Blue Antelope. The Bontebok's inquisitiveness together with its characteristic markings – white "socks" and a white muzzle in an otherwise dark face – set it up as an easy target for early hunters in the 1800s. Bontebok numbers have risen from a seriously endangered 17 to over 200 – the maximum this park can safely sustain. Surplus stock has been passed on to other nature reserves and private landowners over the years. The Bontebok are joined by other antelope, among them the heftily built Red Hartebeest.

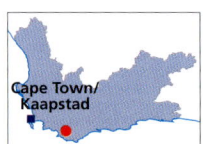

Salmonsdam Nature Reserve

This reserve finds itself at the foot of the Perdeberg mountains. The attractive mountainous landscape is transformed in spring by its plethora of everlasting daisies, doubling its worth to nature enthusiasts as a walking and wildlife-watching destination. An added attraction is its mountain *fynbos* and beautiful waterfalls. Birdwatchers should look out for its more flamboyantly attired birds, particularly the iridescent sunbirds and kingfishers. Although the reserve's name hints at powerful upstream-swimming fish, the area was named, according to local tradition, after Captain Robert Salmon of the HMS *Birkenhead*, which saw a treacherous end at Danger Point in 1852 – a tragic total of 454 lives were lost.

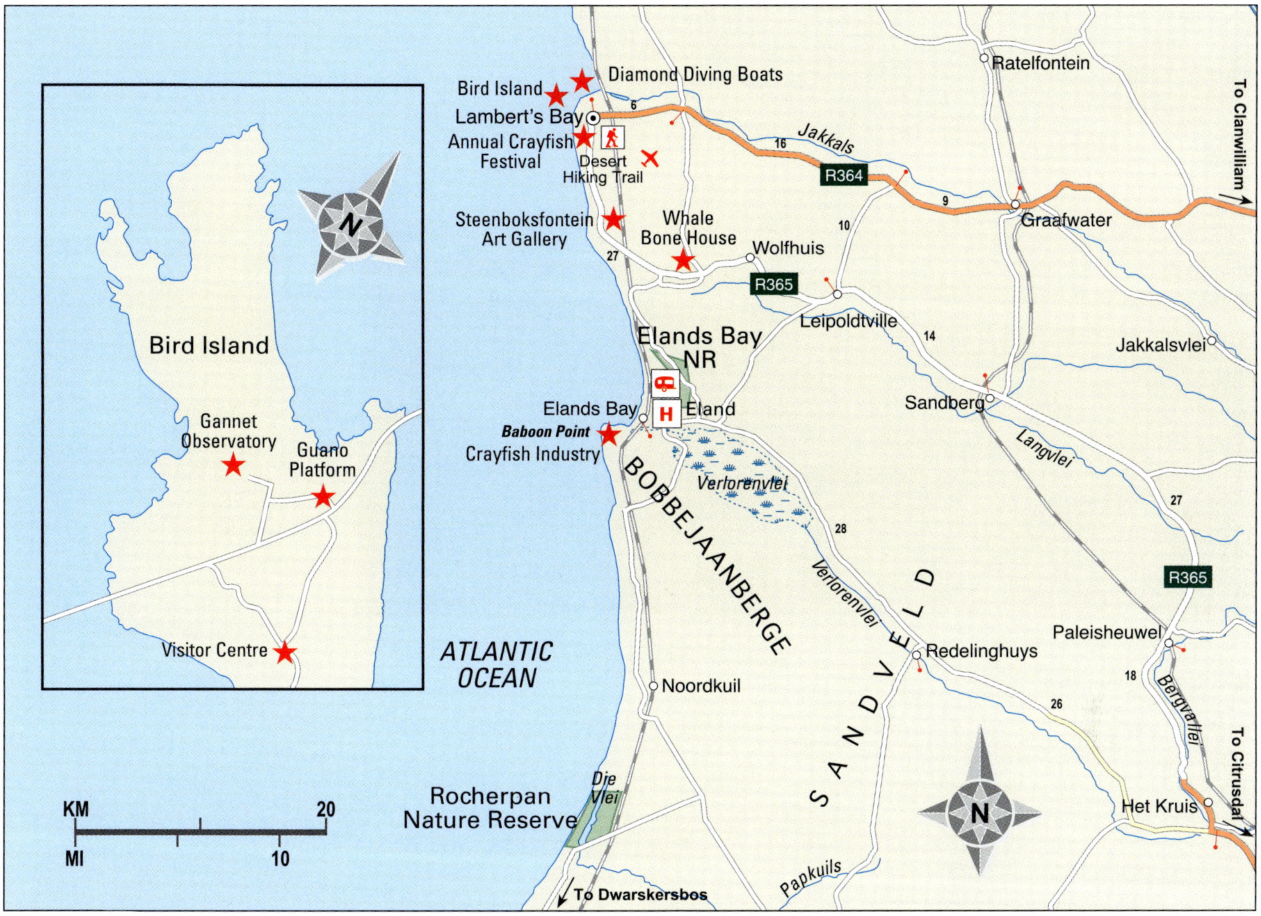

Top Map

To Clanwilliam

Ratelfontein

Diamond Diving Boats
Bird Island
Lambert's Bay
Annual Crayfish Festival
Desert Hiking Trail

Jakkals
R364
16
9
Graafwater

Steenboksfontein Art Gallery
Whale Bone House
Wolfhuis
R365
10
27

Leipoldtville
14
Jakkalsvlei

Elands Bay NR
Elands Bay
Baboon Point
Crayfish Industry
Eland
Sandberg
Langvlei
27

Verlorenvlei
BOBBEJAANBERGE

Verlorenvlei
28
R365
Paleisheuwel

Redelinghuys
18
Bergrivier
To Citrusdal

Noordkuil
26
Het Kruis

SANDVELD
N

Rocherpan Nature Reserve
Die Vlei
Papkuils

KM 20
MI 10

To Dwarskersbos

Bird Island (inset)

Bird Island

ATLANTIC OCEAN

Gannet Observatory
Guano Platform

Visitor Centre

N

BONTEBOK NP

NEAREST TOWN
Swellendam

NEAREST AIRPORT
Cape Town International

SIZE
2786ha

FAUNA/FLORA
1 Bontebok
2 Grey & Common Duiker
3 Red Hartebeest
4 Francolin
5 Denham's (Stanley's) Bustard
6 Secretary Bird
7 Blue Crane
8 African Fish Eagle
9 Gladiolus sp.
10 Erica sp.
11 Protea sp.

MAIN CONTACT DETAILS
028 514 2735
reservations@sanparks.org
www.sanparks.org

ACCOMMODATION INSIDE PARK
Chalavans, campsite
028 514 2735
www.sanparks.org
reservations@sanparks.org

ACCOMMODATION OUTSIDE PARK
028 514 2770
infoswd@sdm.dorea.co.za

SEASONAL INFORMATION

Gate opening times
07:00 – 19:00 (1 Oct to 30 Apr)
07:00 – 18:00 (1 May to 30 Sept)
Day visitors allowed

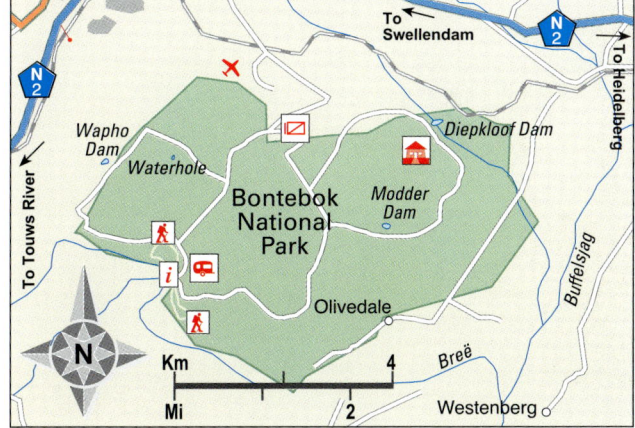

To Swellendam
N2
To Heidelberg
N2
To Touws River
Wapho Dam
Waterhole
Diepkloof Dam
Bontebok National Park
Modder Dam
Buffelsjag
i
Olivedale
Km 4
Mi 2
Breë
Westenberg
N

SALMONSDAM NR

NEAREST TOWN
Stanford

NEAREST AIRPORT
Cape Town International

SIZE
834ha

FAUNA/FLORA
1 Bontebok
2 Klipspringer
3 Grey Duiker
4 Chacma Baboon
5 Verreaux's (Black) Eagle
6 Cape Rockjumper
7 Sunbird sp.
8 Kingfisher sp.
9 Mountain Fynbos
10 Spoonwood
11 Cape Beech

MAIN CONTACT DETAILS
028 314 0062
cncdeon@maxitec.co.za
028 425 5020
capenature@tiscali.co.za
www.capenature.co.za

ACCOMMODATION INSIDE PARK
None

ACCOMMODATION OUTSIDE PARK
028 341 0340
stanfordinfo@overberg.co.za
www.stanfordinfo.co.za

SEASONAL INFORMATION

Closed to the public at present

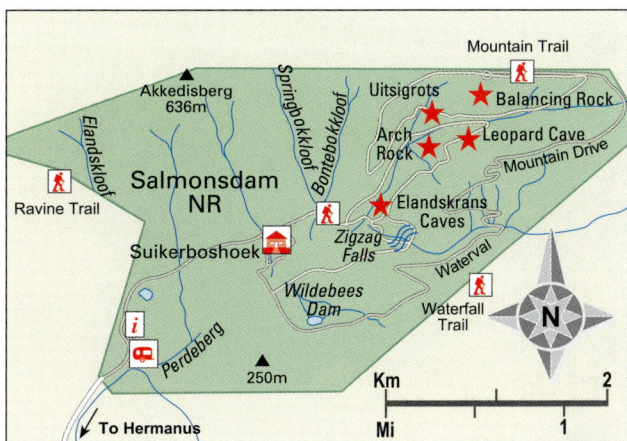

Mountain Trail
Springbokkloof
Bontebokkloof
Uitsigrots
Balancing Rock
Akkedisberg 636m
Arch Rock
Leopard Cave
Mountain Drive
Elandskloof
Salmonsdam NR
Ravine Trail
Elandskrans Caves
Zigzag Falls
Suikerboshoek
Waterval
Wildebees Dam
i
Perdeberg
Waterfall Trail
250m
Km 2
Mi 1
N
To Hermanus

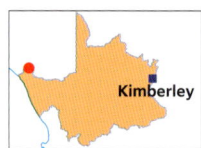

Ai-Ais/Richtersveld Transfrontier Park

AI AIS/RICHTERSVELD TRANSFRONTIER PARK

NEAREST TOWN
Sendelingsdrif

NEAREST AIRPORT
Alexander Bay/Upington

SIZE
6045km²

FAUNA/FLORA
1 Hartmann's Mountain Zebra
2 Suricate (*Meerkat*)
3 Rock Dassie
4 Ground Squirrel
5 Cape Hare
6 Bush Karoo Rat
7 Jackal Buzzard
8 *Halfmens* Tree
9 Quiver Tree
10 *Psammophorous* Plants

MAIN CONTACT DETAILS
027 831 1506
012 428 9111
reservations@sanparks.org
www.sanparks.org

ACCOMMODATION INSIDE PARK
Potjiespram, Richtersberg, De Hoop,
Tatasberg & Ganakouriep Wilderness
Camps, Hiking Trails Base Camp

Ai-Ais Hot Springs Resort
09264 63 262 045
info@nwr.com.na
www.nwr.com.na

ACCOMMODATION OUTSIDE PARK
027 831 1506
richtersveld@sanparks.org
www.sanparks.org

This massive 6045km² territory merges Namibia's Ai-Ais Hot Springs Game Park, into which the Fish River Canyon falls, and South Africa's Richtersveld National Park. The treaty that signed in such a portentous move has succeeded in establishing one of the largest conservation parks in Southern Africa. Fences defining the border between the two countries essentially have been removed, opening the way for a new wave of tourism. In the Richtersveld park, a prime example where negotiations have striven to take into consideration disadvantaged communities, the local Nama have been leasing the land to the national parks board while continuing to live and graze their livestock in the area. They will greatly benefit from the treaty in terms of jobs generated by tourism.

The Richtersveld, an austere, unrelenting landscape of sunburnt rock and desert sand, is nevertheless extraordinary. Giant valleys gouged into ancient rock and presided over by shorn cliffs are primeval in their grandeur. The Orange (Gariep) River delineating the northern border of the Richtersveld yields the only water in this vast barren land.

The Fish River Canyon, second in size to Africa's Blue Nile Gorge (and not the world's second largest canyon, as many claim), is fêted for its tough 5-day, 85km hike between sheer canyon walls and countless switchback bends. Sheared rock faces and eroded cliffs reveal folding and fracturing that dates from 1800 million to 50 million years hence. The hike ends in Ai-Ais, place of natural hot springs bubbling up at 60°C (140°F) – and rudimentary overnight accommodation. Room for improvement here! The Nama name is translated variously as "hot, very hot" to "fire water". With the new transfrontier park in place, tourism authorities are gearing themselves up to the developing of mountain biking, horse and camel trails as well as hiking, river rafting and canoeing.

SEASONAL INFORMATION

Gate opening times
07:00 – 19:00 (1 Oct to 30 Apr)
07:00 – 18:00 (1 May to 30 Sept)
Day visits not recommended

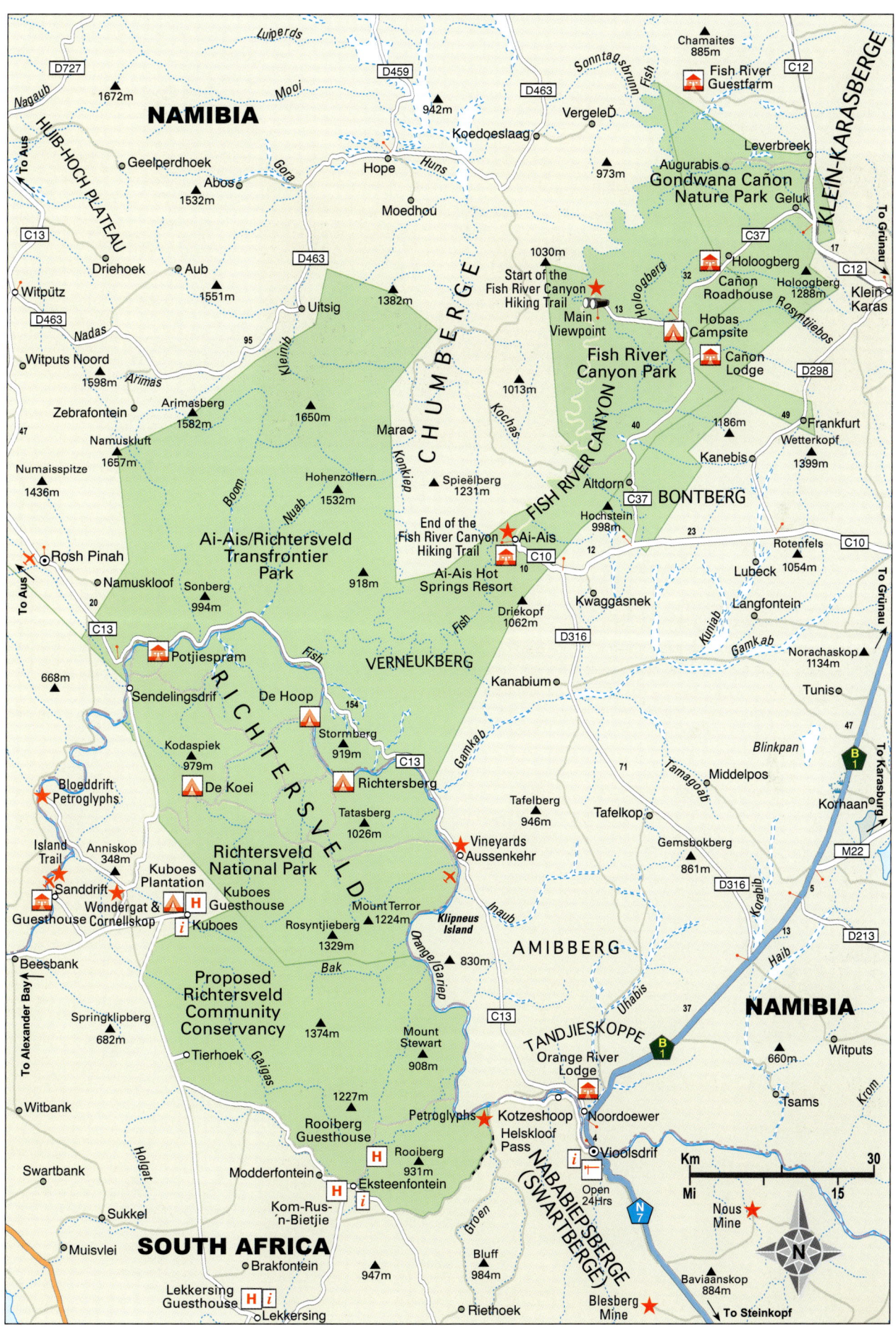

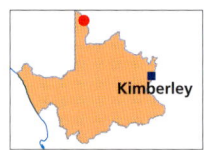

Kimberley

Kgalagadi Transfrontier Park

This was the first of the transfrontier zones to be created in Southern Africa – and it was also among the first in the rest of the world. A fusing of two national parks, South Africa's Kalahari-Gemsbok and Botswana's Mabuasehube–Gemsbok, the vastness of Kgalagadi makes this one of the select few conservation areas of such magnitude left on the globe. Characterised by high orange-red sand dunes rippling like a burnished sea, no permanent rivers have forged across this ancient landscape for thousands of years. The courses of two dry riverbeds, the Auob and Nossob, are testament to this. To overcome this lack of sustaining water, at various points along the riverbeds, wind pumps fill the waterholes which act as a magnet to the wildlife in the coolness of early morning and at the waning of the day. No surprise, then, the derivation of the word "kalahari" from *kgalagadi*, meaning "thirsty land". Eking out an existence on the fringes of the park are tiny hardy communities descended from San hunter-gatherers and nomadic Khoi pastoralists. Together with SA National Parks, they manage this transfrontier territory.

As searing summer temperatures rise to 40°C (104°F) and over, it's best to visit between April and September – although if your skin is armour-plated and you're able to withstand withering heatwaves, January and February bring on great sightings of the dark-maned Kalahari Lion. Kgalagadi is also about taking notice of the finer details – puff adders, barking geckos, Bat-eared Foxes and the endearing Ground Squirrel. Creatures with the most character are the quizzical Suricates, or *Meerkats*, scuttling around then pausing to take stock while rising, ramrod straight, onto their little hindlegs. As an overnight stop, the wilderness camps Bitterpan – rustic shelters on stilts overlooking a waterhole and surrounding red Kalahari sands – and the Kalahari Tented Camp exude the most personality.

KGALAGADI TRANSFRONTIER PARK
NEAREST TOWN
Upington

NEAREST AIRPORT
Upington

SIZE
3,8 million ha

FAUNA/FLORA
1   Black-maned Kalahari Lion
2   Leopard
3   Cheetah
4   Wildebeest
5   Giraffe
6   Gemsbok
7   Springbok
8   Hyena sp.
9   Bat-eared & Cape Fox
10 Suricate
11 Whistling Rat
12 Blueheaded Agama
13 Bateleur Eagle
14 Pygmy Falcon
15 Martial Eagle
16 Camel Thorn
17 Shepherd Tree

MAIN CONTACT DETAILS
054 561 2000
012 428 9111
reservations@sanparks.org
www.sanparks.org

ACCOMMODATION INSIDE PARK
(SOUTH AFRICA)
Traditional Camps:
Twee Rivieren, Mata Mata, Nossob
Wilderness Camps (unfenced):
Kieliekrankie, Urikaruus, Bitterpan,
Gharagab, Grootkolk, Kalahari Tented
012 428 9111
reservations@sanparks.org
www.sanparks.org

ACCOMMODATION INSIDE PARK
(BOTSWANA)
Two Rivers, Polentswa, Rooiputs,
Mabuasehube
09267 318 0774
dwnp@gov.bw

ACCOMMODATION OUTSIDE PARK
054 332 5911
tourism@kharahaismunicipality.co.za
www.kharahaismunicipality.co.za

SEASONAL INFORMATION

Gate opening times
06:00 – 19:30 (Jan, Feb)
06:30 – 19:00 (Mar, Oct)
07:00 – 18:30 Apr, Aug)
07:00 – 18:00 (May)
07:30 – 18:00 (Jun, Jul)
06:30 – 18:30 (Sept)
05:30 – 19:30 (Nov, Dec)

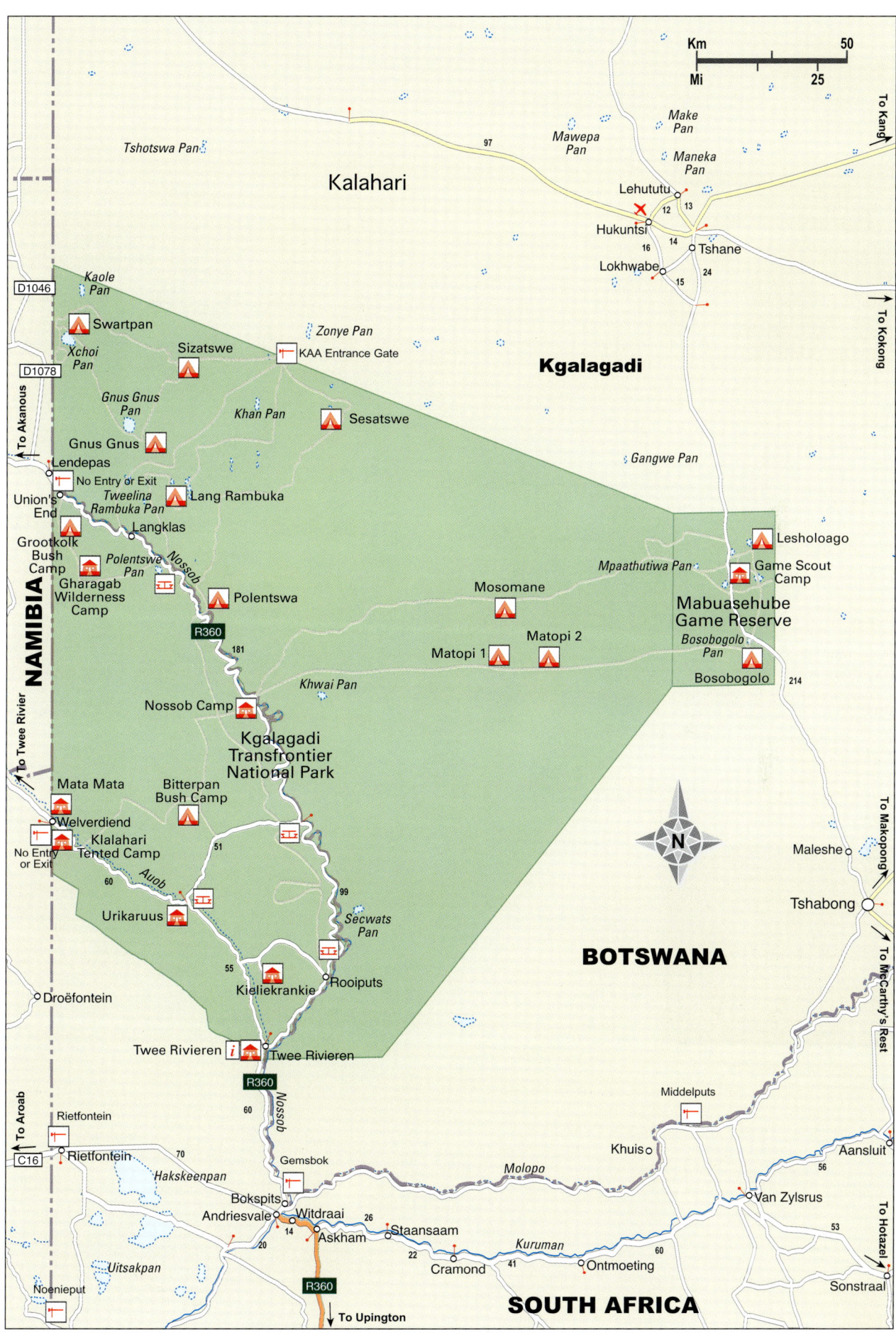

Km 50
Mi 25

Tshotswa Pan

Kalahari

Make Pan
Mawepa Pan
Maneka Pan

To Kang

Lehututu
97
12 13
X
Hukuntsi
16 14 Tshane
Lokhwabe
15 24

To Kokong

D1046
Kaole Pan
Swartpan
Xchoi Pan
Sizatswe
Zonye Pan
KAA Entrance Gate

D1078

To Akanous

Gnus Gnus Pan
Khan Pan
Sesatswe

Kgalagadi

Gnus Gnus
Lendepas
No Entry or Exit
Tweelina Rambuka Pan
Lang Rambuka

Gangwe Pan

Union's End
Langklas
Nossob

Grootkolk Bush Camp
Polentswe Pan
Gharagab Wilderness Camp
Polentswa

R360

181

Lesholoago
Game Scout Camp

Mpaathutiwa Pan

Mabuasehube
Game Reserve

Mosomane

Matopi 2
Matopi 1

Bosobogolo Pan

Bosobogolo
214

Khwai Pan

Nossob Camp

Kgalagadi
Transfrontier
National Park

Mata Mata
Welverdiend
Bitterpan Bush Camp
No Entry or Exit
Klalahari Tented Camp

Auob

51

60

Urikaruus

99

Secwats Pan

N

BOTSWANA

Maleshe

Tshabong

To Makopong

55

Kieliekrankie
Rooiputs

Droëfontein

Twee Rivieren
i Twee Rivieren

To Twee Rivier

R360

60

Nossob

Middelputs

To McCarthy's Rest

To Aroab

Rietfontein

Khuis

Aansluit

C16
Rietfontein

70

Gemsbok

Molopo

56
Van Zylsrus

Hakskeenpan

Bokspits
Andriesvale
Witdraai
26
Staansaam

53
To Hotazel

20 14
Askham
22
Cramond
41
Kuruman
60
Ontmoeting

Uitsakpan

Noenieput

R360

To Upington

SOUTH AFRICA

Sonstraal

NAMIBIA

Kgalagadi

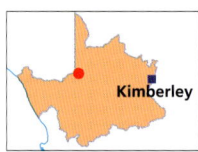

Augrabies Falls National Park

This "place of the great noise" translated from the Khoi name, *Aukoerebis*, alludes to the waterfall, sometimes full and thunderous, sometimes narrow and hemmed-in by bare exposed rock, that occurs along this section of the Orange, or Gariep, River. Part network of islands, channels and cataracts, part exuberant volumes of water, high rainfall can result in up to 19 separate falls. Sharp angles and planes in this blistering rocky landscape translate into deep-cut gorges, cracked ridges and buffed granite boulders. Extreme temperature highs and lows have forced animal and plant life to adapt – witness the region's Giraffes, whose lighter coats reflect heat more efficiently than their counterparts in the rest of the country, while mongoose and rock dassies have learnt to find respite in the shade of fallen trees, rock crevices and burrows. The scaly bark and fleshy, spiky leaves of the sculptural Quiver Trees also manifest adaptation techniques.

AUGRABIES FALLS NP
NEAREST TOWN
Kakamas

NEAREST AIRPORT
Upington

SIZE
46 000ha

FAUNA
1 Giraffe
2 Klipspringer
3 Aardwolf
4 Mongoose sp.
5 Ground Squirrel
6 Rock Dassie
7 Striped Mouse
8 Tent Tortoise
9 Augrabies Flat Lizard
10 Karoo Toad
11 Dusky Sunbird
12 Great Sparrow

MAIN CONTACT DETAILS
054 452 9200
012 428 9111
reservations@sanparks.org
www.sanparks.org

ACCOMMODATION INSIDE PARK
Family cottage, bungalows, camping site
012 428 9111
reservations@sanparks.org
www.sanparks.org

ACCOMMODATION OUTSIDE PARK
Tourist Info, Kakamas
054 431 6300

SEASONAL INFORMATION
Gate opening times
06:00 – 19:00 (summer)
06:30 – 18:00 (winter)
Day visitors allowed

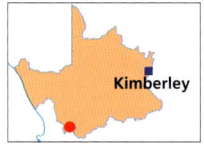

Tankwa Karoo National Park

The area bound by this park is one of the most arid sectors of the Karoo. Up till recently it has been in a veld recovery phase to allow the original vegetation to re-establish itself, and as a result of its lack of tourism infrastructure, the park's main visitors have been scientists and ecologists. Its stark landscape, punctuated by koppies, is often described in terms of moonlike aridity yet in spring, the stony earth is transformed by Karoo succulents – a biome categorised as Tanqua Karoo. The rugged Roggeveld mountains also lend the park a certain unique beauty. It appeals mainly to birding fanatics – among the species are rarities like the Doublebanded and Burchell's Courser – while from the top of the Roggeveld mountains, some have witnessed Black Eagles hunting rock dassies! A night drive could lead to an encounter with the not-so-often spied Aardvark.

TANKWA KAROO NP
NEAREST TOWN
Calvinia

NEAREST AIRPORT
Calvinia

SIZE
80 000ha

FAUNA/FLORA
1 Aardvark
2 Rock Dassie
3 Suricate
4 Mongoose sp.
5 Verreaux's (Black) Eagle
6 Ludwig's Bustard
7 Burchell's Courser
8 Longbilled Lark
9 Coral Aloe

MAIN CONTACT DETAILS
027 341 1927
027 341 2389
conrads@sanparks.org
www.sanparks.org

ACCOMMODATION INSIDE PARK
3 historic houses offering only a roof to sleep under
027 341 1927

ACCOMMODATION OUTSIDE PARK
Tanqua Guest House
027 341 2366
apburger@hantam.co.za

Paulshoek, Varsfontein
027 341 1927

SEASONAL INFORMATION
Entrance to and accommodation inside park is by special arrangement with park management only

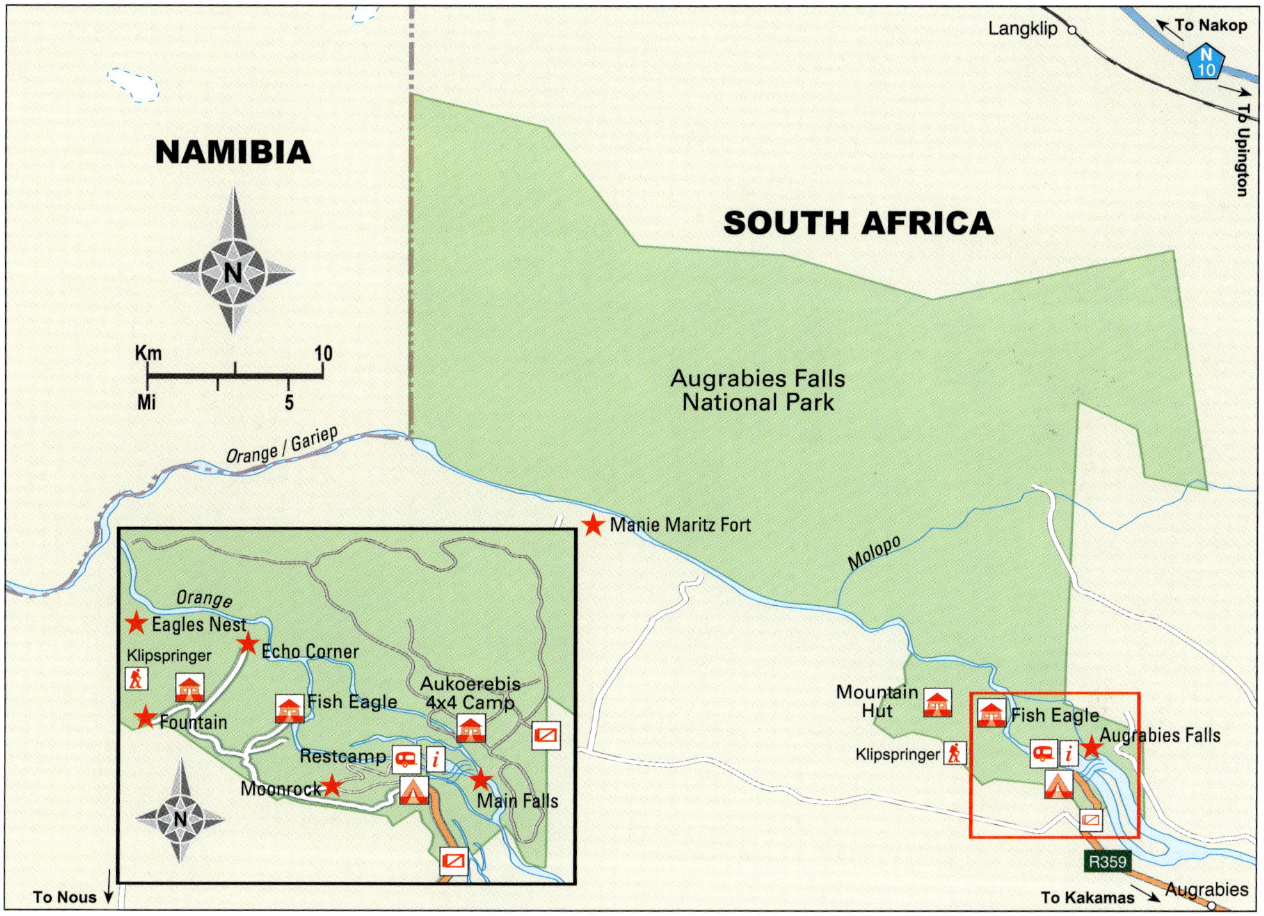

Map 1 (top)

NAMIBIA

N

Km 10

Mi 5

SOUTH AFRICA

Augrabies Falls
National Park

Langklip

To Nakop

N
10

To Upington

Orange / Gariep

★ Manie Maritz Fort

Molopo

Orange

★ Eagles Nest

Klipspringer

★ Echo Corner

★ Fountain

Fish Eagle

Aukoerebis
4x4 Camp

Restcamp i

★ Moonrock

★ Main Falls

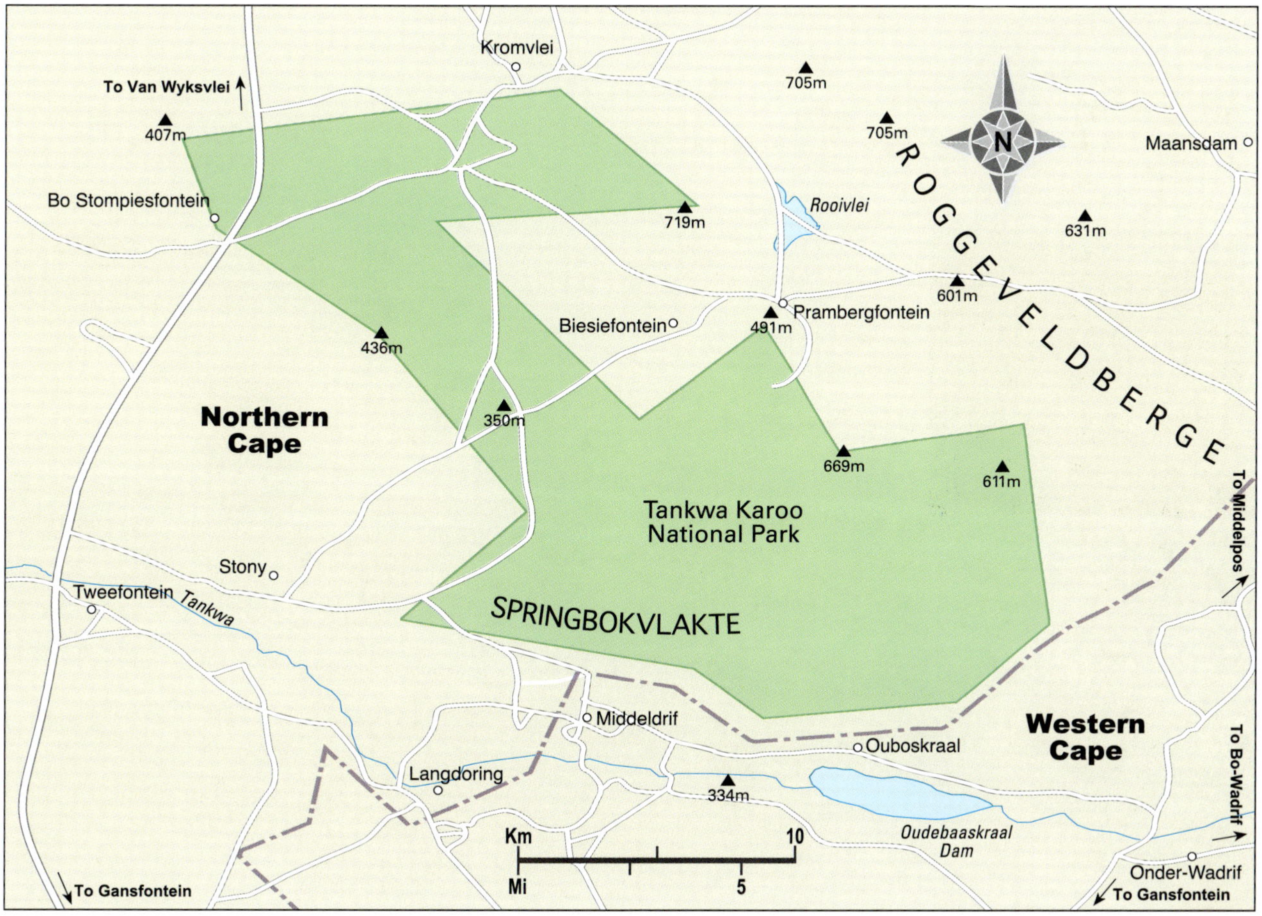

Mountain
Hut

Klipspringer

Fish Eagle

i

★ Augrabies Falls

R359

To Nous

To Kakamas Augrabies

Map 2 (bottom)

Kromvlei

To Van Wyksvlei

▲ 705m

N

ROGGEVELDBERGE

Maansdam

▲ 407m

▲ 705m

Bo Stompiesfontein

Rooivlei

▲ 631m

▲ 719m

▲ 601m

Biesiefontein

Prambergfontein

▲ 436m

▲ 491m

Northern
Cape

▲ 350m

▲ 669m

▲ 611m

To Middelpos

Tankwa Karoo
National Park

Stony

Tweefontein Tankwa

SPRINGBOKVLAKTE

Western
Cape

To Bo-Wadrif

Middeldrif

Langdoring

Ouboskraal

▲ 334m

Oudebaaskraal
Dam

Km 10

Mi 5

To Gansfontein

Onder-Wadrif
To Gansfontein

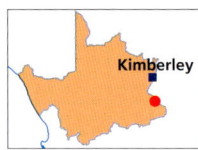

Doornkloof & Rolfontein Nature Reserves

These two nature reserves on the southern shore of Vanderkloof dam are set in a Karoo landscape of giant boulders and dolerite koppies. The confluence of the Seekoei and Orange rivers within **Doornkloof**, though, cuts a cool broad swathe across the dry sculpted landscape. The appeal to free-spirited hikers is that, other than the two- or three-day routes, they can ramble wherever their inclinations take them (pre-arrangement necessary), sleeping in a hut or under the stars in the veld. In Doornkloof, hikers will be surrounded by large antelope but, more exciting, is to come across the secretive Brown Hyena or, on a much smaller scale, the rare South African Hedgehog. **Rolfontein** stands out for its impressive numbers of Eland. Look out, too, for the elegant long-legged Blue Crane, endangered in South Africa and the country's national bird. Along the river, listen for the hollow call of the African Fish Eagle.

DOORNKLOOF NR
NEAREST TOWN
Colesberg

NEAREST AIRPORT (BOTH PARKS)
Kimberley

SIZE
12 000ha

FAUNA
1 Gemsbok
2 Eland
3 Kudu
4 Brown Hyena
5 Bat-eared Fox
6 South African Hedgehog
7 Blue Crane
8 Malachite Kingfisher
9 Red Bishop

MAIN CONTACT DETAILS
051 753 1315

ACCOMMODATION INSIDE PARK
Overnight hut

ACCOMMODATION OUTSIDE PARK
Tourist Info, Colesberg
051 753 0678

ROLFONTEIN NR
NEAREST TOWN
Vanderkloof

SIZE
8000ha

FAUNA/FLORA
1 White Rhino
2 Black Wildebeest
3 Gemsbok
4 Eland
5 Kudu
6 Red Hartebeest
7 Vervet Monkey
8 Blue Crane
9 Sweet Thorn Acacia

MAIN CONTACT DETAILS
053 664 0170

ACCOMMODATION INSIDE PARK
2 hikers' huts, tented camp

053 654 0170

ACCOMMODATION OUTSIDE PARK
Tourist Info, Vanderkloof
053 664 0198

SEASONAL INFORMATION

Gate opening times
Doornkloof NR:
8:00 – 18:00
Entrance fee
Rolfontein NR:
08:00 – 16:00
Permits required

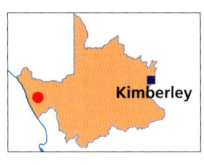

Namaqua National Park, Goegap Nature Reserve

A new initiative by National Parks to protect the fragile ecosystems of Namaqualand, the greater **Namaqua National Park** embraces the Skilpad Wildflower Reserve, which earns its kudos every spring with burnt-orange sheets of ursinia daisies. Added to these are white, yellow and orange *Gousblomme*, Namaqua daisies, Beetle Daisies, gazanias, *vygies*. . . the list is endless. The character of both the Namaqua park and the **Goegap Nature Reserve** is determined by bulky, rounded granite outcrops divided by sandy alluvial valleys. The granite terrain is referred to as the Namaqualand Klipkoppe ("rocky heads") and is part of a 50km fragmented mountain chain; the low-lying plains are called the Sandveld. A feature of Goegap is its expansive collection of endemic succulents. In spring, visitors gain an elevated view of the bright blooms from the back of an open truck in a 3hr guided tour.

NAMAQUA NATIONAL PARK
NEAREST TOWN
Kamieskroon

NEAREST AIRPORT (BOTH PARKS)
Springbok

SIZE
77 000ha

FAUNA
1 Black-backed Jackal
2 Black Harrier
3 Steenbok
4 Klipspringer
5 Aardvark
6 Porcupine
7 Northern Black Korhaan

MAIN CONTACT DETAILS
027 672 1948

ACCOMMODATION INSIDE PARK
None

ACCOMMODATION OUTSIDE PARK
Tourist Info, Kamieskroon
027 672 1627

GOEGAP NATURE RESERVE
NEAREST TOWN
Springbok

SIZE
15 000ha

FAUNA
1 Gemsbok
2 Hartmann's Mountain Zebra

3 Springbok
4 Klipspringer
5 Duiker
6 Ostrich

MAIN CONTACT DETAILS
027 718 9906

ACCOMMODATION INSIDE PARK
Overnight bushcamp, campsite, guesthouse, hut
027 718 9906

ACCOMMODATION OUTSIDE PARK
Tourist Info, Springbok
027 712 2011

SEASONAL INFORMATION

Gate opening times
Namaqua NP:
08:00 – 17:00
Goegap NR:
08:00 – 16:00
Fees payable
Day visitors allowed

Top map (Northern Cape / Free State):

To Hopetown
R369
R48
Diamant
Orange
Vanderkloof
Platberg
1471m
▲1497m
Km 10
N
Mi 5
1330m ▲
16
Rolfontein
Nature Reserve
Reebokrand
1484m ▲
Petrusville
Heilbron
Free State
Grootkop
1487m ▲
Bakenskop
1409m ▲
Uitsig
Knapsakrivier
41
R48
Knapsakberg
1478m ▲
1429m ▲
1375m ▲
32
Vanderkloof
Dam
1352m ▲
R369
Northern
Cape
1448m ▲
Spitskop
1505m ▲
Doornkloof
Nature Reserve
Orange
To Philippolis
Voorspoed
Hartsenberg
1512m ▲
1442m ▲
24
To Colesberg
To Philipstown
Hondeblaf

Bottom map (Namaqualand / Springbok):

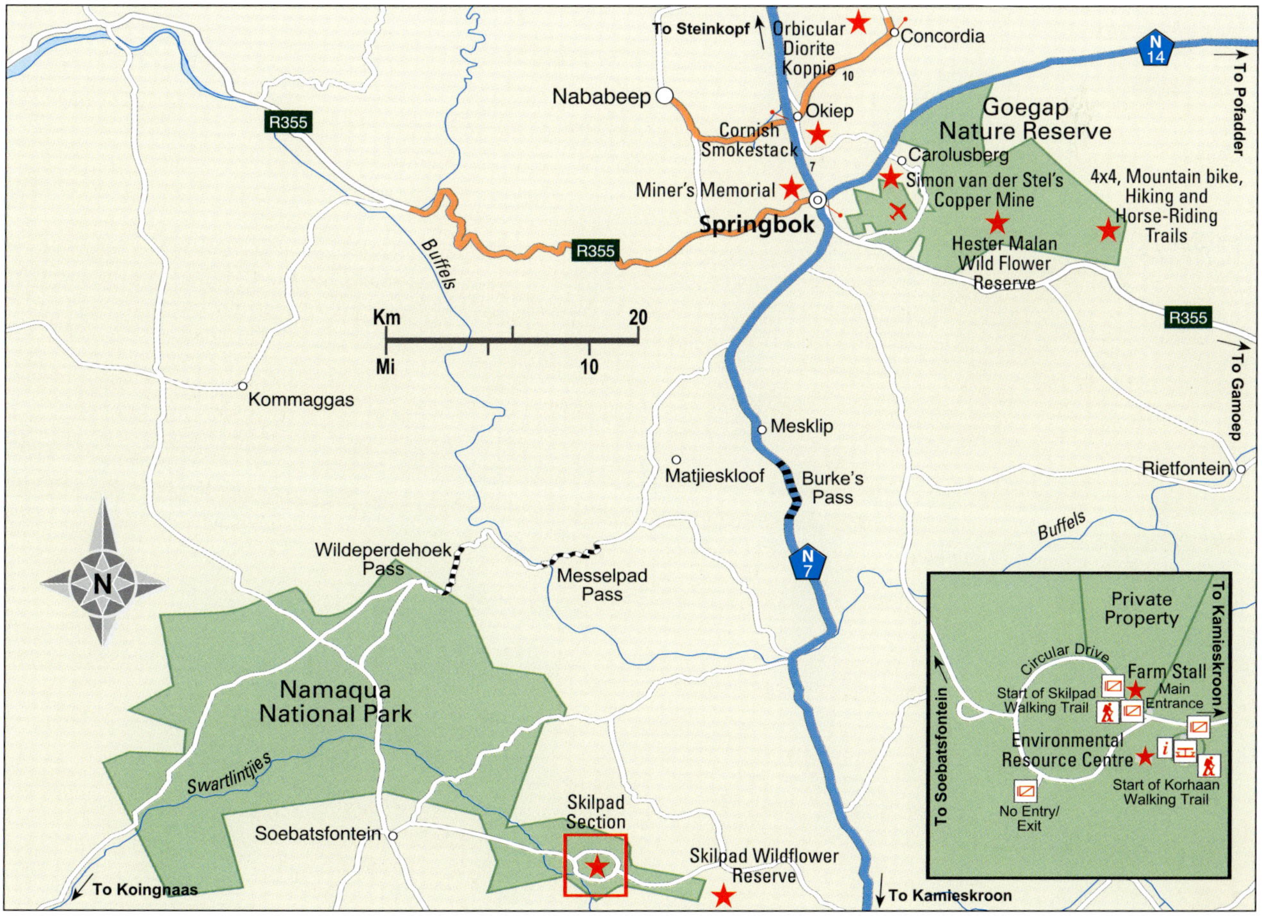

To Steinkopf
Orbicular Diorite Koppie ★
Concordia
N14
To Pofadder
R355
Nababeep
10
Okiep ★
Goegap
Nature Reserve
Cornish Smokestack ★
7
Carolusberg
Simon van der Stel's Copper Mine ★
4x4, Mountain bike, Hiking and Horse-Riding Trails
Miner's Memorial ★
Springbok
Hester Malan Wild Flower Reserve ★
★
R355
To Gamoep
Buffels
Km 20
Mi 10
Kommaggas
Mesklip
Matjieskloof
Burke's Pass
Rietfontein
Buffels
N
Wildeperdehoek Pass
Messelpad Pass
N7
Namaqua
National Park
Swartlintjies
Skilpad Section ★
Skilpad Wildflower Reserve ★
Soebatsfontein
To Koingnaas
To Kamieskroon

Inset (bottom right):

Private Property
To Kamieskroon
Circular Drive
Farm Stall ★
Start of Skilpad Walking Trail
Main Entrance
To Soebatsfontein
Environmental Resource Centre ★
i
Start of Korhaan Walking Trail
No Entry/ Exit

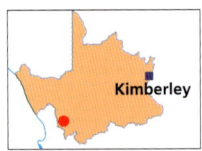

Oorlogskloof & Akkerendam Nature Reserves

The **Oorlogskloof** River flows at the foot of deeply dissected, wide-valleyed gorges which give this reserve its name. Mountains clothed in montane *fynbos* are capped with sharp escarpment edges – a territory that offers experienced hikers cliffs, rock chimneys, eroded plateaus and sculpted sandstone. Ladders and ropes aid hikers in relevant spots. Some of the trails, ranging from day walks to 7-day hikes, involve sharp descents to the river and corresponding ascents up to the cliffs. Needless to say, views from the top are marvellous. A treat are cooling springs and the Bushman rock paintings.

Akkerendam Nature Reserve sprawls across the semi-arid slopes of the Hantamsberg and around the Karee dam. Primarily a bird sanctuary, keen birders are drawn to its wild terrain to track hosts of feathered friends. The claim has been made that over two days, it's possible for twitchers to have ticked off 65 different species in their birding notebooks.

OORLOGSKLOOF NATURE RESERVE
NEAREST TOWN
Nieuwoudtville
NEAREST AIRPORT (BOTH PARKS)
Cape Town International
SIZE
4776ha
FAUNA
1 Cape Fox
2 Smith's Red Rock Rabbit
3 African Weasel
4 Angulate Tortoise
5 Cape Spurfowl (Francolin)
6 Fiscal Shrike
MAIN CONTACT DETAILS
027 218 1159
wpretorius@sp.ncape.gov.za
ACCOMMODATION INSIDE PARK
Huts at Groottuin
Overnight tented camps:
Brakwater, Driefontein, Doltuin,
Pramkoppie, Kareebos, Kameel se Gat,
Swartkliphuis, Olienhoutbos
Overnight shelters:
Suikerbosfontein, Bo-Kloof
🛏 ⚊ 🏕
ACCOMMODATION OUTSIDE PARK
Tourist Info, Nieuwoudtville
027 218 1336

AKKERENDAM NATURE RESERVE
NEAREST TOWN
Calvinia
SIZE
2300ha
AVIFAUNA
1 Booted Eagle
2 Black Harrier
3 Cinnamonbreasted Warbler
4 Namaqua Warbler
5 Fairy Flycatcher
MAIN CONTACT DETAILS
027 341 1712
ACCOMMODATION INSIDE PARK
None
ACCOMMODATION OUTSIDE PARK
Tourist Info, Calvinia
027 341 1712

SEASONAL INFORMATION

Gate opening times
Oorlogskloof NR:
Obtain permit in advance
Day visitors allowed
Akkerendam NR:
Open throughout the year

Vaalbos National Park

This park draws on the alluvial diamond diggings near Kimberley for its character – and adjacent to it is the historic mining village, Sydney-on-Vaal, still with many of its original Victorian buildings intact. Within the park, a tourist route has been developed using material from the diamond diggings. Also unique is the merging of three different ecosystems – the Savannah Grassveld, Kalahari and Karoo biomes – in a single park. The terrain is mainly Kalahari, but look for a crossover between Grassveld and Karoo in the Gras-Holpan sector. The park is named after the most commonly occurring tree, the *Vaalbos*, or Camphor Bush. The picnic and barbecue sites lining the Vaal River and Block dam (Blokdam) are an attractive feature.

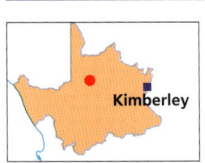

Spitskop Nature Reserve

Consisting mainly of Kalahari desert-like sandy flats interrupted by two rocky outcrops, this reserve's name derives from the prominent rocky koppie near the entrance. Its plains are ideal for game-viewing, and this desert territory is just perfect for the enigmatic Gemsbok. Let yourself be entertained by the nimble Suricates and keep a watch out for puff adders and Cape Cobras. The dormant seeds of spring daisies erupt into their dazzling hues here between August and October. Hikers can observe the wildlife and scenery on foot, staying in an overnight hut if they choose. Picnic spots nestle at the base of Spitskop's granite hill and a telescope can be found at the sheltered viewpoint.

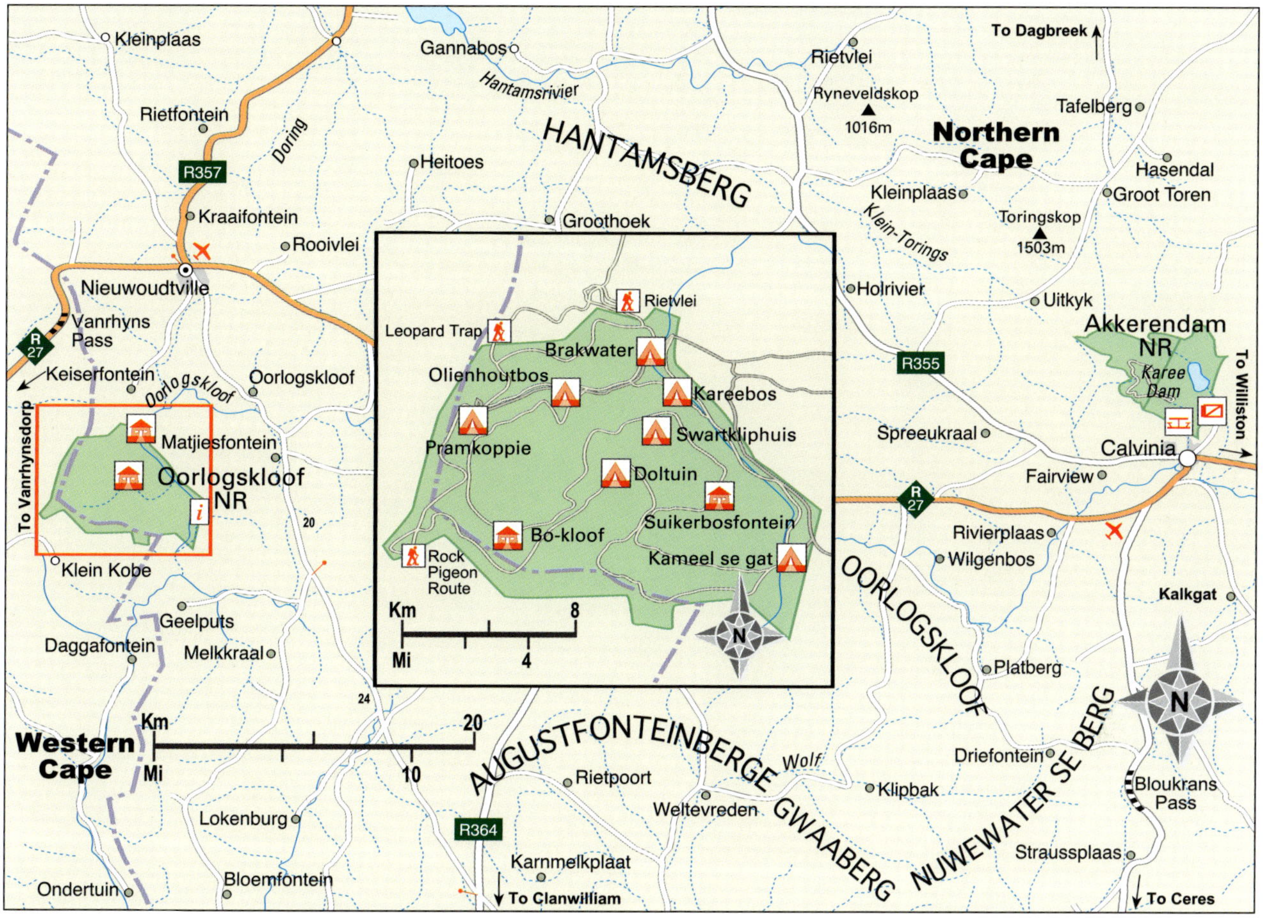

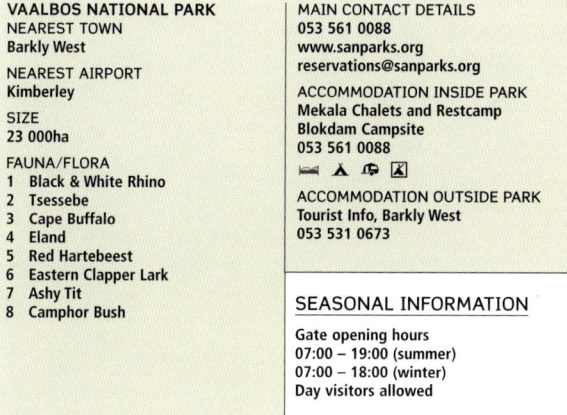

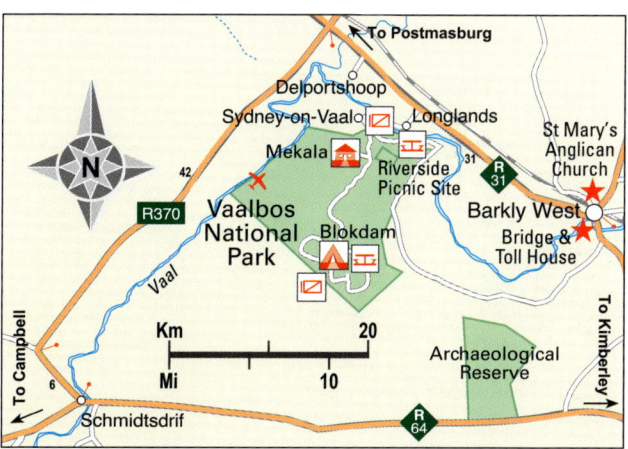

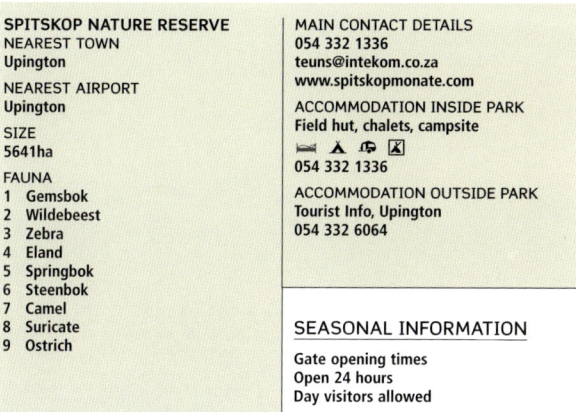

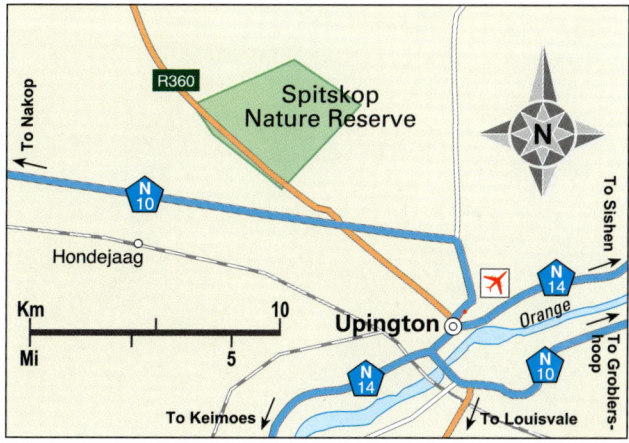

Top map

Kleinplaas
Gannabos
Rietvlei
To Dagbreek
Rietfontein
Hantamsrivier
Ryneveldskop
1016m
Tafelberg
Doring
Heitoes
HANTAMSBERG
Northern Cape
Hasendal
Groot Toren
R357
Groothoek
Kleinplaas
Toringskop
1503m
Kraaifontein
Rooivlei
Holrivier
Uitkyk
Nieuwoudtville
Akkerendam NR
Karee Dam
Vanrhyns Pass
R27
Rietvlei
To Williston
Leopard Trap
Keiserfontein
Oorlogskloof
Brakwater
R355
Matjiesfontein
Spreeukraal
Calvinia
Olienhoutbos
Kareebos
Oorlogskloof NR
Swartkliphuis
Fairview
To Vanrhynsdorp
Pramkoppie
Doltuin
R27
Klein Kobe
Bo-kloof
Suikerbosfontein
Rivierplaas
Wilgenbos
20
Rock Pigeon Route
Kameel se gat
Daggafontein
Geelputs
Km 8
Mi 4
N
Kalkgat
Melkkraal
Platberg
Western Cape
24
AUGUSTFONTEINBERGE
Wolf
Driefontein
NUWEWATER SE BERG
N
Km 20
Mi 10
Rietpoort
Klipbak
OORLOGSKLOOF
GWAABERG
Bloukrans Pass
Lokenburg
Weltevreden
Strausplaas
R364
Karnmelkplaat
To Ceres
Ondertuin
Bloemfontein
To Clanwilliam

Vaalbos National Park (text block)

VAALBOS NATIONAL PARK

NEAREST TOWN
Barkly West

NEAREST AIRPORT
Kimberley

SIZE
23 000ha

FAUNA/FLORA
1 Black & White Rhino
2 Tsessebe
3 Cape Buffalo
4 Eland
5 Red Hartebeest
6 Eastern Clapper Lark
7 Ashy Tit
8 Camphor Bush

MAIN CONTACT DETAILS
053 561 0088
www.sanparks.org
reservations@sanparks.org

ACCOMMODATION INSIDE PARK
Mekala Chalets and Restcamp
Blokdam Campsite
053 561 0088

ACCOMMODATION OUTSIDE PARK
Tourist Info, Barkly West
053 531 0673

SEASONAL INFORMATION

Gate opening hours
07:00 – 19:00 (summer)
07:00 – 18:00 (winter)
Day visitors allowed

Vaalbos map

To Postmasburg
Delportshoop
Sydney-on-Vaal
Longlands
St Mary's Anglican Church
N
Mekala
42
31
R31
R370
Riverside Picnic Site
Barkly West
Vaal
Vaalbos National Park
Blokdam
Bridge & Toll House
To Campbell
6
To Kimberley
Km 20
Mi 10
Archaeological Reserve
Schmidtsdrif
R64

Spitskop Nature Reserve (text block)

SPITSKOP NATURE RESERVE

NEAREST TOWN
Upington

NEAREST AIRPORT
Upington

SIZE
5641ha

FAUNA
1 Gemsbok
2 Wildebeest
3 Zebra
4 Eland
5 Springbok
6 Steenbok
7 Camel
8 Suricate
9 Ostrich

MAIN CONTACT DETAILS
054 332 1336
teuns@intekom.co.za
www.spitskopmonate.com

ACCOMMODATION INSIDE PARK
Field hut, chalets, campsite

054 332 1336

ACCOMMODATION OUTSIDE PARK
Tourist Info, Upington
054 332 6064

SEASONAL INFORMATION

Gate opening times
Open 24 hours
Day visitors allowed

Spitskop map

R360
To Nakop
Spitskop Nature Reserve
N10
N
Hondejaag
To Sishen
N14
N
Orange
Km 10
Mi 5
Upington
To Groblershoop
N14
N10
To Keimoes
To Louisvale

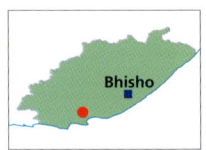
Bhisho

Addo Elephant National Park,
Woody Cape Nature Reserve, Groendal Wilderness Area

Addo was established in the thick valley bushveld surrounding the Sundays River and the Zuurberg mountains to save the last remaining 11 Elephants from overzealous hunters. This successful measure has raised numbers to over 350 today. The gene pool of **Addo National Park**'s elephants differs from any other in the country – believed to be as a result of selective shooting here in the 19th century. Elephant bulls carry small tusks, and most cows are tuskless. Buffalo, too, were forced by hunters to seek refuge in Addo's bushveld, where they turned to nocturnal browsing instead of grazing in the grasslands during the day. The park is dominated by the *Spekboom*.

The **Woody Cape Nature Reserve** has newly been incorporated into the Greater Addo National Park. Its three-in-one combination of ecosystems – forest, coastal dunefields and seashore – mean that only the Succulent Karoo biome is missing from the Addo preserve, making it one of the most diverse conservation areas in the world. The Alexandria dunes, with sharply defined slipfaces, stretch for 50km northward of Algoa Bay and provide an exciting interlude on Addo's Alexandria 2-day hiking trail. Also here are fossil dune ridges marking previous shorelines going back a few million years. Look out for whales and dolphins from the high tops of the dune cliffs.

The **Groendal Wilderness Area** lies within the Groot Winterhoek mountain range, embracing the Swartkops (KwaZungha) River and the Groendal dam at its centre. Kept in its natural state and suffering little impact from farming, hunting and commercialisation, it's a true wilderness in which layers of undulating, green-mantled mountain saddles fade into the far distance. Hikers testing out an array of 4–5-day trails will encounter *fynbos* and isolated pockets of indigenous forest in the ravines; they could also startle a small antelope or two.

ADDO ELEPHANT NP
NEAREST TOWN
Kirkwood

NEAREST AIRPORT (ALL PARKS)
Port Elizabeth

SIZE
145 000ha

FAUNA
1 African Elephant
2 Black Rhino
3 Cape Buffalo
4 Flightless Dung Beetle
5 Red Bishop

MAIN CONTACT DETAILS
042 233 0556/7
reservations@sanparks.org
www.sanparks.org

ACCOMMODATION INSIDE PARK
Hapoor & Domkrag Guesthouses

ACCOMMODATION OUTSIDE PARK
**Mvuba Campsite, Camp Matyholweni,
Narina Bushcamp**
Darlington Lake Lodge: 044 243 3673
Gorah Elephant Camp: 044 532 7818
River Bend Lodge: 042 233 8000
Intsomi Lodge: 046 653 8903/4/5

**WOODY CAPE NATURE RESERVE
(INCORPORATED INTO GREATER
ADDO NP)**
NEAREST TOWN
Port Elizabeth

SIZE
25 000ha

FAUNA/AVIFAUNA
1 Antelope sp.
2 Bushpig
3 Vervet Monkey
4 Narina Trogon
5 Trumpeter Hornbill

MAIN CONTACT DETAILS
046 653 0601

ACCOMMODATION INSIDE PARK
Woody Cape Hut for hikers

ACCOMMODATION OUTSIDE PARK
(ALSO GROENDAL)
Nelson Mandela Bay Tourism (PE)
041 585 8884
info@nmbt.co.za
www.nmbt.co.za

GROENDAL WILDERNESS AREA
NEAREST TOWN
Uitenhage

SIZE
30 000ha

FAUNA/FLORA
1 Grysbok
2 Bushbuck
3 Bushpig

MAIN CONTACT DETAILS
041 992 5418

ACCOMMODATION INSIDE PARK
Campsite

SEASONAL INFORMATION

Gate opening times
Addo Elephant NP:
07:00 – 19:00
Woody Cape NR:
Sunrise to sunset (no later than 19:00)
Groendal Wilderness Area:
08:00 – 16:00
Open throughout the year
Day visitors allowed

To Jeffreys Bay

Witteklip

Groendal Dam

Groendal Wilderness Area

Elands

Swartkops

KwaNobuhle

R334

R102

Uitenhage

Despatch

Bethelsdorp

Ibhayi

New Brighton

Swartkops

PORT ELIZABETH

Bluewater Bay

Coega

R334

R335

To Graaff-Reinet

Glenconnor

Kariega

R75

R336

Addo Elephant National Park

Darlington Dam

Darlington Lake Lodge

Crown Hill

Middlewater

Klipfontein

R400

Mvubu

Kabouga Guesthouse

Kirkwood

Kirkwood

Bluecliff

Sunday's River Citrus Co.

Bontrug

Enon

The Lookout

Sunland

Moth Memorial

Addo

Woodall

The Elephant House

Coerney

Narina

Suurberg

River Bend Lodge

Zuurberg Mountain Inn

R335

Jahleel Island

Brenton Island

St Croix

Algoa Bay

Cannonvale

Colchester

Sundays

Pearson Park Resort

Kinkelbos

Ncanara

Addo Elephant National Park

Tootabi State Farm

N10

To Cradock

(Woody Cape) NR

Paterson

Bellevue

Olifantskop

(Congaskraal) NR

(Dunefields) Reserve

Amakhala Game Reserve

Shamwari Game Reserve

Alicedale

R342

R400

Bushman Sands GR

Riebeek East

Great Fish

To Bedford

Carlisle Bridge

Addo Elephant National Park

(Boschhoek NP)

Seal Island

Bird Island

Nidaros 1930

Woody Cape

Intsomi Lodge

Kwanonqubela

Alexandria

Lalibela GR

N2

R72

Bushmans

Nonqqawuse's Grave

Cape Padrone

Cannon Rocks Holiday Resort

Cannon Rocks

Boknes

Salem

R343

Dias Cross Memorial 1488

Boesmansriviermond

Kenton-on-Sea

Marselle

To Port Alfred

Kariega

Waters Meeting II NR

To Port Alfred

To Peddie

Inset: Botanical Reserve

R335

Coerney

Domkragdam Water Hole

Woodlands Water Hole

Rooidam Water Hole

Gwarriedam Water Hole

Zuurkop

Janwalpan Water Hole

Kadauw Climb out Point

Hapoor Water Hole

Mpunzi Water Hole

Botanical Reserve

Spekboom Climb out Point

Spekboom Wandelpad Trail

To Fort Beaufort

Km 20

Mi 10

51

Tsitsikamma National Park

This must be one of the most gorgeous parcels of wilderness in the land – mountain slopes and deep ravines thick with indigenous trees, restless waves hissing over a cracked rocky coastline, and sensitively designed log cabins tucked into ancient milkwood trees a short wave's length from the ocean. In the Khoi-San tongue this is "the place of much water". They do have a way with words. Most rewarding in this naturalist haven are multiple trails with descriptive names, the longest one – the Otter Trail – needing no introduction.

Latest addition to the Tsitsikamma National Park is a wild, spectacular skyline of unruly jagged peaks separated by the deep-valleyed, meandering Palmiet River – this is Soetkraal. This wilderness tract straddles the Tsitsikamma mountain range between Plettenberg Bay and Misgund in the Langkloof. It is the site of a mesmerising 4x4 trail that climbs and drops, twists and meanders, then ends with camping under the stars.

TSITSIKAMMA NATIONAL PARK
NEAREST TOWN
Plettenberg Bay
NEAREST AIRPORT
George
SIZE
64 712ha
FAUNA/AVIFAUNA
1 Blue Duiker
2 Southern Right Whale
3 Common & Bottlenosed Dolphin
4 Cape Clawless Otter
5 African Black Oystercatcher
6 Cape Cormorant
7 Giant Kingfisher
8 African Finfoot
9 Knysna Woodpecker
10 Knysna Turaco (Lourie)
MAIN CONTACT DETAILS
042 281 1607, 044 382 2095
gardenroute@sanparks.org
nickyr@sanparks.org
www.sanparks.org

ACCOMMODATION INSIDE PARK
Storms River Mouth Restcamp
042 281 1607

Nature's Valley Restcamp
044 531 6700

ACCOMMODATION OUTSIDE PARK
044 533 4065
info@plettenbergbay.co.za
www.plettenbergbay.co.za

SEASONAL INFORMATION
Gate opening times
07:00 – 19:00
Day visitors not allowed in campsites

Camdeboo Nature Reserve
(previously Karoo Nature Reserve)

This reserve has a little of everything: it cradles the charming town of Graaff-Reinet which, with its 200+ national monument buildings, retains a 19th-century air; the Nqewba dam accommodates boats, skiers and shrieking water enthusiasts as well as anglers and birders; wildlife viewing serves up Buffalo, wildebeest and more than a handful of antelope species; and the scenery is staggering, from the Drie Koppe – Lesotho hatlike koppies rising from vast flat plains – to the craggy cliffs of the Valley of Desolation. From view sites visitors can marvel at the spectacle, where, 180 million years ago, molten rock pushed through cracks and fissures of sandstone and shale, cooling to form dolerite. As the sedimentary layers eroded, the dolerite resisted, leaving today's cracked and shattered pillars, pinnacles, buttresses and finely balanced boulders.

CAMDEBOO NATURE RESERVE
NEAREST TOWN
Graaff-Reinet
NEAREST AIRPORT
Port Elizabeth
SIZE
14 500ha
FAUNA/FLORA
1 Cape Buffalo
2 Wildebeest
3 Kudu
4 Springbok
5 Grey/Common Duiker
6 Bat-eared Fox
7 Vervet Monkey
8 Karoo Caterpillar
9 Pale Chanting Goshawk
10 Rock Kestrel
11 Acacia Forest
MAIN CONTACT DETAILS
049 892 3453
reservations@sanparks.org
www.sanparks.org

ACCOMMODATION INSIDE PARK
Hut on Driekoppe Hiking Trail,
Camdeboo Environmental Education
Centre (for school groups)
049 892 3453

ACCOMMODATION OUTSIDE PARK
049 892 4248
info@graaffreinet.co.za
www.graaffreinet.co.za

SEASONAL INFORMATION
Gate opening times
06:30 – 19:00 (Valley of Desolation)
06:30 – 17:30 (Game viewing area)
Day visitors allowed

Map 1 — Tsitsikamma

Klein
Skrik
Braam
Bos
Diep
Joubertskraal

To Haarlem

Misgund
Nuweplaas
Bruinklip

L A N G K L O O F

929m

Opkoms

Baviaanskloof
Wilderness Area

686m

Eastern Cape

R62
Louterwater

13

Kouga

16

Krakeelrivier
Joubertina

Twee Riviere

12

S U U R A N Y S B E R G E

989m

To Kareedouw

Heights

R62
Kompanjiesdrif

Kammiebos

Dwars

955m

Hoëkop
1497m

Western Cape

Formosa Nature Reserve

Lottering

Groot

T S I T S I K A M M A   M T S

Kleinbos

Stormsrivierpiek
1017m

Tsitsikamma Trail

Formosa Nature Reserve

Kruis

Witelskop
1251m

To Oudebos

Tsitsikamma NP

N2

13

Bloukrans Pass

777m

Lottering

Kleinbos

Big Tree

13

Bungee Jumping

Sanddrif

Elands

Hol

Witelsbos

To Plettenberg Bay

10

R102

6

Grootrivier Pass

9

Covie

Bungee Jumping

10

TSITSIKAMMA

T

Kraaibek

4

4

Kleinbos

Stormsrivier

Tsitsikamma Village Inn

H

Paul Sauer Bridge

16

3

Fairview

N2

Witelsbos

Forest Hall

Nature's Valley

Blue Rocks

Clinton's Bank

Tsitsikamma National Park

Blousloep

Beyers Island

Otter Trail

9

Wall Point

Storms River Mouth Rest Camp
Suspension Bridge

202m

Witelsbos State Forest

Groot Bank

Storm Point

Scuba Trail

Vermaak se Krans

Grootkrans

Piet se Baai

Voëlkrans

Skuinsbaai

INDIAN OCEAN

N

Km   16
Mi   8

Map 2 — Graaff-Reinet / Camdeboo

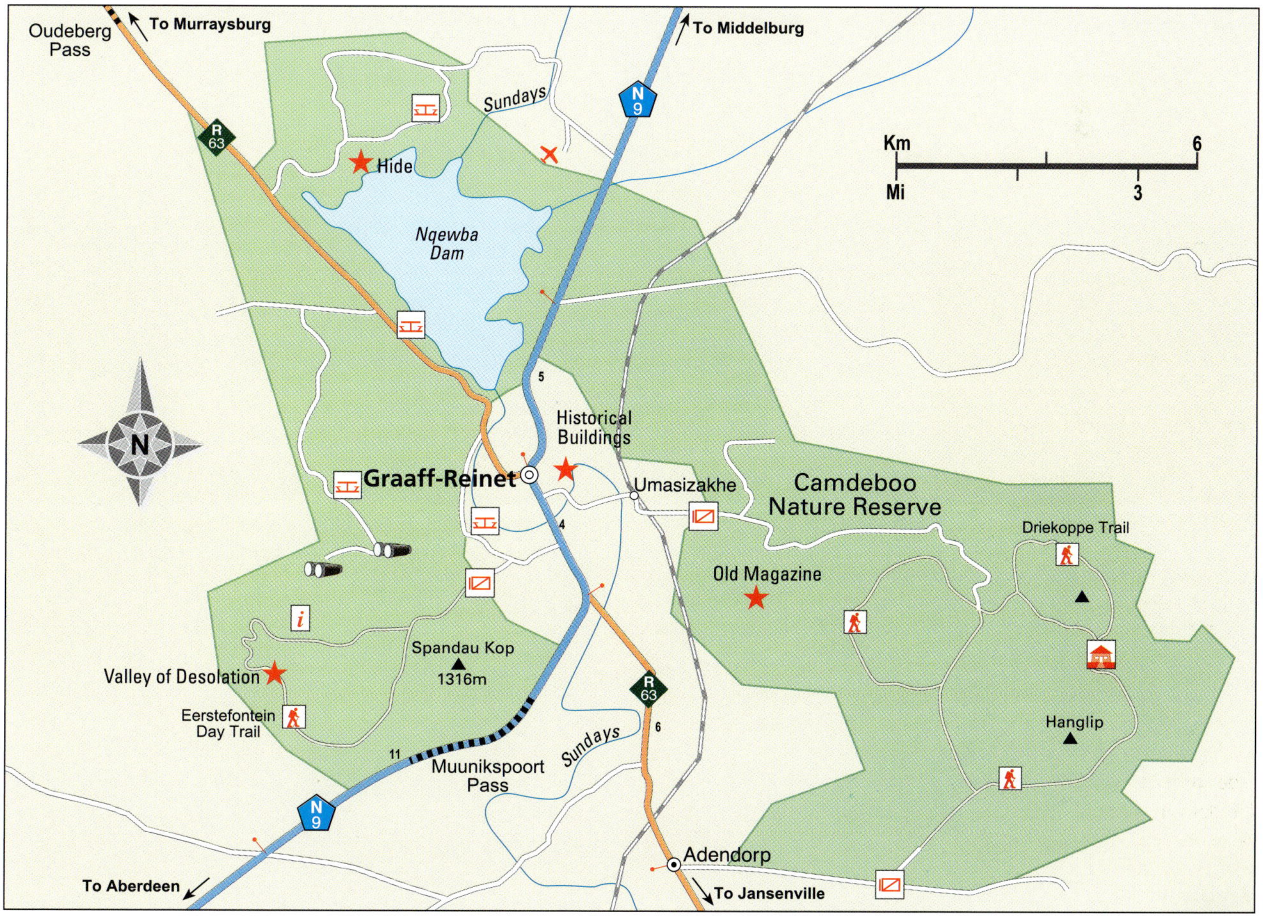

Oudeberg Pass

To Murraysburg

To Middelburg

Sundays

N9

R63

Hide

X

Km   6
Mi   3

Nqewba Dam

5

Historical Buildings

Graaff-Reinet

Umasizakhe

Camdeboo Nature Reserve

Driekoppe Trail

4

Old Magazine

i

Valley of Desolation

Spandau Kop
1316m

Eerstefontein Day Trail

R63

6

Hanglip

11

Muunikspoort Pass

Sundays

N9

Adendorp

To Aberdeen

To Jansenville

Mountain Zebra National Park

This well-watered park, which has the Wilgebooms River running right through the centre, is bounded to one side by the Bankberg's round-topped dolerite hills – defining feature of the Karoo – and a high ridge that merges into the Rooiplaat Plateau. It is thus scenically very pretty besides the appeal of its Cape Mountain Zebra population, which in 1937 was teetering on the brink of extinction. The black stripes of this species are narrower than those of Burchell's (plains) Zebra and they stop short of the belly, leaving it white. Their hides also don't feature the grey-shadow stripes of the Burchell's. Each zebra's stripes, like fingerprints, never match up to any other individual's stripe pattern and even differ on each side of the body. Cape Mountain Zebra prefer the higher grasslands of the plateaus and in winter they are proactive in moving up to mountain slopes and ravines to find grazing.

MOUNTAIN ZEBRA NP
NEAREST TOWN
Cradock
NEAREST AIRPORT
Port Elizabeth
SIZE
30 000ha
FAUNA/FLORA
1   Black Rhinoceros
2   Cape Buffalo
3   Black Wildebeest
4   Cape Mountain Zebra
5   Red Hartebeest
6   Eland
7   Gemsbok
8   Verreaux's (Black) Eagle
9   Martial Eagle
10 Jackal Buzzard
11 Ground Woodpecker
12 *Fynbos*
MAIN CONTACT DETAILS
012 426 5025
www.sanparks.org
reservations@sanparks.org

ACCOMMODATION INSIDE PARK
Mountain Zebra Restcamp,
Doornhoek Guest Cottage,
Family Cottages
012 426 5025

ACCOMMODATION OUTSIDE PARK
048 881 2383
www.cradock.co.za

SEASONAL INFORMATION
Gate opening times
07:00 – 19:00 (1 Oct to 31 Mar)
07:00 – 18:00 (1 Apr to 30 Sept)
Day visitors allowed

East London Coast Conservation Area
Cape Henderson, Gulu, Kwelera, Fort Pato & Umtiza Nature Reserves

The coastline, travelling northwards from East London up to the Transkei's Kei River mouth, is known as the Strandloper Coast. Here, over 400 years ago, Khoi and Gonaqua hunter-gatherers trawled the shoreline, harvesting mussels and other shellfish, leaving behind them today's high dunes – the remains of their *Strandloper* middens. Strung along these shores, the **Gulu**, **Kwelera** and **Cape Henderson nature reserves** all are part of the 60km, 5-day Strandloper Trail which crosses remote, wave-washed beaches, fords river mouths and ducks into remnants of protected indigenous forest. These three reserves, together with **Umtiza** and **Fort Pato** further inland, are part of a concerted effort to preserve the country's threatened forest patches. Fort Pato's forest falls into the Amatole Mist-belt biome, while **Umtiza**'s wooded confines hide Samango Monkeys, rarely seen in South Africa. These reserves are the domain of birdwatchers (Umtiza is known for the gorgeous Narina Trogon), beach anglers and day-picknickers.

EAST LONDON COAST
CONSERVATION AREA
NEAREST TOWN
East London
NEAREST AIRPORT
East London
SIZE
Approx. 3000ha

AVIFAUNA/FAUNA
1   African Black Duck
2   Narina Trogon
3   Yellowthroated Warbler
4   Whitestarred Robin
5   Knysna Woodpecker
6   Knysna Turaco (Lourie)
7   Ashy (Bluegrey) Flycatcher
8   Grey Sunbird
9   Cinnamon & Tambourine Dove
10 Samango Monkey
MAIN CONTACT DETAILS
043 736 9910/09
043 742 4450
info@ecparksboard.co.za

ACCOMMODATION INSIDE PARK
Cape Henderson Hut, campsite
043 742 4450

ACCOMMODATION OUTSIDE PARK
043 722 6015
info@tourismbuffalocity.co.za
www.visitbuffalocity.co.za

SEASONAL INFORMATION
Gate opening times
By arrangement only
Permits required

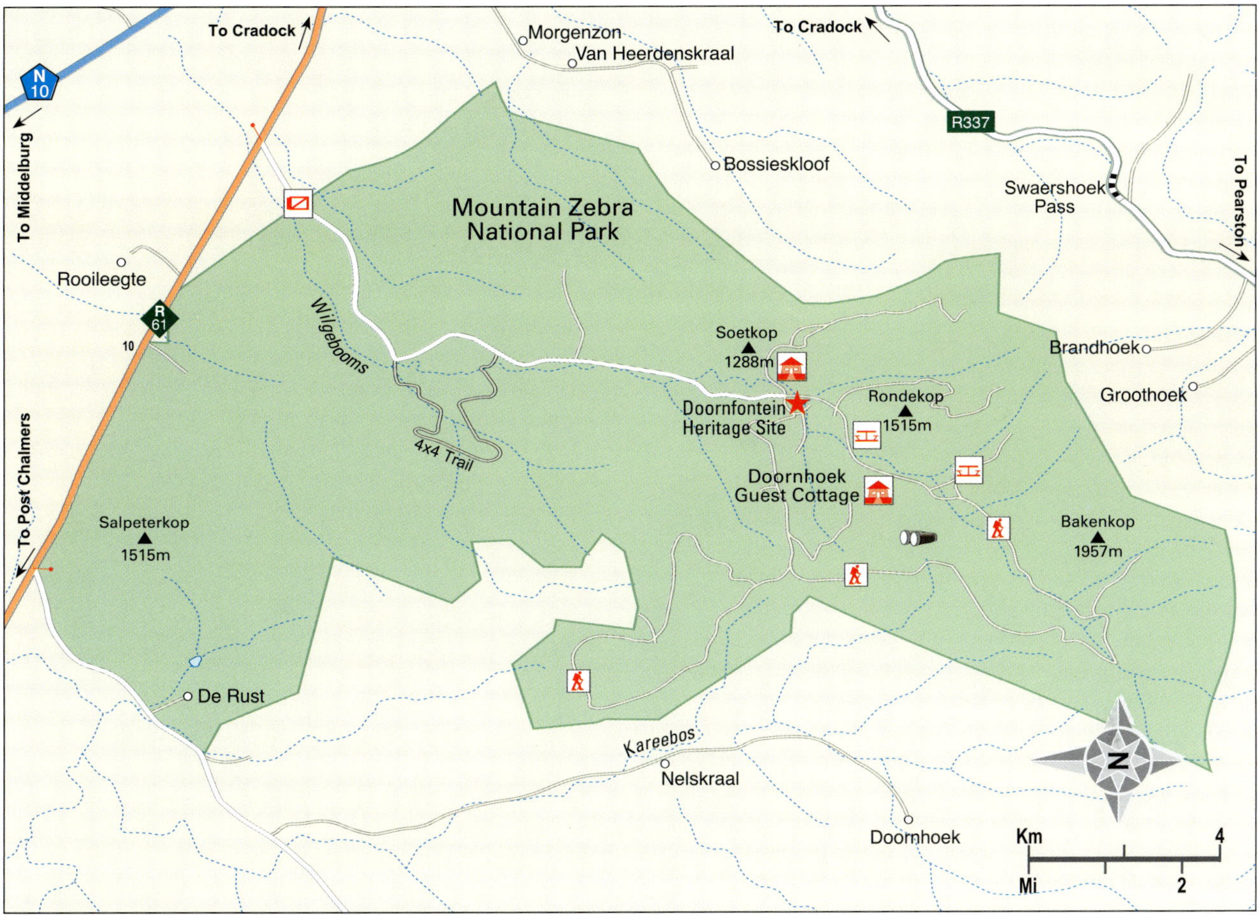

Map 1 — Mountain Zebra National Park

To Cradock

Morgenzon
Van Heerdenskraal

To Cradock

R337

N10

To Middelburg

Bossieskloof

Swaershoek
Pass

To Pearston

Rooileegte

Mountain Zebra
National Park

R61

10

Brandhoek

Soetkop
1288m

Groothoek

Wilgebooms

To Post Chalmers

4x4 Trail

Doornfontein
Heritage Site

Rondekop
1515m

Doornhoek
Guest Cottage

Salpeterkop
1515m

Bakenkop
1957m

De Rust

Kareebos

Nelskraal

Doornhoek

N

Km   4
Mi   2

Map 2 — East London region

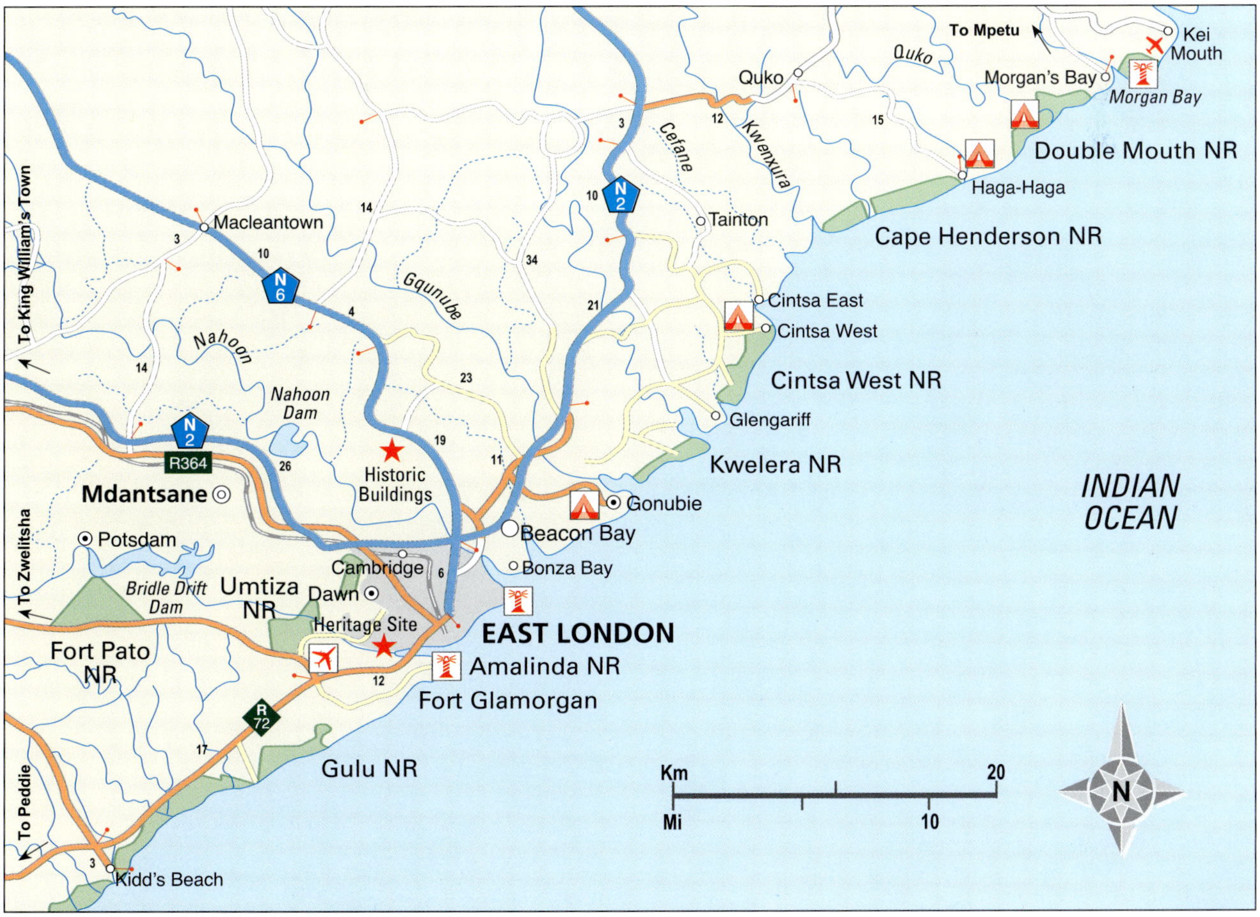

To Mpetu

Quko

Kei
Mouth

Quko

Morgan's Bay

Morgan Bay

Double Mouth NR

3

12

Kwenxura

15

Cefane

Haga-Haga

Cape Henderson NR

To King William's Town

14

Macleantown

10

N2

10

N6

Tainton

3

34

21

Cintsa East
Cintsa West

Gqunube

4

Cintsa West NR

Nahoon

14

23

Glengariff

N2

Nahoon
Dam

Kwelera NR

R364

19

26

11

Historic
Buildings

INDIAN
OCEAN

Mdantsane

Potsdam

Cambridge

Gonubie

Beacon Bay

Bonza Bay

To Zwelitsha

Bridle Drift
Dam

6

Umtiza
NR

Dawn

Fort Pato
NR

Heritage Site

EAST LONDON

Amalinda NR

12

Fort Glamorgan

R72

Gulu NR

To Peddie

17

Km   20
Mi   10

N

3

Kidd's Beach

Great Fish River Reserve Complex
Andries Vosloo Kudu, Sam Knott & Doubledrift Reserves

Three reserves, **Andries Vosloo Kudu**, **Sam Knott** and **Doubledrift**, are linked via a circular touring and wildlife-viewing route and all make up the **Great Fish River Reserve Complex**. In the past, this region witnessed terrible toil and strife between the early Settlers and the Xhosa clans, particularly as the Great Fish River often acted as a boundary between the conflicting territories. Evidence remains in the form of ruined old forts, signalling towers, farmsteads and graves. The tangled valley bushveld is wild and pristine. Kudu are a feature of Andries Vosloo, and in Doubledrift the Great Fish and Kat rivers converge, providing a perfect habitat for hippo to territorially lurk. If you encounter them on land, make sure never to get between them and the water! The luxury lodges in the reserve are onetime homes of the famous Knott family; Mvubu Lodge, on the riverbank, is built of natural materials.

GREAT FISH RIVER RESERVE COMPLEX
NEAREST TOWN
Fort Beaufort
NEAREST AIRPORT
Port Elizabeth
SIZE
45 000ha
FAUNA
1 Black Rhino
2 Cape Buffalo
3 Blue Wildebeest
4 Giraffe
5 Burchell's Zebra
6 Kudu
7 Eland
8 Springbok
9 Steenbok
10 Hippopotamus
MAIN CONTACT DETAILS
040 635 2116
043 742 4450

ACCOMMODATION INSIDE PARK
Andries Vosloo Kudu:
Accommodation for student groups only
046 622 7909
▭
Doubledrift:
Mvubu Lodge & Chalets, Inyathi Game Camp, Mbabala Lodge, Nottingham Lodge, Naudeshoek,
Double Drift Lodge
040 653 8010
▭ ⚲ ⛺ ⚷
Sam Knott:
Sam Knott Cabins
▭ ⚷
ACCOMMODATION OUTSIDE PARK
Tourist Info, Fort Beaufort
046 645 1555

SEASONAL INFORMATION
Gate opening times
Sunrise to sunset
Day visitors allowed

Wild Coast
Hluleka, Silaka, Mkambati, Luchaba, Dwesa & Cwebe Reserves

Scenic beauty common to this chain of coastal protected areas is their luxuriant tropical vegetation, forested belts, wind-tortured rock features, river mouths fanning out into wild seas and sandy shell-strewn shores. **Hluleka Nature Reserve** combines rocky seashore, lagoon and evergreen forest, punctuated with spiky prehistoric-looking strelitzias, scarlet Coral Tree blossoms (in winter) and flat, river lily-pads across which African Jacana delicately tread. In the forests of **Silaka Nature Reserve**, lilies flower on the forest floor and giant trees are draped in mosses, lichens and epiphytic orchids. Walking through grassland above the Msikaba River in the **Mkambati Nature Reserve** leads to breathtaking views of the thickly forested gorge, only place in the world for feathery Pondo Coconut Palms. Mthatha dam in the **Luchaba Game Reserve** draws anglers, birders and water-seeking day-trippers, while in the sister **Dwesa and Cwebe nature reserves**, bounded by ocean and Transkei grasslands, reintroduced crocodiles silently cruise the rivers.

WILD COAST
NEAREST TOWN
Port St Johns, Mthatha
NEAREST AIRPORT (ALL PARKS)
Mthatha
SIZE
Hluleka: 772ha, Silaka: 410ha, Mkambati: 7720ha, Luchaba: 420ha, Dwesa: 3900ha, Cwebe: 2149ha
FAUNA/FLORA (ALL PARKS)
1 Wildebeest
2 Burchell's Zebra
3 Blesbok
4 Cape Clawless Otter
5 Natal Red Rock Rabbit
6 Southern Right Whale
7 Common & Bottlenosed Dolphin
8 Black Duck
9 African Jacana
10 Crowned Crane
11 Denham's (Stanley's) Bustard
12 Narina Trogon
13 Mangrove Kingfisher
14 Coral Tree
15 Natal Fig
16 Pondo Coconut Palm
17 Strelitzia sp.
18 Orchid sp.
19 Watsonia
MAIN CONTACT DETAILS
043 742 4450
info@ecparksboard.co.za
www.ectourism.co.za

ACCOMMODATION INSIDE PARK
Hluluka (043 742 4450)
▭ ⚷
Silaka (043 742 4450),
Dwesa (047 499 7900)
▭ ⚲ ⛺ ⚷
Cwebe (083 996 5343)
▭ ▭ ⚲ ⚷
Mkambati (043 742 4450)
▭ ⚷
Luchaba
None
ACCOMMODATION OUTSIDE PARK
(ALL PARKS)
047 564 1187
tourismpsj@wildcoast.co.za
www.portstjohns.org.za

SEASONAL INFORMATION
Gate opening times
Hluleka NR: 06:00 – 18:00
Silaka NR: 08:00 – 16:30
Mkambati NR: 08:00 – 16:30
Dwesa NR: 08:00 – 16:30
Cwebe NR: 06:00 – 22:00
Luchaba GR: 08:00 – 16:30
Open throughout the year
Day visitors allowed

Map - Upper section

To Bedford
R344
Fort Fordyce Boshoek Outspan
Liddleton
Mpofu Game Reserve
3
12
To Cathcart
Hogsback
Km 20
Mi 10
To Stutterheim
To King William's Town
Keiskammahoek
Sandile Dam
Lingelethu
Fort Fordyce Nature Reserve
16
12
10
24
21
R345
Adelaide
R63
Blinkwater
Martello Tower
13
15
Fort Hare
15
Gaika's Grave 1829
23
19
R352
Fort Beaufort
Bhofolo
Alice
Fort Hare
21
22
23
4
5
Middledrift
17
To Bedford
29
Kat
15
19
19
R57
30
41
10
17
6
R345
Kwa-Pita
Fort Willshire
14
Keiskamma
To King William's Town
Sam Knott NR
Mvubu
Naudeshoek
24
Bothas
21
Doubledrift Game Reserve
Great Fish
24
16
Mbabala
Great Fish River Reserve Complex
Milkwood Tree 1835
Carlisle Bridge
3
17
Bucklands
Double Drift
Breakfast Vlei
12
9
R350
4
8
Fort Brown
Andries Vosloo Kudu NR
16
5
To Grahamstown
Fort Brown
To Grahamstown
Committees
To Peddie

Map - Lower section

To Flagstaff
Holy Cross
Mkambati NR
Umtentu
R396
Tsitsa Bridge
R61
42
Gwe Gwe
St Cuthberts
Tsolo
N2
Sidwadweni
Palmerton
Mkambati Palms
Mkambati
Luchaba Game Reserve
Stoneyridge
37
Lusikisiki
Mkambati
Port Grosvenor
Mthatha Dam
Nobantu
Misty Mount
Libode
Mlengana Pass
Mzimvubu
Magwa Falls
Goss Point
R56
Ntibane
Nduli NR
36
R61
Ntshilini
34
Gemvale
Mbotyi
19
MTHATHA
Rock of Execution
51
Tombo
Lloyds
Buntingville
28
Ngqeleni
Old Bunting
Silaka NR
Port St Johns
11
N2
Viedgesville
22
32
57
Notintsila
H
Boulder Bay
Bityi
7
52
8
Ngqungqu
Dick King 1842
Umtata
Hluleka NR
INDIAN OCEAN
6
24
15
Jojweni
Hluleka
Elliotdale
16
54
Forres Bank 1958
24
Old Morley
Tshani
To Idutywa
Anchorage
Bashee
Coffee Bay
Black Rock
6
Hole In The Wall
Mbolompo Point
Alderley
31
Rothmere
31
Hobeni
Km 30
Mi 15
14
5
The Haven
Cwebe NR
Willowvale
The Haven
Dwesa NR
7
Nyokana
34

Shamwari & Lalibela Game Reserves,
Amakhala Game Reserve

Dense bushveld concealing the entire spectrum of Africa's wildest creatures is the common denominator of this handful of parks. What sets them apart is the ambience and character of their lodge facilities. **Amakhala**, the Xhosa word for aloes, which grow prolifically in the area, outdoes itself with two gracious colonial homesteads, two stone-and-thatch lodges (one of which is a 1930s converted sheep-shearing shed), a historic inn, a Settler farmhouse and an authentic ox-wagon camp. Of **Shamwari**'s five luxury lodges, Longlee Manor is an Edwardian mansion, Eagles Cragg has a spa and serves up a private deck and plunge pool per room – for the discerning traveller, this! – and Bayethe's luxury tented suites bring you closer to nature. At **Lalibela**, thatched canvas-walled safari tents sit on platforms, linked by raised walkways, in the leafy treetops.

SHAMWARI GAME RESERVE
NEAREST TOWN (ALL PARKS)
Grahamstown
NEAREST AIRPORT (ALL PARKS)
Port Elizabeth
SIZE
20 000ha
FAUNA (ALL PARKS)
1   White & Black Rhino
2   African Elephant
3   Cape Buffalo
4   Leopard
5   Cheetah
6   Giraffe
7   Hippopotamus
MAIN CONTACT DETAILS
042 203 1111
www.shamwari.com
ACCOMMODATION INSIDE PARK
Longlee Manor, luxury lodges
ACCOMMODATION OUTSIDE PARK
(ALL PARKS)
046 622 3241
info@grahamstown.co.za
www.grahamstown.co.za

LALIBELA GAME RESERVE
SIZE
7500ha

MAIN CONTACT DETAILS
041 581 8170
res@lalibela.co.za
www.lalibela.co.za
ACCOMMODATION INSIDE PARK
Lodges, campsites

AMAKHALA GAME RESERVE
SIZE
6000ha
MAIN CONTACT DETAILS
042 235 1608
centralres@amakhala.co.za
ACCOMMODATION INSIDE PARK
Colonial homesteads, lodges, safari huts
042 235 1608

SEASONAL INFORMATION
Gate opening times
Shamwari GR, Lalibela GR:
Open 24 hours
No day visitors allowed
Amakhala GR:
08:30 – 16:30
Day visitors allowed

Baviaanskloof Wilderness Area
& Formosa Nature Reserve

This "baboons' gorge" has rising to either side of it the Kouga and **Baviaanskloof** mountains. Its dips and swoops over rugged terrain and across an abundance of rivers are best suited to 4x4s, particularly since the full length of the Baviaanskloof road negotiates five hair-raising passes. Towering rock walls, splashing waterfalls and baboons are the essence of this extensive wilderness. The campsite at Rooihoek is tucked into the foot of red rock crushed into right-angled folds.

Neighbouring Stinkhoutberg rises above the Gamtoos River valley, whose life-giving waters include the Groot, Salt, Kariega and Kouga rivers. *Gamtoos*, in the Khoisan tongue, is roughly translated as "wily as a lion". Intriguing . . . although you're not likely to find Lion here today – but indigenous stinkwoods to wander through and marvel at there are, aplenty. **Formosa**, named after a peak and also the *Erica formosa* species, is beautiful, wild, watered and forested.

BAVIAANSKLOOF WILDERNESS AREA
NEAREST TOWN
Patensie
NEAREST AIRPORT (BOTH PARKS)
Port Elizabeth
SIZE
180 000ha
FAUNA (BOTH PARKS)
1   Cape Buffalo
2   Kudu
3   Chacma Baboon
4   Vervet Monkey
5   Bushpig
6   Honey Badger
7   Mongoose
8   Rock Dassie
9   Mountain Hare
10 Porcupine
MAIN CONTACT DETAILS
042 283 0882, 043 742 4450
info@ecparksboard.co.za
ACCOMMODATION INSIDE PARK
Komdomo Campsite, Doodsklip &
Rooihoek Wilderness Campsites,
Bergplaas & Doornkraal Mountain Huts

ACCOMMODATION OUTSIDE PARK
042 283 0437
info@baviaans.net
www.baviaans.net
FORMOSA NATURE RESERVE
NEAREST TOWN
Kareedouw
SIZE
76 000ha
MAIN CONTACT DETAILS
042 273 1530, 043 742 4450
info@ecparksboard.co.za
ACCOMMODATION INSIDE PARK
No facilities at Formosa, developments due for completion Sept/Oct 2006
ACCOMMODATION OUTSIDE PARK
Tourist Info, Kareedouw
042 288 0303/0756

SEASONAL INFORMATION
Gate opening times
Baviaanskloof & Formosa:
Sunrise to sunset
Day visitors allowed

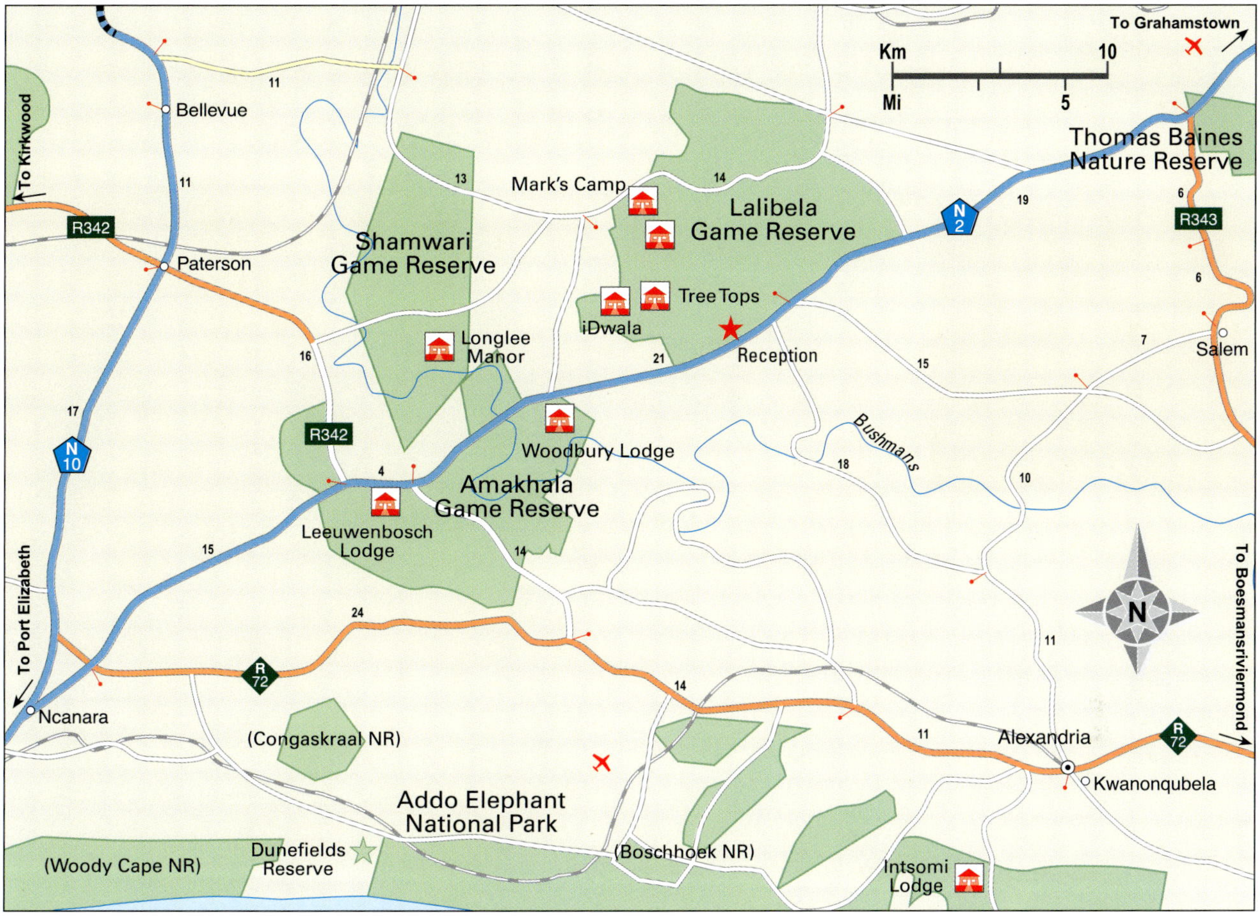

Top map

To Grahamstown

Km | 10
Mi | 5

Bellevue

To Kirkwood

11

R342

Paterson

13

Mark's Camp

Shamwari
Game Reserve

14

Lalibela
Game Reserve

N2

19

Thomas Baines
Nature Reserve

R343

6

6

Tree Tops

iDwala

21

Reception

Salem

7

Longlee
Manor

16

R342

Woodbury Lodge

Bushmans

18

15

Amakhala
Game Reserve

4

Leeuwenbosch
Lodge

N10

17

15

14

10

N

To Boesmansriviermond

24

R72

11

Ncanara

(Congaskraal NR)

14

Alexandria

Kwanonqubela

R72

11

Addo Elephant
National Park

(Boschhoek NR)

(Woody Cape NR)

Dunefields
Reserve

Intsomi
Lodge

Bottom map

To Willowmore

15

Noorspoort
Pass

6

To Klipplaat

To Klipplaat

6

Kleinpoort

13

BAVIAANSKLOOFBERGE

12

19

7

Steytlerville

12

5

35

Blaauwbosch
GR

R75

5

16

To Uitenhage

30

1627m

18

11

Groot

13

12

23

To Uniondale

16

30

28

16

14

17

4

GROOT-WINTERHOEKBERGE

1759m

Mierhoopplaat
NR

10

Nuwekloof
Pass

Baviaanskloof

45

Studtis

36

Western
Cape

Sandvlakte

Colekeplaas

101

Cambria

13

Stinkhoutberg
NR

KOUGABERGE

Baviaanskloof
Wilderness
Area

Eastern
Cape

Kouga Dam

14

Demistkraal

3

Patensie

To Port Elizabeth

To Uniondale

Misgund

56

Andrieskraal

R331

13

Kleinrivier

To Plettenberg Bay

R62

Louterwater

19

Joubertina

15

Krakeelrivier

Twee Riviere

Kammiebos

Kouga

Hol

17

R332

Hankey

Loerie

23

11

20

8

2

Van Stadens
Wild Flower Res.

TSITSIKAMMA
TOLL ROAD

Bloukrans
Pass

Paul Sauer
(Storms River)
Bridge

27

R62

Formosa
NR

Assegaaibos

7

Sandhoek

20

15

R330

12

8

19

T

12

10

T

13

7

14

8

2

8

The
Crags

Nature's
Valley

11

Stormsrivier

28

N2

18

10

Churchill Dam

Clarkson

13

9

Kruisfontein

11

8

11

39

Tsitsikamma
National Park

Kruis

18

Woodlands

R102

20

N2

10

Humansdorp

Jeffreys Bay

Oubosstrand

21

Impofu
Dam

R330

Aston Bay

15

Huisklip
Nature Reserve

19

7

13

15

Paradise Beach

Krombaai

13

16

10

Sea Vista

Oyster
Bay

Slangrivier

8

Cape St Francis NR

Cape St Francis

Cape
St Francis

N

Km | 20
Mi | 10

INDIAN
OCEAN

59

Kariega Game Reserve, Waters Meeting & Thomas Baines Nature Reserves

The unique position of **Kariega**, set high above the river valley of the same name, gives this reserve a special air. At these heights, Martial and Crowned Eagles nest, and you can hear the cry of the African Fish Eagle from the deck of your luxurious log chalet. Visitors can switch from river-level morning cruises aboard the *Kariega Queen* to the elevated ceiling-high valley views of the architecturally designed pub/restaurant. Find your canoe legs in the **Waters Meeting Nature Reserve**, bordering the Kowie River, where a 20km river route finishes conveniently at a hut on Horseshoe Bend. If you keep your voices down, you could have a chance encounter with a vertical-tailed Bushpig or even a graceful Kudu. In neighbouring Kowie Nature Reserve – great for river-bank picnics – look for the rare cycads. And despite the recreational dam in the **Thomas Baines reserve**, you can also get an eyeful of some serious wildlife.

KARIEGA GR
NEAREST TOWN (ALL PARKS)
Grahamstown
NEAREST AIRPORT (ALL PARKS)
Port Elizabeth
SIZE
5000ha
FAUNA/AVIFAUNA (ALL PARKS)
1   African Elephant
2   White Rhino
3   Wildebeest
4   Buffalo
5   Zebra
6   Giraffe
7   Lion
8   Leopard
9   Eland
10 Crowned & African Fish Eagle
11 Jackal Buzzard
12 Blackcollared Barbet
MAIN CONTACT DETAILS
046 636 7904
www.kariega.co.za

ACCOMMODATION INSIDE PARK
Ukhozi, Kariega Lodges

ACCOMMODATION OUTSIDE PARK
(ALL PARKS)
046 622 3241
info@grahamstown.co.za
www.grahamstown.co.za

WATERS MEETING NR
SIZE
34ha
MAIN CONTACT DETAILS
046 624 1235

ACCOMMODATION INSIDE PARK
None

THOMAS BAINES NR
SIZE
1005ha
MAIN CONTACT DETAILS
046 622 7216
ACCOMMODATION INSIDE PARK
Overnight accommodation only for school groups

SEASONAL INFORMATION

Gate opening times
Kariega GR:
10:00 – 15:00
Waters Meeting NR:
07:00 – 16:30
Thomas Baines NR:
08:00 – 17:00
Day visitors allowed

Fort Fordyce & Mpofu Reserves

The prize of **Fort Fordyce**, a small reserve with a prime location on a plateau, is its four crags that are regularly visited by Spiderman-footed rock climbers. Carrying fearful names like Fever Ward, the Labour Ward, Wall of Memories, and the happier More Mojo, three of these crags line the rim of a giant forested amphitheatre. This amphitheatre, and others, was the site of the greatest British military defeat in the Eastern Cape – the early 1850s battle between the Xhosa and the British. For hikers, there are panoramic views which include the Hogsback high country to the east, and groves of yellowwood and milkwood forest.

Spectacular views of the Katberg in the relatively unknown **Mpofu Game Reserve** (*mpofu* means "eland") make this a great start for the Katberg hike, walking trails and pony treks. Look out for unusual exotics like Himalayan Cedar and North American Redwood.

FORT FORDYCE NATURE RESERVE
NEAREST TOWN (BOTH PARKS)
Fort Beaufort
NEAREST AIRPORT (BOTH PARKS)
East London
SIZE
2146ha
FAUNA
1   Black Wildebeest
2   Red Hartebeest
3   Burchell's Zebra
4   Mountain Reedbuck
5   Bushbuck
6   Blue Duiker
7   Chacma Baboon
8   Tree Dassie
MAIN CONTACT DETAILS
046 684 0729

ACCOMMODATION INSIDE PARK
Overnight huts, fully equipped cottages, houses, campsite
046 684 0729

ACCOMMODATION OUTSIDE PARK
(BOTH PARKS)
Tourist Info, Fort Beaufort
046 645 1555

MPOFU GAME RESERVE
SIZE
7500ha
FLORA
1   Dohne Sourveld
2   Valley Bushveld
3   Yellowwood sp.
MAIN CONTACT DETAILS
043 742 4450
info@ecparksboard.co.za

ACCOMMODATION INSIDE PARK
Mpofu, Intloni & Mpunzi Lodges, Mpofu Trail Hut

SEASONAL INFORMATION

Gate opening times
Fort Fordyce NR:
10:00 – 18:00
Mpofu GR:
Sunrise to sunset
Day visitors allowed

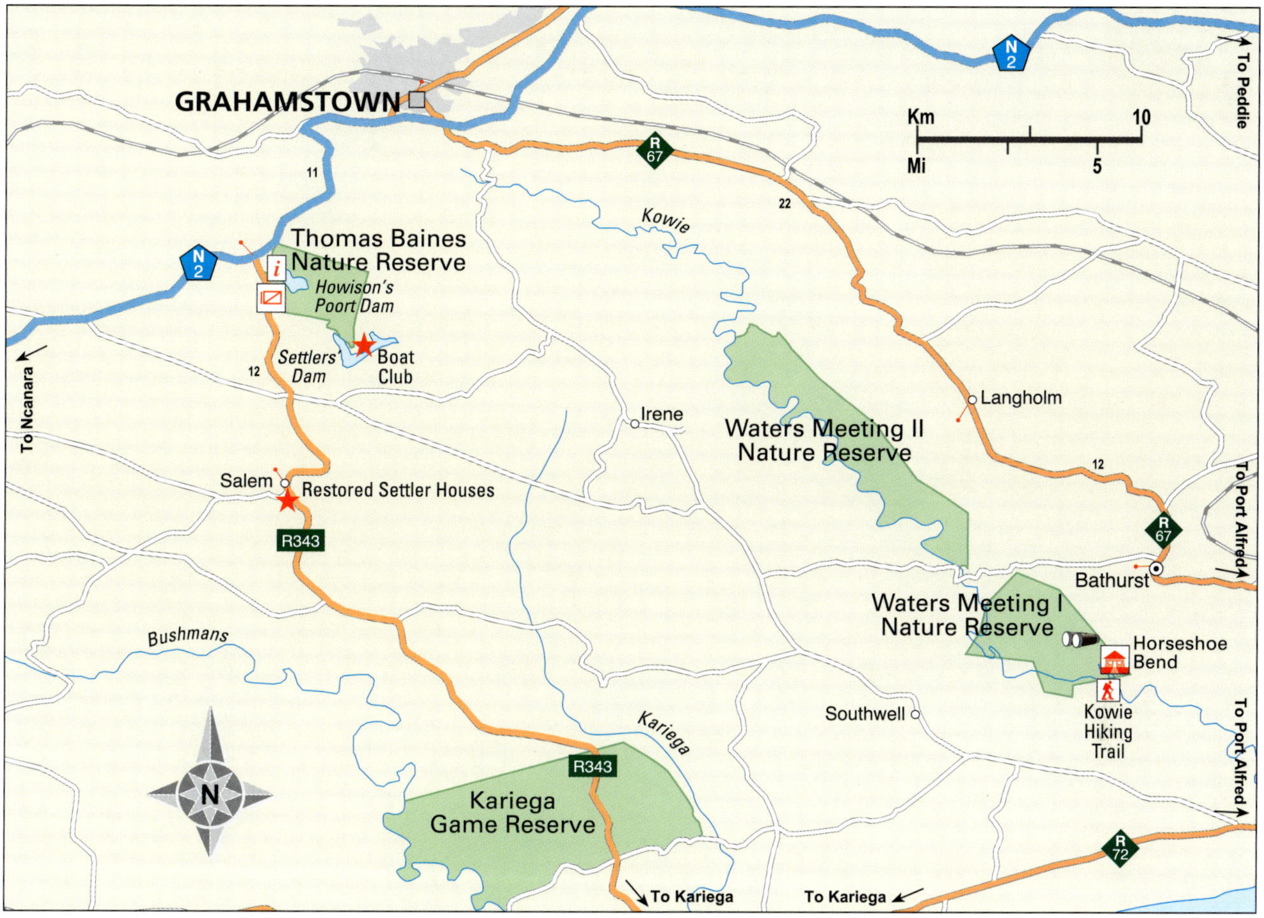

Map 1 (Top)

GRAHAMSTOWN

To Peddie

N2

Km 10
Mi 5

R67

Kowie

11

22

Thomas Baines
Nature Reserve

N2

*Howison's
Poort Dam*

To Ncanara

12

*Settlers'
Dam*

Boat
Club

Irene

Langholm

Waters Meeting II
Nature Reserve

12

To Port Alfred

Salem

Restored Settler Houses

R343

R67

Bathurst

Bushmans

Waters Meeting I
Nature Reserve

Horseshoe
Bend

To Port Alfred

Kariega

Southwell

Kowie
Hiking
Trail

N

R343

Kariega
Game Reserve

R72

To Kariega

To Kariega

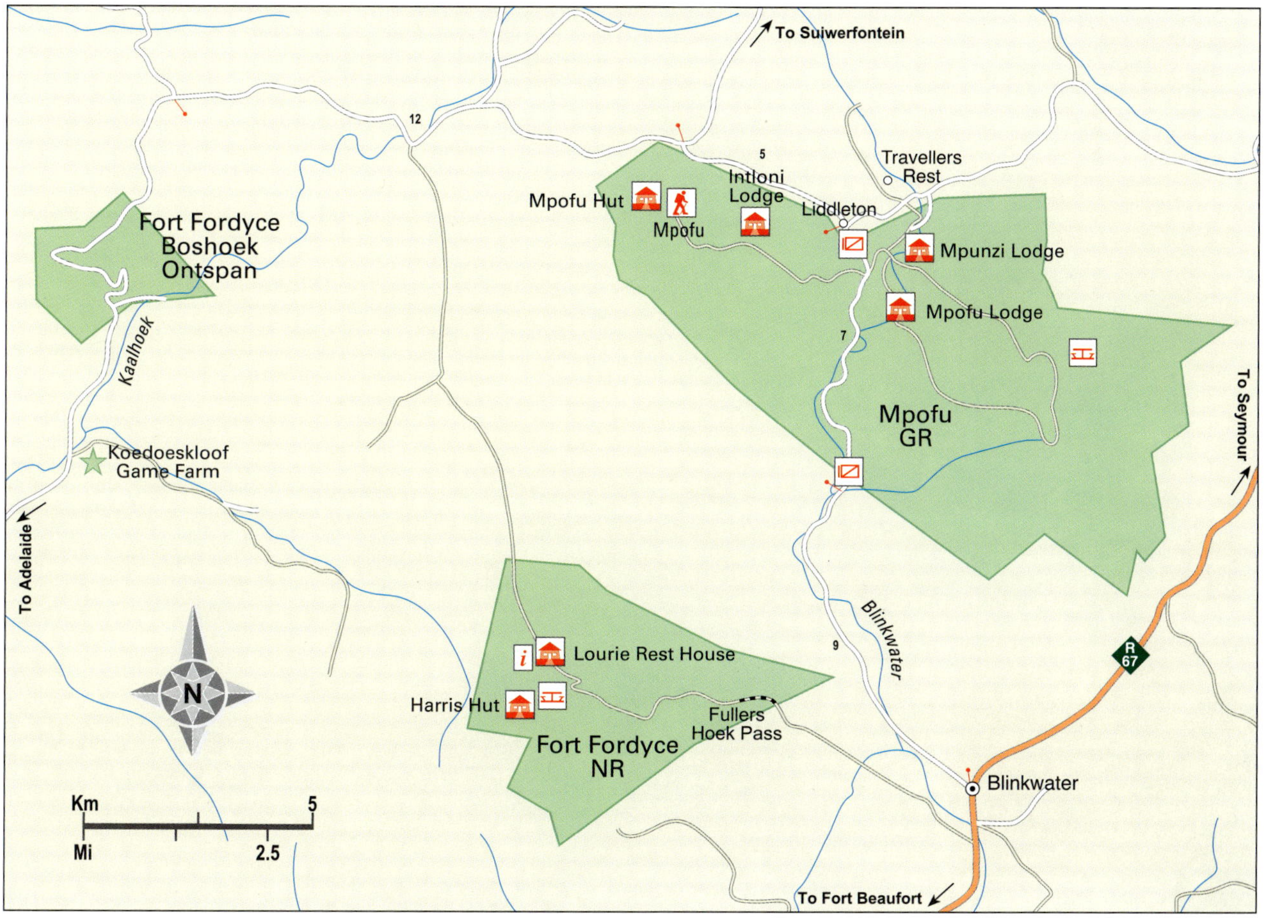

Map 2 (Bottom)

To Suiwerfontein

12

5

Fort Fordyce
Boshoek
Ontspan

Mpofu Hut

Intloni
Lodge

Travellers
Rest

Mpofu

Liddleton

Mpunzi Lodge

Kaalhoek

Mpofu Lodge

To Seymour

7

Koedoeskloof
Game Farm

Mpofu
GR

To Adelaide

N

Blinkwater

Lourie Rest House

9

R67

Harris Hut

Fullers
Hoek Pass

Fort Fordyce
NR

Blinkwater

Km 5
Mi 2.5

To Fort Beaufort

Tsolwana Game Reserve

A conical-shaped hill gives this reserve its name – the Xhosa word *tsolwana* means "sharp little one". The region's semi-arid Karoo-type plains of grassland and scrub-covered hills allow great game-viewing for hikers and sightseers. Visitors can tick off their wildlife checklist from a 4x4, on horseback or on foot as part of game-ranger-led hiking trails. These vary from day trails to 2-day walks, with overnight stops in bush camps. Besides its abundant game, Tsolwana has caves with San paintings. Visitors should also be on the lookout for the reserve's vultures, with their distinctive scrawny necks and collar-feathers.

This reserve opens itself up to the dubious pleasure of hunting, which is permitted in winter under strict supervision. An annual influx of hundreds of overseas trophy hunters descend to bag themselves Mountain Reedbuck, Blesbok and Springbok as well as Guinea Fowl and Grey-winged Francolin.

TSOLWANA GAME RESERVE
NEAREST TOWN
Queenstown
NEAREST AIRPORT
East London
SIZE
8500ha
FAUNA/AVIFAUNA
1 Blesbok
2 Springbok
3 Mountain Reedbuck
4 Aardvark
5 Cape Vulture
6 Blue Crane
7 Guinea Fowl
8 Greywinged Francolin

MAIN CONTACT DETAILS
040 845 1111
ACCOMMODATION INSIDE PARK
Otterford, Indwe, Lily Fountain, Tibet Park Lodges
Fundani, Phumlani Trail Camps
040 845 1111
ACCOMMODATION OUTSIDE PARK
Tourist Info, Queenstown
045 839 2265
sarto@eci.co.za

SEASONAL INFORMATION
Gate opening times
07:30 – 16:30
Day visitors allowed

Kayser's Beach & Kidd's Beach Nature Reserves

The country's concerted efforts to preserve and protect its natural heritage presently include the sleepy beach settlement of **Kayser's Beach** and the little resort town of **Kidd's Beach**. At the former, named after Joseph Franklin Kayser who owned the land in 1928, a ribbon of sand is backed by coastal forest. Its wave-washed rocks are hugely popular among fishermen who, apparently, catch a great variety of fish from here. The same can be said for Kidd's Beach, in this instance named after a former mayor of King William's Town, Charles Kidd. The surf at Kidd's Beach is manned by boardsailors and surfers, and diving expeditions are led among the offshore reefs. The nature reserve status aims to protect both reefs and coastal forest.

Bosberg Nature Reserve

Hikes up the Bosberg mountains lead to an overnight hut on the mountaintop, and the reward for tired walkers is the amazing view across Somerset East. Viewed from the summit of Bloukop ridge, a troop of flat-topped koppies appears to march towards the horizon. You can wash off the heat and sweat in the dam on Bloukop, which is also stocked with trout if you're a dab hand at fly fishing. You could also test out your botany skills on the wealth of indigenous trees in the dense forests by identifying the Wild Olive, Wild Peach, White Stinkwood, and Mountain Cabbage (*Kiepersol*) trees. The mountain heights are watched over by eagles – look out for Booted, Crowned and Black species.

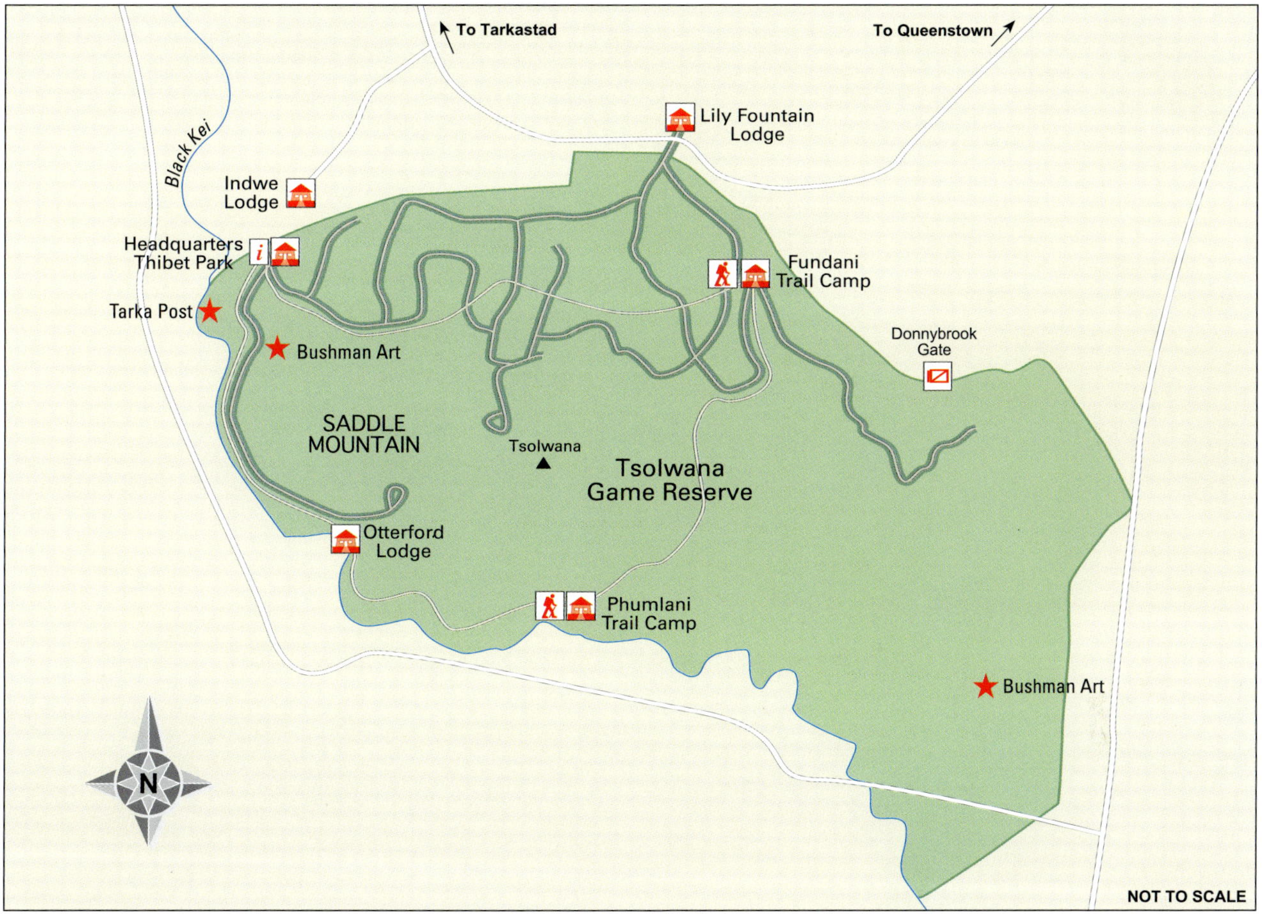

Tsolwana Game Reserve (map)

To Tarkastad

To Queenstown

Black Kei

Lily Fountain Lodge

Indwe Lodge

Headquarters Thibet Park

Tarka Post

Bushman Art

SADDLE MOUNTAIN

Fundani Trail Camp

Donnybrook Gate

Tsolwana

Tsolwana Game Reserve

Otterford Lodge

Phumlani Trail Camp

Bushman Art

N

NOT TO SCALE

KAYSER'S BEACH, KIDD'S BEACH

NEAREST TOWN
East London

NEAREST AIRPORT
East London

SIZE
Information not available

FAUNA/FLORA
1 Bushbuck
2 Large Spotted Genet
3 Striped Polecat
4 Rock Dassie
5 Porcupine
6 Sand Shark
7 Spotted Grunter
8 White Steenbras
9 Kabeljou
10 Sourberry
11 Wild Camphor Bush

MAIN CONTACT DETAILS
043 781 8452/1985

ACCOMMODATION INSIDE PARK
Stone cottages

ACCOMMODATION OUTSIDE PARK
043 722 6015
www.visitbuffalocity.co.za

SEASONAL INFORMATION

Gate opening times
Sunrise to sunset
Day visitors allowed

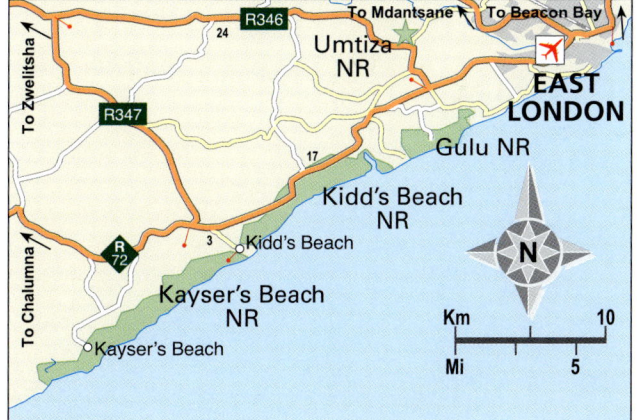

To Mdantsane

To Beacon Bay

R346

To Zwelitsha

Umtiza NR

EAST LONDON

R347

17

Gulu NR

To Chalumna

Kidd's Beach NR

3

Kidd's Beach

Kayser's Beach NR

N

Kayser's Beach

Km 10

Mi 5

BOSBERG NATURE RESERVE

NEAREST TOWN
Somerset East

NEAREST AIRPORT
East London

SIZE
2200ha

FLORA
1 Stinkwood sp.
2 Yellowwood sp.
3 Mountain Cabbage
4 Wild Olive
5 Wild Peach

MAIN CONTACT DETAILS
042 243 0095

ACCOMMODATION INSIDE PARK
Bungalows, campsite

ACCOMMODATION OUTSIDE PARK
042 243 1448/1333
bluecranetourism@isat.co.za
www.somerseteast.co.za

SEASONAL INFORMATION

Gate opening times
Sunrise to sunset
Day visitors allowed

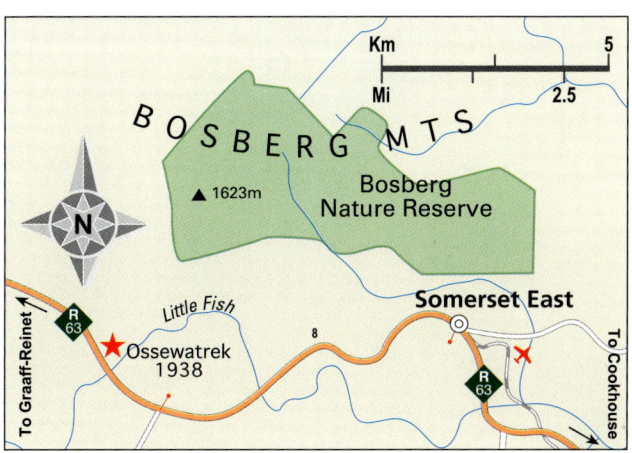

Km 5

Mi 2.5

B O S B E R G   M T S

1623m

Bosberg Nature Reserve

N

To Graaff-Reinet

R63

Little Fish

Ossewatrek 1938

Somerset East

8

R63

To Cookhouse

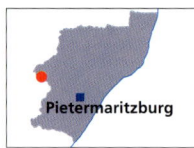

uKhahlamba North & Royal Natal NP
Rugged Glen, Cathedral Peak, Monk's Cowl & iNjasuti

UKHAHLAMBA NORTH
NEAREST TOWN (ALL PARKS)
Bergville

NEAREST AIRPORT (ALL PARKS)
Durban

SIZE
Royal Natal: 8094ha, Rugged Glen: 762ha, Cathedral Peak: 284ha, Monk's Cowl: 11 000ha, iNjasuti: 14 700ha

FAUNA/FLORA (ALL PARKS)
1   Mountain Reedbuck
2   Grey Rhebok
3   Eland
4   Bearded Vulture
5   Black Eagle
6   Yellowwood sp.
7   Protea Savannah

MAIN CONTACT DETAILS
033 845 1000/2
info@kznwildlife.com
www.kznwildlife.com
www.rhino.org.za

ACCOMMODATION INSIDE PARK
Royal Natal & Rugged Glen:
Thendele Hutted Camp, Thendele Lodge, Mahai & Rugged Glen Campsites
036 438 6303/6310

iNjasuti:
Chalets, caravan and tent campsites
036 431 7848/9

Cathedral Peak:
Didima Camp, Cathedral Peak Campsite, Cathedral Peak Hotel
036 488 1888

Monk's Cowl:
Monks Cowl Campsite, Mountain Campsite, Keith's Bush Camp, Cowl's Fork Campsite
036 468 1103

ACCOMMODATION OUTSIDE PARK
Drakensberg Tourism, Bergville
036 448 1557
www.drakensberg.org

Some of the country's most majestic mountainscapes soar dramatically skyward within the Drakensberg's **Royal Natal National Park**. In this section of **uKhahlamba**, "barrier of spears", the Tugela River pole-vaults over the Amphitheatre in five earthward bounds. The Amphitheatre, rising to roughly 1000m in a dramatic 5km curve, is defined to either side by the Eastern Buttress and the Sentinel. Naturally, the walks absorb most people's attention, with 25 to choose from in this park. Gorge Walk, the most popular, has walkers winding along the Tugela, shinning up a chain ladder or wriggling through a 60m Tunnel, then boulder-hopping, before facing awe-inspiring views of the Amphitheatre, creepy Devil's Tooth and Eastern Buttress.

Adjacent to the Royal Natal is the **Rugged Glen reserve**, with its own campsite and dominated by the 2000m Camel's Hump. Trout thrive in an icy river nearby, and nature and horseback trails hold the promise of exhilarating vistas.

Moving southward, an imposing trio, Cathkin Peak, **Monk's Cowl** and Champagne Castle, tower territorially over **iNjasuti**, a remote camp in a spectacular setting. In this rocky terrain, a special point of interest is the rock painting site, Battle Cave. A guided walk to this treasure trove of 750 paintings reveals, among others, animal-headed figures and a battle scene between two rival San clans. Monk's Cowl is the main access point to the Contour Path and to the higher trekking areas of the 'Berg. Plenty of short walks lead from the **Cathedral Peak** hotel to spots with awesome views, while the full day's ascent of the peak of the same name is for only the fittest. The story attached to Champagne Castle concerns two hikers in the 1860s who blamed the quickly depleting levels of a bottle of bubbly for the duo not quite achieving their climbing objective.

SEASONAL INFORMATION

Gate opening times
Royal Natal NP:
05:00 – 19:00 (summer)
06:00 – 18:00 (winter)
Rugged Glen: 06:00 – 22:00
Monk's Cowl:
06:00 – 19:00 (summer)
06:00 – 18:00 (winter)
iNjasuti: 08:00 – 16:30
Cathedral Peak: Open 24 hours

Pietermaritzburg

uKhahlamba Central
Giant's Castle, Kamberg, Lotheni, Highmoor & Mkhomazi

The solid bastion of **Giant's Castle**, towards the southern end of the giant Drakensberg massif, imposes a tangible presence over the game reserve of the same name. Established in the early 1900s to protect dwindling Eland, the reserve today has several hundred of these antelope grazing on rolling grass-covered hills whose tops are encircled by sharp ridges. The eland's significance here is affirmed by their prominence in the prolific San paintings of the Main Caves. Another thrilling presence is the Bearded Vulture, distinctive in its black facial feathers and giant 2.6m wingspan.

Kamberg's central position in the Drakensberg foothills makes it an ideal link to other areas of the 'Berg, including Giant's Castle and Lotheni. Enveloped by chilly-watered trout dams, pretty streams and verdant grassland, its emerald mantle makes it gentler, with an immensely tranquil air. The San rock art at Game Pass Shelter is superlative.

Highmoor Nature Reserve, part of the **Mkhomazi Wilderness Area**, has, as its claim to fame, the record catch of a trout caught in 1998 from Salmo Dam, weighing in at 5.5kg. No guesses as to who visits Highmoor's three dams. With a limit of six anglers per dam at any time, the wide open spaces in their stage-setting of rolling hills and mountains ensure you're the only actors. Even remoter in this part of uKhahlamba is **Lotheni**. Its atmospheric camp at the base of eternally green foothills offers champagne air and solitude to fly fishermen, hikers and mountain bikers. Some of the trails honouring eagles, canyons and Jacob's ladder have caves to hunker down in. Mkhomazi Wilderness is one of the most isolated and least explored areas in this mountain realm. Not attached to the main escarpment, its rolling grasslands are interrupted by a series of elevated ridges (and caves) pointing toward the Midlands.

UKHAHLAMBA CENTRAL
NEAREST TOWN
Winterton

NEAREST AIRPORT
Durban International

SIZE
Giant's Castle: 34 638ha
Highmoor: 15 000ha
Lotheni: 3984ha
Mkhomazi: 50 230ha
Kamberg: 10 000ha

FAUNA/AVIFAUNA
1 **Black Wildebeest**
2 **Eland**
3 **Mountain Reedbuck**
4 **Grey Rhebok**
5 **Grey Duiker**
6 **Chacma Baboon**
7 **Caracal**
8 **Rock Hyrax**
9 **Porcupine**
10 **Black Stork**
11 **Verreaux's (Black) Eagle**
12 **Bearded Vulture**
13 **Bokmakierie**

MAIN CONTACT DETAILS
033 845 1000/2
info@kznwildlife.com
www.kznwildlife.com
www.rhino.org.za

ACCOMMODATION INSIDE PARK
Giant's Castle:
Giant's Castle Camp, Mountain Huts, Rock Lodge
036 353 7130

Kamberg:
Kamberg Camp, Stillerus Cottages, Dondino Berg Cottages, rest huts,
033 267 7108

Highmoor:
033 263 7240

Lotheni:
Lotheni Settlers Homestead, Simes Rustic Cottages, chalets, campsite, hutted camp
033 702 0540

Mkhomazi:
033 266 6444

ACCOMMODATION OUTSIDE PARK
Central Drakensberg Info
036 488 1207
www.drakensberg.org

SEASONAL INFORMATION

Gate opening times
Giant's Castle, Kamberg, Lotheni:
05:00 – 19:00 (Oct to Mar)
06:00 – 18:00 (Apr to Sept)
Highmoor:
06:00 – 18:00
Mkhomazi:
06:00 – 18:00
Day visitors allowed

Km 10

Mi 5

Hillside

LITTLE BERG

iNjasuti Gate

iNjasuti

Giant's Castle
Nature Reserve

Hillside Gate

5

7

Bushmans

KwaMankonjane

Rockmount

8

Hlatikulu

5

Hlatikulu

KwaMkhize

Witteberg Gate

19

Ntabamnyama Track

World's View

Lammergeier
Hide

Crane
Foundation

8

H

Glengarry

uKhahlamba-
Drakensberg Park
(World Heritage Site)

Giant's
Lodge

Giant's Hutted
Camp

12

5

Popple
Peak
3377m

Bannerman
Hut

Highmoor
Dam

Highmoor

Highmoor
State Forest

6

Main
Cave

Giant's Castle Two Huts Hike

Mt Durnford
3275m

Vulture
Hide

Mooi

Kamberg

Emeweni Falls

Nzinga

Giant's
Castle
3314m

Kamberg
NR

Sheba's
Breasts
2321m

Nzinga

Sinclair's
Shelter
Cave

LESOTHO

Ash
Cave

The Tent
3130m

Yellowwood
Cave

Lotheni

Mkhomazi
NR

Cyprus
Cave

McKenzie
Cave

3314m

Root Family
Farm

Gelib
Tree

Lotheni
NR

Loteni

14

Carter's
Hill
1935m

Mokhotlong

Lynx Cave

Nhlothimbe

Pingpong
Cutting

Lower Loteni

Vergelegen
NR

The Pyramid
2009m

Highland
Nook

16

Mkomazi

Vergelegen

Forest
Station

Mqatsheni

Stepmore

SOUTH AFRICA

uKhahlamba-
Drakensberg Park
(World Heritage Site)

Mkhomazana

5

Mzimkhulu
Wilderness
Area

Sani Top
Chalets

Twelve
Apostles
2914m

22

Mkomazana

Snow Hill
1763m

Sani Pass

Sani Pass

H

Sani Pass

4

Cobham
NR

Good Hope
Cave

Sani Lodge

To Underberg

N

DRAKENSBERG

Pietermaritzburg

uKhahlamba South
Himeville, Vergelegen Nature Reserve, Cobham, Coleford, Garden Castle & Bushman's Nek Valley

UKHAHLAMBA SOUTH
NEAREST TOWN
Underberg

NEAREST AIRPORT
Durban International

SIZE
Garden Castle/Bushman's Nek Valley:
35 300ha
Cobham: 52 000ha
Vergelegen: 21 000ha
Himeville: 104ha
Coleford: 1272ha

FAUNA/FLORA
1 Black Wildebeest
2 Eland
3 Oribi
4 Mountain Reedbuck
5 Grey Rhebok
6 Duiker
7 Blesbok
8 Jackal sp.
9 Serval
10 Cape Clawless Otter
11 *Themeda* & *Festuca* Grassland
12 *Protea dracomontana*
13 Tree Fern sp.

MAIN CONTACT DETAILS
033 845 1000/2
info@kznwildlife.com
www.kznwildlife.com
www.rhino.org.za

ACCOMMODATION INSIDE PARK
Garden Castle/Bushman's Nek Valley:
Hermit's Wood Campsite
033 701 1823

Cobham:
Cobham Campsite
033 702 0831

Vergelegen:
Bird's Nest Overnight Cave
033 702 0831

Himeville:
No accommodation
033 702 0007

Coleford:
No accommodation
033 701 1972

ACCOMMODATION OUTSIDE PARK
Southern Drakensberg Publicity
033 701 1471
www.drakensberg.org

The rolling, grassy foothills of the southern Drakensberg where these reserves find themselves are less about the dominating majesty of the northern massif and more about mirror-like lakes teeming with trout, waterfalls, streams, and peaceful treed campsites with mountain backdrops like cardboard cutouts against the skyline. A contiguous area of reserves, starting with **Vergelegen, Cobham, Himeville**, and the Swamp Nature Reserve close by, attracts anglers, hikers, birders and picknickers, most of whom take advantage of the prettily located campsites near water and under trees. Waterbirds at The Swamp include the rare Wattled Crane; Vergelegen offers the most direct route to the Drakensberg's highest peak, Thabana Ntlenyana, in Lesotho; and Cobham, dominated by Hodgson's Peaks, which also enclose the Giant's Cup, has excellent rock art sites which can be viewed with a knowledgeable guide. Cobham is a territory of upland tarns and lakes – one sector has been named the Lake District – where lush tree ferns flourish.

South of Himeville, four dams and the Ngwangwane and Ndawana rivers in the **Coleford Nature Reserve** are stocked with Rainbow Trout. Its beautiful setting is great for picnics, walks and horse trails and the Coleford Camp looks out over the Ngwangwane valley.

Garden Castle Nature Reserve looks to the distinctive Rhino Peak to the north and Garden Castle Peak to the south. Sandstone buttresses and unusual formations make this dramatic hiking territory. The well-trodden 5-day Giant's Cup trail, which starts from the Sani Pass road and follows the line of the escarpment, crosses the Cobham and Garden Castle reserves, finishing at the lovely **Bushman's Nek Valley**.

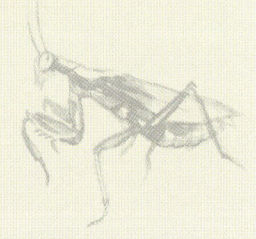

SEASONAL INFORMATION

Gate opening times
Himeville, Vergelegen, Cobham,
Garden Castle & Bushman's Nek Valley:
05:00 – 19:00 (1 Oct to 31 Mar)
06:00 – 18:00 (1 Apr to 30 Sept)
Day visitors allowed
Entrance fee
Coleford:
Closed to the public

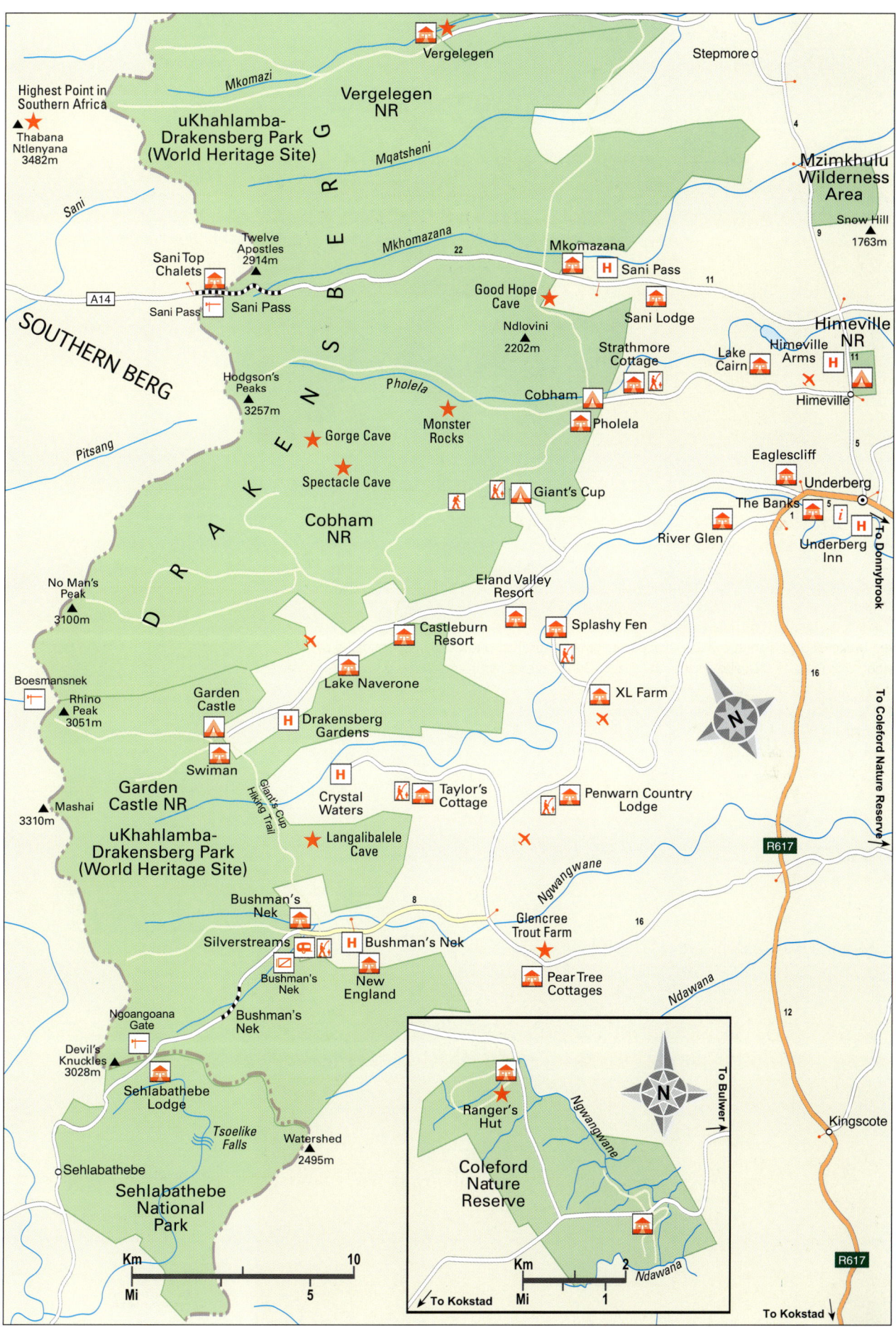

Highest Point in
Southern Africa

▲★ Thabana
Ntlenyana
3482m

Mkomazi

uKhahlamba-
Drakensberg Park
(World Heritage Site)

Vergelegen

Vergelegen
NR

Mqatsheni

Stepmore

Mzimkhulu
Wilderness
Area

4

Sani

Snow Hill
1763m

9

Twelve
Apostles
2914m

Mkhomazana

22

Mkomazana

H Sani Pass

11

Sani Top
Chalets

A14

Sani Pass

Sani Pass

Good Hope
Cave ★

Sani Lodge

Himeville
NR

Himeville
Arms H 11

SOUTHERN BERG

Hodgson's
Peaks
▲ 3257m

Pholela

Ndlovini
2202m

Strathmore
Cottage

Cobham

Pholela

Lake
Cairn

Himeville

Pitsang

Gorge Cave ★

Monster
Rocks ★

Eaglescliff

Underberg

★ Spectacle Cave

Giant's Cup

The Banks

i

5

H

To Donnybrook

Cobham
NR

River Glen

Underberg
Inn

D R A K E N S B E R G

No Man's
Peak
▲ 3100m

Eland Valley
Resort

Castleburn
Resort

Splashy Fen

16

Boesmansnek

Rhino
Peak
▲ 3051m

Garden
Castle

Lake Naverone

XL Farm

Swiman

H Drakensberg
Gardens

Garden
Castle NR

uKhahlamba-
Drakensberg Park
(World Heritage Site)

Mashai
3310m

Crystal
Waters

H

Taylor's
Cottage

Penwarn Country
Lodge

R617

Langalibalele
Cave

Giant's Cup Hiking Trail

8

Ngwangwane

16

To Coleford Nature Reserve

Bushman's
Nek

Silverstreams

H Bushman's Nek

Glencree
Trout Farm

Bushman's
Nek

New
England

Pear Tree
Cottages

Ndawana

Ngoangoana
Gate

Bushman's
Nek

Devil's
Knuckles
▲ 3028m

12

Sehlabathebe
Lodge

Tsoelike
Falls

Watershed
2495m

Ranger's
Hut ★

To Bulwer

Sehlabathebe

Coleford
Nature
Reserve

Kingscote

Sehlabathebe
National
Park

Km   10

Mi   5

Km   2

Ndawana

To Kokstad

Mi   1

To Kokstad

To Kokstad

R617

Pietermaritzburg

Greater St Lucia Wetland Park

The Greater St Lucia Wetland Park, both a World Heritage Site and a Ramsar Wetland Site, is a tapestry of lagoons, swamps and waterways, reeds and papyrus, and high forested dunes (among the world's tallest). Beginning with the southern reaches, the restcamp in the Mapelane Nature Reserve sits at both the Mfolozi River mouth and on a sweeping bay with an offshore reef – the grand prize is fishing from rock, surf and ski-boat. Forested dunes yield Vervet Monkeys and birds for Africa. A shallow lake in reed and papyrus sandflats on the Mfolozi River make up the Lake Eteza Nature Reserve, which draws birders to check out its waterfowl. Stretching north of St Lucia to Cape Vidal, Mfabeni's tall dunes of Natal Wild Banana, Natal Fig, and White and Coastal Red Milkwood trees are a treat, as are the orientating views from Mission Rocks over Charters Creek, Fanie's Island and False Bay. Light-tackle boat angling and bird-watching at all three of these spots is flavour of the day, but the overriding pleasure is setting out on self-guided birding trails and hunkering in hides with a backdrop of grazing Waterbuck and Reedbuck, while hippo snort from the pans. The St Lucia Marine Reserve extends from just south of Cape Vidal to 11km north of Jesser Point and Sodwana, and 3 nautical miles out to sea. A marine sanctuary that loops between Leven Point and Red Sands forbids any fishing. In this marine reserve are reef forests of 100 different species of coral fostering brilliant tropical fish. And in November, Leatherback and Loggerhead Turtles emerge to lay their eggs on the beaches. Sodwana Bay, in the north, positively bristles with game-fishermen and scuba divers – this is South Africa's showy diving mecca, its offerings ranging from Flute-mouthed Butterflyfish to Honeycomb Moray Eels.

GREATER ST LUCIA WETLAND PARK

NEAREST TOWN
St Lucia

NEAREST AIRPORT
Richards Bay

SIZE
328 000ha

FAUNA
1 African Elephant
2 Black Rhino
3 Buffalo
4 Waterbuck
5 Kudu
6 Nyala
7 Impala
8 Nile Crocodile
9 Hippo
10 Humpback Whale
11 Bottlenosed & Dusky Dolphin
12 Leatherback & Loggerhead Turtle
13 Lesser & Greater Flamingo
14 Pelican
15 Heron sp.
16 Tern sp.
17 Stork sp.

MAIN CONTACT DETAILS
033 845 1000/2
info@kznwildlife.com
www.kznwildlife.com
www.rhino.org.za

ACCOMMODATION INSIDE PARK
Cape Vidal:
Self-contained log cabins, campsites
035 590 9012
🛏 🍴 🏕 🔥 🅺

Sodwana Bay NP:
Sodwana Bay Lodge, cabins, campsite
035 571 0117
🛏 🏕 🔥 🅺

St Lucia Marine Sanctuary:
Sugarloaf & Eden Park
St Lucia Wilderness Base Camp
035 590 9002
🛏 🏕 🔥 🅺

Mfabeni/Mission Rocks:
Mount Tabor Rustic Campsite
035 590 9002
🛏 🏕 🔥 🅺

Charters Creek:
Charters Creek Camp
035 550 9000/1513
🛏 🏕 🔥

False Bay Park:
Dugandlovu Rustic Camp
035 562 0425
🛏 🏕 🔥 🅺

Fanie's Island, Lake eTeza:
None

Mapelane:
Log cabins, campsite
035 590 1407
🛏 🏕 🔥 🅺

ACCOMMODATION OUTSIDE PARK
Tourist Info, St Lucia
035 550 4059

SEASONAL INFORMATION

Gate opening times
Cape Vidal, Mfabeni/Mission Rocks:
05:00 – 19:00 (summer)
06:00 – 18:00 (winter)
Sodwana Bay, St Lucia:
Open 24 hours
Charters Creek, False Bay:
06:00 – 19:00 (summer)
06:00 – 18:00 (winter)

Pietermaritzburg

Hluhluwe-iMfolozi Park

This park was once the exclusive hunting preserve of Zulu kings Dingiswayo and Shaka, implying a degree of informal "protection" in its earliest days under their first "conservation" laws – and in the south of the park, game pits in which animals were trapped can still be seen today. iMfolozi is more famously credited for rescuing the White Rhino from extinction when it was proclaimed a Reserved Area for Game in 1895. By 1960, numbers had risen to 700 and needed to be translocated to other parks. Operation Rhino was the name given to the project, and although the first rhino, transferred to Mkhuze, didn't survive, by 2000 over 3500 rhino had been translocated around the world. A count in July 2003 turned up 1687 White and 400 Black Rhino.

The **iMfolozi** sector of this combined park is drier, resulting in open acacia-savannah plains and woodlands contained by the Black and White Mfolozi rivers. A feature of the park is its self-guided trails, in vehicles and on foot, and more primitive wilderness trails accompanied by guides across territory that has no roads – only the tracks made by animals. Here, sleeping under the stars or in tented camps, the sights and sounds of nature dominate, and intricate wildlife patterns that would otherwise elude you in a car can be closely observed.

The higher-rainfall **Hluhluwe** sector delivers deep valleys, palm-fringed rivers, rolling hills and tracts of forest. Here visitors are likely to find large herds of game, and will be thrilled with sightings of the Big Five. A not-so-common feature is the plethora of picnic sites permitting visitors to leave their vehicles for some wildlife viewing. The attractive thatched Hilltop Camp has outstanding views over Hluhluwe. Here, Hlaza Hide, sited at what was once a summerhouse, and a waterhole lit softly at night encourage discreet close encounters of the animal kind.

HLUHLUWE-IMFOLOZI PARK
NEAREST TOWN
uLundi

NEAREST AIRPORT
Richards Bay

SIZE
96 000ha

FAUNA
1   African Elephant
2   White & Black Rhino
3   Buffalo
4   Blue Wildebeest
5   Giraffe
6   Lion
7   Leopard
8   Cheetah
9   Zebra
10 Hyena sp.
11 Jackal sp.
12 Wild Dog
13 Nyala
14 Kudu
15 Mountain Reedbuck
16 Impala
17 Duiker
18 Warthog

MAIN CONTACT DETAILS
033 845 1000/2
info@kznwildlife.com
www.kznwildlife.com
www.rhino.org.za

ACCOMMODATION INSIDE PARK
Restcamps, Bush Lodges
Hilltop Camp
Mpila Camp
Mthwazi, Muntulu, Munywaneni,
Masinda Lodges
Gqoyeni, Hlatikulu Bush Lodges

ACCOMMODATION OUTSIDE PARK
Tourist Info, uLundi
035 874 5607

SEASONAL INFORMATION

Gate opening times
05:00 – 19:00 (Nov to Feb)
06:00 – 18:00 (Mar to Oct)

To Mkuze
Mbedle 443m
To Nongoma
Ngxongwane
5
R618
17
Bombolo 678m
Dukumbane
Mduna
Ngweni
N2
Mhlosinga
To Mtubatuba
Dukumbane 645m
Makowe 555m
Buxedeni
18
R618
N
Mona
Mthwazi
Hilltop
Memorial Gate
Hluhluwe Dam
Hlabisa
Nzimane
Thiyeni Hide
Muntulu
Munywaneni
Hluhluwe
Ntondweni 378m
Hluhluwe-iMfolozi Park
22
Kwasithole 311m
Bhejane Hide
Nyalazi Gate
339m
Mbulunga
Sontuli
Black Mfolozi
Gqoyeni
Mpila
Nselweni
Masinda
9
Machibini
Nyalazi
Mambeni Gate
Somkele
14
R618
eMdoneni Lodge
H
Mphafa Hide
eNqolothi Gate
Shaka's Hunting Pits
Mfolozi
To St Lucia
3
Mtubatuba
Paradiso
H
uMunywana
River View
Munywana
Sanagonyana
10
Lake eTeza Nature Reserve
Lake Teza
Mvamanzi
Teza
19
Makhwezini
Msuzduze
18
16
N2
Dondotsha
11
Ntambanana
Km
20
Mi
10
KwaMbonambi
To eMpangeni

Maputaland
Kosi Bay & Lake Sibaya

MAPUTALAND
NEAREST TOWN (BOTH PARKS)
St Lucia

NEAREST AIRPORT (BOTH PARKS)
Richards Bay

SIZE
Kosi Bay: 10 000ha
Lake Sibaya: 77.5km^2

AVIFAUNA
Kosi Bay:
1 Nile Crocodile
2 Hippopotamus
3 Loggerhead & Leatherback Turtle
4 Humpback Whale

Lake Sibaya:
1 Hippopotamus
2 Nile Crocodile
3 Woodward's Batis
4 Reed & Whitebreasted Cormorant
5 Giant & Malachite Kingfisher
6 Pygmy Goose

MAIN CONTACT DETAILS
033 845 1000/2
info@kznwildlife.com
www.kznwildlife.com
www.rhino.org.za

ACCOMMODATION INSIDE PARK
Kosi Bay
Nhlange, Bhanga, Sihadla
Madlangwe Camp, campsite, chalets
035 592 9876

Lake Sibaya
None, use Mabibi Campsite
035 574 8998

Thonga Beach Lodge
035 474 1473

ACCOMMODATION OUTSIDE PARK
Tourist Info, St Lucia
035 550 4059

The expansive coastal plain of Maputaland is cradled on the landward side by the Lebombo mountains to the north and the Ubombo mountains to the south. People drawn to the remote watery wilderness of **Kosi Bay** love the silence of solitude and are content to leave behind all the trappings of modern, civilised life. Kosi's name belies its character – it is, in fact, an estuary linking four interconnected lakes strung out southward along the coast. Angling absorbs most visitors, including the local Thonga fishermen whose wooden palisade fish traps scar the waters in wavy curves – a distinctive Kosi Bay signature. aManzimnyama, the southernmost lake, is fringed with giant-leaved Kosi (Raffia) Palms, whose fleshy fruit and leafy fronds provide food and nesting sites to the rare black-and-white Palmnut Vulture. Also protected here, in the Coastal Forest Nature Reserve, are five different mangrove species not to mention Lala Palms, Waterberry trees, mahoganies and milkwoods. Dwindling numbers of breeding sea turtles have led to the creation of the coastal sanctuary, extending from the high-water mark to 3 nautical miles out to sea. December is Loggerhead and Leatherback Turtle egg-laying month. The campsite in Mabibi Bay is so remote, only 4x4s will get you there, and a wooden boardwalk is your only link to the beach. You are likely to be the only souls there, which means the rock pools, snorkelling and surf angling are as pristine as you'll get. Nearby, in the crystal waters of **Lake Sibaya** – South Africa's largest freshwater lake – visitors could come face to face with hippo and crocodile, and they will tick off countless birds from their lists. The Ozabeni campsite under shady trees gives on to a flat, low-lying area of 11 hippo- and croc-filled small lakes and pans which drain into northern Lake St Lucia.

SEASONAL INFORMATION

Gate opening times
Kosi Bay:
05:00 – 19:00 (summer)
06:00 – 18:00 (winter)
Lake Sibaya:
Gate opening times
06:00 – 18:00
Day visitors allowed

MOZAMBIQUE

Manhoca

5

MUZI

Mloli

25

Tembe
Elephant
Reserve

22

Tembe Elephant
Lodge

8

Sihangwane

14

Phelandaba

Sileza

24

Mpophomeni

SOUTH AFRICA

R
22

N

Manaba

15

3

Mseleni

2

20

21

17

14

Tshongwe

22

Mabaso
Plantation

Mbazwana
Inn

H

R
22

Muzi
Pan

Sodwana Bay
State Forest

Mantuma

Ozabeni
Section

uMzunduzi

Mkhuze Game
Reserve

Nsumo
Pan

Phinda
Resource Reserve

Mkuze
Swamp

To Hluhluwe

Ponta do Ouro

Manhoca

Ponta do Ouro

Kosi Bay

Makhawulani

15

Kosi Bay
Nature
Reserve

R
22

KuMpungwini

7

Kosi Bay
Lodge

Lake Kosi
(Lake Nhlanga)

eMangusi

Boteler
Point

aManzimnyama

Kosi Bay Forest Lodge

Malangeni

Dog Point

Maputaland
Marine Reserve

Black Rock

Mvelabusha

Rocktail Bay
Lodge

Coastal Forest
Reserve

Island Rock

Phambuka Safari Camp

Mabibi Camp

Hully Point

Lake Sibaya

INDIAN
OCEAN

Baya Camp

Gobey's Point

Seven-Mile Reef

Mbazwana
Plantation

14

Five-Mile Reef

Sodwana Bay
Lodge

Sodwana Bay

Mbazwana

Two-Mile Reef

Sodwana Chalets

Jesser Point

Sodwana Bay
National Park

Algea Reef

27

Adlam's Reef

St Lucia Marine
Sanctuary

Lake
Bhangazi

Greater
St Lucia
Wetland Park
(WHS)

Km   10

Mi   5

75

Pietermaritzburg

Queen Elizabeth Park, Midmar, Albert Falls, Karkloof, Blinkwater & Craigie Burn NR

Just outside Pietermaritzburg, the small nature reserve of **Queen Elizabeth Park** is an apt base for the KZN Wildlife headquarters. A profusion of luscious tropical cycads provides an inviting setting for rambles and picnics, and naturally-growing endangered Hilton Daisies prettify the grasslands where small antelope graze, while Crown Eagles keep a watchful eye.

Midmar Dam is a little livelier, where the animated voices of yachtsmen, waterskiers and board-sailors are carried in the air across the busy waters. Despite this hyperactivity, nothing short of White Rhino and Blue Wildebeest can be seen ambling contentedly in the surrounding nature reserve. Two reserves lying adjacent to one another feature lovely waterfalls, Albert and Karkloof. Both are great for trails and picnics, but Albert Falls dam's reputation for some of the world's best bass fishing keeps its shores bristling with keen fishermen. Naturalists revel in the call of the Fish Eagle, also lured here by the dam's bounty. The **Albert Falls reserve** prides itself on the true bushveld feel of its little game park. The 88m tumble of the **Karkloof** falls ends in a valley of plantation forests; walkers here should keep their eyes open for the endemic Karkloof Blue Butterfly, emblem of the nearby Midlands Meander. Rietvlei, a tranquil farming district beyond the Midlands Meander, has around and within its confines the **Blinkwater** and **Craigie Burn nature reserves**. Grasslands, plantations, waterfalls and Mist-belt Podocarpus forests (containing all three yellowwood species) add interest to hiking trails here. The clear Craigie Burn dam, backed by high hills and fed by the Nyamvubu River, keeps water-loving families entertained. In Blinkwater, endangered Wattled Crane breed near Island Dam – so no swimming allowed! Look out for dainty little Oribi, which, when alarmed, go into a series of straight-legged vertical leaps, sometimes referred to as "stotting".

QUEEN ELIZABETH PARK
NEAREST TOWN (ALL PARKS)
Pietermaritzburg

NEAREST AIRPORT (ALL PARKS)
Durban International

SIZE
93ha

FAUNA/FLORA
1 Zebra
2 Impala
3 Hilton Daisy
4 Cycad sp.

MAIN CONTACT DETAILS (ALL PARKS)
033 845 1000/2
www.kznwildlife.com

ACCOMMODATION INSIDE PARK
None

ACCOMMODATION OUTSIDE PARK
(ALL PARKS)
033 345 1348/9
info@pmbtourism.co.za
www.pmbtourism.co.za

MIDMAR DAM NATURE RESERVE
SIZE
1000ha

FAUNA
1 White Rhino
2 Blue Wildebeest
3 Hippopotamus

ACCOMMODATION INSIDE PARK
Chalets, rustic cabins, campsite
033 330 2067

ALBERT FALLS NATURE RESERVE
SIZE
950ha

FAUNA
1 White Rhino
2 Antelope sp.

ACCOMMODATION INSIDE PARK
Notuli Campsite, rondawels, chalets

KARKLOOF NATURE RESERVE
SIZE
2800ha

AVIFAUNA
1 Crowned Eagle
2 Cape Parrot

ACCOMMODATION INSIDE PARK
Rockwood Forest Lodge, The Leopards Lodge, Retreat & Brook Cottages
033 502 9094

CRAIGIE BURN & BLINKWATER NR
SIZE
Craigie Burn: 330ha
Blinkwater: 350ha

FAUNA/AVIFAUNA
1 Oribi
2 Blue Swallow
3 Crested Guinea Fowl

ACCOMMODATION INSIDE PARK
None

SEASONAL INFORMATION
Gate opening times
Queen Elizabeth: 06h00 – 18h00
Albert Falls:
05h00 – 19h00 (summer)
05h30 – 18h00 (winter)
Midmar Dam: Open 24 hours
Karkloof & Craigie Burn:
Sunrise to sunset
Day visitors allowed
Blinkwater: No public access

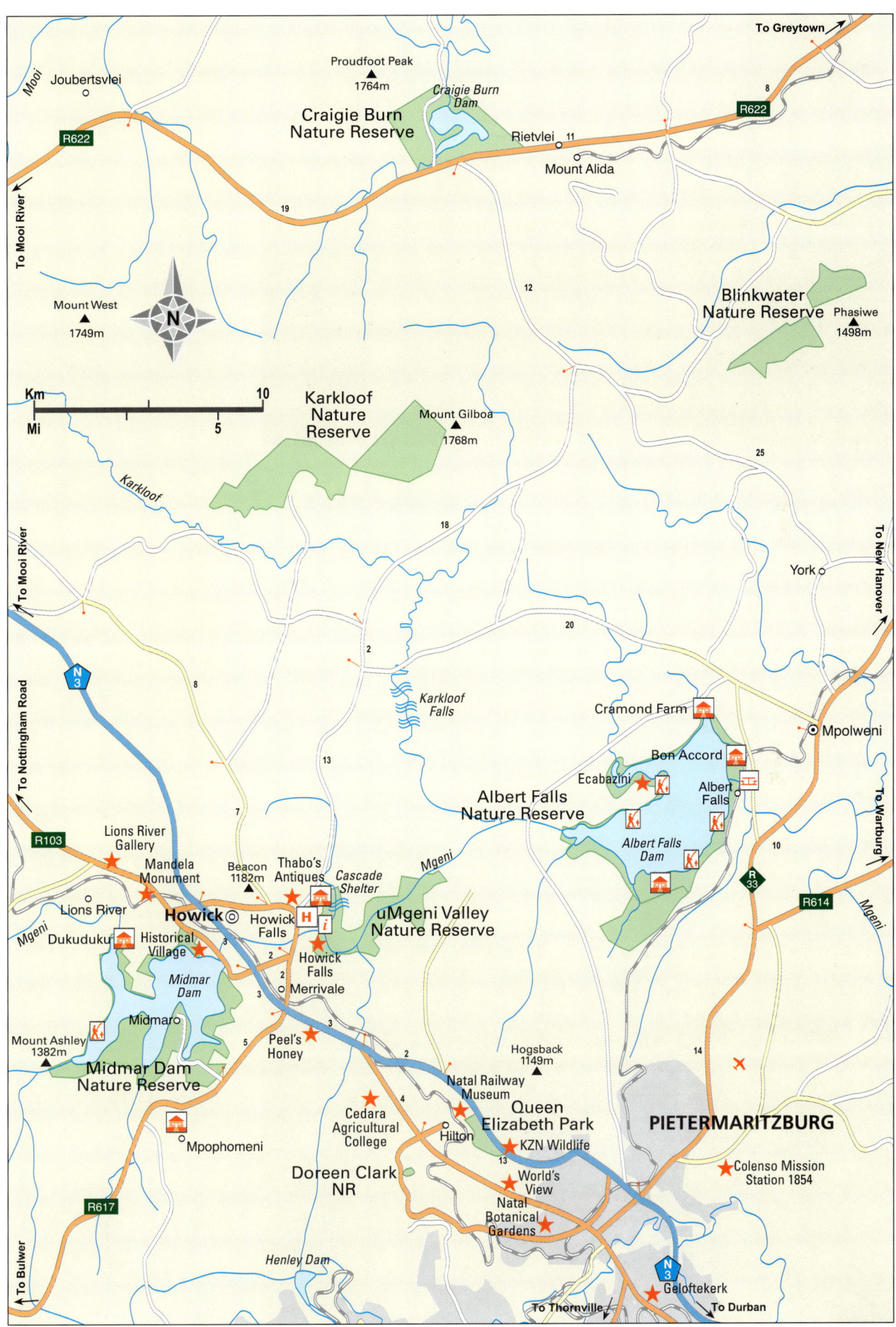

To Greytown

R622

8

Mooi

Joubertsvlei

R622

Proudfoot Peak
1764m

Craigie Burn
Dam

Craigie Burn
Nature Reserve

Rietvlei   11

Mount Alida

19

To Mooi River

Mount West
1749m

N

Km   10

Mi   5

Karkloof
Nature
Reserve

Mount Gilboa
1768m

12

Blinkwater
Nature Reserve   Phasiwe
1498m

25

Karkloof

18

York

To New Hanover

To Mooi River

N3

8

2

Karkloof
Falls

20

Cramond Farm

Bon Accord

Ecabazini

Mpolweni

Albert Falls
Nature Reserve

Albert
Falls

To Nottingham Road

R103

Lions River
Gallery

Mandela
Monument

Beacon
1182m

Thabo's
Antiques

Cascade
Shelter

Mgeni

13

7

Albert Falls
Dam

10

R33

R614

Mgeni

Lions River

Dukuduku

Historical
Village

Howick   Howick
Falls

H

i

uMgeni Valley
Nature Reserve

Mgeni

Midmar
Dam

2

Howick
Falls

Merrivale

Midmaro

3

Mount Ashley
1382m

Midmar Dam
Nature Reserve

Peel's
Honey

5

3

2

Hogsback
1149m

14

Mpophomeni

Cedara
Agricultural
College

4

Natal Railway
Museum

Hilton

Queen
Elizabeth Park

KZN Wildlife

PIETERMARITZBURG

Doreen Clark
NR

13

World's
View

Colenso Mission
Station 1854

R617

Natal
Botanical
Gardens

To Bulwer

Henley Dam

N3

Geloftekerk

To Thornville

To Durban

To Wartburg

Pietermaritzburg

Durban
Beachwood Mangroves, uMhlanga Lagoon, Bluff, Kenneth Stainbank, Krantzkloof & North Park Nature Reserves

Beachwood Mangroves, a mangrove swamp forest at the mouth of the Umgeni River, is so valuable it's become a National Monument. This protected area's three main habitats are birdy heaven – dune scrub, the swamp of Black, Red and White Mangroves, and grassland and reedbed fringes support species ranging from Southern Tchagra through Mangrove Kingfisher (in winter) to three different cisticolas. Birders unite! Don't forget to look for the single-clawed Fiddler Crabs and mudskippers propelling themselves with their pectoral fins across the mud. Meanwhile, at **uMhlanga Lagoon**, on the southern bank of the uMhlanga River, two trails through estuarine, dune and coastal forest make it possible to check off 60 species on a single visit in summer, 40 species in winter.

In the Bluff suburb of Durban is the large pan and adjacent forest of the **Bluff Nature Reserve**. Two bird hides edging the pan and a self-guided trail meandering around it bring bird-watchers into close proximity with waterbirds and waders, among them spoonbills and cormorants which nest in the reedbeds in late winter and spring. **North Park**, named after the family who owned the property and whose graves lie in the reserve, is unusual for its 102 recorded tree species, of which 48 are considered rare. You will also be surrounded by the delicate fluttering wings of a myriad butterfly species.

Krantzkloof Nature Reserve offers a change of pace with its dramatic gorge channelling the eMolweni River. Trails encountering kloofs, waterfalls and streams – with picnic spots – lead to viewpoints, one of which faces a massive cliff face that's visited by Lanner and Peregrine Falcon.

A bequest from **Kenneth Stainbank** of forest and grassland tracts has brought this nature reserve of Zebra, small antelope, mongoose and monkeys into existence. Four walking trails, a sometimes challenging mountain-bike route and picnic sites keep everyone happy.

BEACHWOOD MANGROVES
NEAREST TOWN (ALL PARKS)
Durban

NEAREST AIRPORT (ALL PARKS)
Durban International

MAIN CONTACT DETAILS (ALL PARKS)
033 845 1000/2
info@kznwildlife.com
www.kznwildlife.com
www.rhino.org.za

SIZE
76ha

AVIFAUNA/FLORA
1   Mangrove Kingfisher
2   Water Dikkop
3   Swamp (Natal) Nightjar
4   Black, Red & White Mangrove
☒

ACCOMMODATION INSIDE PARK (ALL PARKS)
None

ACCOMMODATION OUTSIDE PARK (ALL PARKS)
031 304 4934
funinsun@iafrica.com
www.durbansouthafrica.co.za

UMHLANGA LAGOON NR
SIZE
26ha

FAUNA
1   Duiker
2   Bushbuck
☒

BLUFF NATURE RESERVE
SIZE
45ha

FAUNA
1   Wader sp.
2   Spoonbill sp.
3   Cormorant sp.
4   Vervet Monkey
☒

KENNETH STAINBANK NR
SIZE
253ha

FAUNA/FLORA
1   Zebra
2   Monkey sp.
3   Bushbaby
4   Natal Fig Tree
☒

KRANTZKLOOF NATURE RESERVE
SIZE
600ha

FAUNA/FLORA
See Kenneth Stainbank NR
☒

NORTH PARK
SIZE
52ha

FAUNA
1   Duiker
2   Banded Mongoose
3   Rock Dassie

SEASONAL INFORMATION

Gate opening times
Beachwood Mangroves: 07:00 – 16:00
uMhlanga Lagoon NR: 06:00 – 18:00
Bluff NR: 07:00 – 17:00
Kenneth Stainbank:
06:00 – 18:00 (summer)
06:00 – 18:30 (winter)
Krantzkloof NR: 06:00 – 18:00
North Park: 07:00 – 16:30

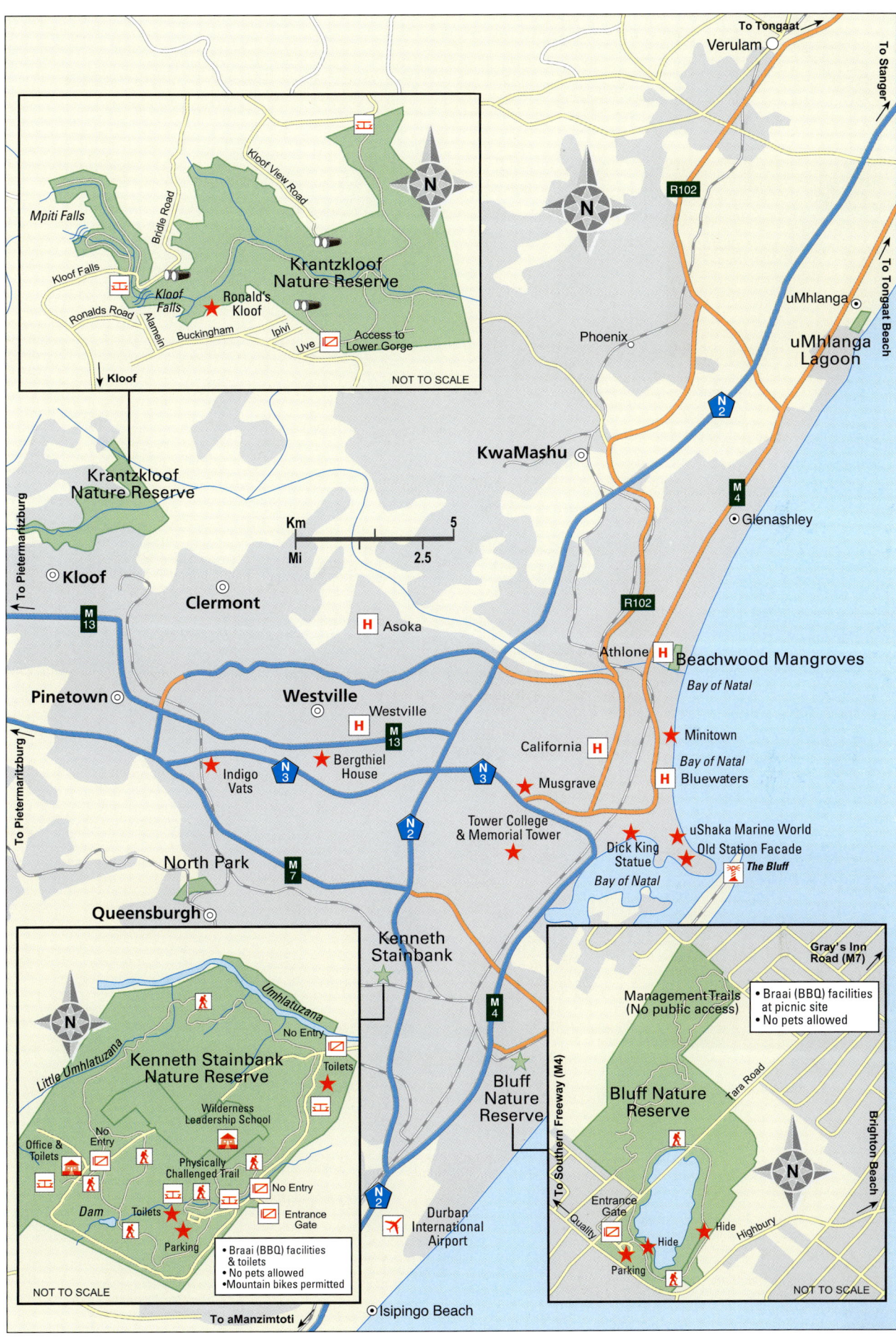

Krantzkloof Nature Reserve (inset map)

Mpiti Falls
Kloof Falls
Kloof Falls
Ronalds Road
Bridle Road
Kloof View Road
Alamein
Buckingham
Ipivi
Uve
Ronald's Kloof
Access to Lower Gorge

Krantzkloof
Nature Reserve

↓ **Kloof**

NOT TO SCALE

To Tongaat →
Verulam
To Stanger
R102
To Tongaat Beach →
uMhlanga
Phoenix
uMhlanga
Lagoon
N2
KwaMashu
M4
Glenashley

Krantzkloof
Nature Reserve

To Pietermaritzburg
Kloof
M13
Clermont

Km ———— 5
Mi ———— 2.5

Asoka

Athlone
Beachwood Mangroves
Bay of Natal

Pinetown
Westville
M13
Westville
Bergthiel House
N3
Indigo Vats
California
Minitown
Bay of Natal
Bluewaters

Musgrave
N3
N2
Tower College & Memorial Tower
uShaka Marine World
Old Station Facade
Dick King Statue
The Bluff
Bay of Natal

North Park
M7
Queensburgh

Kenneth
Stainbank

M4

Bluff
Nature
Reserve

Kenneth Stainbank Nature Reserve (inset map)

Umhlatuzana
Little Umhlatuzana
No Entry
Toilets
Kenneth Stainbank
Nature Reserve
Wilderness
Leadership School
Office &
Toilets
No Entry
Physically
Challenged Trail
No Entry
Dam
Toilets
Entrance
Gate
Parking

N

• Braai (BBQ) facilities
  & toilets
• No pets allowed
• Mountain bikes permitted

NOT TO SCALE

To aManzimtoti →
Isipingo Beach

N2
Durban
International
Airport

Bluff Nature Reserve (inset map)

Gray's Inn
Road (M7)

Management Trails
(No public access)

• Braai (BBQ) facilities
  at picnic site
• No pets allowed

Bluff Nature
Reserve

Tara Road
Brighton Beach

To Southern Freeway (M4)
Entrance
Gate
Quality
Hide
Hide
Hide
Highbury
Parking

N

NOT TO SCALE

Chelmsford & Ncandu Nature Reserves

In this nature reserve on the Ngagane River, the **Chelmsford** (Ntshingwayo) dam is a haven for boating and watersports but is known too for its carp and bass fishing. "Non-petrol-heads" will be happy to find wildlife of the calibre of White Rhino and Wildebeest in the surrounding grasslands, and birders will be quite overwhelmed. On the reserve's bird list are special species, like larks intriguingly named Spikeheeled, Pinkbilled or Eastern Clapper Lark – all of which should make non-bird-watchers instant converts.

Along the Muller's Pass road in Normandien, the **Ncandu** River rushes over a series of exposed rocks creating a waterfall of cascades, rivulets and watery mist that sustains bushes clinging to the fall's rocky crevices. The surrounding picturescape of green-mantled mountains with its pockets of dense riverine forest, wildflower-strewn paths and rocky mountain streams is lovely terrain for the many walking trails that exist in the area, with overnighting in caves or huts.

CHELMSFORD NATURE RESERVE
NEAREST TOWN (BOTH PARKS)
Newcastle

NEAREST AIRPORT (BOTH PARKS)
Durban International

SIZE
6014ha

FAUNA
1 White Rhino
2 Red Hartebeest
3 Blesbok
4 Oribi
5 Springbok
6 Lark sp.

MAIN CONTACT DETAILS
033 845 1000/2
info@kznwildlife.com
www.kznwildlife.com
www.rhino.org.za

ACCOMMODATION INSIDE PARK
Leokop & Sandford Campgrounds
Chelmsford Camp
Richgate

ACCOMMODATION OUTSIDE PARK
(BOTH PARKS)
034 315 3318
info@newcastle.co.za
www.tourismnewcastle.co.za

NCANDU NATURE RESERVE
SIZE
1800ha

FAUNA
1 Red Hartebeest
2 Blesbok
3 Oribi
4 Springbok

ACCOMMODATION INSIDE PARK
None

SEASONAL INFORMATION

Gate opening times
Both reserves:
05:00 – 20:00 (Oct to Mar)
06:00 – 19:00 (Apr to Sept)

Mkhuze Game Reserve
& Phinda Resource Reserve

Backed up against the Ubombo mountains and linked to the St Lucia wetlands via the Mkhuze Swamp, the **Mkhuze reserve** is fêted as much for its birdlife as for its wild animals. Particularly memorable are its riverine forests of giant Sycamore Figs lining the Mkuze River and the eerie groves of sallow-hued Fever Trees fringing the Nhlonhlela Pan. The atmospheric Fig Forest Walk takes in a bit of both: twisted, entwined sycamore trunks versus the ghoulish-yellow sheen of "fevered" trunks. The country's only regular breeding colony of Pinkbacked Pelicans nests in the Fever Trees lining the Nsumo Pan. **Phinda**, adjoining Mkhuze has, to its credit, the full Big Five after extensive efforts to restore the once-cultivated reserve land to its original wilderness. Perhaps its greatest magic lies in its ultraluxury lodges, notably Forest Lodge – raised glass-walled chalets that "float" among the Torchwood Trees, allowing the secrets of the surrounding wilderness in.

MKHUZE GAME RESERVE
NEAREST TOWN (BOTH PARKS)
St Lucia

NEAREST AIRPORT (BOTH PARKS)
Richards Bay

SIZE
40 000ha

FAUNA/FLORA
1 African Elephant
2 Black & White Rhino
3 Giraffe
4 Cheetah
5 Antelope sp.
6 Zebra
7 Hippopotamus
8 Nile Crocodile
9 Hyena sp.
10 Giant Fig Tree
11 Fever Tree

MAIN CONTACT DETAILS
035 573 9004/1, 082 799 1491

ACCOMMODATION INSIDE PARK
Mantuma Main Camp,
Umkhumbe Tented Bush Lodge,
Nhlonhlela Bush Lodge

ACCOMMODATION OUTSIDE PARK
(BOTH PARKS)
Tourist Info, St Lucia
035 550 4059

PHINDA RESOURCE RESERVE
SIZE
18 500ha

FAUNA/AVIFAUNA
1 African Elephant
2 Black & White Rhino
3 Buffalo
4 Lion
5 Leopard
6 Pel's Fishing Owl
7 African Finfoot

MAIN CONTACT DETAILS
035 562 0271
phinda@ccafrica.com
www.ccafrica.com

ACCOMMODATION INSIDE PARK
Phinda Forest Lodge, Mountain Lodge
Phinda Vlei Lodge, Rock Lodge
Phinda Zuka Lodge, Getty House

SEASONAL INFORMATION

Gate opening times
Mkhuze GR:
05:00 – 19:00 (Oct to Mar)
06:00 – 18:00 (Apr to Sept)
Day visitors allowed
Phinda Resource Reserve:
05:30 – 19:00 (Oct to Mar)
Day visitors allowed by arrangement

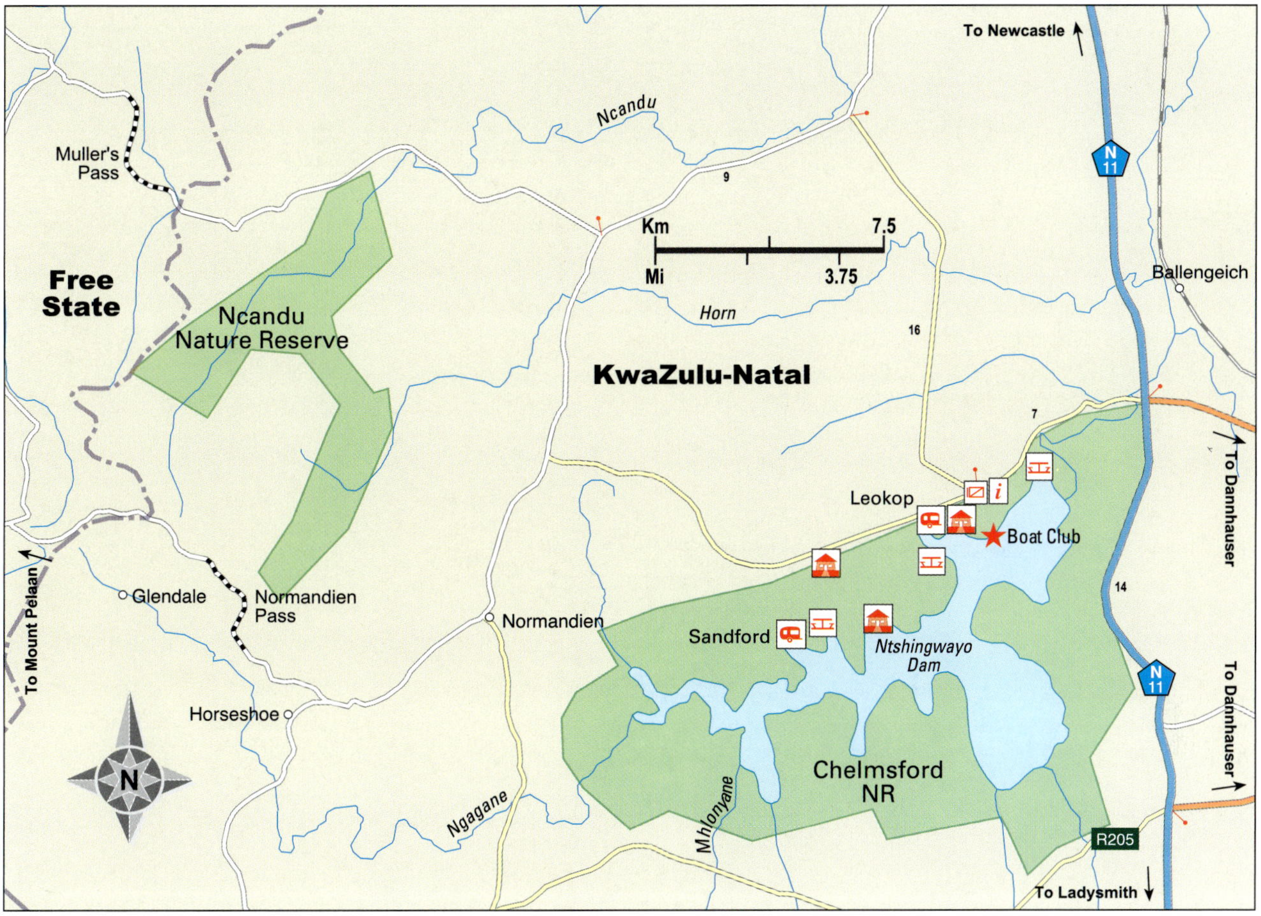

Map 1 (Top) — KwaZulu-Natal / Chelmsford

To Newcastle

Ncandu

N11

9

Muller's Pass

Free State

Ballengeich

Km 7.5

Mi 3.75

Horn

16

Ncandu Nature Reserve

KwaZulu-Natal

7

Leokop

To Dannhauser

★ Boat Club

i

To Mount Pelaan

Glendale

Normandien Pass

Normandien

Sandford

14

Ntshingwayo Dam

N11

Horseshoe

To Dannhauser

Mhlonyane

Chelmsford NR

N

Ngagane

R205

To Ladysmith

Map 2 (Bottom) — Mkhuze Game Reserve / Phinda

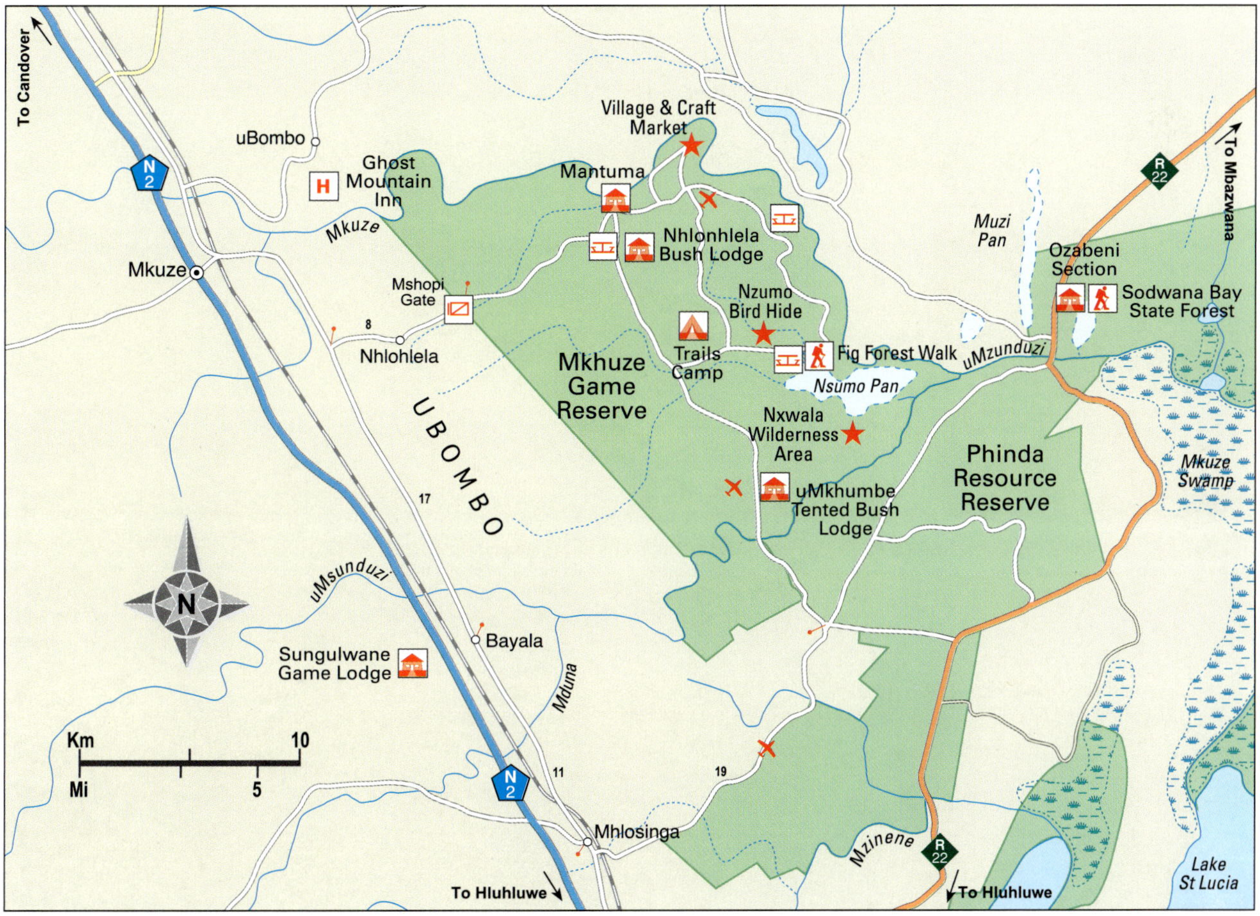

To Candover

N2

Village & Craft Market ★

uBombo

Ghost Mountain Inn

Mantuma

Muzi Pan

R22

To Mbazwana

Mkuze

H

Nhlonhlela Bush Lodge

Ozabeni Section

Sodwana Bay State Forest

Mkuze

Mshopi Gate

Nzumo Bird Hide ★

Mkuze Game Reserve

Trails Camp

Fig Forest Walk

uMzunduzi

8

Nhlohlela

U B O M B O

Nsumo Pan

Mkuze Swamp

Nxwala Wilderness Area ★

Phinda Resource Reserve

uMkhumbe Tented Bush Lodge

N

uMsunduzi

Sungulwane Game Lodge

Bayala

17

Mduna

Lake St Lucia

Km 10

Mi 5

N2

11

19

Mhlosinga

Mzinene

R22

To Hluhluwe

To Hluhluwe

eMakhosini-Opathe Heritage Park, Thakazulu Game Reserve & Ntendeka Wilderness Area

A merging of Opathe Game Reserve, established to protect Black Rhino, and a wilderness stretch encompassing the Valley of the Kings, the **eMakhosini-Opathe Heritage Park** is steeped in Zulu history. Shaka was born in the eMakhosini valley; he and six of his regal forebears lie buried here, remembered within the park by a memorial encircled with seven different animal horns. Situated at the edge of the eMakhosini valley, the lovely surrounds rise and dip from mountain upland through mistbelt grassland to valley bushveld. **Thakazulu Game Reserve**, in the lush valley created by the Black Umfolozi and Thaka rivers, shares a similar beauty – which can be appreciated on a challenging, all-terrain 4x4 trail. At Tangami Safari Spa, the natural mineral mudbath is one of only five in the world. **Ntendeka**'s wilderness is isolated and breathtakingly beautiful – dramatic cliffs and exquisite waterfalls display orchids, Ngome lilies, giant-leafed *Streptocarpus* and spreading tree ferns that resemble umbrellas.

EMAKHOSINI-OPATHE
NEAREST TOWN (ALL PARKS)
uLundi

NEAREST AIRPORT (ALL PARKS)
Richards Bay

SIZE
24 000ha

FAUNA
1 Cape Buffalo
2 Zebra
3 Nyala
4 Blue Crane

MAIN CONTACT DETAILS
035 870 2050/5000

ACCOMMODATION INSIDE PARK
None

ACCOMMODATION OUTSIDE PARK
(ALL PARKS)
Tourist Info, uLundi
035 874 5607

THAKAZULU GAME RESERVE
SIZE
12 000ha

AVIFAUNA
1 Martial & Verreaux's (Black) Eagle
2 African Hawk Eagle
3 Bearded Woodpecker
4 Secretary Bird

MAIN CONTACT DETAILS
034 982 2133 ext 2229
www.vryheid.co.za

ACCOMMODATION INSIDE PARK
Tangami Safari Spa, chalets, campsite

NTENDEKA WILDERNESS AREA
SIZE
5250ha

FAUNA/FLORA
1 Samango Monkey
2 Caracal
3 Porcupine
4 White Stork
5 Bald Ibis
6 Ngome Lily
7 Tree Fuchsia

MAIN CONTACT DETAILS
034 967 9100

ACCOMMODATION INSIDE PARK
Campsite

SEASONAL INFORMATION

Gate opening times
eMakhosini-Opathe:
05:00 – 19:00 (summer)
06:00 – 18:00 (winter)
Ntendeka Wilderness Area:
07:30 – 18:00
Day visitors allowed

Tembe Elephant & Ndumo Game Reserves

Just a 5.5km-broad strip of land – the Mbangweni Corridor – divides these two reserves, which are likely to merge sometime in the future. **Tembe**'s reputation rests on its elephants, **Ndumo**'s on its bird count – at around 430 species, the highest in South Africa. Ndumo's initial aim was to protect the Hippopotamus, whose numbers have increased considerably, but today the croc count exceeds that of this gregarious semi-aquatic mammal. Ten vehicles (4x4s only) are permitted into Tembe daily. Of interest is Tembe's protected sand forest, the country's largest. A specially enclosed sector laid with two self-guided trails helps naturalists identify species such as Lebombo Wattle, Zulu Podberry and False Tamboti. Try also to spot an elusive Suni Antelope. For guests at the stilted Ndumo Wilderness Camp on the edge of Banzi Pan, nature walks through forests of fig trees and 4x4 excursions around the pans are considered a first-class wilderness experience.

TEMBE ELEPHANT RESERVE
NEAREST TOWN (BOTH PARKS)
St Lucia

NEAREST AIRPORT (BOTH PARKS)
Richards Bay

SIZE
30 000ha

FAUNA
1 African Elephant
2 White & Black Rhino
3 Giraffe
4 Waterbuck
5 Nyala
6 Eland
7 Zebra
8 Hippopotamus
9 Nile Crocodile
10 Neergard's Sunbird

MAIN CONTACT DETAILS
031 202 9090
031 267 0144
www.tembe.co.za

ACCOMMODATION INSIDE PARK
Tembe Lodge, tented camp
031 202 9090

ACCOMMODATION OUTSIDE PARK
(BOTH PARKS)
Tourist Info, St Lucia
035 550 4059

NDUMO GAME RESERVE
SIZE
10 117ha

FAUNA
1 African Elephant
2 White & Black Rhino
3 Cape Buffalo
4 Lion
5 Leopard
6 Dung Beetle

MAIN CONTACT DETAILS
035 591 0004
035 591 0058/32

ACCOMMODATION INSIDE PARK
Ndumo Camp, chalets, hutted camp

SEASONAL INFORMATION

Gate opening times
Tembe Elephant GR:
06:00 – 18:00
Ndumo GR:
08:00 – 18:00
Day visitors allowed

Map 1 (Upper)

To Mahlangazi →

Langkrans

Ngome

R618

Cetshwayo's Refuge

Ntendeka Wilderness Area

R618

★ Enyokeni Palace

White Mfolozi

9

14

Swart uMfolozi

Kwa Phenyane

Nongoma

6

10

R618

To Hlabisa →

9

7

Calvert

Glückstadt

R34

23

Tangami Safari Spa ★

Black Mfolozi

R66

25

Thakazulu GR

13

Goedgeloof

Komvoorhoogte

Thaka

Bayeni

Black Mfolozi

Sigubudu

N

Mcna

Barklieside

52

Nhlazatshe

Nkonjeni Mission Hospital ★

29

Mahlabatini

9

White Mfolozi

41

Km   25

Mi   12

R34

Denny Dalton

uLoliwe

uLundi

✕ Mpande's Grave

Ntshamanzi

Hluhluwe-iMfolozi Park

To Dundee

20

Nsubeni

15

9

Site of Cetshwayo's Palace ★

R68

20

Babanango

Grave of Dinizulu ★

10

3

29

eMakhosini-Opathe Heritage Park

White Mfolozi

Fort Louis

8

9

To Ntambanana →

uMunywana

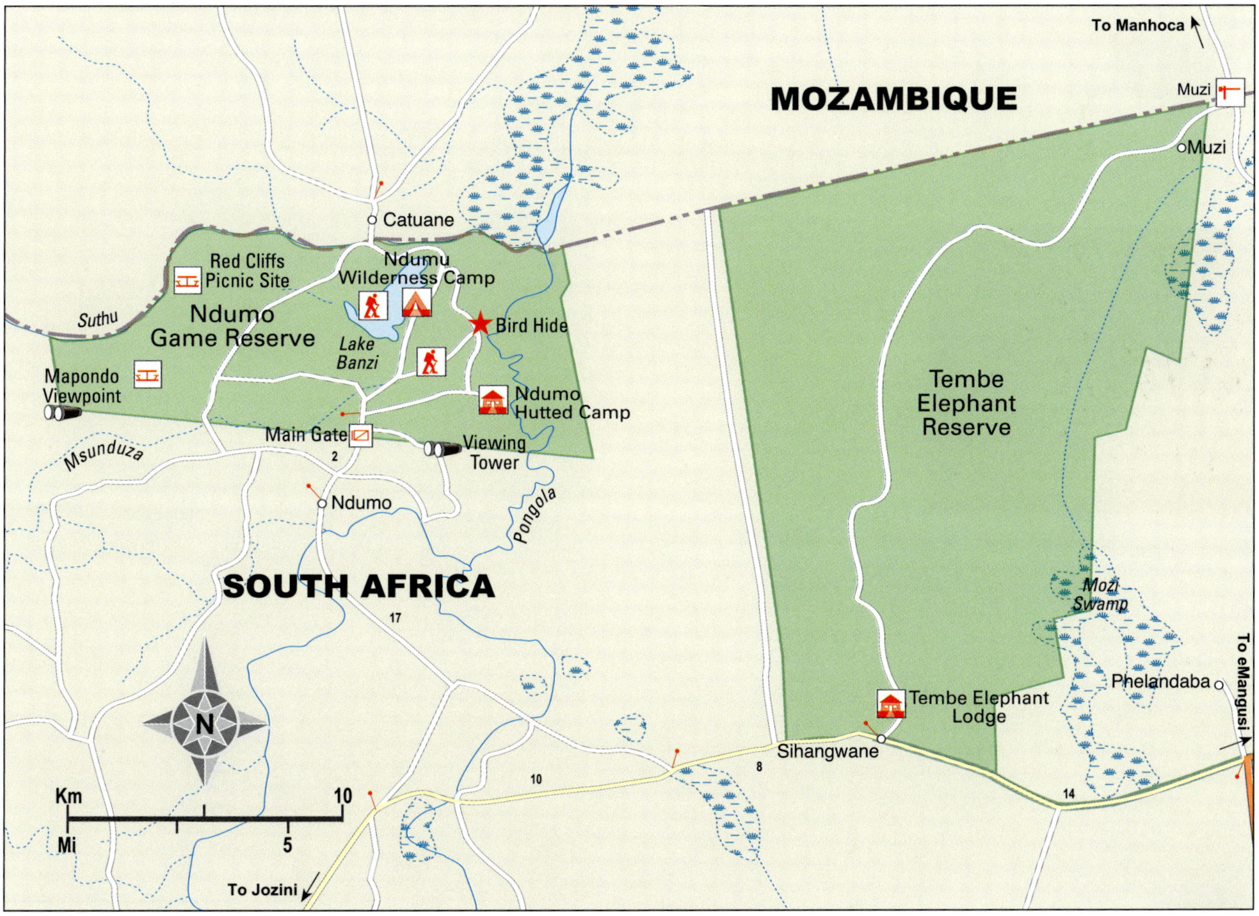

To Melmoth ↓   To Melmoth ↓

Map 2 (Lower)

To Manhoca ↑

MOZAMBIQUE

Muzi

Muzi

Catuane

Red Cliffs Picnic Site

Ndumu Wilderness Camp

Suthu

Ndumo Game Reserve

Lake Banzi

★ Bird Hide

Tembe Elephant Reserve

Mapondo Viewpoint

Ndumo Hutted Camp

Main Gate

Viewing Tower

Msunduza

2

Ndumo

Pongola

SOUTH AFRICA

17

Mozi Swamp

To eMangusi →

Phelandaba

Tembe Elephant Lodge

Sihangwane

8

14

Km   10

Mi   5

10

N

To Jozini ↓

Pietermaritzburg

Ithala Game Reserve,
Vryheid Hill, Klipfontein & Pongola Bush Nature Reserves

Ruggedly beautiful **Ithala Game Reserve**, bordering on the Pongola River, is one of South Africa's best kept secrets. So is the environmentally sensitive Ntshondwe Camp, built of stone, wood and thatch under acacias, Wild Figs and Cabbage Trees at the foot of Ngotshe plateau's russet-pink sandstone cliffs. Just as nice are the reserve's scenic picnic sites and croc-free rivers to swim in. Also on the Pongola River, the wild, remote **Pongola Bush Nature Reserve** has the highest mountains in Zululand with, of course, the most all-encompassing views. An isolated mountaintop stone cottage will appeal to solitude-seekers. **Vryheid Hill Nature Reserve**, set in an area steeped in Zulu and Anglo-Boer history, is a place of sweeping views, grassland orchids and wildflowers. The removal of exotic bluegums and wattles where the Mfolozi River feeds into the dam of the **Klipfontein Nature Reserve** is successfully creating an artificial wetland and bird sanctuary here.

ITHALA GAME RESERVE
NEAREST TOWN (ALL PARKS)
Vryheid
NEAREST AIRPORT (ALL PARKS)
Richards Bay
SIZE
29 653ha
FAUNA
1   Black & White Rhino
2   Giraffe
3   Zebra
MAIN CONTACT DETAILS
(ALL PARKS)
034 983 2540, 033 845 1000/2
info@kznwildlife.com
www.kznwildlife.com
ACCOMMODATION INSIDE PARK
Ntshondwe Lodge, Doornkraal Camp,
Mbizo, Mhlangeni, Thalu Bush Camps
034 983 2540
ACCOMMODATION OUTSIDE PARK
(ALL PARKS)
034 982 2133
information@vhd.dorea.co.za

VRYHEID HILL NATURE RESERVE
SIZE
950ha
FAUNA/FLORA
1   Red Toad
2   Krantz Aloe

ACCOMMODATION INSIDE PARK
Ntingonono Environmental Centre
034 981 4341

KLIPFONTEIN NATURE RESERVE
SIZE
4562ha
AVIFAUNA
1   Crowned Crane
2   Greenbacked Heron
ACCOMMODATION INSIDE PARK

PONGOLA BUSH NR
SIZE
950ha
AVIFAUNA
1   Whitebacked Vulture
2   Burchell's Starling
ACCOMMODATION INSIDE PARK

SEASONAL INFORMATION
Gate opening times
Ithala & Vryheid Hill:
06:00 – 18:00
Klipfontein:
Sunrise to sunset
Day visitors allowed

Pietermaritzburg

Weenen Game Reserve,
Wagendrift Nature Reserve & Moor Park

Wagendrift Nature Reserve is named after a drift across the Bushmans River, once used by transport wagons travelling between Port Natal and the Witwatersrand's goldfields. While fishermen and boats congregate at the dam, trailists and naturalists wander in **Moor Park**, a part of the nature reserve. History and ecology combine in a trail along a 1903-built irrigation furrow, and in the exposed fossilised trees at the dam's southern end. Southern Africa's first known Iron Age settlement (AD1300) on Makhabeni Hill, overlooking Moor Park, made it into the Guinness Book of World Records. The small **Weenen Game Reserve** is an example of dynamite in small packages. Meaning "place of weeping" in memory of Zulu-massacred Voortrekkers, park scenery varies from the high-walled gorge cut by the Bushmans River to valleys of wild thornveld backed by distant hills. Included in the package are White and Black Rhino and 251 bird species.

WEENEN GAME RESERVE
NEAREST TOWN
Weenen
NEAREST AIRPORT (ALL PARKS)
Durban International
SIZE
5000ha
FAUNA
1   Black & White Rhino
2   Giraffe
3   Zebra
MAIN CONTACT DETAILS
036 354 7013
ACCOMMODATION INSIDE PARK
Nyandu Environmental Tented Camp,
Weenen Cottages
ACCOMMODATION OUTSIDE PARK
Tourist Info, Weenen
036 354 1711

**WAGENDRIFT NATURE RESERVE
(INCORPORATES MOOR PARK)**
NEAREST TOWN
Estcourt
SIZE
980ha
FAUNA/AVIFAUNA
1   Black Wildebeest
2   African Fish Eagle
3   Verreaux's (Black) Eagle

MAIN CONTACT DETAILS
036 352 5520
ACCOMMODATION INSIDE PARK
Wagendrift: Chalets, campsite
Moor Park: None
ACCOMMODATION OUTSIDE PARK
Tourist Info, Estcourt
036 352 3000

SEASONAL INFORMATION
Gate opening times
All parks:
06:00 – 18:00
Day visitors allowed

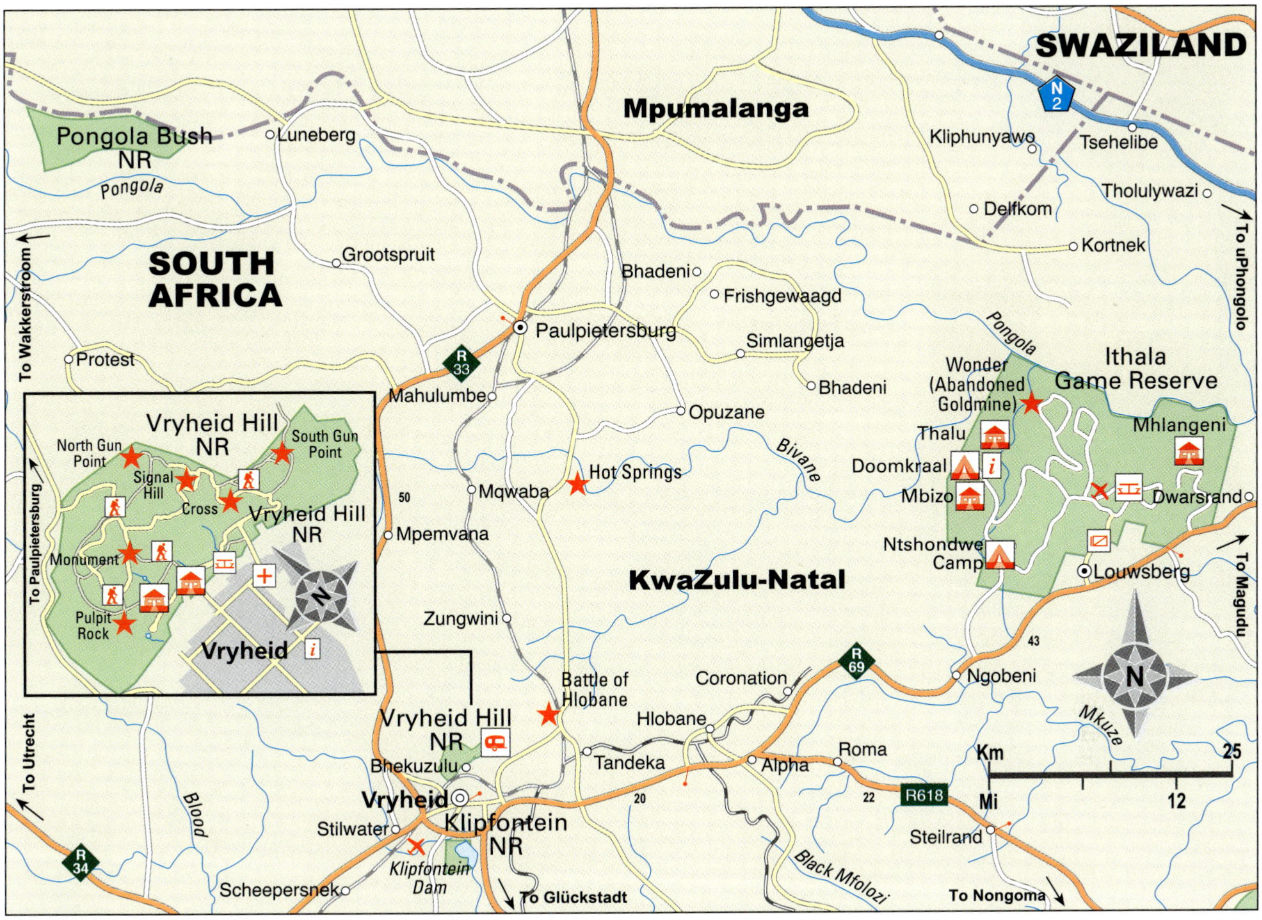

SWAZILAND

Mpumalanga

Kliphunyawo
Tsehelibe
Tholulywazi
Delfkom
Kortnek
To uPhongolo

Pongola Bush
NR
Luneberg
Pongola
Grootspruit

**SOUTH
AFRICA**

Protest
To Wakkerstroom

Paulpietersburg
R33
Mahulumbe
Bhadeni
Frishgewaagd
Simlangetja
Bhadeni
Opuzane
Bivane

Wonder
(Abandoned
Goldmine)
**Ithala
Game Reserve**
Thalu
Mhlangeni
Doomkraal
Mbizo
Dwarsrand
Ntshondwe
Camp
Louwsberg
To Magudu
Pongola

Hot Springs
Mqwaba

To Paulpietersburg

**Vryheid Hill
NR**
North Gun
Point
South Gun
Point
Signal
Hill
Cross
**Vryheid Hill
NR**
Monument
N
Pulpit
Rock
Vryheid
i

Mpemvana

KwaZulu-Natal

50

Zungwini

43

Ngobeni

Mkuze

Battle of
Hlobane
Coronation
R69
Vryheid Hill
NR
Hlobane
Km
25
Bhekuzulu
Tandeka
Alpha
Roma
Mi
12
Vryheid
20
22
R618
Stilwater
**Klipfontein
NR**
Steilrand
Scheepersnek
*Klipfontein
Dam*
To Glückstadt
To Nongoma
Black Mfolozi
R34
Blood
To Utrecht

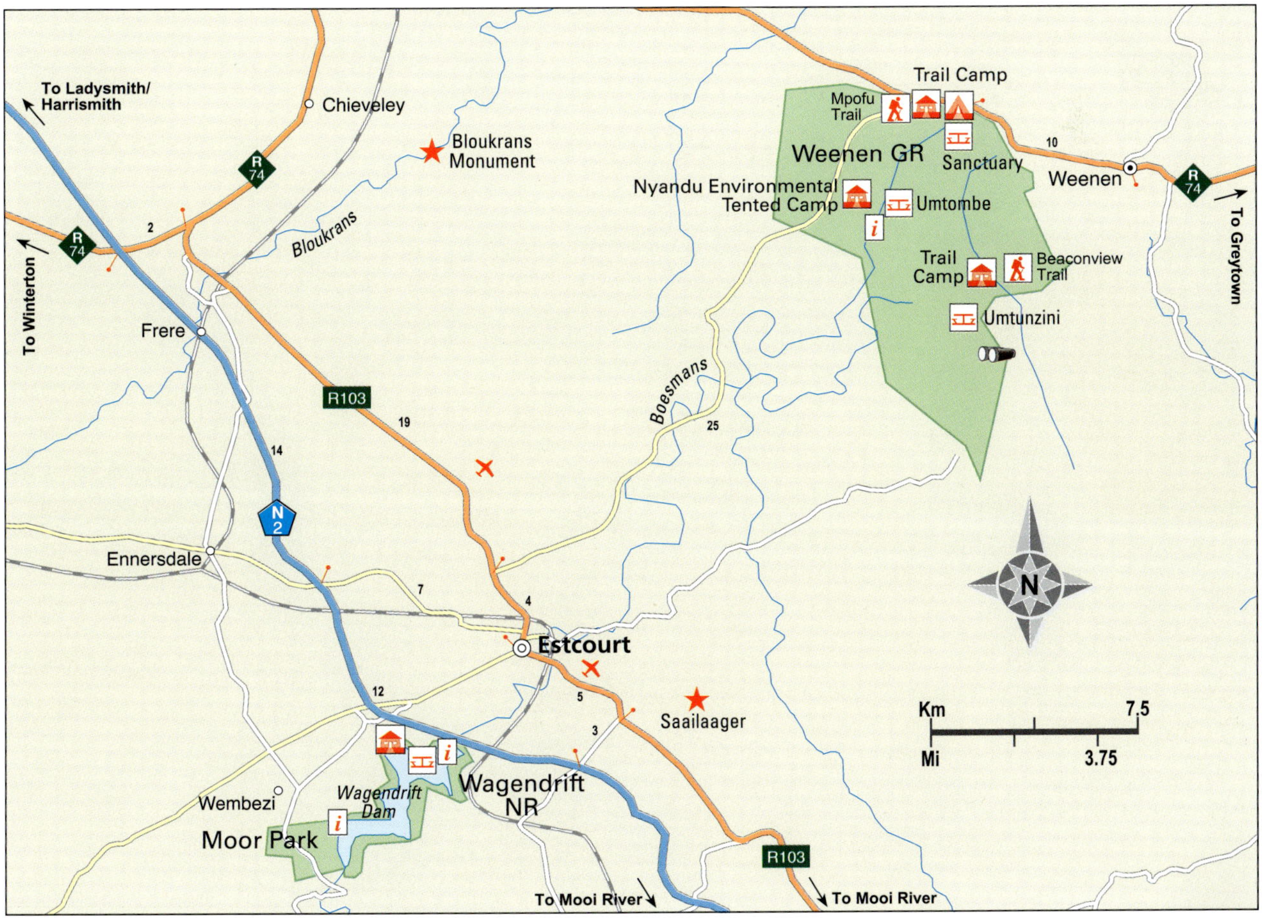

To Ladysmith/
Harrismith
Chieveley
Bloukrans
Monument
Trail Camp
Mpofu
Trail
R74
Weenen GR
Sanctuary
10
Weenen
R74
To Greytown
Bloukrans
Nyandu Environmental
Tented Camp
Umtombe
i
2
R74
To Winterton
Frere
Trail
Camp
Beaconview
Trail
R103
19
Boesmans
Umtunzini
14
25
N2
Ennersdale
7
4
Estcourt
5
12
Saailaager
3
*Wagendrift
Dam*
Km
7.5
**Wagendrift
NR**
Mi
3.75
Wembezi
i
Moor Park
R103
To Mooi River
To Mooi River

85

Oribi Gorge & uMtamvuna Nature Reserves,
uVongo River Nature Reserve

All these nature reserves straddle KwaZulu's holiday-atmosphere South Coast – today dubbed the Hibiscus Coast for its green, luxuriant subtropical environs. **Oribi Gorge Nature Reserve** is perhaps the most spectacular (in the true sense of the word). Walking trails descend into the 400m-deep gorge cut by the uMzimkulwana River for 24km, or trace its high edge. Lined with dense coastal bush and forests, this is the realm of eagles and kingfishers – and elusive Leopard. Also offering Nature's drama in the form of forested cliffs and a river-forged valley, the **uMtamvuna Nature Reserve** promises sightings of Cape Vultures soaring above their nesting sites. Orchids, ferns and tropical shrubs in **uVongo River Nature Reserve** and an arboretum of hundreds of exotic and indigenous coastal trees in Skyline Nature Reserve uphold KwaZulu-Natal's reputation for lush, thriving, humidity-loving natural vegetation.

ORIBI GORGE NATURE RESERVE
NEAREST TOWN
Port Shepstone

NEAREST AIRPORT (ALL PARKS)
Margate

SIZE
1850ha

FAUNA
1 Leopard
2 Oribi

MAIN CONTACT DETAILS
039 679 1644, 033 845 1000/2

ACCOMMODATION INSIDE PARK
Oribi Gorge Camp, chalets, rustic huts

ACCOMMODATION OUTSIDE PARK
039 682 2455
portshepstone@hibiscuscoast.org.za

UMTAMVUNA NATURE RESERVE
NEAREST TOWN
Port Edward

SIZE
3247ha

FAUNA/AVIFAUNA
1 Samango Monkey
2 Cape Vulture

MAIN CONTACT DETAILS
039 311 2383

ACCOMMODATION INSIDE PARK

ACCOMMODATION OUTSIDE PARK
039 313 1211
portedward@hibiscuscoast.org.za

UVONGO RIVER NR
NEAREST TOWN
Margate

SIZE
28ha

AVIFAUNA
1 Narina Trogon

MAIN CONTACT DETAILS
039 315 7378

ACCOMMODATION INSIDE PARK
None

ACCOMMODATION OUTSIDE PARK
Hibiscus Coast Tourism
039 317 4630, 039 312 1222/3/4

SEASONAL INFORMATION

Gate opening times
Oribi NR: 06:30 – 19:30
uMtamvuna NR & uVongo River:
Sunrise to sunset
Day visitors allowed

Richards Bay Game Reserve,
uMlalazi & aMatikulu Nature Reserves

The **aMatikulu Nature Reserve** is one of the few places in Southern Africa where Giraffe and Kudu graze on forested dunes overlooking the Indian Ocean. Hippos, crocodiles and sharks lurk in the lagoon at the uMlalazi River mouth, where the **uMlalazi Nature Reserve** offers Raffia Palms, Black and White Mangroves, and mudflats with crabs and crustaceans. In the **Richards Bay Game Reserve**, Thulasihleka, a large reed-lined pan, is one of Richard's Bay's "hottest" waterbird spots. New, rare migrants include the endangered Goliath and Squacco Herons. Cradled in the bend of the Enseleni River, whose waters conceal crocodiles and hippos, the eNseleni Nature Reserve has a 5km self-guided weekend walk among grazing antelope and Blue Wildebeest. Visit Dlinza Forest and eNtumeni nature reserves for hard-wood forests, grassy glades, leafy ferns, sinuous forest climbers, dainty buck and birds. Harold Johnson Nature Reserve, onetime site of Fort Pearson and the Ultimatum Tree, has an interesting 2km educational Zulu and Boer "Remedies and Rituals" trail.

RICHARDS BAY GAME RESERVE
NEAREST TOWN
Richards Bay

NEAREST AIRPORT (ALL PARKS)
Richards Bay

SIZE
1200ha

AVIFAUNA
1 Goliath & Squacco Heron
2 Whitebacked Duck

MAIN CONTACT DETAILS
035 753 2211, 033 845 1000

ACCOMMODATION INSIDE PARK
None

ACCOMMODATION OUTSIDE PARK
Tourist Info, uMhlathuze
035 907 5018

UMLALAZI NATURE RESERVE
NEAREST TOWN (ALSO AMATIKULU)
eMpangeni

SIZE
1028 ha

FLORA
1 Raffia Palm
2 Mangrove sp.

MAIN CONTACT DETAILS
035 340 1836/9

ACCOMMODATION INSIDE PARK
Inkwazi & Indaba Camps, log cabins

ACCOMMODATION OUTSIDE PARK
(ALSO aMATIKULU)
Tourist Info, eMpangeni
035 792 1283

AMATIKULU NATURE RESERVE
SIZE
2100ha

FAUNA
1 Giraffe
2 Hippopotamus
3 Nile Crocodile
4 African Finfoot

MAIN CONTACT DETAILS
032 453 0155

ACCOMMODATION INSIDE PARK
Zangozolo Tented Camp

SEASONAL INFORMATION

Gate opening times
Richards Bay:
Sunrise to sunset
uMlalazi NR:
05:00 – 22:00
aMatikulu NR:
07:00 – 17:00
Day visitors allowed

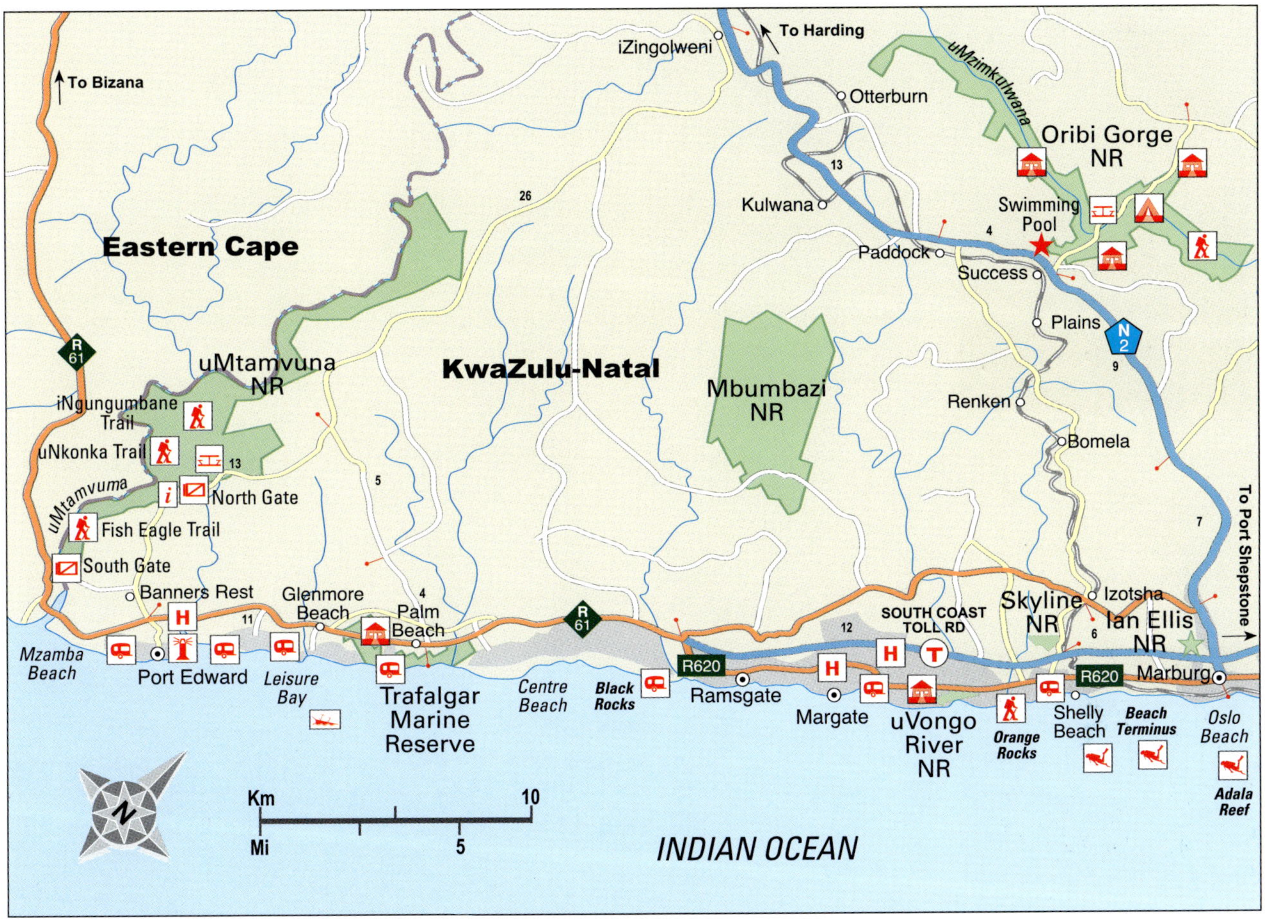

Top Map

To Harding

To Bizana

iZingolweni

Otterburn

uMzimkulwana

Oribi Gorge NR

Kulwana

13

Swimming Pool

Paddock

4

Success

Eastern Cape

26

Plains

N2

KwaZulu-Natal

uMtamvuna NR

Mbumbazi NR

Renken

iNgungumbane Trail

Bomela

uNkonka Trail

13

To Port Shepstone

R61

uMtamvuma

North Gate

5

7

Fish Eagle Trail

i

South Gate

Banners Rest

Glenmore Beach

4

Skyline NR

Izotsha

Ian Ellis NR

Palm Beach

6

Mzamba Beach

H

11

R61

12

SOUTH COAST TOLL RD

Marburg

Port Edward

Leisure Bay

Trafalgar Marine Reserve

Centre Beach

Black Rocks

R620

Ramsgate

H

T

Skyline

R620

Margate

uVongo River NR

Orange Rocks

Shelly Beach

Beach Terminus

Oslo Beach

Adala Reef

Km 10
Mi 5

N

INDIAN OCEAN

Bottom Map

To KwaMbonambi

eNseleni

Nkwalini

R34

27

9

12

N2

12

eNseleni NR

R66

Bulawayo Site of Shaka's Kraal

R34

eMpangeni

Ngwelezana

2

17

Richards Bay

21

Mhlatuzana

Ngoye Forest

R102

Mhlatuzi Lagoon

To eNtumeni

22

Dlinza Forest NR

Cowards Bush Monument

12

Felixton

Richards Bay Game Reserve

eNtumeni NR

eShowe

Fort KwaMondi

KwaDlangezwa

eSikhawini

28

Port Durnford Lighthouse

R66

Nsingweni

15

Port Durnford

10

Mtunzini

Raffia Palms

Battle of Gingindlovu

26

8

eMoyeni

18

Siyaya

uMlalazi NR

INDIAN OCEAN

Gingindlovu

Indaba Camp Site

aMatikulu

6

9

Nyoni

R102

18

Tugela

7

21

aMatikulu NR

N2

Mandini

3

N

Tugela

Harold Johnson NR

To Darnall

Km 20
Mi 10

Spioenkop Dam Nature Reserve

The mountain of Spioenkop stands sentinel over the thorn savannah and tranquil waters of the Spioenkop dam and nature reserve. An ever-present reminder of the famous Battle of Spioenkop in 1900, when the British were humiliatingly defeated by the Boers during the South African War, its 360-degree views reinforce its role in earlier times as an effective lookout point. Across the dam on the southern horizon, the Drakensberg mountains cut their dramatic silhouette, and across the plains to the north lies Ladysmith. The reserve's most exhilarating excursions are horse trails that thread among long, sinuous-necked giraffe and sometimes even square-lipped White Rhino. The animals are far more tolerant of horses than people on foot, ensuring more thrilling encounters.

Pongolapoort Nature Reserve

The Pongolapoort (Jozini) lake and its nature reserve are both part of the greater Pongolapoort Biosphere Reserve, all defined by the gorgeous Lebombo mountains and the curves of the Pongola River as it enters the lake. Avid fishermen are lured to these waters specifically for their bounty of Tigerfish – this is the only lake in South Africa home to the "striped waterdog". The reason: the lake lies in a subtropical zone, so species tend to match those of Central Africa. Variety here is also greater than other freshwater lakes as a result of floods that dumped exotics, such as bass and carp, into its waters. Semi-submerged trees and grazing wildlife at the water's edge have earned Pongolapoort comparisons with Zimbabwe's Lake Kariba.

Mount Currie Nature Reserve

Set in a part of KwaZulu-Natal known as East Griqualand, Mount Currie's grassy, protea-covered slopes and parcels of montane forest provide a verdant contrast to the boating playground of Crystal dam, which happens to be fed by the waters of Crystal Spring. When, back in 1863, some 2000 Griqua men, women and children, with their 20 000 head of stock, emerged from the mountains, they found life-giving water, wildlife and verdant pastures. Their graves and a National Monument at the *laager* site are reminders of these hardy pioneers. A climb of Mount Currie brings hikers closer to the reserve's Bearded Vultures and other prolific raptors; look out for the distinctive white and brown-spotted chest of the fierce Martial Eagle.

Vernon Crookes Nature Reserve

Vernon Crookes, characterised by grassland marching over layer upon layer of rolling hills interspersed with wooded valleys, is surrounded by fields of sugarcane, gum plantations and tribal lands. In the reserve, spring surprises the senses with myriad delicate wildflowers. High grassland ridges give on to wonderful views of the ocean, while Crowned and Martial Eagles, both of which nest in the reserve, keep a sharp eye on grassland prey from their elevation in the thermals. At Vernon Crookes Camp, a rustic treehouse claiming to offer a lounge/dining area, kitchen and three bedrooms (and 21 beds!) sounds an intriguing way to get some shuteye. The birdlife is so outstanding, it seems, 100 species can easily be recorded in a summer morning's birding!

SPIOENKOP DAM NR

NEAREST TOWN
Bergville

NEAREST AIRPORT
Durban International

SIZE
6000ha

FAUNA
1 White Rhino
2 Kudu
3 Giraffe
4 Black-backed Jackal
5 Brown Hyena
6 Aardwolf
7 Mountain Reedbuck
8 Steenbok

MAIN CONTACT DETAILS
036 488 1578

ACCOMMODATION INSIDE PARK
iPhika Tented Bushcamp, chalets, campsite

ACCOMMODATION OUTSIDE PARK
Tourist Info, Bergville
036 448 1557/1296

SEASONAL INFORMATION

Gate opening times
06:00 – 19:00
Day visitors allowed

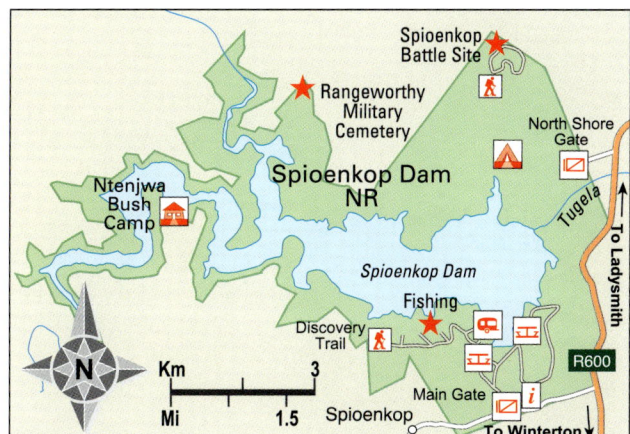

PONGOLAPOORT NR

NEAREST TOWN
St Lucia

NEAREST AIRPORT
Richards Bay

SIZE
1600ha

FAUNA
1 Hippopotamus
2 Nile Crocodile
3 Zebra
4 Kudu
5 Nyala
6 Impala

MAIN CONTACT DETAILS
034 435 1012/1123

ACCOMMODATION INSIDE PARK
Campsite

ACCOMMODATION OUTSIDE PARK
uMhlathuze Tourism Office
035 907 508

SEASONAL INFORMATION

Gate opening times
05:00 – 19:00 (summer)
06:00 – 18:00 (winter)
Day visitors allowed

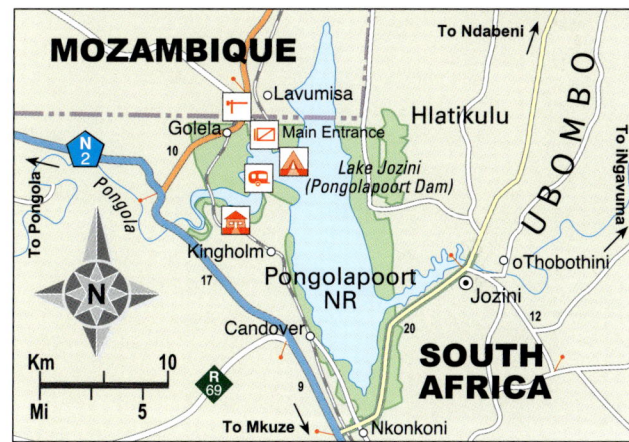

MOUNT CURRIE NR

NEAREST TOWN
Kokstad

NEAREST AIRPORT
Durban International

SIZE
1750ha

FAUNA
1 Martial Eagle
2 Bearded Vulture
3 Protea sp.

MAIN CONTACT DETAILS
039 727 3844

ACCOMMODATION INSIDE PARK
Cottages, campsite

ACCOMMODATION OUTSIDE PARK
Tourist Info, Kokstad
039 747 9077

SEASONAL INFORMATION

Gate opening times
06:00 – 18:00
Day visitors allowed

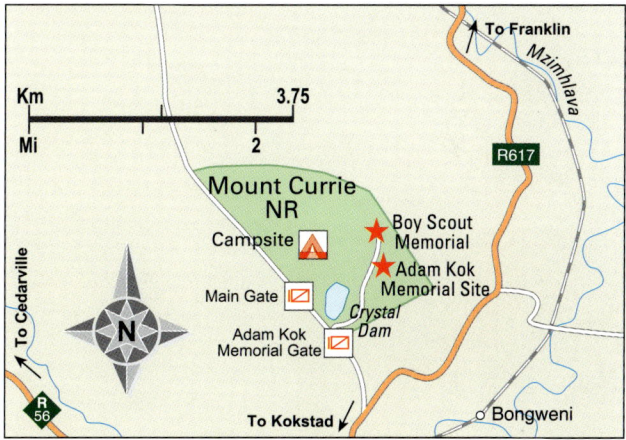

VERNON CROOKES NR

NEAREST TOWN
uMzinto

NEAREST AIRPORT
Margate

SIZE
2189ha

FAUNA
1 Zebra
2 Oribi
3 Blesbok
4 Impala
5 Grey Duiker
6 Vervet Monkey
7 Caracal
8 Crowned & Martial Eagle

MAIN CONTACT DETAILS
039 974 2222, 083 293 3622

ACCOMMODATION INSIDE PARK
Nyengelezi Camp

ACCOMMODATION OUTSIDE PARK
Tourist Info, uMzinto
039 976 1364

SEASONAL INFORMATION

Gate opening times
06:00 – 18:00 (summer)
06:00 – 17:00 (winter)
Day visitors allowed

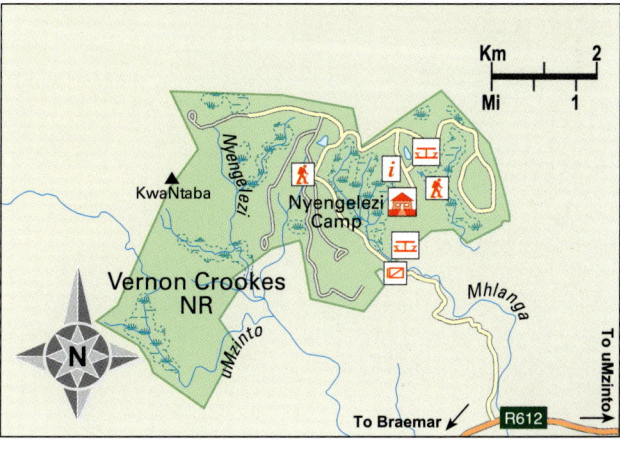

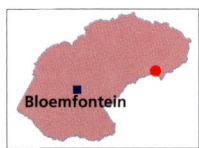

Golden Gate Highlands National Park

Nature has excelled herself in the gigantic sandstone buttresses that rear into the sky in this park. Over roughly 200 million years, layer upon layer of sandstone, shale, mudstone and silt, with lava intrusions forming sills and dykes, have left behind the Golden Gate's dramatic cliffs. In early morning or late evening light, iron oxides in the sandstone turn from rust-red and copper to amber and bronze. Most prominent are The Sentinel (or Brandwag) and the Golden "gateway" to the park; others are shaped like mushrooms and a statesman's nose. A guided walk to Cathedral Cave, whose 30m domed ceiling is reminiscent of a soaring church interior, reveals a stream tumbling down from the cave roof. The walk is off-limits in breeding season, as rare Bald Ibis nest here. Walks of varying length and difficulty guarantee the unsurpassed scenery of the Golden Gate park itself and the Drakensberg and Lesotho's Maluti mountains.

GOLDEN GATE HIGHLANDS NP
NEAREST TOWN
Clarens

NEAREST AIRPORT
Bloemfontein

SIZE
11 600ha

FAUNA/FLORA
1   Black Wildebeest
2   Burchell's Zebra
3   Eland
4   Oribi
5   Blesbok
6   Springbok
7   Bearded Vulture
8   Bald Ibis
9   Oldwood Tree

MAIN CONTACT DETAILS
058 255 0000/0012
reservations@sanparks.org
www.sanparks.org

ACCOMMODATION INSIDE PARK
Glen Reenen Rest Camp,
Wilgenhof Environmental Education
Centre (For youth groups),
Highlands Mountain Retreat,
Qwa Qwa Rest Camp,
Noordt Brabant Guest House

ACCOMMODATION OUTSIDE PARK
Tourist Info, Clarens
058 256 1173

SEASONAL INFORMATION

Gate opening times
05:00 – 22:00
Day visitors allowed

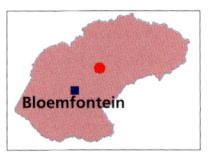

Willem Pretorius & Erfenis Dam Nature Reserves

In spite of the Aventura public holiday resort on the Allemanskraal Dam at the centre of the **Willem Pretorius Nature Reserve**, the range of wildlife here is pretty impressive, counting White Rhino and Gemsbok among its mammals, and Caracal and Black-backed Jackal among its predators. A lesser-known attraction is the well-preserved ruin of a prehistoric settlement on the summit of Doringberg, belonging to the long-vanished Leghoya people, it seems. It once was characterised by diminutive huts and cattle *kraals* of stone, the stone-slab roofing probably dictating the huts' size. One of the settlements has been restored and is a National Monument. The **Erfenis Dam Nature Reserve** is fairly new. The dam, initially constructed for irrigation, has been discovered by anglers and men who like messing around in powerboats. An added bonus is wildlife in the small 400ha nature reserve, which includes weighty species such as Black-backed Jackal and Red Hartebeest.

WILLEM PRETORIUS NR
NEAREST TOWN
Winburg

NEAREST AIRPORT (BOTH PARKS)
Bloemfontein

SIZE
12 005ha

FAUNA/FLORA
1   White Rhino
2   Gemsbok
3   Black-backed Jackal
4   Caracal
5   Leopard Tortoise
6   Egyptian Goose
7   Wild Olive Tree
8   Sweet Thorn Acacia

MAIN CONTACT DETAILS
057 651 4003/4

ACCOMMODATION INSIDE PARK
Education Centre, bushcamp, campsites, self-contained chalets

ACCOMMODATION OUTSIDE PARK
Tourist Info, Winburg
051 881 0003

ERFENIS DAM NATURE RESERVE
NEAREST TOWN
Theunissen

SIZE
400ha

FAUNA/FLORA
1   Black Wildebeest
2   Red Hartebeest
3   Tsessebe
4   Burchell's Zebra
5   Mountain Reedbuck
6   Steenbok
7   African Fish Eagle
8   Wild Olive Tree

MAIN CONTACT DETAILS
057 733 2125

ACCOMMODATION INSIDE PARK
Caravan park, bush camp

ACCOMMODATION OUTSIDE PARK
Tourist Info, Theunissen
057 733 0106

SEASONAL INFORMATION

Gate opening times
Willem Pretorius NR:
07:00 – 18:30
Erfenis Dam NR:
06:00 – 21:00
Day visitors allowed

Map 1 — Golden Gate Highlands National Park

SOUTH AFRICA

Little Caledon

Spitskop

Bridal Veil Falls

Wilgenhof Environmental Education Centre

Bushman Cave

Woodhouse Kop

Rondawelkop

To Kestell

To Harrismith

R712

Golden Gate Highlands National Park

Brandwag

Glen Reenen

R712

To Clarens

Holkrans Cave

Buffelspruit

Cathedral Cave

Swartkop

Rhebok Hut

Rhebok Hiking Trail

R O O I B E R G E

Generaalskop

Ribbokkop

Snowhills

Monantsa Pass

To Phuthaditjhaba

Sefako

LESOTHO

Caledon

To Lebono

Km 50 / Mi 25

N

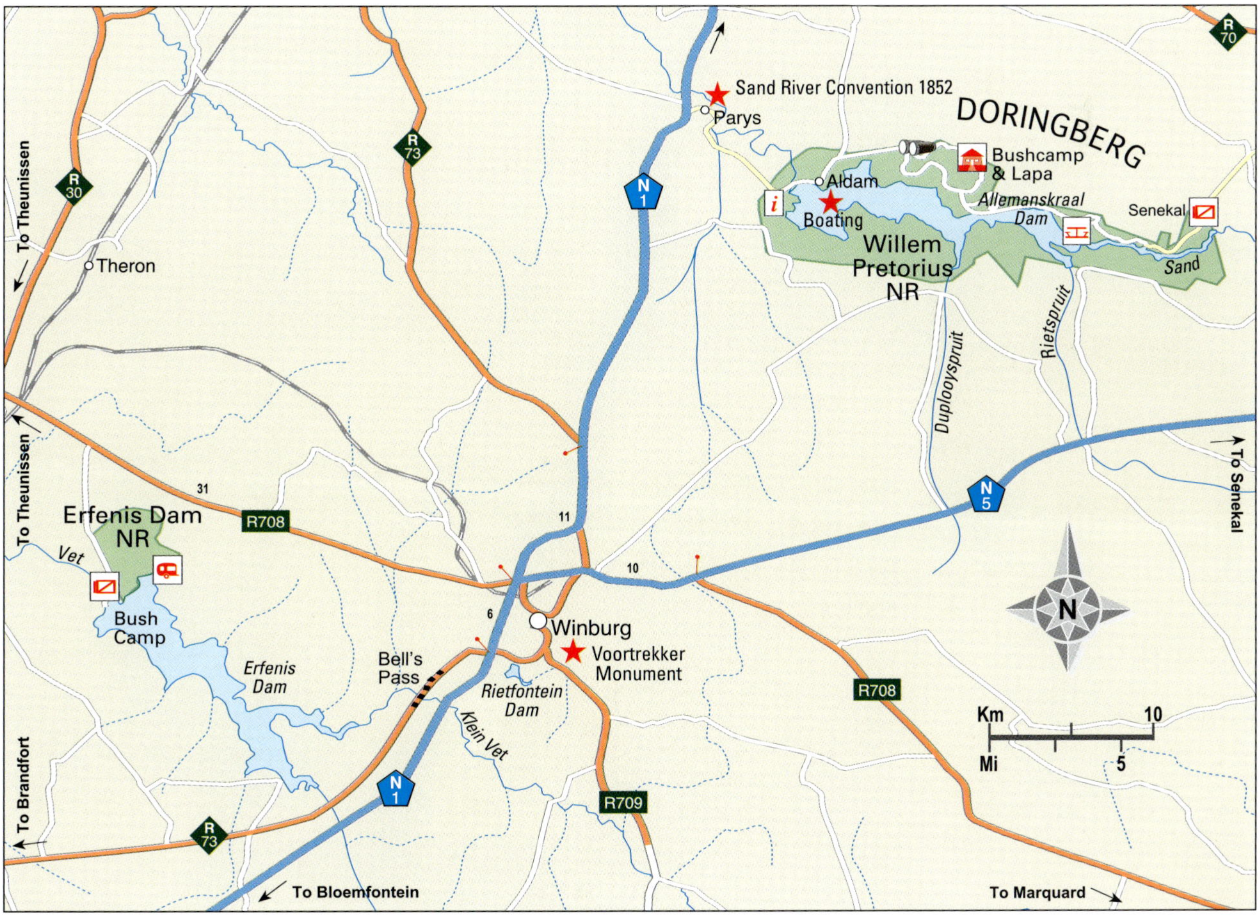

Map 2 — Winburg / Willem Pretorius NR

R70

To Theunissen

R73

N1

Sand River Convention 1852

Parys

DORINGBERG

Bushcamp & Lapa

Aldam

i

Boating

Allemanskraal Dam

Senekal

Sand

R30

Theron

Willem Pretorius NR

Rietspruit

Duplooyspruit

To Senekal

N5

To Theunissen

Erfenis Dam NR

31

R708

Vet

11

Bush Camp

10

Erfenis Dam

Bell's Pass

6

Winburg

Voortrekker Monument

Rietfontein Dam

R708

To Brandfort

Klein Vet

N1

R73

R709

To Bloemfontein

To Marquard

Km 10 / Mi 5

N

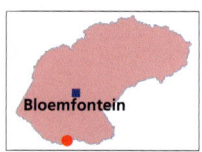

Gariep Dam Nature Reserve,
Oviston & Tussen-die-Riviere Reserves

From **Gariep Dam Nature Reserve**, a tour of the 13.2km of tunnels through the Gariep dam wall, and down 1000 steps, takes you to the bedrock foundation of the Orange River. The central section of the wall, holding back 6000 million cubic litres of water, is arched to deflect the thrust of the water towards the outer solid-rock foundations. The water pressure is so tremendous, the wall in fact gives under it. These and other fascinating facts are revealed on your guided walk. On the southern side of the Gariep dam, different ways to experience the **Oviston Nature Reserve**'s wildlife vary from hikes to horse or mountainbike rides. Tops of the three summer nature trails in the **Tussen-die-Riviere Game Reserve** – which in winter is a hunting reserve – is the Klipstapel hiking trail; an intriguing feature is a field of eroded dolerite pillars balancing precariously on their bases.

GARIEP DAM NR
NEAREST TOWN
Bethulie

NEAREST AIRPORT (ALL PARKS)
Bloemfontein

SIZE
13 000ha

FAUNA
1 Black Wildebeest
2 Cape Mountain Zebra

MAIN CONTACT DETAILS
051 754 0026/48
gariepnr@telkomsa.net

ACCOMMODATION INSIDE PARK

ACCOMMODATION OUTSIDE PARK
Tourist Info, Bethulie
051 763 0522/0643

OVISTON NATURE RESERVE
NEAREST TOWN
Venterstad

SIZE
16 000ha

FAUNA
1 Black Wildebeest
2 Springbok

MAIN CONTACT DETAILS
051 655 0000, 084 581 0155

ACCOMMODATION INSIDE PARK

ACCOMMODATION OUTSIDE PARK
Tourist Info, Venterstad
051 654 0224/5

TUSSEN-DIE-RIVIERE GR
NEAREST TOWN
Bethulie

SIZE
22 000ha

FAUNA
1 Gemsbok
2 Aardwolf

MAIN CONTACT DETAILS
051 763 1000, 762 2803

ACCOMMODATION INSIDE PARK

ACCOMMODATION OUTSIDE PARK
See Gariep Dam NR

SEASONAL INFORMATION

Gate opening times
Gariep Dam NR:
07:00 – 18:00
Oviston NR:
08:00 – 16:30
Tussen-die-Riviere GR:
07:00 – 18:00

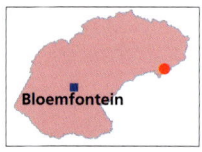

Sterkfontein Dam Nature Reserve

Great, flat sheets of water and the pummelled peaks of the Drakensberg foothills make this mountain reserve particularly special. Grass-covered slopes, scrub-filled kloofs and, higher up, dense Afromontane forests in a few mountain gorges make the walks quite enchanting. Trees entwined with wild grape form a dense leafy canopy beneath which ferns and mosses thrive, the fronds of tree ferns drape lushly from their hosts, and in the dampness, tree trunks wear a mantle of fungi and lichens. Besides the reserve's mountain-loving buck and antelope, Bald Ibis together with the Whitebellied and Blue Korhaan are evident on grassy slopes, as is the Secretary Bird, mincing through the grassland on long thin legs. A major attraction is a vulture restaurant, best viewed from Oliviershoek Pass outside the reserve, with great sightings of Cape and Bearded Vulture. While you're at it, look out for Black and Martial Eagles planing on the air thermals.

STERKFONTEIN DAM NR
NEAREST TOWN
Harrismith

NEAREST AIRPORT
Bloemfontein

SIZE
18 000ha

FAUNA/FLORA
1   Mountan Reedbuck
2   Oribi
3   Martial Eagle
4   Jackal Buzzard
5   Cape & Bearded Vulture
6   Bald Ibis
7   Whitebellied & Blue Korhaan
8   Secretary Bird
9   Tree Fern sp.
10 Yellowwood sp.

MAIN CONTACT DETAILS
058 622 3520
www.freestatetourism.gov.za

ACCOMMODATION INSIDE PARK
Fully equipped chalets, campsite

ACCOMMODATION OUTSIDE PARK
Tourist Info, Harrismith
058 622 3525

SEASONAL INFORMATION

Gate opening times
06:00 – 22:00
Day visitors allowed

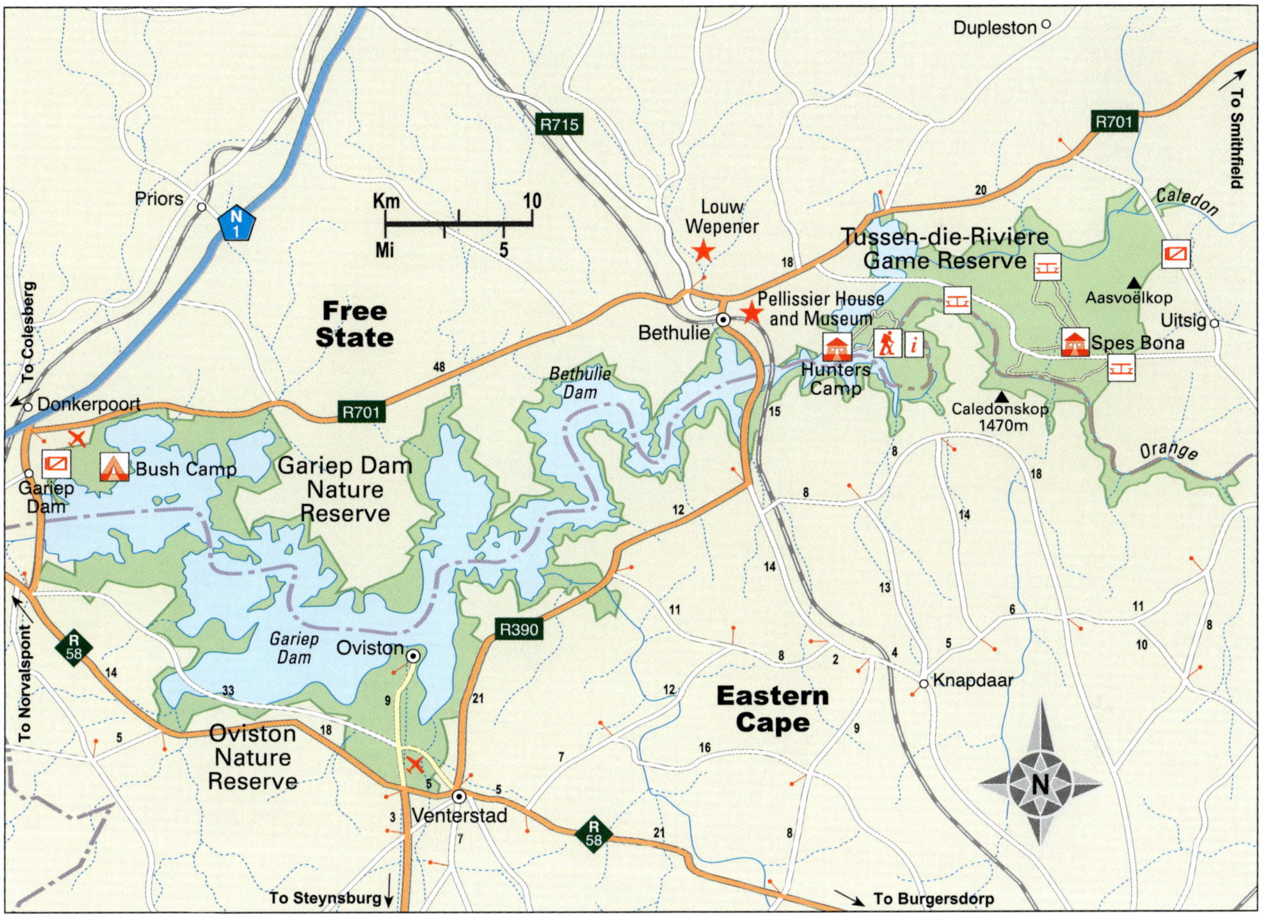

Map 1 (Free State / Eastern Cape — Gariep Dam area)

Dupleston

To Smithfield

R715

R701

Caledon

20

Priors

N1

Km 10

Mi 5

Louw Wepener

Tussen-die-Riviere Game Reserve

Free State

18

Pellissier House and Museum

Bethulie

Aasvoëlkop

Uitsig

Spes Bona

Hunters Camp

To Colesberg

48

Bethulie Dam

15

Caledonskop 1470m

Orange

R701

Donkerpoort

8

Bush Camp

Gariep Dam Nature Reserve

18

Gariep Dam

12

14

8

13

6

11

8

To Norvalspont

R58

14

Gariep Dam

Oviston

R390

11

5

10

33

12

14

5

9

21

Eastern Cape

2

Knapdaar

9

5

Oviston Nature Reserve

18

12

16

9

N

3

Venterstad

5

7

7

8

5

R58

21

To Steynsburg

To Burgersdorp

Map 2 (Free State / KwaZulu-Natal — Sterkfontein Dam area)

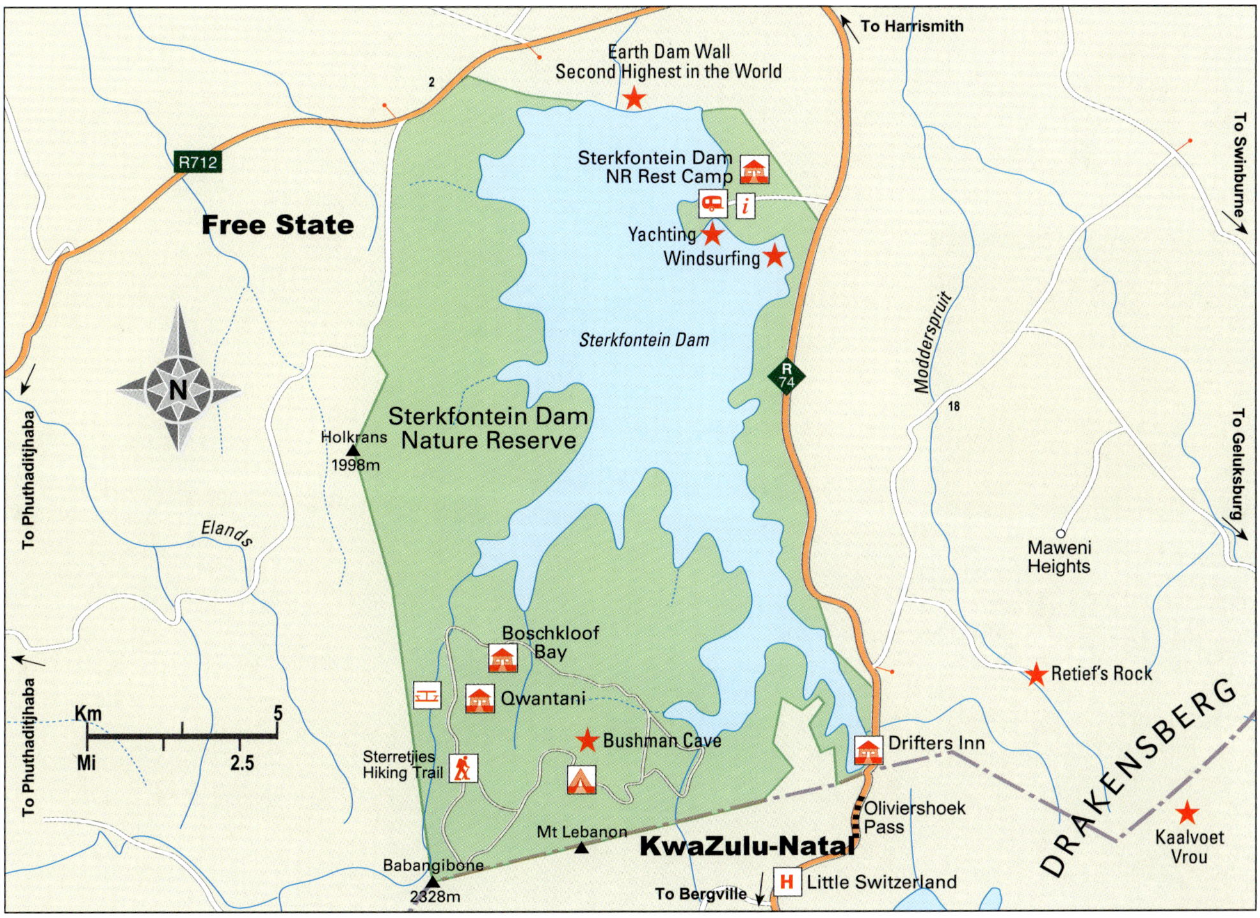

To Harrismith

Earth Dam Wall Second Highest in the World

2

R712

Free State

Sterkfontein Dam NR Rest Camp

To Swinburne

Yachting

Windsurfing

Modderspruit

R74

Sterkfontein Dam

18

To Phuthaditjhaba

Holkrans 1998m

Sterkfontein Dam Nature Reserve

Elands

To Geluksburg

Maweni Heights

To Phuthaditjhaba

Boschkloof Bay

Retief's Rock

DRAKENSBERG

Km 5

Mi 2.5

Qwantani

Bushman Cave

Sterretjies Hiking Trail

Drifters Inn

Oliviershoek Pass

Mt Lebanon

KwaZulu-Natal

Kaalvoet Vrou

Babangibone 2328m

H Little Switzerland

To Bergville

93

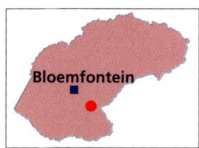

Caledon & Rustfontein Dam Nature Reserves

These two reserves are set in the Free State landscape of endless rolling grassland and cultivated belts of tassel-topped maize and bright-faced sunflowers. Both focus on bodies of water, although **Caledon Nature Reserve**'s tranquil dam pulls in anglers rather than boatsmen. Greatly appealing to nature-lovers are the bushcamp night shelters – wooden cabins on decks floated on the water, with benches and a *lapa* on the shore. The surrounding grassy hills – emerald in summer, amber-yellow in winter – and rocky-walled ravines are a soul-soothing escape from life's tribulations. Twitchers will enjoy the waterbirds or can spend time tracking the grazing wild animals, among them Black Wildebeest and Zebra. **Rustfontein Dam Nature Reserve** has, as its setting, tree-studded koppies and grassy hillsides against which water-lovers ski, surf and sail, and anglers cast their lines for that anticipated big catch.

CALEDON NR
NEAREST TOWN
Wepener

NEAREST AIRPORT (BOTH PARKS)
Bloemfontein

SIZE
2300ha

FAUNA
1 Black Wildebeest
2 Burchell's Zebra
3 Blesbok
4 Springbok
5 Mountain Reedbuck
6 Black Stork

MAIN CONTACT DETAILS
051 583 2000

ACCOMMODATION INSIDE PARK
No facilities at present – closed for renovations, due to reopen 2007/2008

ACCOMMODATION OUTSIDE PARK
Tourist Info, Wepener
051 583 1131

RUSTFONTEIN DAM NR
NEAREST TOWN
Bloemfontein

SIZE
393ha

FAUNA
1 Black Wildebeest
2 Burchell's Zebra
3 Springbok

MAIN CONTACT DETAILS
051 528 2926

ACCOMMODATION INSIDE PARK
🏕 ⛺ 🎣

ACCOMMODATION OUTSIDE PARK
Tourist Info, Bloemfontein
051 405 8489
www.bloemfontein.co.za

SEASONAL INFORMATION

Gate opening times
Caledon NR:
Closed for renovations
Rustfontein Dam NR:
08:00 – 18:00

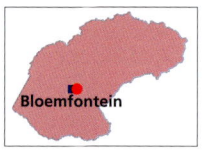

Bloemfontein
Naval Hill, Signal Hill & Grant's Hill

Three hills, all with commanding views of Bloemfontein's city spreading out below. . . The panoramas are good from the flat crest of **Naval Hill**, also a game reserve – the only known one in South Africa to be located within city limits. And not to be sneezed at, either, is its range of wildlife, extending to Blue Wildebeest, Giraffe and a number of small antelope. It's also the site of the Lamont Hussey Observatory, today converted into a theatre. From **Signal Hill**, your views could be enhanced by glimpses of a jackal, little Mountain Reedbuck or a mischievous *Meerkat*. On the top of **Grant's Hill**, a Neo-Dutch-style mansion named Oliewenhuis, after the abundantly growing Wild Olive trees on the surrounding hills, once served as an official statesmen's residence. Today an art museum, its magnificent grounds grant access to walking trails around Grant's Hill. Do check out the mythologically-inspired outdoor African carousel.

**NAVAL HILL (FRANKLIN NR),
SIGNAL HILL & GRANT'S HILL**
NEAREST TOWN
Bloemfontein

NEAREST AIRPORT
Bloemfontein

SIZE
Information not available

FAUNA
1 Blue Wildebeest
2 Red Hartebeest
3 Eland
4 Giraffe
5 Jackal sp.
6 Springbok
7 Blesbok
8 Mountain Reedbuck
9 *Meerkat* (Suricate)

MAIN CONTACT DETAILS
051 405 8489
🎣

ACCOMMODATION INSIDE PARK
None

ACCOMMODATION OUTSIDE PARK
Tourist Info, Bloemfontein
051 405 8489
information@bloemfontein.co.za
www.bloemfontein.co.za

SEASONAL INFORMATION

Gate opening times
Sunrise to sunset

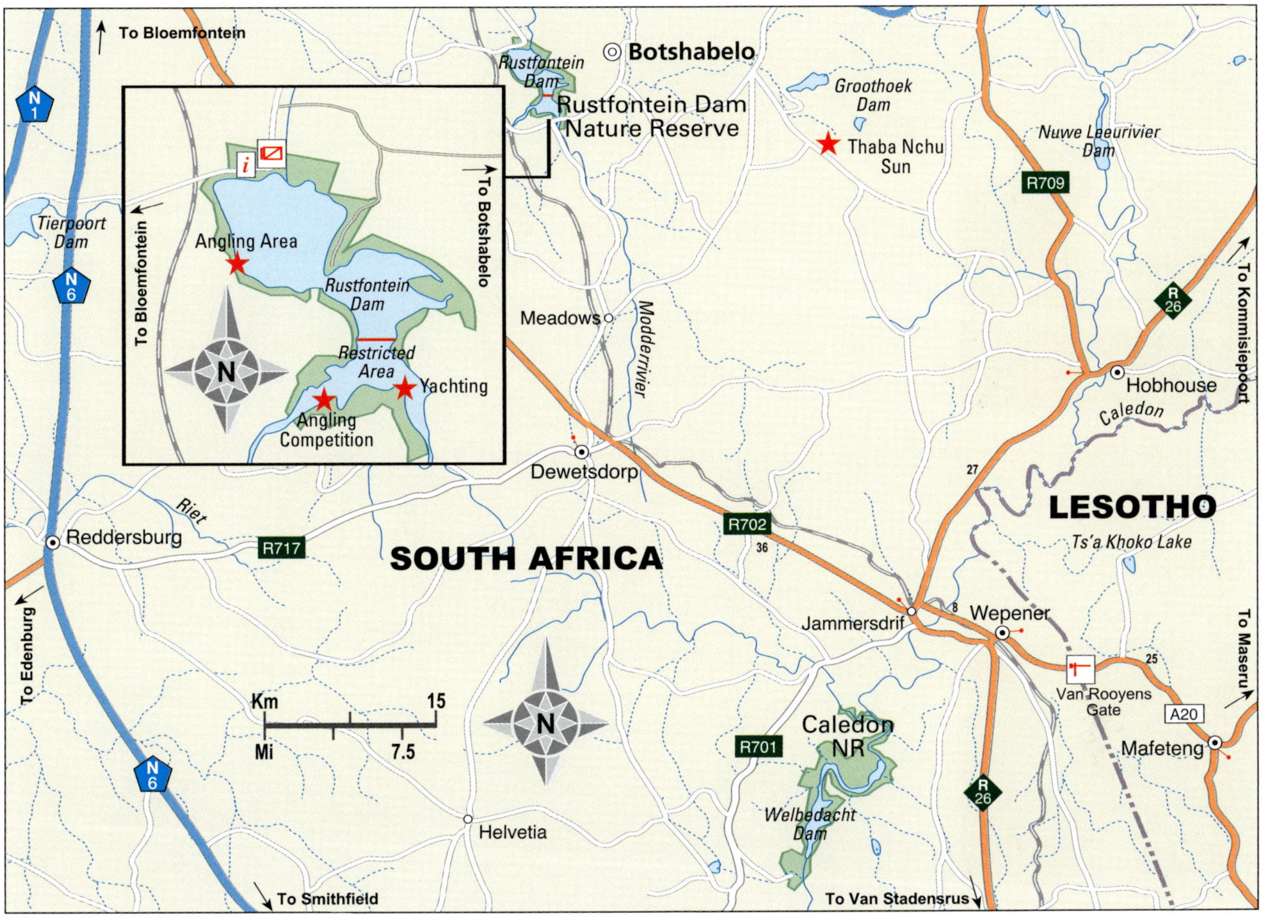

Map 1 (Regional)

To Bloemfontein

N1

Botshabelo ⊙

Rustfontein Dam

Rustfontein Dam Nature Reserve

Groothoek Dam

Thaba Nchu Sun ★

Nuwe Leeurivier Dam

R709

N6

Tierpoort Dam

To Bloemfontein

Inset map:
- *i*
- Angling Area ★
- *Rustfontein Dam*
- *Restricted Area*
- Yachting ★
- Angling Competition ★
- **N** (compass)

To Botshabelo

R **26**

To Kommisiepoort

Meadows

Modderrivier

Hobhouse ⊙

Caledon

SOUTH AFRICA

Riet

To Bloemfontein

Reddersburg ⊙

R717

Dewetsdorp ⊙

LESOTHO

Ts'a Khoko Lake

R702

36

27

To Edenburg

8

Jammersdrif

Wepener ⊙

To Maseru

25

Van Rooyens Gate

A20

N6

Km 15

Mi 7.5

N (compass)

R701

Caledon NR

Mafeteng ⊙

R **26**

Helvetia ⊙

Welbedacht Dam

To Smithfield

To Van Stadensrus

Map 2 (City - Bloemfontein)

To Boshof

To Soutpan

Preller Square ★

Van Andel St

Morgan St

Waverley Rd

Christian Brothers College

Poulteney St

Bays Village ★

Rhyn Ave

Clarens St

Gelderland

Maas St

Franklin St

General Hertzog St

Gordon Smit St

Massey St

Winter St

Wilcocks Rd

Kmdt Senekal St

Albrecht St

Prophet St

Dickie Clark St †

Oliver St

Webb St

Waverley Rd

Essex St

Hindon St

General v Schoor St

Kidger St

Goodale St

Page St

Prettyman Rd

Browne St

York Rd

Sowden St

Innes Ave

To Noordhoek

Baton St

Kestell St

Whites Rd

Milner Rd

Grant's Hill

Capt. Goodman St

Kommandant Senekal St

Lady Smith St

Louis Botha St

Peter Cr.

Lamont Hussey Observatory Theatre ★

1465m ▲

Capt. Dawson St

Paul Roux St

Harry Smith St

McEwan

Deville Dr.

Stewart Cr.

Fischer St

1481m ▲

General Hertzog St

Papenfus Pl

Oliewenhuis Art Gallery ★

Deane Ave

Unie Ave

Km 0.5

Mi 0.25

Naval Hill (Franklin NR)

White Horse ★

N (compass)

Reyger St

Brebner Rd

Premier's Residence ★

High St

Residence of Chief Justice ★

Aliwal St

Orchid House ★

To Noordhoek

Connor Ave

Bompart St

Brill St

Andries Pretorius

Gruis St †

† †

Piet Retief St

President Steyn Ave

Arboretum Ave

8th St †

7th St

Fragrance Gardens ★

Sarel Cilliers

Reid St

Signal Hill

6th St

5th St

1499m ▲

Lombard St

Barlow St

M **30**

President Reitz Ave

Westdene Tennis Club ★

4th St

3rd St

Holiday Inn Garden Court

Fawkes St

Bree St

Brompton Rd

Cromwell Rd

Ambulance St

Meiring St

Truter St

†

Collins Rd

2nd St

H

† †

†

1st Ave

Keilner St

Barnes St

1st St

To Oranjesig

To Buitesig

95

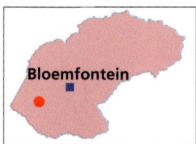

Kalkfontein Dam Nature Reserve

Heat and dust and the dry Free State air combine daily to create smouldering burnt-orange sunsets beyond the small koppies and ridges of this nature reserve. Campers and anglers are drawn like magnets to the clear waters of the Kalkfontein dam, in which yellowfish (Small- and Largemouth species), Orange River Mudfish, barbel and carp try to evade the anglers' hooks. Waterbirds also flock to these waters including, in season, tall spindly-legged Greater and Lesser Flamingos, all pretty in pink. The hook-beaked Osprey competes with anglers as it lazily flies across the water surface before plunge-diving to snap up its hapless prey.

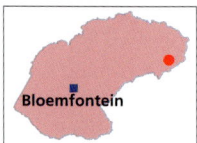

Mt Everest Game Reserve
(Eagle Mountain Game Lodge)

Previously a private game reserve, this territory today sustains small antelope and buck but nothing more dramatic than that. What it does have to offer is rock climbing on the Mt Everest sport crags composed of cave sandstone. Originally yielding difficult stretches suitable only for experienced rock climbers willing to test their boundaries, a series of easy bolted lines has since been laid out by the KwaZulu-Natal mountain club. There's a huge sense of humour at play where routes are concerned. One, named Ostrich Egg Boulder (no prizes as to what this particular rock resembles), has route sections with titles like Eggstacy, Green Eggs and Ham, Cholesterol Bomb and Just Yolking. Makes you want to take up rock climbing simply to join in the fun.

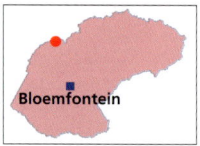

Sandveld Nature Reserve

Situated between the arms of the Bloemhof Dam Nature Reserve, Sandveld lies along one side of the Bloemhof dam, at the meeting of the Vaal and Vet rivers. Besides its wetlands, Kalahari thornveld is another of its diverse range of habitats, ensuring enormous variety in its birdlife. Those who are happier with horns and hooves will be well satisfied tracking down wildlife in the nature reserve, and the soft-sand beaches fringing the dam are particularly pleasing to fishermen and watersport-lovers. Things to look out for are the diminutive Pygmy Falcon, which sometimes commandeers communal nests built by the Social Weavers, and Whitebacked Vultures which breed in large nests on the top of the Camel Thorn trees.

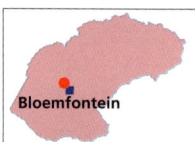

Soetdoring Nature Reserve

Named (in Afrikaans) after the prolific Sweet Thorn acacias flanking the Modder River to the east, this reserve stops in the west at the Krugersdrif dam. Being so close to Bloemfontein, these waters are the focus of powerboats, water-skiers and fishermen. There are plenty of large and small antelope in the reserve, but it's fun to try to spot the smaller creatures like Leguaans, Water Mongoose and (very shy!) otters in the dam and river, or the Small Spotted Genet and African Wildcat in the hills. Guided night excursions will let you into the secret life of the reserve's nocturnal animals. Unique accommodation in a thatched complex among the Sweet Thorns comes in the form of modified train coaches and a *lapa*.

KALKFONTEIN DAM NR

NEAREST TOWN
Fauresmith

NEAREST AIRPORT
Bloemfontein

SIZE
162ha

AVIFAUNA
1 South African Shelduck
2 Caspian Tern
3 Greater & Lesser Flamingo
4 Osprey

MAIN CONTACT DETAILS
051 722 1441

ACCOMMODATION INSIDE PARK
None

ACCOMMODATION OUTSIDE PARK
Tourist Info, Fauresmith
051 723 0020

SEASONAL INFORMATION

Gate opening times
06:00 – 18:00
Day visitors allowed

MOUNT EVEREST GAME RESERVE

LOCATION
Harrismith

NEAREST AIRPORT
Johannesburg International

SIZE
1200ha

FAUNA
1 Small Antelope sp.

MAIN CONTACT DETAILS
058 623 0235

ACCOMMODATION INSIDE PARK
Eagle Mountain Game Lodge
058 623 0235
Self-catering chalets, campsite

ACCOMMODATION OUTSIDE PARK
Tourist Info, Harrismith
058 622 3525

SEASONAL INFORMATION

Gate opening times
07:00 – 22:00
Day visitors allowed

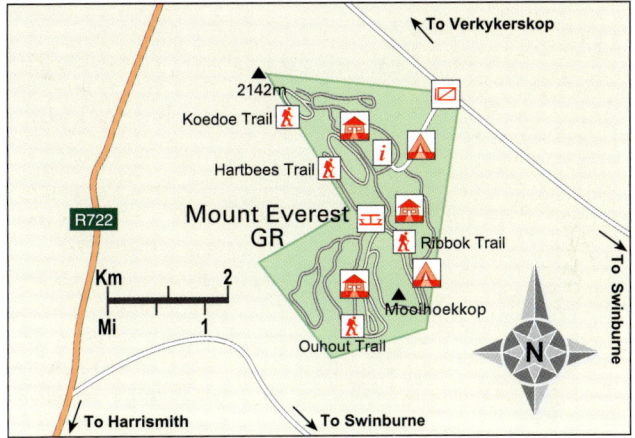

SANDVELD NATURE RESERVE

NEAREST TOWN
Bloemhof

NEAREST AIRPORT
Bloemfontein

SIZE
37 700ha

FAUNA/AVIFAUNA
1 Buffalo
2 White Rhino
3 Blue Wildebeest
4 Giraffe
5 Tsessebe
6 Kudu
7 Aardwolf
8 Heron sp.
9 Lesser & Greater Flamingo
10 Pygmy Falcon
11 Whitebacked Vulture

MAIN CONTACT DETAILS
053 433 1701/2

ACCOMMODATION INSIDE PARK
Fully-equiped chalets, campsite

ACCOMMODATION OUTSIDE PARK
Tourist Info, Bloemhof
053 433 1017

SEASONAL INFORMATION

Gate opening times
06:00 – 18:00
Day visitors allowed

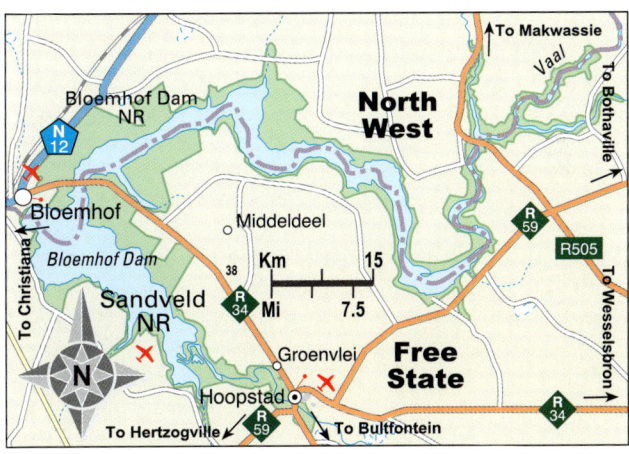

SOETDORING NATURE RESERVE

NEAREST TOWN
Bloemfontein

NEAREST AIRPORT
Bloemfontein

SIZE
7500ha

FAUNA/FLORA
1 White Rhino
2 Gemsbok
3 Eland
4 Springbok
5 Genet
6 African Wildcat
7 Cape Clawless Otter
8 Water Mongoose
9 Leguaan
10 Tortoise sp.
11 Sweet Thorn Acacia

MAIN CONTACT DETAILS
051 433 1167

ACCOMMODATION INSIDE PARK
Madinokgwe Train Camp, bush camp

ACCOMMODATION OUTSIDE PARK
Tourist Info, Bloemfontein

SEASONAL INFORMATION

Gate opening times
07:00 – 17:00
Day visitors allowed

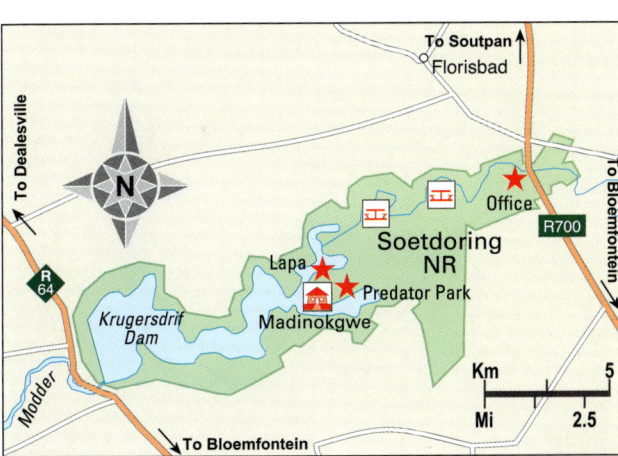

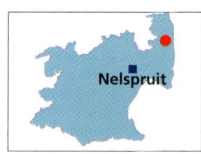

Nelspruit

Kruger National Park (Mpumalanga)
& Surrounding Reserves

KRUGER NP (MPUMALANGA)
NEAREST TOWN
Nelspruit

NEAREST AIRPORT
Kruger Mpumalanga International (KMIA)

SIZE (ENTIRE PARK)
2 million ha

FAUNA/AVIFAUNA (ALL PARKS)
1   African Elephant
2   Black & White Rhino
3   Buffalo
4   Giraffe
5   Lion
6   Leopard
7   Cheetah
8   Zebra
9   Hippopotamus
10 Wild Dog
11 Spotted Hyena
12 Saddlebilled Stork
13 Kori Bustard
14 Eagle sp.
15 Lappetfaced Vulture
16 Pel's Fishing Owl
17 Ground Hornbill
18 Greyheaded Bush Shrike

MAIN CONTACT DETAILS
013 735 4152
012 428 9111/426 5000

ACCOMMODATION INSIDE PARK
Orpen, Satara, Skukuza, Lower Sabie, Pretoriuskop, Crocodile Bridge, Berg-en-dal, Roodewal, Maroela, Tamboti, Talamati, Singita, Imbali, Rhino, Jock, Biyamiti, Lukimbi, Mpanamana & Balule Camps

ACCOMMODATION OUTSIDE PARK
Tourist Info, Nelspruit
013 755 1988

LONDOLOZI GR
MAIN CONTACT DETAILS
011 809 4300, 013 735 5653

SABI SAND GR
MAIN CONTACT DETAILS
013 735 5102

MTHETHOMUSHA GR
MAIN CONTACT DETAILS
013 794 7025, 759 5432

Transfrontier parks aside, **Kruger** is South Africa's largest national park and one of the best wildlife sanctuaries in the world. Its three distinct vegetation sectors each offer a divergent experience. The southern sector, although highly-trafficked due to its accessibility, yields some of the park's best game-viewing, and its granite koppies and woodland, spliced by the verdant Sabie River, create scenic surrounds. Buzzing **Skukuza Camp** – park headquarters – acts as director of operations with its airport, petrol station, shops, and museums. The drive from here to **Pretoriuskop Camp** is a winner for wildlife spotting, while **Berg-en-dal Camp** prettily lives up to its name, offering dipping valleys and granite domes. Bordering Kruger's southwestern corner, **Mthethomusha Game Reserve** is the result of a partnership between community and conservation. The late chief of the Mphakeni tribe handed over low-potential agricultural land for sustainable development – a pioneering approach that focuses on close community involvement in conservation. Today, this reserve's rugged granite crags and woodland vegetation sustain the Big Five.

The phalanx of private reserves hugging the unfenced western border of Kruger's southern sector all vie hotly with one another for ultraluxury in surrounds, service, and sleeping arrangements. One of these, **Sabi Sand Game Reserve**, contained to the south by the Sabie River and traversed by the Sand River, itself contains a plethora of smaller private reserves, among them the well-known **Sabi Sabi**, **Mala Mala** and **Londolozi**. With no fences between Kruger and these reserves, the wildlife is superlative, with a particular emphasis on the gorgeous big cats, Leopard and Cheetah. Entirely unique is the ecologically designed Sabi Sabi Earth Lodge, excavated into a slope and finished in a straw, stone and pigment plaster. One suite has as its headboard a sculptural, rough-hewn tree with spreading branches; dinner is heralded by resonant blasts of a kudu horn and taken in a reed *boma* lit by paraffin lamps.

SEASONAL INFORMATION

Gate opening times
Orpen, Paul Kruger, Phabeni, Numbi, Malelane & Crocodile Bridge Gates:
05:30 – 18:30 (Nov to Mar)
06:00 – 17:30 (Apr to Jul)
06:00 – 18:00 (Aug & Sept)
05:30 – 18:00 (Oct)

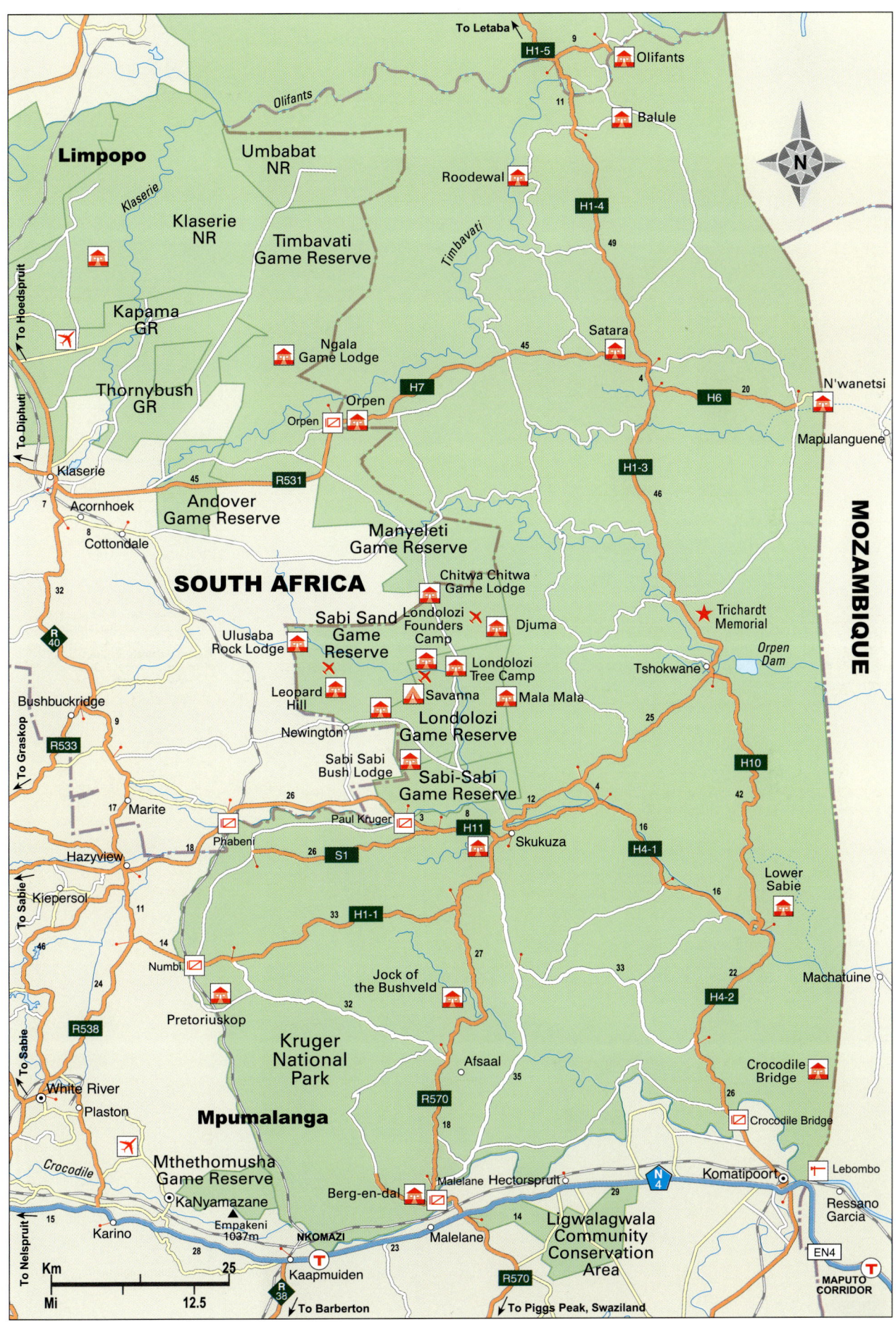

Limpopo

To Letaba

H1-5 9

Olifants

11

Balule

Olifants

Umbabat NR

Roodewal

Timbavati

H1-4

49

Klaserie

Klaserie NR

Timbavati Game Reserve

N

Kapama GR

To Hoedspruit

Satara

45

H7

Ngala Game Lodge

Orpen

4

H6 20

N'wanetsi

To Diphuti

Thornybush GR

Orpen

Mapulanguene

Klaserie

R531

H1-3

7

Acornhoek

45

Andover Game Reserve

46

8

Cottondale

Manyeleti Game Reserve

32

SOUTH AFRICA

Chitwa Chitwa Game Lodge

Trichardt Memorial

R40

Sabi Sand Game Reserve

Londolozi Founders Camp

Djuma

Orpen Dam

Ulusaba Rock Lodge

Londolozi Tree Camp

Tshokwane

Bushbuckridge

Leopard Hill

Savanna

Mala Mala

9

R533

Newington

Londolozi Game Reserve

25

To Graskop

Sabi Sabi Bush Lodge

H10

17

Marite

Sabi-Sabi Game Reserve

12

4

42

18

Phabeni

26

Paul Kruger

3

8

H11

Hazyview

26

S1

Skukuza

H4-1

16

Kiepersol

To Sabie

11

16

Lower Sabie

46

14

H1-1

33

Numbi

Jock of the Bushveld

27

33

22

24

32

Machatuine

R538

Pretoriuskop

Afsaal

35

H4-2

To Sabie

Kruger National Park

Crocodile Bridge

White River

Mpumalanga

R570

26

Plaston

18

Crocodile Bridge

MOZAMBIQUE

Mthethomusha Game Reserve

Lebombo

Crocodile

KaNyamazane

Berg-en-dal

Malelane Hectorspruit

N4

Komatipoort

To Nelspruit

Empakeni 1037m

NKOMAZI

29

Ressano Garcia

15

Karino

28

14

Ligwalagwala Community Conservation Area

Km   25

Kaapmuiden

23

Malelane

EN4

Mi   12.5

R38

R570

MAPUTO CORRIDOR

To Barberton

To Piggs Peak, Swaziland

99

Nelspruit

Blyde River Canyon Nature Reserve

This reserve stretches for some 60km along the Greater Drakensberg escarpment, where what's claimed as the world's third deepest canyon can be found. Eons ago, when the supercontinent Gondwana broke up with Madagascar and Antarctica splitting away, the weight of a vast shallow sea covering the eastern part of Southern Africa caused tilting of the continent edge. When magma intruded the sea floor, its additional weight forced the centre of the basin downward, intensifying the height of the outer rim and creating today's dramatic escarpment. Once this sea, already ancient by the time Gondwana split up, had retreated, it left layer upon layer of dolomite and sandstone sediments accumulated over millions of years. A route along the escarpment summit, between Graskop and Blydepoort dam, allows visitors into the fantasy world of Nature's sculpting prowess and the astounding vistas she's created. First off, just outside reserve bounds, is The Pinnacle, a free-standing cracked buttress of Black Reef quartzite; next is God's Window, where awe-inspiring views generally reserved for the Supreme Being drop some 700m into the valley and across the deeply forested canyon as far as the eyes can see. Then, into the reserve, the Bourke's Luck Potholes mark the meeting of two rivers, Blyde and Treur ("joy" and "sadness"), whose swirling, pebble-carrying waters scooped hollows into the red and yellow dolomite rock. Early prospectors once extracted sizable quanties of gold from here. Finally, detaching themselves from the far wall of the canyon are the Three Rondavels, with eroded dolerite walls stained fiery orange by lichens and vegetated domed quartzite caps. A number of trails through the reserve taking in unsurpassed scenery could bring you into close proximitiy with five of Southern Africa's six primate species, Samango and Vervet Monkeys, nocturnal Greater and Lesser Bushbabies, and Chacma Baboons.

BLYDE RIVER CANYON NR
NEAREST TOWN
Graskop

NEAREST AIRPORT
Kruger Mpumalanga International (KMIA)

SIZE
30 000ha

FAUNA/AVIFAUNA
1 Leopard
2 Hippopotamus
3 Nile Crocodile
4 Oribi
5 Grey Rhebok
6 Klipspringer
7 Red Duiker
8 Bushbuck
9 Bush Pig
10 Chacma Baboon
11 Samango & Vervet Monkey
12 Rock Dassie
13 Greater & Lesser Bushbaby
14 Knysna Turaco (Lourie)
15 Purple Crested Turaco (Lourie)
16 Owl sp.
17 Buzzard sp.
18 Peregrine & Lanner Falcon
19 Blue Swallow

MAIN CONTACT DETAILS
013 761 6019, 013 752 8476
www.panoramainfo.co.za
www.mpumalanga.com

ACCOMMODATION INSIDE PARK
Aventura Blydepoort, Aventura Swadini Resort, Belvedere GuestHouse, 3 huts for hikers

ACCOMMODATION OUTSIDE PARK
Tourist Info, Graskop
013 767 1377
www.panoramainfo.co.za

SEASONAL INFORMATION
Gate opening times
07:00 – 17:00
Day visitors allowed

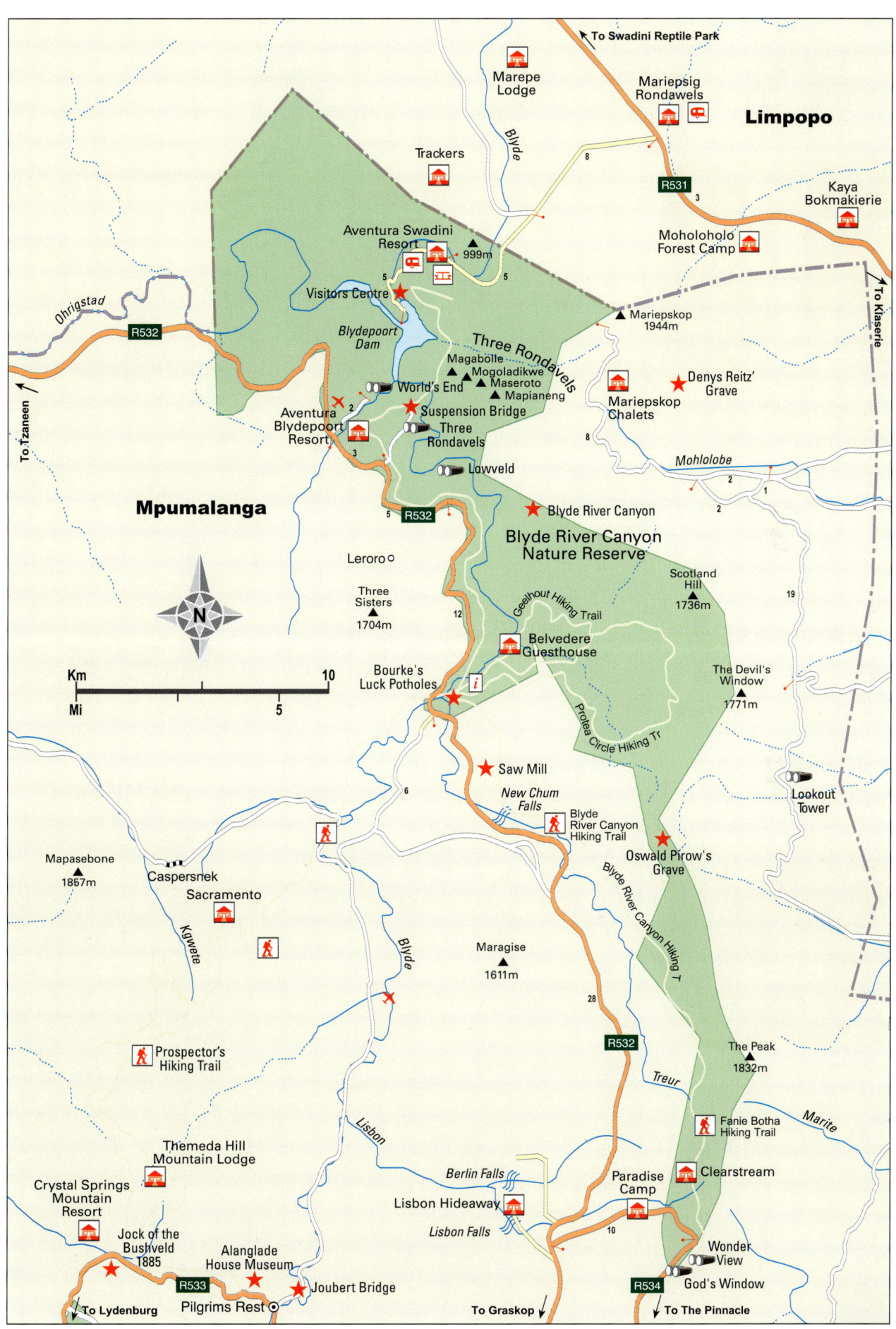

Limpopo

To Swadini Reptile Park

Marepe
Lodge

Mariepsig
Rondawels

R531

Kaya
Bokmakierie

Trackers

Blyde

8

3

Moholoholo
Forest Camp

Aventura Swadini
Resort

999m

To Klaserie

Visitors Centre

5

5

Mariepskop
1944m

Ohrigstad

R532

Blydepoort
Dam

Three Rondavels

Magabolle
Mogoladikwe
Maseroto
Mapianeng

Denys Reitz'
Grave

Mariepskop
Chalets

To Tzaneen

World's End

Suspension Bridge

8

Aventura
Blydepoort
Resort

2

Three
Rondavels

Mohlolobe

3

Lowveld

2

Mpumalanga

5

R532

Blyde River Canyon

1

2

Leroro

Blyde River Canyon
Nature Reserve

Scotland
Hill
1736m

Three
Sisters
1704m

Geelhout Hiking Trail

19

Belvedere
Guesthouse

12

The Devil's
Window
1771m

Km

10

Bourke's
Luck Potholes

Mi

5

Protea Circle Hiking Tr

Lookout
Tower

Saw Mill

Mapasebone
1867m

Caspersnek

New Chum
Falls

Blyde
River Canyon
Hiking Trail

6

Sacramento

Oswald Pirow's
Grave

Kgwete

Maragise
1611m

Blyde River Canyon Hiking T

Prospector's
Hiking Trail

Blyde

28

R532

The Peak
1832m

Treur

Marite

Fanie Botha
Hiking Trail

Lisbon

Themeda Hill
Mountain Lodge

Clearstream

Crystal Springs
Mountain
Resort

Berlin Falls

Paradise
Camp

Jock of the
Bushveld
1885

Lisbon Hideaway

Lisbon Falls

10

Wonder
View

Alanglade
House Museum

God's Window

R533

Joubert Bridge

To Graskop

R534

To Lydenburg

Pilgrims Rest

To The Pinnacle

Jericho Dam & Morgenstond Dam Nature Reserves

Highly commendable efforts are presently being made by South Africa's conservation authorities to preserve threatened natural resources – evident in the proclaiming of many new nature reserves around the country. Two recent land transfers from Water Affairs and Forestry to Nature Conservation have centred on the **Jericho** and **Morgenstond dams** in a move to preserve the high-altitude Grassland Biome in which they lie. Morgenstond feeds into Jericho, and the surrounding lands once comprised abandoned maize fields. The hope is that their recovery back to pristine grassland will attract back three globally threatened Grassveld bird species, the Rudd's and Botha's Lark and the Yellowbreasted Pipit. In the meanwhile, competitive anglers cast their flies and artificial lures into Jericho dam for its Smallscale Yellowfish. Catches here have made it into fly-angling recordbooks.

JERICHO DAM NR
NEAREST TOWN (BOTH PARKS)
Ermelo

NEAREST AIRPORT (BOTH PARKS)
Kruger Mpumalanga International
(KMIA)

SIZE
2186ha

AVIFAUNA/FLORA (BOTH PARKS)
1   Wattled & Crowned Crane
2   Rudd's & Botha's Lark
3   Yellowbreasted Pipit
4   Grassland Biome

MAIN CONTACT DETAILS
017 846 9796, 082 786 7959

ACCOMMODATION INSIDE PARK
Basic facilities

ACCOMMODATION OUTSIDE PARK
(BOTH PARKS)
Tourist Info, Ermelo
082 786 7959

MORGENSTOND DAM NR
SIZE
Information not available

MAIN CONTACT DETAILS
082 786 7959

ACCOMMODATION INSIDE PARK
None

SEASONAL INFORMATION

Gate opening times
Jericho Dam NR:
06:00 –18:00
Morgenstond Dam NR:
Sunrise to sunset
Day visitors allowed

Songimvelo Game Reserve & Ligwalagwala

Sprawled in the knucked folds of the Barberton's ancient mountains and neighbouring onto the forests lining the border with Swaziland, **Songimvelo Game Reserve's** beautiful landscapes offer refuge to a diversity of animals. They slake their thirst in the broad Komati River as it winds across the valley floor and into Swaziland on its quest to find the sea. A herd of elephants introduced from Kruger National Park have settled nicely into their new habitat, and the predators' slot is filled by wily Brown Hyena, Black-backed Jackal and the ever-beautiful Leopard. Plans are afoot to link Songimvelo with Swaziland's Malolotja Nature Reserve to create a transfrontier conservation area.

Ligwalagwala is a nature-based tourism development between the parks board and the farmers and communities displaced by the Driekoppies dam construction. This protected area aims to nurture all of the Big Five, and has already made an impressive start.

SONGIMVELO GR
NEAREST TOWN
Barberton

NEAREST AIRPORT (BOTH PARKS)
Kruger Mpumalanga International
(KMIA)

SIZE
96 000ha

FAUNA/FLORA
1   African Elephant
2   White Rhino
3   Blue Wildebeest
4   Leopard
5   Giraffe
6   Zebra
7   Hippopotamus
8   Brown Hyena
9   Black-backed Jackal
10 Shelley's Francolin
11 Cycad sp.

MAIN CONTACT DETAILS
017 884 0047

ACCOMMODATION INSIDE PARK
Kromdraai Camp

ACCOMMODATION OUTSIDE PARK
Tourist Info, Barberton
013 712 2121
www.lowveld.info.com

LIGWALAGWALA
NEAREST TOWN
Nelspruit

SIZE
15 000ha

FAUNA
1   African Elephant
2   Lion

MAIN CONTACT DETAILS
013 752 7001

ACCOMMODATION INSIDE PARK
5 exclusive lodges

ACCOMMODATION OUTSIDE PARK
Tourist Info, Nelspruit
013 755 1988
www.lowveld.info.com

SEASONAL INFORMATION

Songimvelo GR:
08:00 – 18:00
Ligwalagwala:
Sunrise to sunset
Day visitors allowed

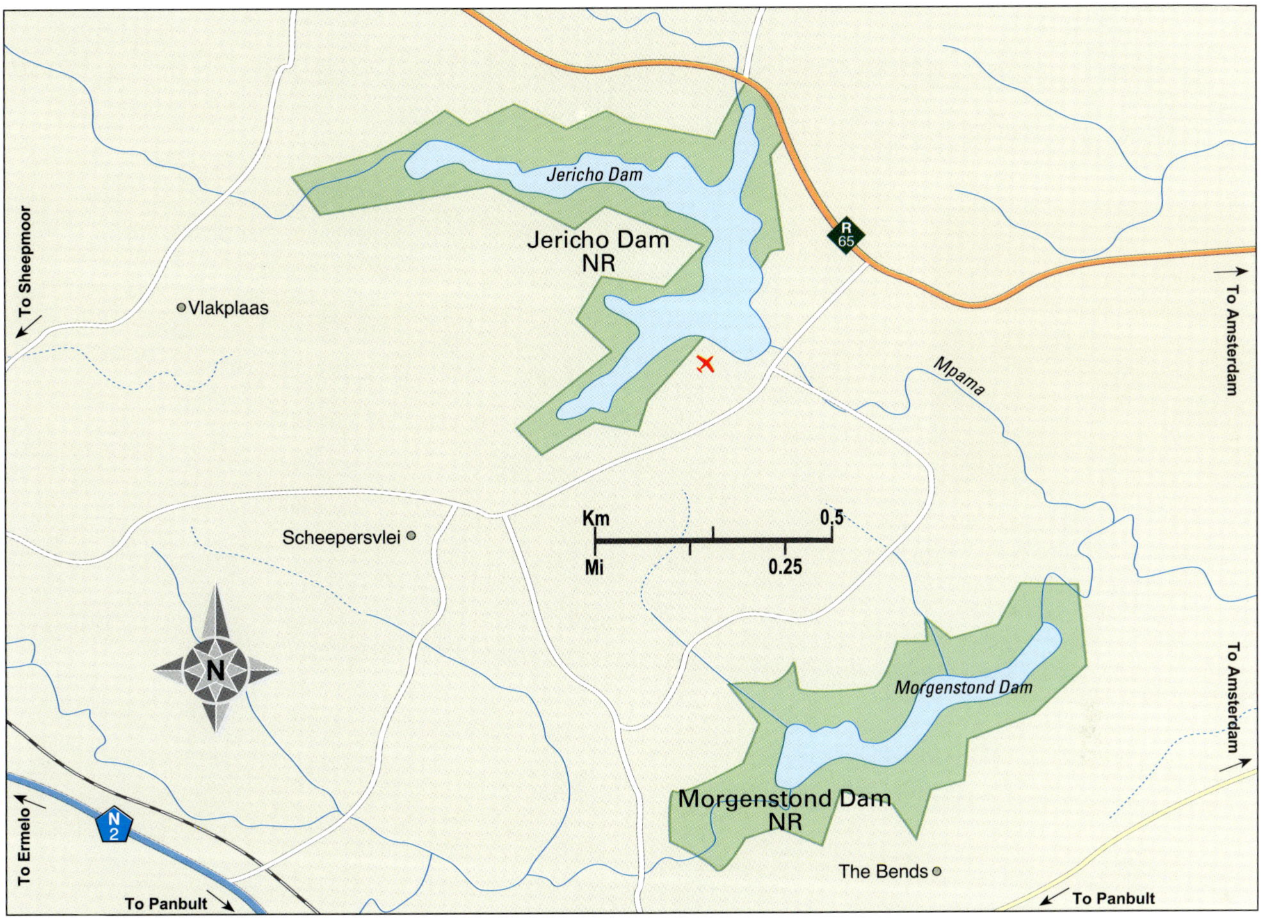

Map 1 (top)

To Sheepmoor

Jericho Dam

Jericho Dam NR

R 65

To Amsterdam

Vlakplaas

Mpama

To Amsterdam

Scheepersvlei

Km
Mi
0.5
0.25

N

Morgenstond Dam

To Ermelo

N 2

Morgenstond Dam NR

To Panbult

The Bends

To Panbult

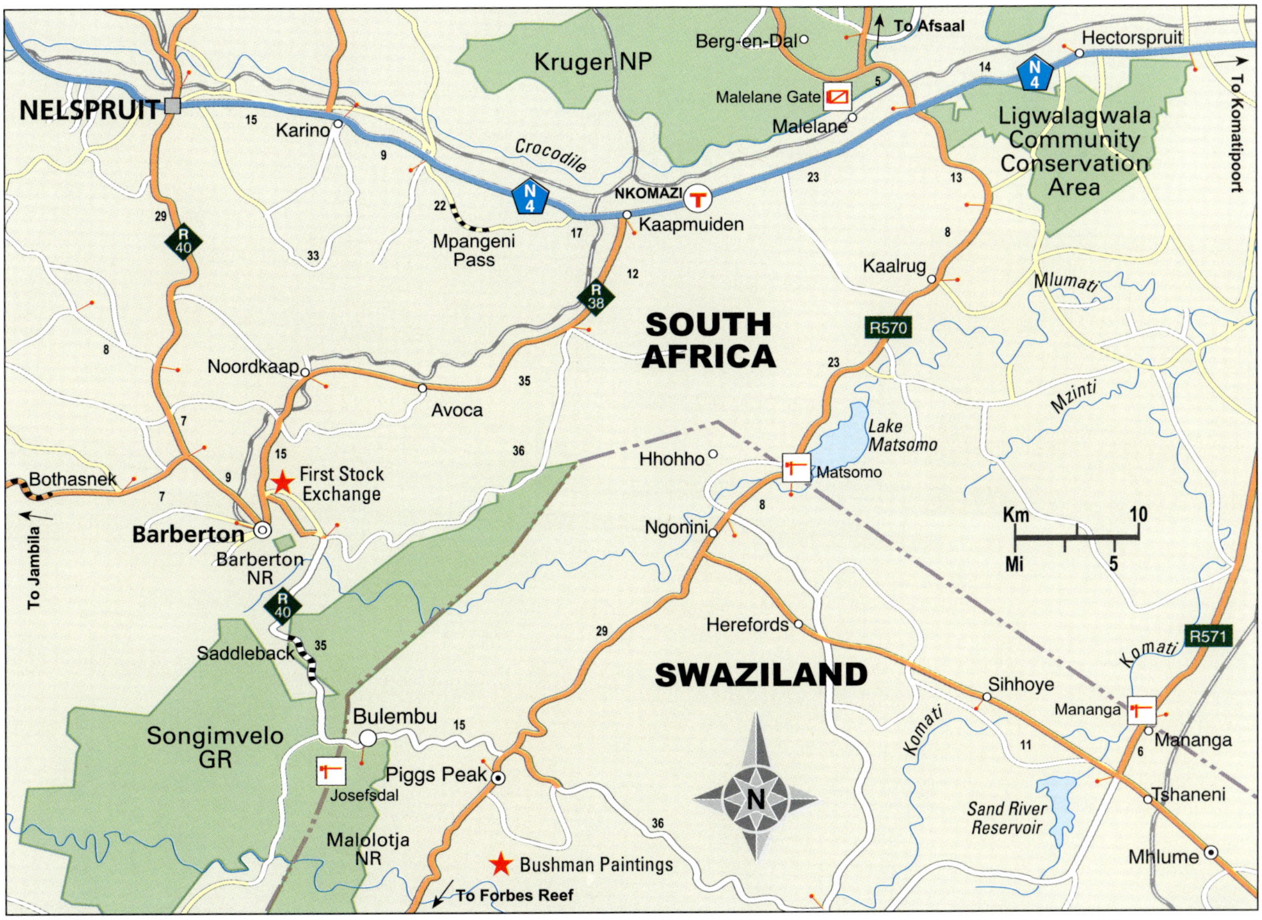

Map 2 (bottom)

To Afsaal

Kruger NP

Berg-en-Dal

Hectorspruit

N 4

NELSPRUIT

Malelane Gate

5

14

N 4

To Komatipoort

15

Karino

9

Crocodile

Malelane

Ligwalagwala Community Conservation Area

29

R 40

22

Mpangeni Pass

N 4

17

NKOMAZI

Kaapmuiden

23

13

Kaalrug

8

Mlumati

33

12

R 38

SOUTH AFRICA

R 570

8

Noordkaap

35

Avoca

23

Mzinti

7

36

Lake Matsomo

Bothasnek

9

15

First Stock Exchange

Hhohho

Matsomo

Km
Mi
10
5

To Jambila

7

Barberton

8

Ngonini

Barberton NR

R 40

R 571

35

Saddleback

29

Herefords

Komati

SWAZILAND

Sihhoye

Songimvelo GR

Bulembu

15

Mananga

11

6

Mananga

Josefsdal

Piggs Peak

N

Tshaneni

Malolotja NR

Sand River Reservoir

Bushman Paintings

Mhlume

To Forbes Reef

36

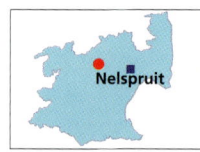

Dullstroom & Verloren Vallei Nature Reserves

Dullstroom's cool, misty, sub-alpine climate – some say, reminiscent of the Scottish Highlands – fosters the country's only (besides Blyde River reserve) high-lying, moist grasslands. Settled in the Steenkampsberg, Dullstroom's handful of cold, clear rivers flowing from the mountains have made this a trout-fishing paradise; they also feed marshlands, the most important being **Verloren Vallei**, today a Ramsar site consisting of over 30 wetlands. All three of South Africa's rare crane species – the Blue, Crowned and Wattled Cranes – live in the wetlands, with captive breeding occurring at Verloren Vallei. Claims are made that over 200 different wildflower species flourish around Dullstroom – naturalists will revel in the aloes, pink gladioli, orchids, tree ferns, red Fire Lilies, and white, pink and golden Arum Lilies. Look out for the huge, bright pink heads of the Tumbleweed flowers, which, when they dry, are barrelled along by the wind, scattering seeds as they tumble.

DULLSTROOM NATURE RESERVE
NEAREST TOWN (BOTH PARKS)
Dullstroom

NEAREST AIRPORT (BOTH PARKS)
Kruger Mpumalanga International
(KMIA)

SIZE
400ha

FLORA/FAUNA
1 Arum Lily sp.
2 Aloe sp.
3 Gladiolus sp.
4 Orchid sp.
5 Trout sp.

MAIN CONTACT DETAILS
(BOTH PARKS)
013 254 0799, 083 484 4933

ACCOMMODATION INSIDE PARK
Chalets, campsite

ACCOMMODATION OUTSIDE PARK
(BOTH PARKS)
Tourist Info, Dullstroom
013 254 0020
www.dullstroom.info.com

VERLOREN VALLEI NR
SIZE
5891ha

FAUNA/FLORA
1 Side-striped Jackal
2 Mountain Reedbuck
3 Wattled, Crowned & Blue Crane
4 Redwinged Francolin
5 Cape Eagle Owl
6 Ground Orchid
7 Aloe sp.
8 Watsonia sp.
9 Gladiolus sp.

ACCOMMODATION INSIDE PARK
None

SEASONAL INFORMATION

Gate opening times
Dullstroom NR:
Sunrise to sunset
Day visitors allowed
Verloren Vallei NR:
No public access

Gustav Klingbiel, Lydenburg & Sterkspruit Nature Reserves

All three reserves lie in the vicinity of the spectacular Long Tom Pass, which from its summit drops 1100m over 8km in dramatic curves – this sets the scene for the type of mountain scenery hikers can expect on the walks and trails within these reserves. Thornveld and bushveld on the low-lying areas, montane grassland on hills and plateaus, and little pockets of mountain forest in the ravines make sure the birdlife is scintillating. Buck and small antelope are plentiful, particularly in **Gustav Klingbiel Nature Reserve**, which also has larger animal species. Here, the Klipgatspruit carves a deep valley through the mountains. Archaeological ruins – stone-walled villages and agricultural terraces dating to the Later Iron Age – and remnants of Anglo-Boer War forts lie in Gustav Klingbiel. Also here is the Lydenburg Museum, which holds replicas of sixth-century terracotta heads unearthed in the Sterkspruit valley; they are Southern Africa's earliest known forms of African clay sculpture.

**GUSTAV KLINGBIEL &
LYDENBURG NR**
NEAREST TOWN (ALL PARKS)
Lydenburg

NEAREST AIRPORT (ALL PARKS)
Kruger Mpumalanga International
(KMIA)

SIZE
2200ha

FAUNA
1 Blue Wildebeest
2 Leopard
3 Eland
4 Kudu
5 Oribi
6 Small Antelope sp.

MAIN CONTACT DETAILS
013 235 2213, 013 235 2121

ACCOMMODATION INSIDE PARK
Overnight huts

ACCOMMODATION OUTSIDE PARK
(ALL PARKS)
Tourist Info, Lydenburg
013 235 2213, 082 779 3748

STERKSPRUIT NR
SIZE
2060ha

FAUNA
1 Leopard
2 Oribi
3 Grey Rhebok
4 Mountain Reedbuck
5 Red & Grey Duiker
6 Gurney's Sugarbird

MAIN CONTACT DETAILS
013 235 2075

ACCOMMODATION INSIDE PARK
None

SEASONAL INFORMATION

Gate opening times
Gustav Klingbiel & Lydenburg NR:
08:00 – 16:00 (Mon to Fri)
08:00 – 17:00 (Sat to Sun)
Day visitors allowed
Sterkspruit NR:
No public access

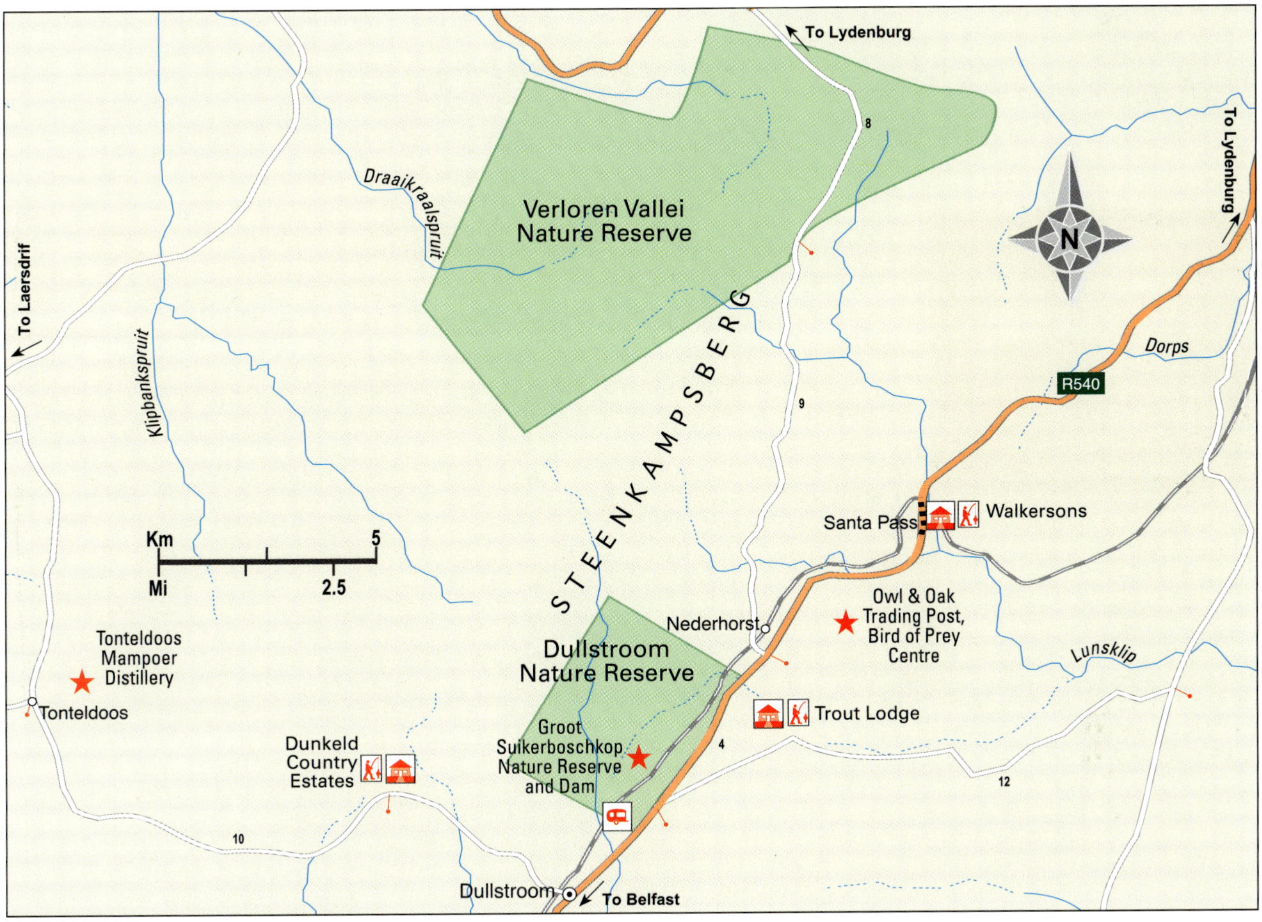

Map 1 (top)

To Lydenburg

To Lydenburg

To Lydenburg

To Laersdrif

Draaikraalspruit

Verloren Vallei
Nature Reserve

S T E E N K A M P S B E R G

8

9

R540

Dorps

Lunsklip

Klipbankspruit

Km 5
Mi 2.5

Santa Pass · Walkersons

Tonteldoos
Mampoer
Distillery

Tonteldoos

Nederhorst

Dullstroom
Nature Reserve

Owl & Oak
Trading Post,
Bird of Prey
Centre

Trout Lodge

4

12

Dunkeld
Country
Estates

Groot
Suikerboschkop
Nature Reserve
and Dam

10

Dullstroom · To Belfast

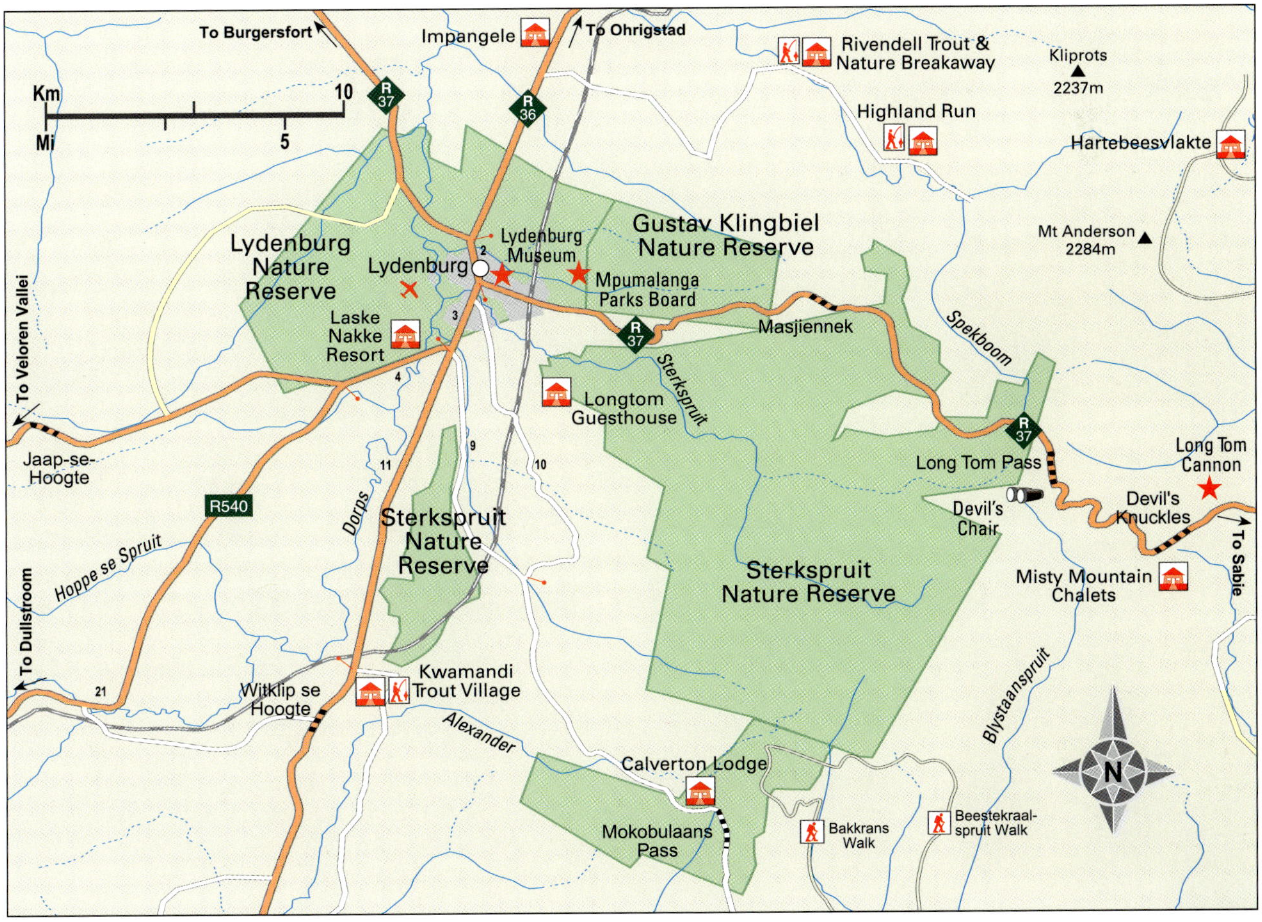

Map 2 (bottom)

To Burgersfort

Impangele · To Ohrigstad

Rivendell Trout &
Nature Breakaway

Kliprots
2237m

R37

R36

Highland Run

Hartebeesvlakte

Km 10
Mi 5

Lydenburg
Nature
Reserve

Gustav Klingbiel
Nature Reserve

Mt Anderson
2284m

Lydenburg
Museum

Lydenburg

2

To Veloren Vallei

Laske
Nakke
Resort

Mpumalanga
Parks Board

3

R37

Masjiennek

Spektboom

R37

Longtom
Guesthouse

Sterkspruit

Long Tom Pass

R37

Long Tom
Cannon

Jaap-se-
Hoogte

4

9

10

Devil's
Chair

Devil's
Knuckles

To Sabie

R540

Hoppe se Spruit

Dorps

11

Sterkspruit
Nature
Reserve

Sterkspruit
Nature Reserve

Misty Mountain
Chalets

To Dullstroom

21

Witklip se
Hoogte

Kwamandi
Trout Village

Alexander

Blystaanspruit

Calverton Lodge

Mokobulaans
Pass

Bakkrans
Walk

Beestekraal-
spruit Walk

Ohrigstad Dam & Mt Sheba Nature Reserves

Within 10km of its source in the foothills of Mauchsberg, the Ohrigstad River is dammed by the wall of the **Ohrigstad dam**. With the misty uplands of the Greater Drakensberg escarpment all around, the setting is inspiring. It's a great spot at which to don your bird-watching boots, unpack your fishing rod or settle in with your picnic basket. The tranquillity will not be shattered by noisy recreational powerboating, although angling from motorised boats does get the nod – and there are yellowfish, barbel, tilapia and carp all gullibly waiting to take the bait. . .

The overwhelming serenity and beauty of tall Afromontane forests, exotic-looking cycads and giant old yellowwoods is tempered by the impassive lines of **Mt Sheba**'s quartzite ridge and rocky outcrops. Forest birds here are a twitcher's dream, and naturalists will love the labelled trees and rare clivias, gladioli and disas – one is even called *Disa extinctoria*.

OHRIGSTAD DAM NR
NEAREST TOWN (BOTH PARKS)
Pilgrims Rest

NEAREST AIRPORT (BOTH PARKS)
Kruger Mpumalanga International (KMIA)

SIZE
2563ha

FAUNA
1   Rhino
2   Klipspringer
3   Duiker
4   Mountain Reedbuck

MAIN CONTACT DETAILS
013 238 0302

ACCOMMODATION INSIDE PARK
Ohrigstad Dam Guest House
🛏 ⊠

ACCOMMODATION OUTSIDE PARK (BOTH PARKS)
Tourist Info, Pilgrims Rest
013 768 1060

MT SHEBA NR
SIZE
400ha

AVIFAUNA
1   Crowned Eagle
2   Secretary Bird
3   Redwinged Francolin
4   African Emerald Cuckoo

MAIN CONTACT DETAILS
013 768 1241
www.mountsheba.co.za

ACCOMMODATION INSIDE PARK
Timeshare units managed by RCI
011 258 0341
Mt Sheba Hotel
🛏 ⊠

SEASONAL INFORMATION

Gate opening times
Ohrigstad Dam NR:
06:00 – 18:00
Mt Sheba NR:
06:00 – 18:00
Day visitors allowed

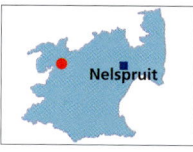

Loskop Dam Game Reserve

Not that far from the bustle of city life, the massive Loskop dam stretches for some 23km along the Waterberg foothills. Visitors with a taste for resort activity can stay at the nearby Aventura complex. The game reserve around Loskop's shores penetrates the Olifants River valley, straddling highveld and bushveld. While anglers try their luck on bass, carp, tilapia, yellowfish and barbel, the local parks board has been busy reintroducing wild animals into the reserve, even Leopard prowl the rocky terrain – although don't count on seeing these shy cats. Loskop made history some 40 years ago when the first White Rhino calf to be born outside Kwazulu-Natal saw its first beginnings here, after its parents were reintroduced from iMfolozi Game Reserve.

Nooitgedacht Dam Nature Reserve

This highveld-grassland reserve on the Komati River is another that has seen its transferral from Water Affairs and Forestry to Nature Conservation. Interesting terrain that incorporates savannah grassland, riverine forest, high mountains and woodland makes the hiking trails out of the ordinary. From the topmost vantage point on the Magaliesberg, expansive views encompass the valley cut by the Magalies River to the Klein Swartberg mountain summit of Buffelspoort. No wonder, then, that the sky is the dominion of eagles – look for the powerful wing-beats of Tawny, Martial and Verreaux's (Black) Eagles, while in the valley, the sharp yellow talons of African Fish Eagles plunge into the river-waters. Cape, Lappetfaced and Whitebacked Vultures are enticed to the reserve's vulture restaurant.

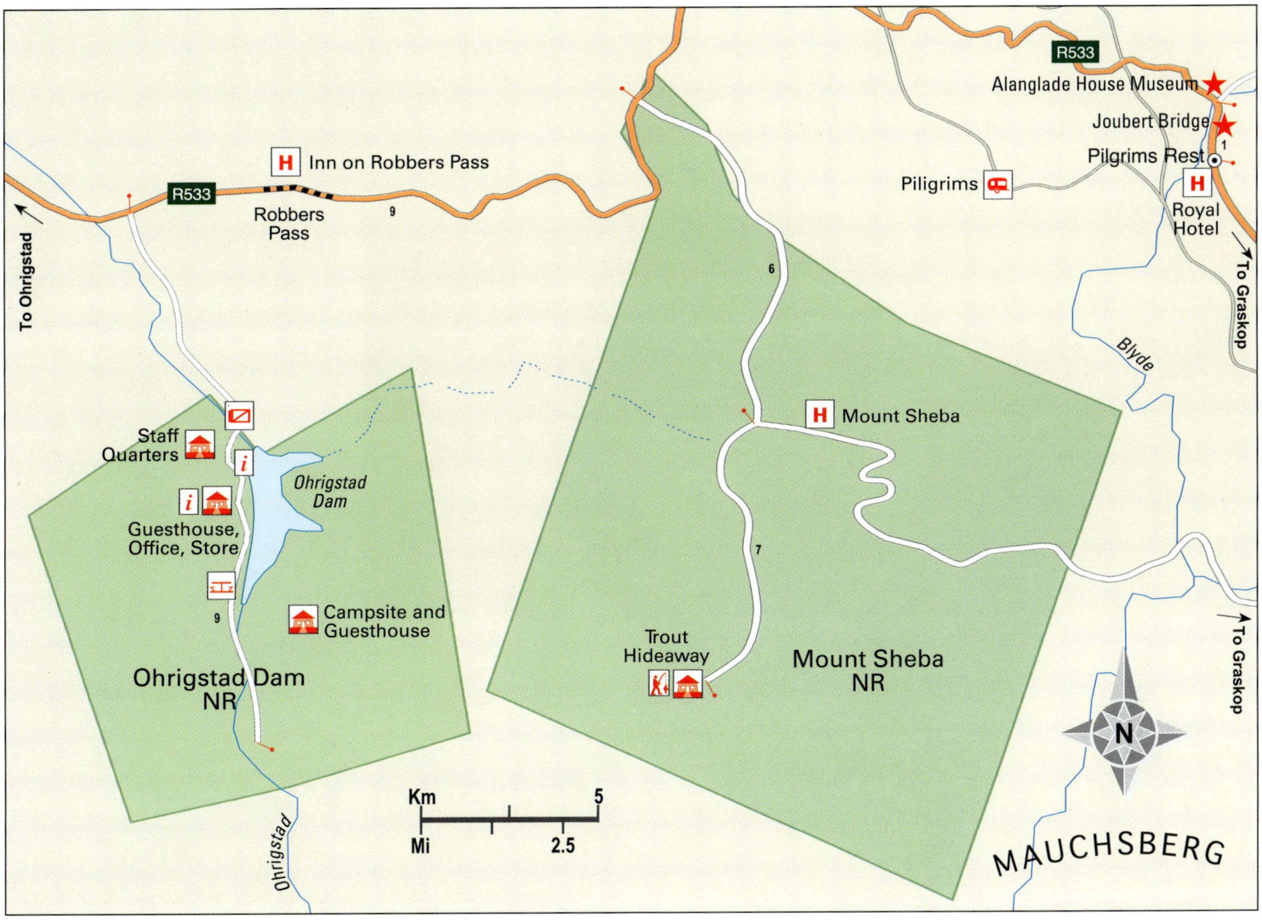

Top Map

To Ohrigstad

R533

H Inn on Robbers Pass

Robbers Pass

9

R533

Alanglade House Museum ★

Joubert Bridge ★

Piligrims

Pilgrims Rest

1

H Royal Hotel

To Graskop

6

Blyde

□

Staff Quarters

i

i

H Mount Sheba

Ohrigstad Dam

Guesthouse, Office, Store

7

Campsite and Guesthouse

9

Trout Hideaway

Mount Sheba NR

Ohrigstad Dam NR

To Graskop

Ohrigstad

N

Km 5

Mi 2.5

MAUCHSBERG

Loskop Dam GR

LOSKOP DAM GR

NEAREST TOWN
Groblersdal

NEAREST AIRPORT
Kruger Mpumalanga International (KMIA)

SIZE
15 000ha

FAUNA
1 White Rhino
2 Buffalo
3 Leopard
4 Giraffe
5 Kudu
6 Sable Antelope
7 Nile Crocodile

MAIN CONTACT DETAILS
013 262 2762, 013 262 4184

ACCOMMODATION INSIDE PARK
Hippo and Crocodile Hut, Fish Eagle Hut, 3 mountain huts

ACCOMMODATION OUTSIDE PARK
Tourist Info, Groblersdal
013 261 3032

SEASONAL INFORMATION

Gate opening times
Open 24 hours

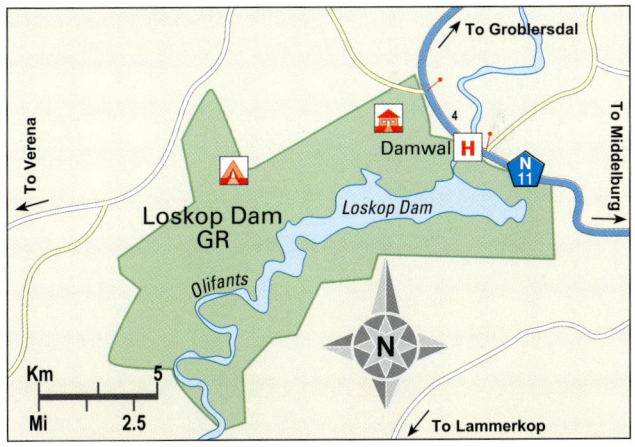

To Groblersdal

To Verena

4

Damwall **H**

N11

To Middelburg

Loskop Dam GR

Loskop Dam

Olifants

N

Km 5

Mi 2.5

To Lammerkop

Nooitgedacht Dam NR

NOOITGEDACHT DAM NR

NEAREST TOWN
Carolina

NEAREST AIRPORT
Kruger Mpumalanga International (KMIA)

SIZE
3420ha

FAUNA/AVIFAUNA
1 Red Hartebeest
2 Zebra
3 Springbok
4 Grey Rhebok
5 Steenbok
6 Tawny & Verreaux's (Black) Eagle
7 African Fish Eagle
8 Lappetfaced & Whitefaced Vulture
9 Blue Crane
10 Egyptian Goose

MAIN CONTACT DETAILS
017 843 2603

ACCOMMODATION INSIDE PARK
Campsite

ACCOMMODATION OUTSIDE PARK
Tourist Info, Carolina
017 843 1552/1055

SEASONAL INFORMATION

Gate opening times
06:00 – 18:00

Komati

Witkloofspruit

R33

Nooitgedacht Dam

To Waterval-Boven

Nooitgedacht Dam Nature Reserve

N

R36

Km 5

Mi 2.5

To Carolina

To Carolina

■Pretoria

Cradle of Humankind
Heia Safari Ranch, Rhino & Lion, The Cradle, & Hartbeeshoek Reserves

Some of the world's richest concentrations of hominid fossil-bearing sites exist at the Cradle of Humankind, a strip of dolomitic limestone caves that has yielded over 850 hominid fossil remains. Nearby, **Heia Safari Game Reserve**, lying under the protective watch of the Swartkop mountains, isn't exactly your wild bushveld experience – giraffe lope through the hotel grounds and zebra drink at the crystalline-blue pool! However, you do experience Zulu culture, reenacted through drumming, harmonised voices and tribal dance while you sip traditional beer from a calabash and eat from *potjies*. At the **Rhino & Lion reserve**, the success of a breeding programme for endangered Cape Wild Dog – an addition to the introduced White Rhino, Lion and Cheetah – has led to breeding iniatives for Bengal Tiger, Puma and the very rare White Lion. Check out the three wildlife webcams from their website! Guided horse trails at **The Cradle Nature Reserve** wind through riverine forest and grassland in a setting of rugged ridges and hazy mountains. The Black Reef stone ridge on which some of the reserve lies – part of the geological formation called the Transvaal Supergroup and once the bed of an ancient sea – contains stromatolites, caves and fossils; these are seen on the Heritage Trails. The holiday resort-ish game-viewing experience continues in the **Hartbeeshoek reserve**, which, from the comfort of the Hartbeeshoek resort, offers day and evening wildlife tours. Hikers and birders can get closer to Nature by exploring on foot, with the ever-present Magaliesberg at their elbows. Hartbeeshoek has achieved fame as a modern-day Woodstock, after the first revival in 1999. Each year, the hordes flock to "shoo-wow" over the music and New Age lifestyle stalls.

HEIA SAFARI GR

NEAREST TOWN (ALL PARKS)
Johannesburg

NEAREST AIRPORT (ALL PARKS)
Johannesburg International

SIZE
650ha

FAUNA
1 White Rhino
2 Hippopotamus
3 Giraffe
4 Burchell's Zebra

MAIN CONTACT DETAILS
011 919 5000

ACCOMMODATION INSIDE PARK
Hotel Heia, bungalows

ACCOMMODATION OUTSIDE PARK
(ALL PARKS)
011 832 2780
www.gauteng.net

RHINO AND LION RESERVE

SIZE
1600ha

FAUNA
1 White Rhino
2 Buffalo
3 Lion
4 Wild Dog

MAIN CONTACT DETAILS
011 957 0109
www.rhinolion.co.za

ACCOMMODATION INSIDE PARK
Luxury chalets, tented camp

THE CRADLE NR

SIZE
3000ha

FAUNA
1 White Rhino
2 Giraffe
3 Burchell's Zebra
4 Eland

MAIN CONTACT DETAILS
011 659 1622
www.thecradle.co.za

ACCOMMODATION INSIDE PARK
Thatched chalets, Forest Camp

HARTBEESHOEK GR

SIZE
390ha

FAUNA
1 Giraffe
2 Burchell's Zebra
3 Kudu
4 Blesbok

MAIN CONTACT DETAILS
011 251 0992, 082 870 8182
zingela@intekom.co.za

ACCOMMODATION INSIDE PARK
Chalets, campsite

SEASONAL INFORMATION

Gate opening times
Heia Safari GR: Open 24 hours
Rhino and Lion Reserve:
08:00 – 16:00 (weekdays)
08:00 – 16:30 (weekends/holidays)
The Cradle NR: sunrise to sunset
Day visitors by arrangement only
Hartbeeshoek GR: 09:00 – 17:00
Day visitors allowed

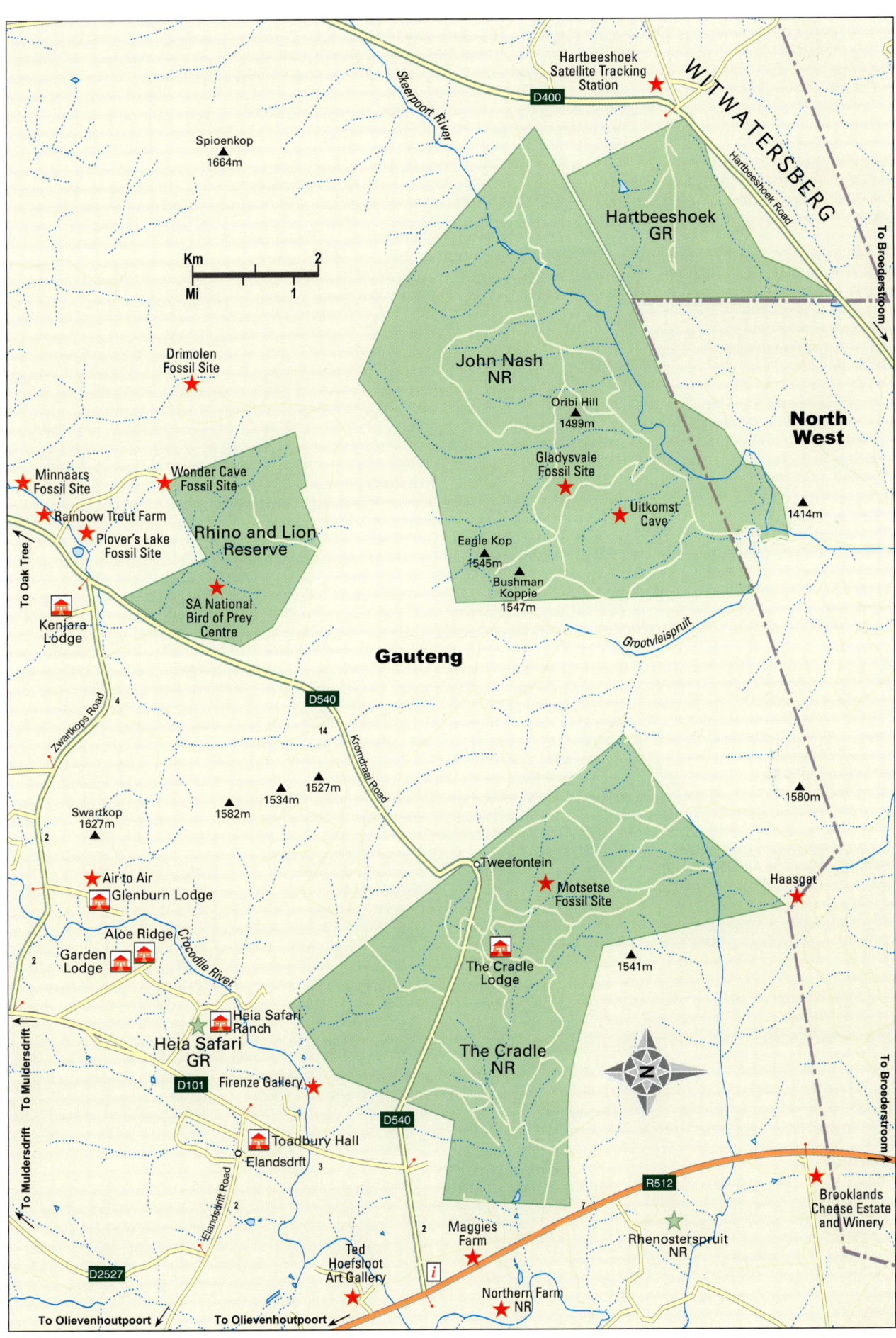

Km 2
Mi 1

Spioenkop
▲
1664m

Skeerpoort River

Hartbeeshoek
Satellite Tracking
Station ★

D400

WITWATERSBERG

Hartbeeshoek Road

Hartbeeshoek
GR

To Broederstroom

Drimolen
Fossil Site
★

John Nash
NR

Oribi Hill
▲
1499m

North
West

Gladysvale
Fossil Site
★

Uitkomst
Cave ★

▲
1414m

Minnaars
Fossil Site ★

Wonder Cave
Fossil Site ★

Rhino and Lion
Reserve

Eagle Kop
▲
1545m

Bushman
Koppie ▲
1547m

Rainbow Trout Farm ★

To Oak Tree

Plover's Lake
Fossil Site ★

★
SA National
Bird of Prey
Centre

Gauteng

Grootvleispruit

Kenjara
Lodge

D540

Zwartkops Road

4

14

Kromdraai Road

▲
1527m

1534m ▲

2

Swartkop
1627m ▲

1582m ▲

▲
1580m

Air to Air ★
Glenburn Lodge

Tweefontein

Motsetse
Fossil Site ★

Haasgat ★

Aloe Ridge

Crocodile River

The Cradle
Lodge

▲
1541m

2

Garden
Lodge

Heia Safari
Ranch

Heia Safari
GR

The Cradle
NR

N

To Muldersdrift

D101

Firenze Gallery ★

To Muldersdrift

D540

Toadbury Hall

Elandsdrft

Elandsdrift Road

3

To Broederstroom

2

R512

D2527

2

7

Brooklands
Cheese Estate
and Winery ★

Ted
Hoefsloot
Art Gallery

i

Maggies
Farm ★

Rhenosterspruit
NR

To Olievenhoutpoort

To Olievenhoutpoort

Northern Farm
NR ★

Suikerbosrand Nature Reserve

The backbone of this reserve, the Suikerbosrand mountains, features two geological systems: basalt rock that millions of years ago intruded the earth's crust and horizontal bands of the more friable sandstone. A selection of hiking trails of differing lengths explores rocky crags, grassy plains and wooded kloofs – the longest one traverses most of the reserve's expanse. Both mountains and reserve take their name from the Transvaal Suikerbos (Sugarbush), or *Protea caffra*, which grows profusely on the sandstone soils. The heat of summer is blistering at midday, so early starts are wise. Be prepared for reverberating thunderstorms that roll around the sky as the heat buildup releases its pent-up energy. Those who have a penchant for contemplation and stillness rather than the motion of one foot placed after another can retreat to a stone and wood meditation hut beside Sedaven dam (it is not part of the trails).

SUIKERBOSRAND NR
NEAREST TOWN
Heidelberg
NEAREST AIRPORT
Johannesburg International
SIZE
13 337ha
FAUNA/FLORA
1 Black Wildebeest
2 Red Hartebeest
3 Cheetah
4 Oribi
5 Eland
6 Kudu
7 Zebra
8 Brown Hyena
9 Blesbok
10 Springbok
11 Mountain Reedbuck
12 Duiker
13 *Protea caffra*

MAIN CONTACT DETAILS
011 904 3933

ACCOMMODATION INSIDE PARK
Heidelbergkloof Campsite, Kareekloof Campsite, meditation hut, camps for youth groups, hiking trail huts

ACCOMMODATION OUTSIDE PARK
Tourist Info, Heidelberg
016 349 1261

SEASONAL INFORMATION
Gate opening times
07:00 – 18:00
Day visitors allowed

Johannesburg
Klipriviersberg Nature Reserve & Rondebult Bird Sanctuary

No-one would ever believe that the **Klipriviersberg reserve** is 11km out of the Jozi city centre. Its expanse of open veld modified with koppies has great wheeling skies, birds flitting and chittering about and the trickling of the Bloubosspruit meandering through. Stone Age artefacts dating back 250,000 years have been discovered in these "stone river mountains" but the lack of permanent dwelling-site evidence suggests Stone Age peoples hunted but didn't settle here. Ancient stone circles do exist, believed to date from about 1500. **Rondebult**'s wetlands have earned their reputation for excellent birding. A mix of grassland, marshland and reedbeds radiating from the sanctuary's three large pans promises variety in size, shape, colour and bird behaviour. Eight hides dotted around the water make things easy. Pink-infused Greater Flamingo are special visitors, as is the occasional Marsh Owl (on winter days), with its almost comical diving-mask-like face.

KLIPRIVIERSBERG NR
NEAREST TOWN
Johannesburg
NEAREST AIRPORT (BOTH PARKS)
Johannesburg International
SIZE
690ha
FAUNA/FLORA
1 Black-backed Jackal
2 Cape Fox
3 Cape Clawless Otter
4 Small-spotted Genet
5 Yellow Mongoose
6 Porcupine
7 Scrub Hare
8 Tree Squirrel
9 *Acacia karoo* (Sweet Thorn)
10 Cabbage Tree
11 White Stinkwood
12 Puzzle Bush (*Deurmekaarbos*)

MAIN CONTACT DETAILS
011 682 1494
www.veld.org

ACCOMMODATION INSIDE PARK
(BOTH PARKS)
None

ACCOMMODATION OUTSIDE PARK
Tourist Info, Johannesburg
011 832 2780
www.gauteng.net

RONDEBULT BIRD SANCTUARY
NEAREST TOWN
Germiston
SIZE
94ha
AVIFAUNA
1 Greater Flamingo
2 Blackcrowned Night Heron
3 African Wattled Plover
4 Little Bittern
5 African (Ethiopian) Snipe
6 Marsh Owl

MAIN CONTACT DETAILS
011 874 5911

ACCOMMODATION OUTSIDE PARK
011 456 0111, 011 820 4004

SEASONAL INFORMATION
Gate opening times
Klipriviersberg NR:
Sunrise to sunset
Rondebult Bird Sanctuary:
08:00 – 16:00

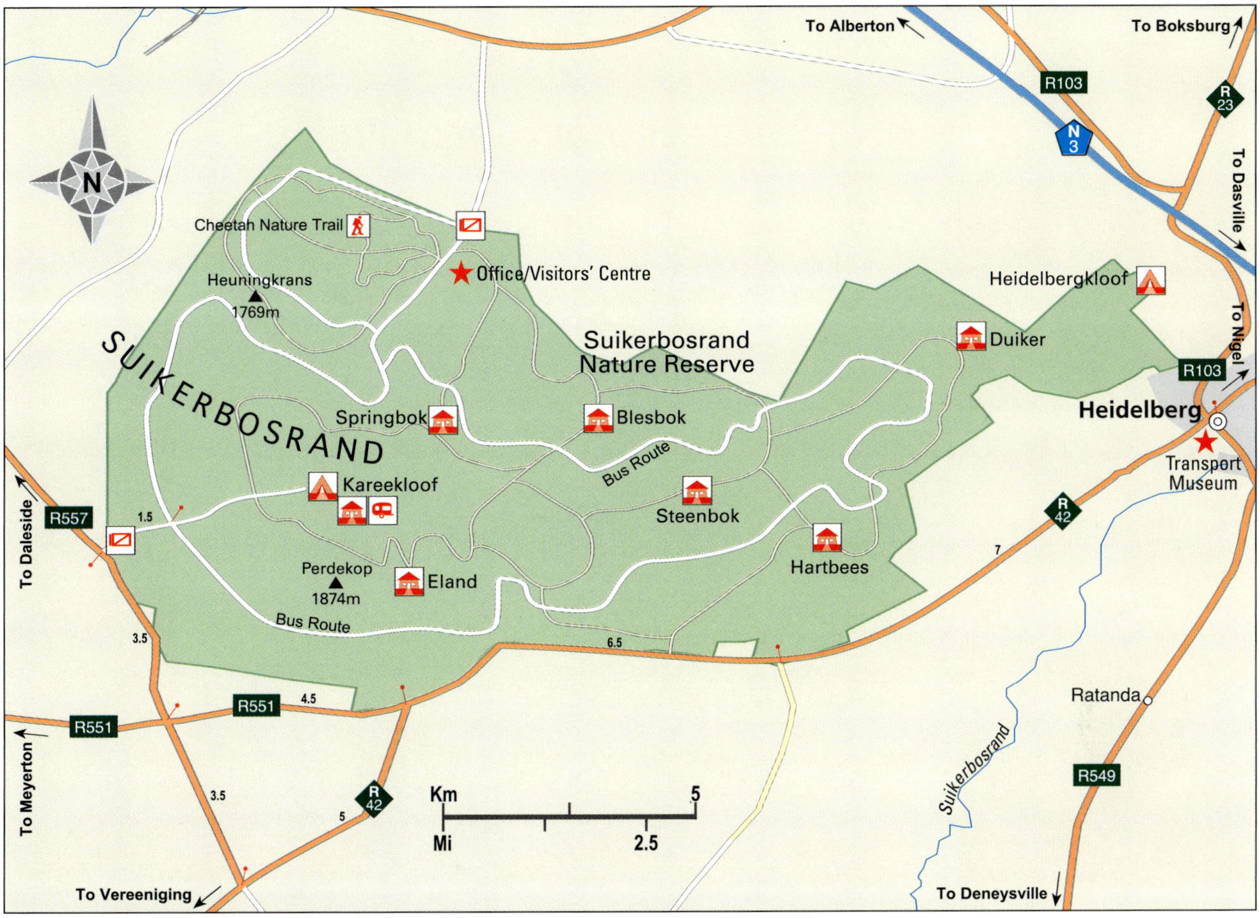

Suikerbosrand Nature Reserve

To Alberton
To Boksburg
R103
R23
N3
To Dasville
To Nigel

SUIKERBOSRAND
Suikerbosrand Nature Reserve

Cheetah Nature Trail
Office/Visitors' Centre
Heuningkrans 1769m
Heidelbergkloof
Duiker
R103
Springbok
Blesbok
Heidelberg
Transport Museum
Bus Route
Kareekloof
Steenbok
R42
Perdekop 1874m
Eland
Hartbees
Bus Route
Ratanda
Suikerbosrand

To Daleside
R557
1.5
3.5
6.5
7
R551
4.5
To Meyerton
R551
3.5
R42
5

Km
Mi
5
2.5
R549

To Vereeniging
To Deneysville

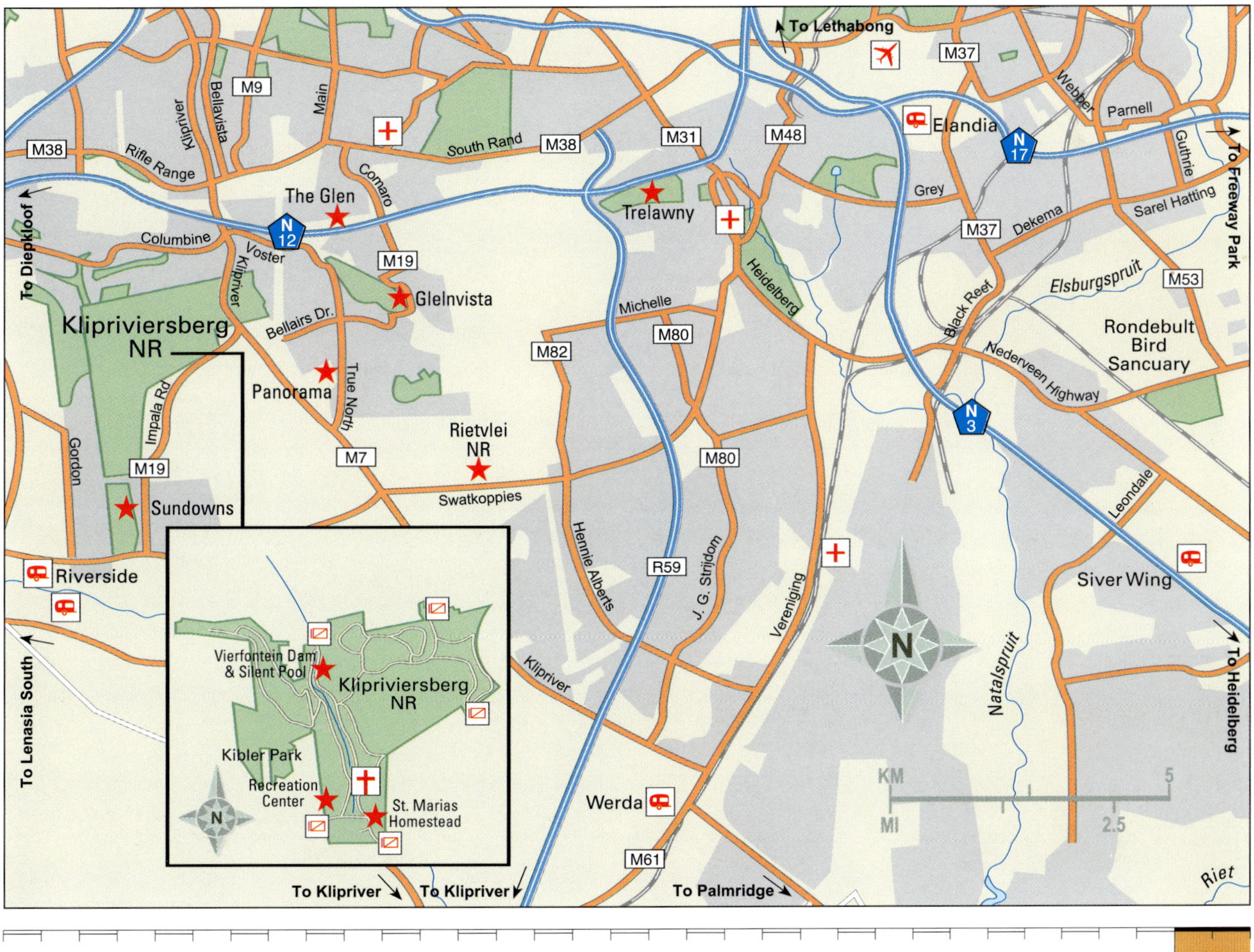

Kliprivier / Johannesburg South

To Lethabong
M37
M9
Bellavista
Main
South Rand
M38
M38
M31
M48
Elandia
Webber
Parnell
Guthrie
To Freeway Park
N17
Kliprivier
Rifle Range
The Glen
Comaro
Trelawny
Grey
N12
Columbine
Voster
Kliprivier
M19
Glelnvista
Bellairs Dr.
M37
Dekema
Sarel Hatting
Klipriviersberg NR
Panorama
True North
M82
Michelle
M80
Heidelberg
Black Reef
Elsburgspruit
M53
Rondebult Bird Sancuary
N3
M7
Rietvlei NR
M19
Sundowns
Swatkoppies
Gordon
Impala Rd
Nederveen Highway
Riverside
Leondale
Siver Wing
To Lenasia South

Vierfontein Dam & Silent Pool
Klipriviersberg NR
Kibler Park
Recreation Center
St. Marias Homestead

Hennie Alberts
Kliprivier
R59
J. G. Strijdom
Vereeniging
Natalspruit
Werda
M80
N

KM
MI
5
2.5

To Diepkloof
To Kliprivier
To Kliprivier
To Palmridge
M61
To Heidelberg
Riet

Bronkhorstspruit Dam Nature Reserve

The Bronkhorstspruit dam forms the centrepiece to this reserve, which, despite its appeal to naturalists and bird-lovers also hosts a number of resorts clustering around its fringes. Weekends bustle with anglers, boat-owners, windsurfers and sun-worshippers, particularly at Bronkhorstbaai with its cafeteria, clipped grass and swimming pools. The dam's surrounding reedbeds, eucalyptus copses and grasslands are a brilliant place for enthusiastic beginner birders to notch up a host of common waders and grassland LBJs (little brown jobs) in their clean white notebooks. When the water level drops in the reedbeds, waders love the muddy shoreline, and standing on the bridge across the Bronkhorstspruit River, you're sure to get a good look-see at the Whitethroated Swallow, Pied Kingfisher or Hamerkop.

Roodeplaat Dam Nature Reserve & Leeuwkloof Valley Conservancy

The **Roodeplaat dam** lies in the Dinokeng area – "place of rivers" in the language of the Tswana and Pedi people. Wildlife in the thornveld reserve on the dam's eastern shore includes prolific grazers, while special bird encounters could have you being entertained by the protracted grating chatter of different warbler species. At certain times of the year, hundreds of small fish struggle up the little stream in the reserve and are snatched up by Giant, Pied and Malachite Kingfishers. Also in Dinokeng, land owned by a collection of farmers has gone into the formation of the **Leeuwkloof Valley Conservancy**. Once roamed by Lion (and hunted by Paul Kruger, according to legend), its 240 grazers today can be tracked on foot, horses, mountainbikes and 4x4s.

Rietvlei Nature Reserve

Despite lying within the limits of the city, Rietvlei is one of the world's largest urban nature reserves. A restocking programme has focused on wildlife that is endemic to the Highveld, and its open grasslands make it a pleasure for visitors wanting a successful game-watching experience. A family unit of five hippos is a recent introduction; sleek, lissome Cheetah also stalk the grasslands. The birds are no small-fry either – standing tall and not easy to miss are Blue Crane, Secretary Bird, and Goliath and Greenbacked Heron. Picknickers can settle in at the Marais dam, upstream from Rietvlei, concealing themselves in the bird hide for unobtrusive bird-spotting. Overnight hiking and horse trails are accompanied by reserve staff.

Krugersdorp Game Reserve

Situated little more than a 40-minute drive from central Johannesburg, this reserve is a treat for urban moles. Rolling plains, rocky outcrops and a densely wooded valley offer a scenic change of pace to those wearied by their glass, brick and mortar landscapes. Wild animals here that stray from the norm are the rarer Roan and Sable Antelope with their scimitar-like horns, and Tsessebe. Unusual, too, is the 100ha Lion enclosure in the centre of the reserve. Conference-goers will be tickled to find that some of the rooms look onto a dam in which two hippos, rescued during the drought of 1992, spray and snort. With walking no longer allowed, day and night excursions in open Land Rovers make up for this.

BRONKHORSTSPRUIT DAM NR

NEAREST TOWN
Bronkhorstspruit

NEAREST AIRPORT
Johannesburg International

SIZE
908ha

AVIFAUNA
1 Redchested Flufftail
2 Whitebacked Duck
3 Great Crested Grebe
4 Orange River Francolin
5 Caspian Tern
6 Marsh Owl
7 Pied Kingfisher
8 Hamerkop
9 Whitethroated Swallow

MAIN CONTACT DETAILS
013 932 1621

ACCOMMODATION INSIDE PARK

ACCOMMODATION OUTSIDE PARK
Tourist Info, Bronkhorstspruit
013 932 6200

SEASONAL INFORMATION

Gate opening times
06:00 – 18:00
Day visitors allowed

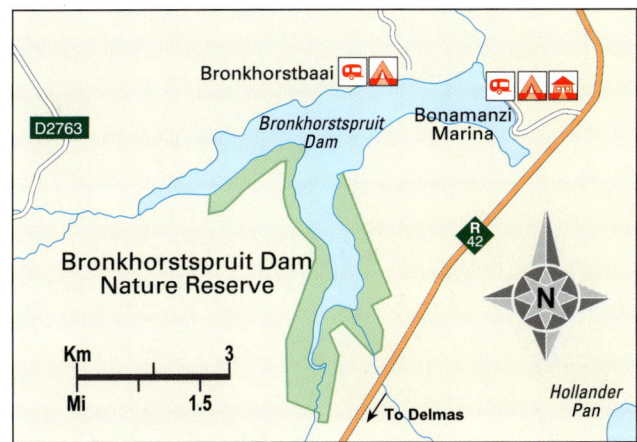

ROODEPLAAT DAM NR

NEAREST TOWN (BOTH PARKS)
Pretoria

NEAREST AIRPORT (BOTH PARKS)
Johannesburg International

SIZE
1695ha

FAUNA/AVIFAUNA
1 Burchell's Zebra
2 Impala
3 Giant, Pied & Malachite Kingfisher

MAIN CONTACT DETAILS
012 808 5131/3519

ACCOMMODATION INSIDE PARK

ACCOMMODATION OUTSIDE PARK
(BOTH PARKS)
Tourist Info, Pretoria
012 337 4430

LEEUWKLOOF VALLEY CONS.

SIZE
400ha

FAUNA
1 Kudu
2 Caracal

MAIN CONTACT DETAILS
012 735 1274

ACCOMMODATION INSIDE PARK
None

SEASONAL INFORMATION

Gate opening times
Roodeplaat Dam NR:
06:00 – 20:00
Leeuwkloof Valley Cons:
Open sunrise to sunset

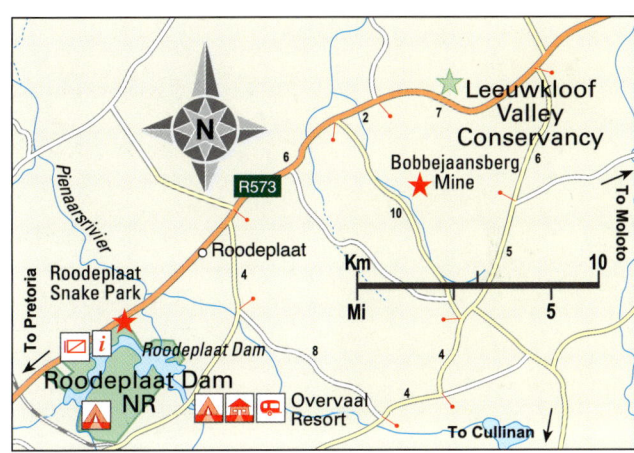

RIETVLEI NATURE RESERVE

NEAREST TOWN
Pretoria

NEAREST AIRPORT
Johannesburg International

SIZE
4000ha

FAUNA/AVIFAUNA
1 White Rhino
2 Buffalo
3 Cheetah
4 Burchell's Zebra
5 Red Hartebeest
6 Hippopotamus
7 Brown Hyena
8 Springbok
9 Secretary Bird
10 Goliath & Greenbacked Heron
11 African Finfoot
12 Blue Crane

MAIN CONTACT DETAILS
012 345 2274/5103/5104

ACCOMMODATION INSIDE PARK
Self-catering chalets, campsite

ACCOMMODATION OUTSIDE PARK
Tourist Info, Pretoria
012 337 4430

SEASONAL INFORMATION

Gate opening times
08:00 – 17:00 (Sept to Mar)
06:00 – 16:00 (Apr to Aug)
Day visitors allowed

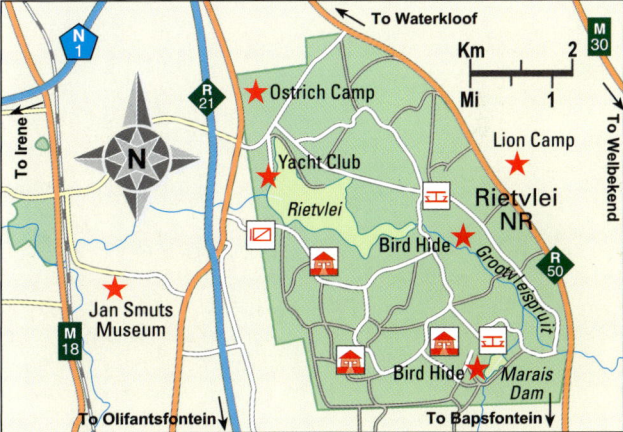

KRUGERSDORP GAME RESERVE

NEAREST TOWN
Krugersdorp

NEAREST AIRPORT
Johannesburg International

SIZE
1500ha

FAUNA
1 White Rhino
2 Buffalo
3 Giraffe
4 Lion
5 Black Wildebeest
6 Roan & Sable Antelope
7 Tsessebe
8 Gemsbok
9 Burchell's Zebra
10 Hippopotamus

MAIN CONTACT DETAILS
011 950 9900

ACCOMMODATION INSIDE PARK
Ngonyama Lion Lodge, self-catering
chalets, rondavels, campsite

ACCOMMODATION OUTSIDE PARK
Tourist Info, Krugersdorp
011 953 3727

SEASONAL INFORMATION

Gate opening times
08:00 – 18:00
Day visitors allowed

Marievale Bird Sanctuary

A zone of open pans and waterways fed by the Blesbokspruit, Marievale Bird Sanctuary is a refreshing preserve in the midst of mining and agricultural activity going on all around. Worthy of a Ramsar wetland site rating, its neck-collar of reedbeds and grasslands has birding enthusiasts regularly passing through because rare bird species are so frequently reported. At least 140 people have been known to line up with binoculars and scopes to home in on onetime unusual visitor, the Buffbreasted Sandpiper! It's one of the few places in Gauteng to watch the Black Egret play its unique trick of shading the water with its circular winged canopy. This enables it to spear an unsuspecting fish minus the irritating reflective glare of sunlight bouncing off the water's surface.

Nooitgedacht Game Ranch, Plumari Africa Reserve

Nooitgedacht Game Ranch, presided over by the Magaliesberg's highest reaches, delivers the entire wildlife experience – from Gemsbok and Wildebeest to hyena, from raptors to a vulture restaurant. Guests at **Plumari**'s game lodge, once known as De Ou Waenhuis, have a degree of exclusivity in that the chalets are limited to only 17. Meals are eaten in view of the hippo dam and the line-up in the surrounding reserve includes many major wild animals bar Lion and Elephant. Bushman rock carvings and Stone Age tools are a bonus. A major attraction is the private collection (one of the largest in South Africa) of painstakingly restored ox-carts and wagons dating between 1800 and 1900. The reserve is immensely proud of the birth of a White Rhino – the first to be born in the Magaliesberg in a century.

Rhenosterspruit & Diepsloot Nature Reserves

The **Rhenosterspruit reserve** sprawls in the Winsome valley, where the views expand to the Magaliesberg mountains. Water is not in short supply here, as the reserve's rolling grasslands straddle the Jukskei, Crocodile and Hennops rivers, which cut a broad tranquil band across the undulating open veld. Besides the wildlife here, a less usual sight for hikers are the Ostriches, loping straight-necked through the grasslands; be wary – their kick is capable of delivering a powerful knockout strike! The green, poplar-treed oasis of Northern Farm has been turned into the **Diepsloot Nature Reserve**. *SA Birding* calls it one of Johannesburg's best-kept secrets because of its wealth of feathered friends – all of 300 recorded species. The acacia woodland lures the magically named Fairy Flycatcher.

Tswaing Nature Reserve

The **Tswaing Crater** ("place of salt" in Tswana) was gouged out of the earth when a blazing stony meteorite slammed down some 220,000 years ago. Also known as the Zoutpan Crater, the 200m-deep, 1.4km-diameter indentation cradles a lake rich in dissolved carbonates and sodium chloride – the only impact crater in southern Africa to do so. Waterbirds congregate on its marshes.

MARIEVALE BIRD SANCTUARY

NEAREST TOWN
Nigel

NEAREST AIRPORT
Johannesburg International

SIZE
1000ha

FAUNA/AVIFAUNA
1 Blesbok
2 Cape Hare
3 Buffbreasted Sandpiper
4 Black Egret
5 Spurwing Goose
6 Great White Heron
7 South African Shelduck
8 Pectoral Sandpiper
9 Moorhen

MAIN CONTACT DETAILS
011 355 1980, 011 355 1903

ACCOMMODATION INSIDE PARK
Overnight chalets
🛏 🖼

ACCOMMODATION OUTSIDE PARK
Tourist Info, Nigel
011 456 0117/3

SEASONAL INFORMATION

Gate opening times
05:30 – 19:30 (Oct to Mar)
06:30 – 18:00 (Apr to Sept)
Day visitors allowed

NOOITGEDACHT GAME RANCH

NEAREST TOWN (BOTH PARKS)
Rustenburg

NEAREST AIRPORT (BOTH PARKS)
Johannesburg International

SIZE
2000ha

FAUNA
1 Giraffe
2 Secretary Bird

MAIN CONTACT DETAILS
082 449 9075

ACCOMMODATION INSIDE PARK
Tented Ingwe Bush Camp
🛏 🖼

**ACCOMMODATION OUTSIDE PARK
(BOTH PARKS)**
Tourist Info, Rustenburg
014 597 0904/5

PLUMARI AFRICA RESERVE

SIZE
4000ha

FAUNA
1 Hippopotamus
2 Warthog

MAIN CONTACT DETAILS
011 794 3797

ACCOMMODATION INSIDE PARK
Plumari Game Lodge
🛏 🖼

SEASONAL INFORMATION

Gate opening times
Nooitgedacht GR:
Sunrise to sunset
Plumari Africa:
07:00 – 16:30 (summer)
07:00 – 16:00 (winter)

RHENOSTERSPRUIT NR

NEAREST TOWN
Pretoria

NEAREST AIRPORT (BOTH PARKS)
Johannesburg International

SIZE
10 000ha

AVIFAUNA
1 Ostrich

MAIN CONTACT DETAILS
011 701 3076, 082 657 2120

ACCOMMODATION INSIDE PARK
🛏 🅰 🚲

DIEPSLOOT NR

NEAREST TOWN
Johannesburg

SIZE
350 – 400ha

AVIFAUNA
1 Fairy Flycatcher

MAIN CONTACT DETAILS
011 464 1002

ACCOMMODATION INSIDE PARK
None

**ACCOMMODATION OUTSIDE PARK
(BOTH PARKS)**
Tourist Info, Pretoria
012 337 4430

SEASONAL INFORMATION

Gate opening times
Rhenosterspruit NR:
06:00 – 18:00
Diepsloot NR:
Sunrise – 17:00 (weekends)

TSWAING CRATER NR

NEAREST TOWN
Johannesburg

NEAREST AIRPORT
Johannesburg International

SIZE
2000ha

AVIFAUNA
1 Waterbird sp.

MAIN CONTACT DETAILS
012 790 2302, 083 505 2271

ACCOMMODATION INSIDE PARK
Lekgotla Chalets, campsite
🛏 🅰 🖼

ACCOMMODATION OUTSIDE PARK
Tourist Info, Pretoria
012 337 4430
www.tshwane.gov.za

SEASONAL INFORMATION

Gate opening times
08:00 – 16:00
Day visitors allowed

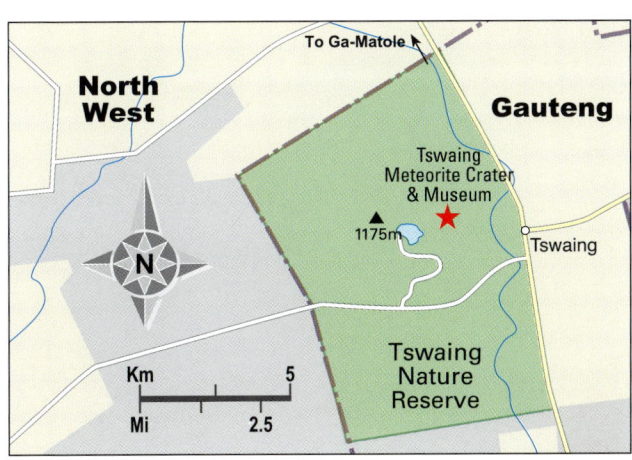

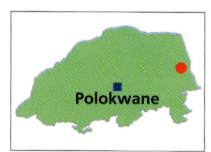

Polokwane

Kruger National Park (Limpopo)
& Surrounding Reserves

Kruger's northern sector is the hottest, driest and wildest. It is also the remotest and least visited, so visitors who revel in solitude and a sense of true wilderness should point their GPSs northward. Quite different from the rest of the park, this is a place of Mopane forests, giant Jackal-berry and Nyala-berry trees, fat Baobabs and great herds of grey lumbering – but nimble-footed – elephant. **Punda Maria** Camp is buffered by sand forest with nearby groves of unruly Baobab trees, while **Mopani** and **Shingwedzi**, both fronting onto water, settle into their Mopane veld surrounds. Minimal human disturbance translates into the presence here of rarer species, such as Lichtenstein's Hartebeest, the tiny Suni Antelope, and endangered Wild Dog. Verdant riverine forest lining the Luvuvhu River hides Samango Monkeys and hints at the superlative birdlife both in the forests and in the woodlands. Visitors won't miss the ubiquitous Lilacbreasted Roller with its panoply of iridescent hues . . . turquoise through royal blue and aquamarine to lilac-mauve. Up in the tangled north, the Mutale Falls safari camp in **Makuya Game Reserve** is perched on a river where a gorge waits to be swum and abseiled, and a 1000-year-old Baobab (biggest in the world, they claim) causes great bewonderment. Finally, in the 80km corridor, Madimbo, a bushland zone bordering Zimbabwe, lies untamed **Matshakatini Nature Reserve**. The corridor has recently seen much of its land handed back to communities who once benefited from it.

Of the private reserves that snugly border Kruger's central sector, **Letaba Ranch** and **Andover Game Reserve** are examples of truly wild, undeveloped areas that greatly benefit from Kruger's migratory wildlife trundling down ancient routes to fresh pastures. At Ndlopfu, in wild **Umbabat Nature Reserve**, guests report sightings of Leopard and Lion from their private decks, while at **Klaserie Nature Reserve** you can choose between East African style – billowing gauzy nets in safari tents on raised wooden platforms – or a tree-house lodge balanced in the branches. In **Timbavati Game Reserve**, an overnight wilderness hike or a drive at sparrow's peep to watch the copper sunrise, followed by a high-class breakfast, brings you up close and personal with Nature. Cherry on the top comes from Royal Malewane Lodge at **Thornybush Game Reserve**, which makes helicopters and executive jets available to its guests; it also retains one of only two Master Trackers in the country. **Kapama Game Reserve** sends willing guests off on a dawn or dusk ramble on elephant-back. Finally, the utter remoteness of **Manyeleti Game Reserve** – Shangaan for "place of the stars" – encourages the more adventurous to join a rustic trails camp, where they shower under the Southern Cross and dine around a blazing campfire.

KRUGER NP (LIMPOPO)
NEAREST TOWN
Phalaborwa

NEAREST AIRPORT
Phalaborwa

SIZE (ENTIRE PARK)
2 million ha

FAUNA/AVIFAUNA
1   African Elephant
2   Black & White Rhino
3   Buffalo
4   Giraffe
5   Lion
6   Leopard
7   Cheetah
8   Lichtenstein's Hartebeest
9   Suni Antelope
10 Wild Dog
11 Samango Monkey
12 Spotted Hyena
13 Kori Bustard
14 Lappetfaced Vulture
15 Ground Hornbill
16 Lilacbreasted Roller

MAIN CONTACT DETAILS
013 735 6873
012 428 9111/426 5000

ACCOMMODATION INSIDE PARK
Punda Maria, Shingwedzi, Mopani,
Letaba & Olifants, Sirheni, Shimuwini,
Bateleur & Boulders Camps

ACCOMMODATION OUTSIDE PARK
Tourist Info, Phalaborwa
015 781 0111

MAKUYA GR
MAIN CONTACT DETAILS
015 295 3025/2829

ANDOVER GR
MAIN CONTACT DETAILS
015 793 2183, 015 290 7300

MANYELETI GR
MAIN CONTACT DETAILS
015 290 7300

TIMBAVATI GR
MAIN CONTACT DETAILS
015 793 0415

KLASERIE NR
MAIN CONTACT DETAILS
015 793 3000

UMBABAT NR
MAIN CONTACT DETAILS
015 290 7300

THORNYBUSH GR
MAIN CONTACT DETAILS
015 793 1976

KAPAMA GR
MAIN CONTACT DETAILS
015 793 1038

LETABA RANCH GR
MAIN CONTACT DETAILS
015 295 3025

SEASONAL INFORMATION

Gate opening times
Pafuri, Punda Maria &
Phalaborwa Gates:
05:30 – 18:30 (Nov to Mar)
06:00 – 17:30 (Apr to Jul)
06:00 – 18:00 (Aug & Sept)
05:30 – 18:00 (Oct)

ZIMBABWE

Km | 50 | Vouzela
Mi | 25 | 208 | Vouga

Limpopo

Matshakatini
Nature Reserve

To Tshipise

R525
Masisi
Pafuri Gate
H1-9
Thulamela
Ruins
Pafuri
Limpopo
12
19

Nwandedi
GR
Serena
Baobab
Hill
H1-8

Mutale
Luvuvhu

Nwandedi
Dam

Makuya
Game Reserve

SOUTH AFRICA
Punda
Maria
Klopperfontein
Drift
41

To Wyllie's Poort

*Lake
Fundudzi*
Mhinga
Punda
Maria Gate
H13-1
15

Mutshindudi
R524
21

Thohoyandou
Xigalo
Mavamba
Malamulele
67

H1-7

Sirheni
Bushveld
Camp

MOZAMBIQUE

Tshakhuma
Levubu
Muswani
Phugwane
50

Luvuvhu
R524

Vuwani
52
*Nsami
Dam*
Kojalingo
Shingwidzi
Shingwedzi

R578
Klein-Letaba
Babangu
Bateleur
Bushveld
Camp

To Makhado
Ha-Magoro
*Middle-Letaba
Dam*
Giyani
Kruger
National
Park

H1-6
73

Singuedeze

Hildreth Ridge
R81
34
Nkomo
43
Mopani

Great Limpopo
Transfrontier
Reserve

To Mooketsi
R529
Dzumeri
Boulders
30
Giriyondo

Molototsi
Ga-Modjadji
Modjadji
NR
Malekatla
34
Mineral Springs
Hans Merensky
Nature Reserve
Letaba
Ranch
Game
Reserve
Shimuwini
Bushveld Camp
32

La Cotte
Letaba

Ndzalama
Wildlife
Resort
Mulati
Lulekani
Phalaborwa
Gate
H14
22
H1-6
Letaba
Letaba

28
R71
Letsitele
R71
41
Selati
Game Reserve
Namakgale
11
9
Phalaborwa
H1-9
43
H1-5
24

To Tzaneen
35
19
Gravelotte
Olifants
9

R36
Leydsdorp
26
Makalali
Private
Reserve
32
Olifants
11
Balule

Ofcolaco
R526
37
Umbabat
NR
Roodewal
H1-4

Trichardtsdal
Mica
Balule
Nature
Reserve
Klaserie
NR
Timbavati
Game Reserve
49

Legalameetse
NR
44
Makutsi
Conservancy
R36
25
R525
27
Kapama
GR
Klaserie
Ngala
Game Lodge
Orpen
Satara
45

Penge
Blyde Olifants
Conservancy
Hoedspruit
Timbavati
H7
4
H6

DRAKENSBERG
Diphuti
18
15
Thornybush
GR
Orpen
Gate

JG Strijdom
Tunnel
Abel Erasmus
Pass
32
R531
24
Klaserie
R531
45
H1-3

Echo
Caves
Branddraai
*Blydepoort
Dam*
Andover
Game Reserve

R37
7
28
Longsight
R36
20
R532
*Blyde River
Canyon NR*
R40
Acornhoek
Cottondale
8
Manyeleti
Game Reserve
Mpumalanga

Burgersfort
Voortrekker
Fort
Tricardt
Memorial

To Polokwane
To Lydenburg
Moroneo
Ohrigstad
To Graskop
To Hazyview

Limpopo

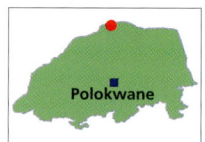

Polokwane

Mapungubwe National Park

One of South Africa's newest parks has started its life already as a UNESCO World Heritage Site – the country's sixth. Edging onto the confluence of the Limpopo and Shashe rivers, 360-degree views from the top of its small, free-standing, oval-shaped mountain encompass the lands of Botswana and Zimbabwe; plans for a transfrontier park are afoot, linking to the Tuli Block and Tuli Safari Area. At Mapungubwe ("place of the stone of wisdom" according to one translation, although there are several theories!) signs of human occupation from AD850 – some two centuries before Great Zimbabwe – to the 13th century show it to have been a powerful state, trading with Arabia and India via East African ports. Impregnable buttresses, boulder-strewn koppies, Wild Fig roots strangling rocky crevices, and greasy-grey Baobabs imbue this space with spirit. Archaeological treasures – a gold-foil rhino (Shona symbol of power), sceptre and ornaments, trade glass beads and Chinese ceramics – are presently displayed at Pretoria University.

MAPUNGUBWE NP
NEAREST TOWN
Musina

NEAREST AIRPORT
Musina

SIZE
28 000ha

FAUNA/FLORA
1   African Elephant
2   White Rhino
3   Wild Dog
4   Brown Hyena
5   Python sp.
6   Black Mamba
7   Scorpion sp.
8   Pel's Fishing Owl
9   Baobab
10 Wild Fig Tree
11 Nyala-berry Tree

MAIN CONTACT DETAILS
015 534 2014

ACCOMMODATION INSIDE PARK
Leokwe Camp, Limpopo Forest Tented Camp, Tshugulu Lodge, Vhembe Wilderness Camp
🛏 ⛺ ⊠

ACCOMMODATION OUTSIDE PARK
Tourist Info, Musina
015 534 3500
musinatourism@limpopo.co.za
www.limpopotourism.org.za

SEASONAL INFORMATION

Gate opening times
06:00 – 18:00
Day visitors allowed

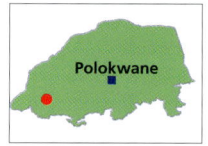

Polokwane

Marakele National Park
& Ben Alberts Nature Reserve

The all-new **Marakele National Park**, a merging of the original park, Welgevonden Game Reserve and the privately owned Marakele contractual park, reinforces an admirable aim by SANParks to increase South Africa's protected areas to 10% of land mass by 2010. Settled among the stony crags of the imposing Waterberg mountains, the landscape is one of twisted Cedar trees, tall-standing cycads, mophead tree ferns and soaring eagles. In summer, spot the wingspans of Blackbreasted Snake and Brown Snake Eagles with their black-on-white detailing. The 900 breeding pairs of Cape Vulture make this Africa's largest colony. The nearby **Ben Alberts Nature Reserve** delivers its fair share of wildlife, but most fascinating is the vulture restaurant outside the reserve bounds. Viewed from the anonymity of a hide little more than a couple of wingspans away, an abbatoir serves up a carnivorous feast daily as the graceful yet powerful birds swoop in for the treat.

MARAKELE NP
NEAREST TOWN (BOTH PARKS)
Thabazimbi

NEAREST AIRPORT (BOTH PARKS)
Johannesburg International

SIZE
20 000ha

FAUNA/FLORA
1   African Elephant
2   White Rhino
3   Tsessebe
4   Kudu
5   Eland
6   Chacma Baboon
7   Vervet Monkey
8   Cape Vulture
9   Blackbreasted Snake Eagle
10 Cedar Tree
11 Cycad sp.
12 Tree Fern sp.

MAIN CONTACT DETAILS
014 777 1745

ACCOMMODATION INSIDE PARK
Bontle Campsite, Tlopi Tented Camp
⛺ ⛽ ⊠

ACCOMMODATION OUTSIDE PARK
(BOTH PARKS)
Tourist Info, Thabazimbi
014 777 1745

BEN ALBERTS NATURE RESERVE
SIZE
2000ha

FAUNA
1   Kudu
2   Nyala
3   Cape Vulture

MAIN CONTACT DETAILS
014 777 1670

ACCOMMODATION INSIDE PARK
Chalet for overnight visitors
🛏

SEASONAL INFORMATION

Gate opening times
Marakele NP:
07:30 – 18:00 (summer)
07:30 – 17:00 (winter)
Day visitors allowed
Ben Alberts NR:
Day visitors not allowed

Map 1 (Mapungubwe NP region)

BOTSWANA

Northeast
Tuli Conservation
Area

ZIMBABWE

To Tuli

To Beitbridge

Shashe River

Limpopo River

Maloutswa
Game Hide

Vhembe
Wilderness
Camp

Limpopo River

Rhodes Drift
Lodge

Confluence

Shroda
Dam

Limpopo
Forest

Mapungubwe
NP

Pontdrif

Limpopo
Valley

Leokwe
Restcamp

R572

To Musina

Little Muck
Lodge

Museum & Interpretation
Centre

Park Entrance

Little Muck
Game Hide

SOUTH AFRICA

Tshugulu
Lodge

11

13

To Baines Drift

1

Tshugulu Gate

19

Km 10

Mi 5

① Tshugulu eco-route
② Khongoni Loop
③ Kanniedood Loop

N

R572

To Evangelina

To Bandur

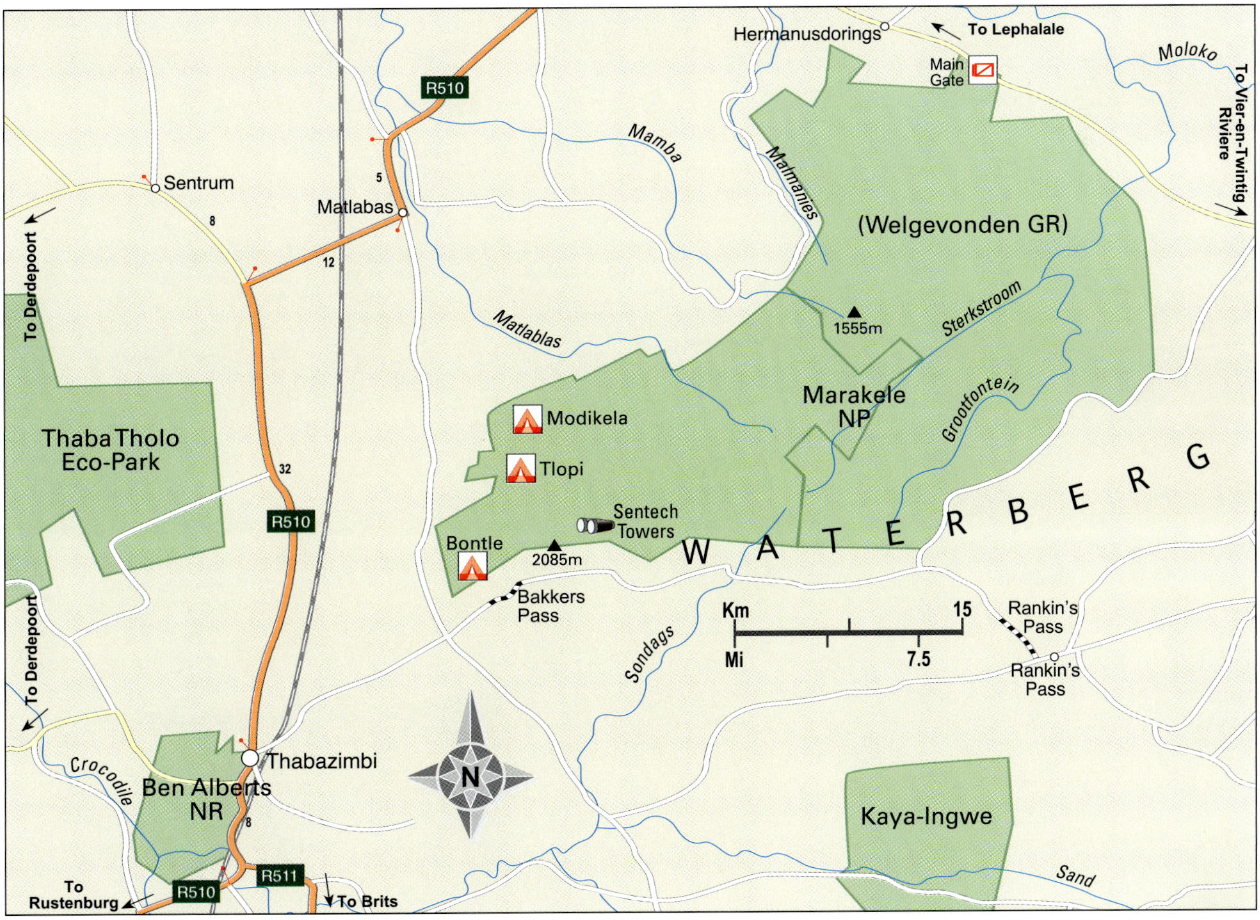

Map 2 (Marakele NP region)

Hermanusdorings

To Lephalale

Moloko

Main
Gate

To Vier-en-Twintig
Riviere

R510

Mamba

Sentrum

Malmanies

(Welgevonden GR)

Matlabas

5

8

12

1555m

Sterkstroom

Matlablas

Grootfontein

Thaba Tholo
Eco-Park

32

Modikela

Marakele
NP

R510

Tlopi

W A T E R B E R G

Sentech
Towers

Bontle

2085m

Km 15

Mi 7.5

Rankin's
Pass

Bakkers
Pass

Rankin's
Pass

Sondags

N

Crocodile

Thabazimbi

Ben Alberts
NR

Kaya-Ingwe

8

Sand

To
Derdepoort

To Derdepoort

R510   R511

To Brits

To
Rustenburg

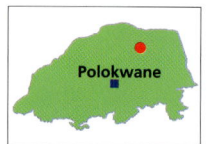

Ben Lavin, Honnet, Nwanedi & Musina Reserves

The Manavhela community, proudly sharing their Venda heritage, run the **Ben Lavin reserve** spread out at the foot of the Soutpansberg. A network of game-viewing roads can be explored night and day on foot, by car or mountain-bike, or as part of an overnight hiking trail. Then it's chilled sundowners, gazing across the Doorn River, a Sicklebush braai fire crackling fragrantly nearby. Resort and reserve life are inextricably entwined at two Aventura destinations, the **Honnet** and **Nwanedi game reserves**. Aventura Tshipise ("something warm") in Honnet alludes to the 44°C thermal waters that can be indulged in after a 4x4 or horseback tour. Nwanedi's resort sits snugly at the base of a giant dam wall where, at times, sheets of water hurtle over. Also intriguing is a row of volcanic-shaped hills, scoured by sharp vertical ridges. In the **Musina reserve**, the sky is filled with the dishevelled roots of over 100 Baobabs, which are protected here.

BEN LAVIN NR
NEAREST TOWN
Makhado

NEAREST AIRPORT (ALL PARKS)
Polokwane

SIZE
2500ha

FAUNA/FLORA
1   Giraffe
2   Bronzewinged Courser

MAIN CONTACT DETAILS (ALL PARKS)
015 539 0624, 015 290 7300
www.golimpopo.com

ACCOMMODATION INSIDE PARK
Lodges, luxury tents, huts, campsite
🛏 ⛺ 🍴 🅿

ACCOMMODATION OUTSIDE PARK
Tourist Info, Makhado
015 516 3415

HONNET GR
NEAREST TOWN (ALSO NWANEDI, MUSINA)
Musina

SIZE
22 000ha

FAUNA/FLORA (ALSO NWANEDI, MUSINA)
1   Wildebeest
2   Tsessebe
3   Giraffe

4   Burchell's Zebra
5   Baobab

ACCOMMODATION INSIDE PARK
None

ACCOMMODATION OUTSIDE PARK (ALSO NWANEDI, MUSINA)
Tourist Info, Musina
015 534 3500

NWANEDI GR
SIZE
9000ha

ACCOMMODATION INSIDE PARK
Protea Nwanedi, rondawels, campsite
🛏 ⛺ 🍴 🅿

MUSINA NR
SIZE
4910ha

ACCOMMODATION INSIDE PARK
None

SEASONAL INFORMATION

Gate opening times
Ben Lavin NR:
06:00 – 20:30
Honnet GR:
Open 24 hours
Nwadeni GR:
Sunrise to sunset
Musina NR:
06:00 – 18:00

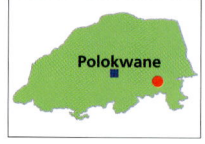

Blyde Olifants Conservancy, Balule & Makalali Reserves

In the conservancy spanning the see-through waters of the **Blyde** and the more turbulent and powerful **Olifants** River, private farm fences were dismantled to encourage natural migration – a move mimicked in the other three reserves. Hippos and crocodiles, bush-willow woodland and giant boulder outcrops, and the brooding Drakensberg escarpment are a magic combination. At **Balule**, after a bushwalk led by a Shangaan tracker, guests can sit in the thatched *lapa*, watching wildlife slake their thirst at the pan. The cough of a lion sometimes carries thrillingly across the night air. Still under development, **Makutsi**'s 1000ha naturally expanded to 3000ha when boundaries with Makgokolo were removed, in line with conservation and ecotourism plans. **Makalali**'s innovative African architecture, sensitively hand-crafted by local artisans on the Makhutswi riverbank, clearly sets this reserve apart – it is all earth walls, thatched spires and wooden-stilt *salas* (day-rooms) set among the Jackal-berry trees.

BLYDE OLIFANTS CONSERVANCY
NEAREST TOWN (ALL PARKS)
Phalaborwa

NEAREST AIRPORT (ALL PARKS)
Phalaborwa

SIZE
17 000ha

FAUNA/FLORA
1   Hippopotamus
2   Nile Crocodile
3   Bald Ibis
4   Peregrine Falcon
5   African Finfoot
6   Marula Tree

MAIN CONTACT DETAILS (ALL PARKS)
015 290 7300
info@golimpopo.com
www.golimpopo.com

ACCOMMODATION INSIDE PARK
Tshukudu, Lissataba Camps
🛏 🅿

ACCOMMODATION OUTSIDE PARK (ALL PARKS)
Tourist Info, Phalaborwa
015 781 0111

BALULE NR
SIZE
35 000ha

FAUNA
1   African Elephant

2   White Rhino
3   Buffalo
4   Lion
5   Leopard

ACCOMMODATION INSIDE PARK
Mfubu Lodge, Mohlabetsi, Ezulwini, Tulani, Drifters Lodges
🛏 🅿

MAKALALI PRIVATE RESERVE
SIZE
24 500ha

FAUNA
1   African Elephant
2   White Rhino
3   Cheetah
4   Lion
5   Hippopotamus

ACCOMMODATION INSIDE PARK
Makalali Game Lodge, guesthouses
🛏 🅿

SEASONAL INFORMATION

Gate opening times
Blyde Olifants Conservancy & Balule NR:
Sunrise to sunset
Makalali Private Reserve:
06:00 – 19:00
Day visitors allowed

Top map

ZIMBABWE

Limpopo

To Masisi

R572 — Musina (Messina)

Musina NR

Baobab Trees

R508

Nzhelele

R525

Nwanedi GR

Luphephe Dam

Nwanedi Dam

Tshi-hovho-hovho Falls

Tshipise

Honnet GR

SOUTH AFRICA

To Evangelina

R578 — To Elim

Sand

Mopane

N1

Nzhelele Dam

Dzata Ruins

Mutale

Lake Funduzi

To Punda Maria

Hide — i — Hide

To Fort Edward

To Carlow

R523

Waterpoort

Masekwaspoort

BAOBAB TOLL ROAD — T — Oorwinning

Wyllie's Poort

R523

Mutshindudi

Thohoyandou

Luvuvhu

S O U T P A N S B E R G

Wyllie's Poort

Verwoerd Tunnels

Mara

Stonehenge — i

Makhado (Louis Trichardt)

Ratombo — Tshakhuma

Levubu

Buysdorp

R522

Km 25
Mi 12.5

To Bandelierkop

Ben Lavin NR

R578 — Elim

Albasini Dam

Borchers

Vuwani

N

51 · 17 · 15 · 14 · 27 · 7 · 18 · 19 · 9 · 29 · 41 · 22 · 13 · 13 · 4 · 16 · 15 · 12 · 18 · 28 · 37 · 19 · 4

Bottom map

R71

Namakgale

To Phalaborwa

Gravelotte

Selati Game Reserve

Leydsdorp

Ga-Selati

R526

Km 10
Mi 5

R40

Cycad Reserve

Tulani

Tintshaba — Mfubu

Darisandi

To Tzaneen

Ofcolaco

Makutsi Conservancy

Makalali Private Reserve

Mica

Balule Nature Reserve

Trichardtsdal

Edeni

Makutsi Safari Farm

Makalali Game Lodge

Sorabi Rock Lodge

Tantris

Ingwe Game Farm

R36

R525

Blyde Olifants Conservancy

Mohlabetsi

Tshukudu

Kapama Game Reserve

D R A K E N S B E R G

Lissataba

Olifantstenk

Blyde

Tshukudu Game Lodge and Bush Camp

Monsoon Centre

River Lodge — H

Swadini Reptile Park

Hoedspruit

H — Fort Coepieba

Eastgate

Dublin Farm Cottages

Diphuti — Baobab Tree

Otters Den

Manoutsa Park

The Trading Post

To Branddraai

To Klaserie

To Klaserie

N

41 · 11 · 32 · 37 · 8 · 17 · 8 · 6 · 7 · 11 · 12 · 4 · 15 · 14 · 25 · 27 · 10 · 5 · 18 · 15

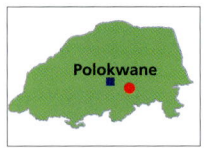

Wolkberg Wilderness Area & Lekgalameetse Nature Reserve

The feeling of walking on green-carpeted mountaintops at the very top of the world makes the **Wolkberg Wilderness** – this "mountain of the clouds" – a hiker's Shangri-La. For competent and agile rock climbers only, there are no paths or marked sites to pitch your tent – but there are massive buttresses, vertical quartzite cliffs, interlocking spurs, thickly forested kloofs and a river gorge flanked by perpendicular aloe-clothed cliffs. **Lekgalameetse**, fittingly "the place of much water", embraces the Downs Nature Reserve. Under its moist canopy of giant yellow-woods and Natal Mahoganies, amid the flutter of rare butterflies (many still to be classified), epiphytic orchids drape exotically from the branches and clivias smoulder, dark crimson-red through off-white. Contiguous with these protected areas, to the west, lies Bewaarkloof Nature Reserve, a wild broken territory of dolomite and ironstone and deep incised valleys, covered with proteas, bushwillow and acacias.

WOLKBERG WILDERNESS AREA
NEAREST TOWN (BOTH PARKS)
Tzaneen
NEAREST AIRPORT (BOTH PARKS)
Polokwane
SIZE
22 009ha
FAUNA/FLORA
1　Grey Rhebok
2　Vervet & Samango Monkey
3　Caracal
4　Wolkberg Butterfly
5　Wild Fig Tree
6　Cape Beech Tree
MAIN CONTACT DETAILS (BOTH PARKS)
015 290 7300
info@golimpopo.com
www.golimpopo.com
ACCOMMODATION INSIDE PARK
Campsite
⛺ 🅿
ACCOMMODATION OUTSIDE PARK (BOTH PARKS)
Tourist Info, Tzaneen
015 307 6513/7244

LEKGALAMEETSE NR
SIZE
18 718ha
FAUNA/FLORA
1　Leopard
2　Samango Monkey
3　Bushbaby
4　Yellowwood sp.
5　Mahogany sp.
6　Orchid sp.
7　Clivia sp.
ACCOMMODATION INSIDE PARK
Log cabins, wooden chalets
🛏 🅿

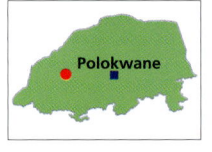

Waterberg Biosphere
Lapalala Wilderness, Mokolo Dam & D'Nyala Reserves

The Waterberg massif, stretching more than 150km from the Marakele National Park in the southwest to the Masebe National Reserve in the northeast, rises in flat sedimentary layers out of the bushveld lowlands. As the sun sinks into the horizon, the iron and manganese in the rock faces glows orange-red, then purple. The early Voortrekkers found rivers and streams flowing abundantly from the recesses of the massif, cliffs glistening with water – hence the mountain's name. A mass of protected areas falls under the **Waterberg Biosphere** (a UNESCO World Heritage Site), among them **Lapalala**, famous for its Black Rhino breeding programme and that of other endangered species such as Roan Antelope. Many people have emerged from Lapalala's Wilderness School, informed and inspired. Boats and fishermen sometimes dodge hippos and crocodiles at the dam on the **Mokolo** River, and **D'Nyala**'s suitably wild bushveld has recently become part of the Limpopo 4x4 Off-road Challenge.

LAPALALA WILDERNESS GR
NEAREST TOWN (ALL PARKS)
Lephalale
NEAREST AIRPORT (ALL PARKS)
Polokwane
SIZE
36 000ha
FAUNA
1　Black Rhino
2　Roan Antelope
3　Hippopotamus
MAIN CONTACT DETAILS
014 755 4395
reservations@lapalala.com
www.lapalala.com
ACCOMMODATION INSIDE PARK
Kolobe Lodge, Rhino Camp, Lapotedi, Haasjeveld Farmhouse, Lookout Safari Bushcamp
🛏 ⛺ 🅿
ACCOMMODATION OUTSIDE PARK (ALL PARKS)
Tourist Info, Lephalale
014 736 2193

MOKOLO DAM NR
SIZE
4600ha
FAUNA/FLORA
1　Roan Antelope
2　Sharpe's Grysbok
3　Protea sp.

MAIN CONTACT DETAILS
014 763 5447
ACCOMMODATION INSIDE PARK
Campsite
⛺ 🔥 🅿

D'NYALA NR
SIZE
8000ha
FAUNA
1　White Rhino
2　Giraffe
3　Nyala
MAIN CONTACT DETAILS
015 290 7300
info@golimpopo.com
www.golimpopo.com
ACCOMMODATION INSIDE PARK
Chalets
🛏 🅿

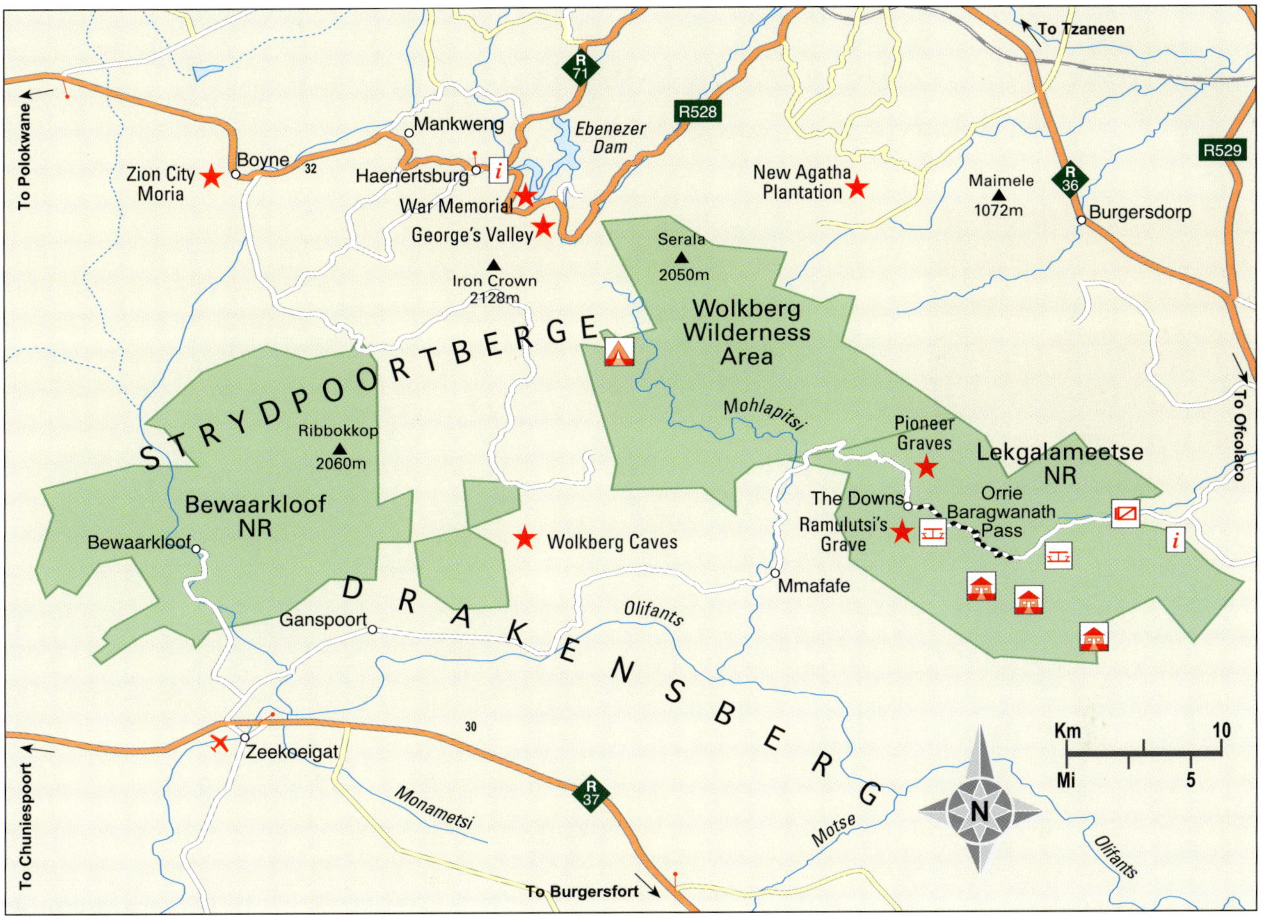

Map 1 (top):

To Tzaneen

R71

To Polokwane

Mankweng

R528

Ebenezer Dam

R529

Zion City Moria ★

Boyne 32

Haenertsburg

New Agatha Plantation ★

Maimele 1072m

R36

Burgersdorp

War Memorial ★

George's Valley ★

Serala 2050m

Iron Crown 2128m

S T R Y D P O O R T B E R G E

Wolkberg Wilderness Area

Mohlapitsi

To Ofcolaco

Ribbokkop 2060m

Pioneer Graves ★

Lekgalameetse NR

Bewaarkloof NR

Bewaarkloof

Wolkberg Caves ★

The Downs

Ramulutsi's Grave ★

Orrie Baragwanath Pass

D R A K E N S B E R G

Ganspoort

Olifants

Mmafafe

To Chuniespoort

Zeekoeigat

30

Monametsi

R37

Km 10

Mi 5

N

Motse

Olifants

To Burgersfort

Map 2 (bottom):

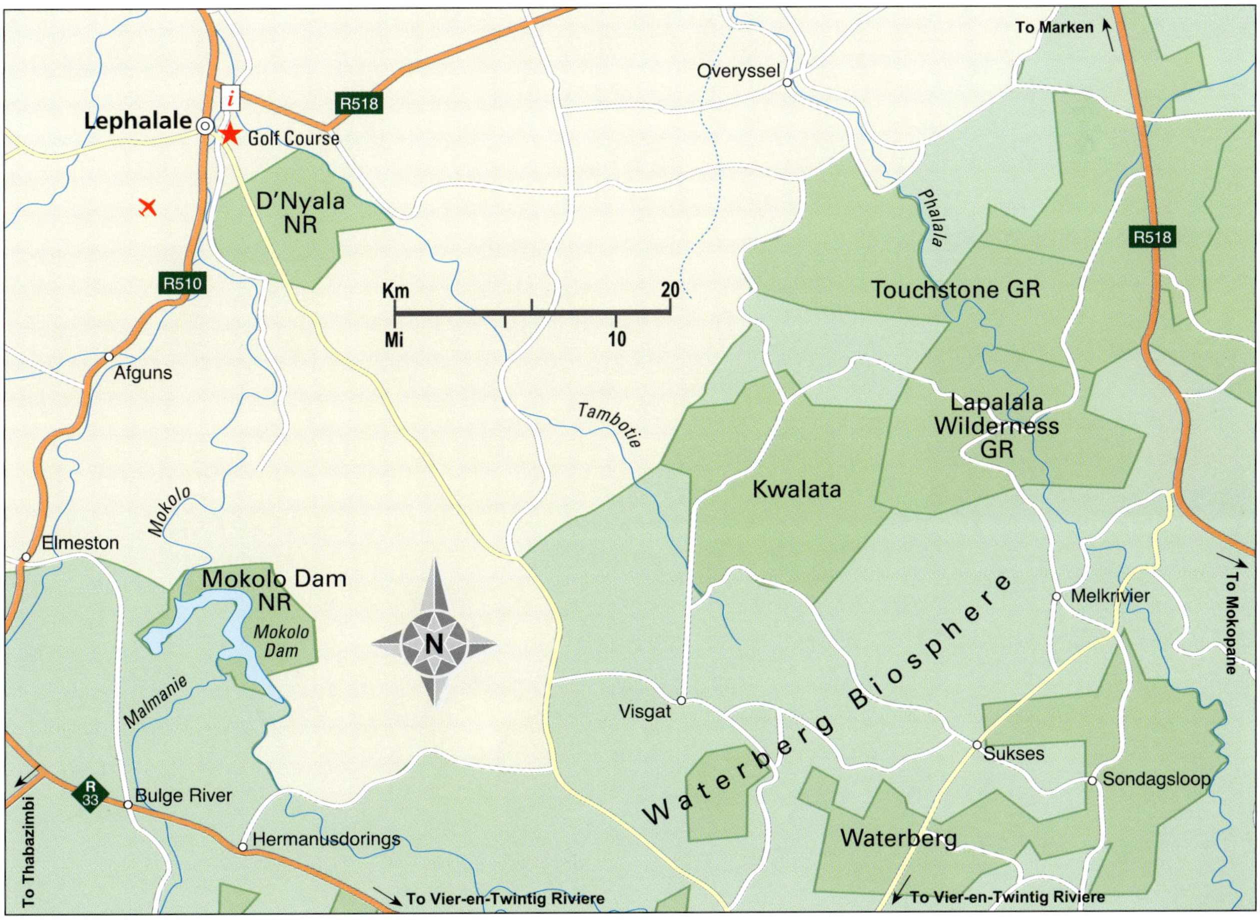

To Marken

Overyssel

Lephalale

R518

i

Golf Course ★

Phalala

R518

D'Nyala NR

Touchstone GR

R510

Km 20

Mi 10

Afguns

Tambotie

Lapalala Wilderness GR

Kwalata

Elmeston

Mokolo

Mokolo Dam NR

Mokolo Dam

N

Melkrivier

To Mokopane

W a t e r b e r g   B i o s p h e r e

Malmanie

Visgat

Sukses

Sondagsloop

R33

Bulge River

Waterberg

To Thabazimbi

Hermanusdorings

To Vier-en-Twintig Riviere

To Vier-en-Twintig Riviere

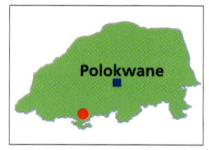

Nylsvlei, Rust de Winter, Mabalingwe & Mabula Reserves

Although Roan Antelope and Tsessebe relish the vlei expanse of the **Nylsvlei Nature Reserve**, the country's largest flood plain, most people flock here for its gregarious gaggle of waterbirds – they have been known to number 80,000 in particularly wet seasons. Twenty-three of the waterfowl species are on the Red Data (endangered) list. Staying in birdie heaven, **Rust de Winter Nature Reserve** specialises in birdlife that thrives in broadleaved woodland and thornveld. With names like Scalyfeathered Finch and Pearlspotted Owl, you can't go wrong! At Itaga lodge in **Mabalingwe Game Reserve** ("place of the spotted leopard", although don't hold your breath about glimpsing one), an electric fence keeps mischievous elephants from stripping the Marula trees. . . Visitors can espy **Mabula reserve**'s wild animal entourage while suspended beneath a giant balloon, and at Shakama Game Farm (depending on numbers), a star-gazing expert is invited in to reveal the wonders of the firmament.

NYLSVLEI NR
NEAREST TOWN (ALL PARKS)
Bela-Bela
NEAREST AIRPORT (ALL PARKS)
Polokwane
SIZE
4000ha
FAUNA
1 Roan Antelope
2 Tsessebe
3 Waterbird sp.
MAIN CONTACT DETAILS
(ALL PARKS)
015 290 7300
info@golimpopo.com
www.golimpopo.com
ACCOMMODATION INSIDE PARK

ACCOMMODATION OUTSIDE PARK
(ALL PARKS)
Tourist Info, Bela-Bela
014 736 3694

RUST DE WINTER NR
SIZE
3000ha
AVIFAUNA
1 Pearlspotted Owl
2 Scalyfeathered Finch
ACCOMMODATION INSIDE PARK

MABALINGWE GR
SIZE
12 500ha
FAUNA/FLORA (ALSO MABULA)
1 African Elephant
2 Rhino
3 Buffalo
4 Lion
5 Leopard
ACCOMMODATION INSIDE PARK
Tlou Lodge, Itaga Game Lodge,
Kubu, Ingwe, Pitsi, Kalahari Camps

MABULA GR
SIZE
12 000ha
ACCOMMODATION INSIDE PARK
Mabula Game Lodge
021 689 2221

SEASONAL INFORMATION

Gate opening times
Nylsvlei & Rust de Winter NR:
06:00 – 18:00
Day visitors allowed
Mabalingwe & Mabula GR
Sunrise to sunset
Day visitors allowed by arrangement

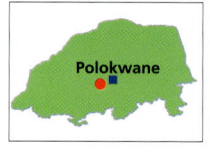

Percy Fyfe, Doorndraai Dam & Polokwane Reserves

The breeding efforts of the **Percy Fyfe Nature Reserve** make it a dead-cert for future generations to get to admire the graceful sweeping arc of a Roan or Sable Antelope's horns or the heavy-headed gaze of an Addo Buffalo. In the **Doorndraai Dam Nature Reserve**, a dam set in a landscape of hills draws plenty of campers who vie with one another for the reserve's spoils – anglers and watersports participants stick to the water, bird-watchers flee to the woodlands, and off-roaders head for the hills in a cloud of dust. Adjacent to the city of the same name, the **Polokwane Game Reserve** lies in the way of the Tropic of Capricorn; luckily, though, the 1300m plateau on which it sits nicely tempers the heat. The reserve safeguards the Pietersburg Plateau False Grasslands, including the open red-grass plains where the very uncommon Shortclawed Lark dips and swoops. One for the twitchers!

PERCY FYFE NR
NEAREST TOWN (ALSO DOORNDRAAI)
Mokopane
NEAREST AIRPORT (ALL PARKS)
Polokwane
SIZE
2500ha
FAUNA
1 Buffalo
2 Roan & Sable Antelope
3 Tsessebe
MAIN CONTACT DETAILS
(ALSO DOORNDRAAI)
015 290 7300
info@golimpopo.com
www.golimpopo.com
ACCOMMODATION INSIDE PARK
Youth Camp

ACCOMMODATION OUTSIDE PARK
(ALSO DOORNDRAAI)
Tourist Info, Mokopane
015 491 9740

DOORNDRAAI DAM NR
SIZE
7000ha
FAUNA
1 Tsessebe
2 Sable Antelope
3 Mountain Reedbuck

ACCOMMODATION INSIDE PARK
Campsite

POLOKWANE GR
NEAREST TOWN
Polokwane
SIZE
3200ha
FAUNA
1 White Rhino
2 Shortclawed Lark
MAIN CONTACT DETAILS
015 290 2010/2331
ACCOMMODATION INSIDE PARK
Union Campsite, chalets

ACCOMMODATION OUTSIDE PARK
Tourist Info, Polokwane
015 290 7300

SEASONAL INFORMATION

Gate opening times
Percy Fyfe NR:
08:00 – 18:00
Doorndraai Dam NR:
06:00 – 20:00
Polokwane GR:
07:00 – 18:00 (Sept to Mar)
08:00 – 17:00 (Apr to Aug)
Day visitors allowed

Top Map

To Mokopane

Mookgophong (Naboomspruit)

Atoom

Loubad

R101

HOEKBERGE

Sand

R33

31

Donkerpoort Dam

Thabo Kwena Crocodile Farm

i

9

Park Office

N1

Nyl

Nylsvlei Nature Reserve

Middelfontein

Shakama Game Farm

19

Modimolle (Nylstroom)

10

12

Rooiberg

Mabula Game Reserve

Limpopo

Strijdom House & Reformed Church

Km 20

Mi 10

14

Mabalingwe Game Reserve

R101

23

R516

33

Platrivier Dam

Hot Mineral Springs

19

KRANSKOP TOLL ROAD

Holme Park

36

R33

R516

26

Mabula

Bela-Bela (Warmbaths)

9

27

Tuinplaas

Leeupoort

Hetbad/Warmbaths NR

i

Blockhouse

Settlers

R516

To Marble Hall

Riet

Ngobi

R101

R576

Katsibane

Plat

Marapyane

Mogohlwaneng

Magareng

Gotwane

N

Bamokgoko

Loding

Borakalalo National Park

Bollantlokwe

Kwa-Phake

Phake

North West

Moratele

Klipvoor Dam

Pienaars

Kgomo-Kgomo

Pienaars

Masobe

Rust de Winter

Mdala NR

Tolwane

Tladistat

Tshwane

Pienaarsrivier

N1

Rantebeng

North West

Makapaanstad

Dertig

Rust de Winter Nature Reserve

Rust de Winter Dam

Legonyane

To Thabazimbi

To Pretoria

Bottom Map

GaMabotsha

To Makhado

Seshego

10

To Marken

N11

Wit

Mapela

21

Ga-Mashashane

Bloed

Polokwane (Pietersburg)

16

R518

Km 20

Mi 10

Polokwane GR

14

Mogalakwena

Rooisloot

Park Office

N1

Marabastad Fort

Rietkolk

Percy Fyfe Nature Reserve

Kuschke NR

Bakoni Malapa Northern Sotho Open-Air Museum

Sterkwater

21

Ana Trees

35

First Gold Refinery

31

R37

Lakalaka

Mahweleng

ZEBEDIELA

R101

Nuwe Smitsdorp

N

T

9

33

Gladdeklipkop

Sterk

Mokopane (Potgietersrus)

9

Makapaan Cave

R519

Mmadikiri

6

8

Chuene Crocodile Farm

6

12

16

Moorddrif Monument 1854

8

Nkumpi Dams

Louis Trichardt's Trek 1836

11

Doorndraai Dam

Park Office

19

Zebediela

11

Doorndraai Dam Nature Reserve

NYL

T

Drummondlea

25

Citrus Plantations

25

R518

Nuku Hut

N1

R518

Nkumpi

R519

22

R101

Haakdoring

N11

R519

To Mookgophong

To Roedtan

To Roedtan

To Glen Cowie

To Zeekoeigat

To Lebowakgomo

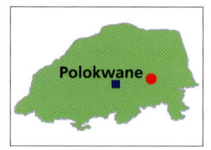

Selati, Hans Merensky & Ndzalama Reserves

Selati Game Reserve, another conservancy formed by 15-odd owners and situated north of the Olifants River, and Modjadji Nature Reserve are kingdoms in which cycads (and, in Modjadji, successive generations of the rain-making queen) reign. These "living fossils" are so called because scientists believe their sturdy trunks and dense sprouting green crowns dominated the landscape along with prehistoric dinosaurs about 150 million years ago. They bear cones, some of which weigh up to 34kg! Selati's *Encephalartos dyerianus* occurs naturally nowhere else in the world, while Modjadji's palm forest of *Encephalartos transvenosus* is totally unique. In spite of **Hans Merensky Nature Reserve**'s tourist leanings – a *kraal* museum, an Aventura resort – its trails across dolerite rocky ridges, dams, woodlands and grasslands are inspiring. **Ndzalama Wildlife Reserve** – place of the "sacred rock" – invites you to commune with Nature in its rustic bushcamp of stone and Mopane wood tucked into granite rock.

SELATI GR
NEAREST TOWN
Phalaborwa
NEAREST AIRPORT (ALL PARKS)
Phalaborwa
SIZE
30 000ha
FAUNA
1   White Rhino
2   Leopard
3   Cheetah
MAIN CONTACT DETAILS (ALL PARKS)
015 290 7300
www.golimpopo.com
ACCOMMODATION INSIDE PARK
Campsite
ACCOMMODATION OUTSIDE PARK
Tourist Info, Phalaborwa
015 781 0111

HANS MERENSKY NR
NEAREST TOWN (ALSO NDZALAMA)
Gravelotte
SIZE
5182ha
FAUNA
1   Kudu
2   Impala
3   Hippopotamus

ACCOMMODATION INSIDE PARK
Aventura Eiland Resort
015 386 8000
ACCOMMODATION OUTSIDE PARK
(ALSO NDZALAMA)
Tourist Info, Gravelotte
015 780 6300
NDZALAMA WILDLIFE RESERVE
SIZE
8000ha
FAUNA
1   African Elephant
2   White Rhino
ACCOMMODATION INSIDE PARK
Ndzalama Lodge, Shanatsi & Leopard Bushcamps

SEASONAL INFORMATION
Gate opening times
Selati GR:
06:00 – 18:00
Day visitors allowed
Hans Merensky NR:
07:30 – 18:00
Day visitors allowed
Ndzalama:
Open 24 hours
No day visitors allowed

Wonderkop & Maleboch Nature Reserves

Wonderkop Nature Reserve is a core part of the Waterberg Biosphere, although a little less developed than some. In a similar way, **Maleboch Nature Reserve** (like Blouberg below) has powerful potential to eventually join with other small game ranches in a conservancy-style preserve where fences fall and wild animals roam freely for grazing. Most of these reserves and ranches, in turn, fit into the greater Soutpansberg conservation area, and parks boards are hard at work to keep them protected. Key to it all is the Sourveld grass of the bushveld, not much favoured by cattle and sheep as pasture, but perfect for wildlife. This is a land of euphorbias and Cabbage Trees, and of bristling acacias – Spike- and Hook-thorn, Flame and Sweet Thorn.

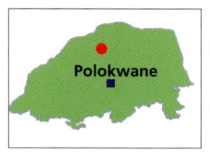

Soutpansberg
Blouberg & Langjan Nature Reserves

The dramatic uplands of the **Soutpansberg**, a richly potential area dubbed recently the "Golden Horseshoe", cuts a broad west-east swathe across the Limpopo landscape. A great proportion is made up of privately owned ranches and game and nature reserves, and the Waterberg Biosphere is a part of it. In the west of the Soutpansberg, at its foot, lie the broad salt pans that give the range its name. Its varied habitats allow for great contrasts. Kalahari-type veld and russet sand dunes in **Langjan Nature Reserve** nurture a naturally occurring herd of Gemsbok, while the rocky mountain cliffs of **Blouberg Nature Reserve** sustain a Cape Vulture breeding colony. Also cared for here are captive owls, raptors and vultures beyond rehabilitation.

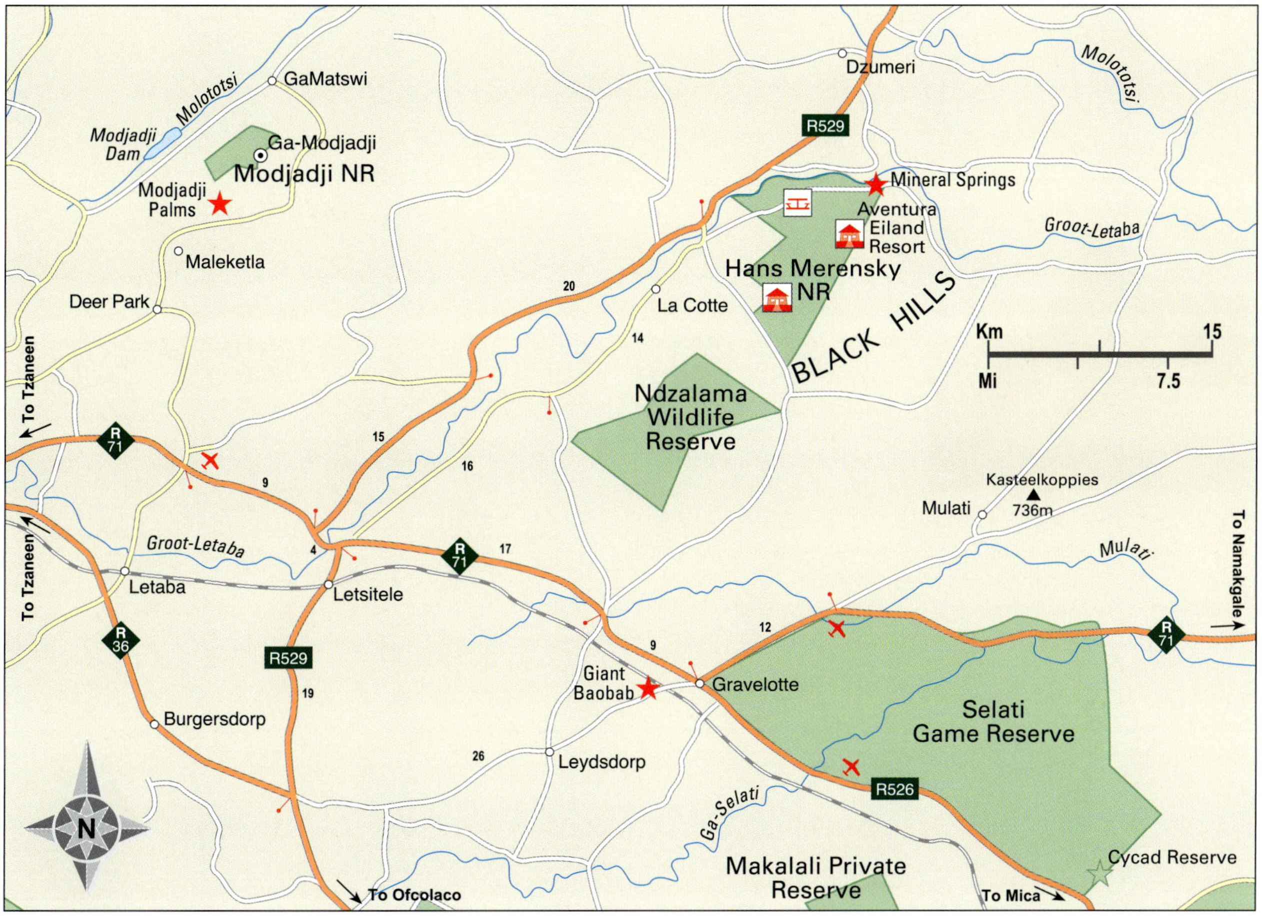

Map (top)

GaMatswi • Dzumeri • Molototsi • R529 • Molototsi

Modjadji Dam • Ga-Modjadji • Modjadji NR • Mineral Springs • Aventura Eiland Resort • Hans Merensky NR • Groot-Letaba

Modjadji Palms • Maleketla • La Cotte • BLACK HILLS

Deer Park • 20 • 14 • Ndzalama Wildlife Reserve

Km 15 / Mi 7.5

To Tzaneen • R71 • 9 • 15 • 16 • Kasteelkoppies 736m • Mulati • To Namakgale

To Tzaneen • Groot-Letaba • Letaba • Letsitele • R71 • 17 • 4 • Mulati • R71

R36 • R529 • 19 • 9 • 12 • Selati Game Reserve

Burgersdorp • Giant Baobab • Gravelotte • 26 • Leydsdorp • R526 • Cycad Reserve

N • Ga-Selati • Makalali Private Reserve • To Mica

To Ofcolaco

Left text column

WONDERKOP NR
NEAREST TOWN (BOTH PARKS)
Polokwane

NEAREST AIRPORT (BOTH PARKS)
Polokwane

SIZE
16 100ha

FAUNA/FLORA (BOTH PARKS)
1 Roan Antelope
2 Cape Vulture
3 Black (Verreaux's) Eagle
4 Euphorbia sp.
5 Cabbage Tree

MAIN CONTACT DETAILS
(BOTH PARKS)
015 290 7300
www.golimpopo.com

ACCOMMODATION INSIDE PARK
(BOTH PARKS)
None

ACCOMMODATION OUTSIDE PARK
(BOTH PARKS)
Tourist Info, Polokwane
015 290 7300

MALEBOCH NR
SIZE
5000ha

SEASONAL INFORMATION

Gate opening times
Wonderkop NR:
Sunrise to sunset
Maleboch NR:
06:00 – 18:00
Day visitors not allowed

To Tom Burke • R561 • Mogalakwena • Maleboch NR • My Darling • Vergelegen • Blouberg • 963m • Glen Alpine Dam • Driekoppies • Baltimore • Woudkop • N • To Mogwadi • Wonderkop NR • Km 20 / Mi 10 • N11 • R561 • Steilwater • Mokodung • To Marken • To Mokopane

---

Lower left text column

BLOUBERG NR
NEAREST TOWN (BOTH PARKS)
Makhado

NEAREST AIRPORT (BOTH PARKS)
Polokwane

SIZE
9360ha

AVIFAUNA
1 Cape Vulture

MAIN CONTACT DETAILS
(BOTH PARKS)
015 290 7300

ACCOMMODATION INSIDE PARK
Tamboti Bushcamp, chalets, campsite

ACCOMMODATION OUTSIDE PARK
(BOTH PARKS)
Tourist Info, Makhado
015 516 3415

LANGJAN NR
SIZE
4500ha

FAUNA
1 Gemsbok

ACCOMMODATION INSIDE PARK
None

SEASONAL INFORMATION

Gate opening times
Blouberg NR:
07:30 – 16:00
Day visitors allowed
Langjan NR:
07:30 – 16:00
Day visitors allowed

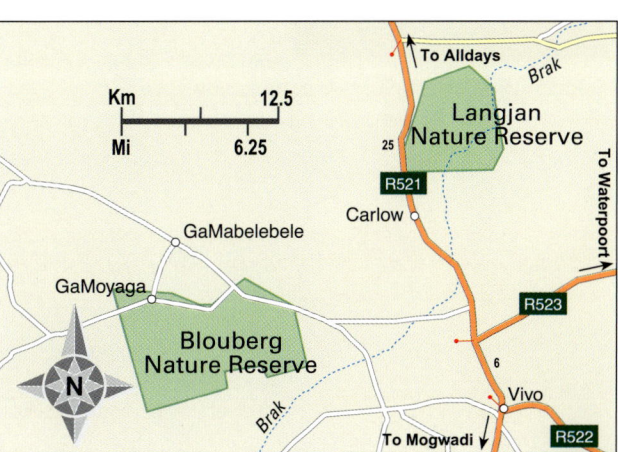

To Alldays • Brak • Langjan Nature Reserve • Km 12.5 / Mi 6.25 • 25 • To Waterpoort • R521 • GaMabelebele • Carlow • GaMoyaga • N • R523 • Blouberg Nature Reserve • 6 • Vivo • Brak • To Mogwadi • R522

Mafikeng

Pilanesberg National Park,
Metani Game Ranch & Vaalkop Dam Nature Reserve

Pilanesberg's unique feature has got to be its siting on an extinct volcanic crater. Concentric rings of broken hills rise 600m above the great grassland expanses, the result some 1300 million years ago of molten lava forging its way up through the earth's crust. Thanks in part to Operation Genesis, at the time the largest game translocation undertaken in the world, Pilanesberg today boasts a complement of virtually every mammal of Southern Africa. Neighbouring **Metani Game Ranch** encourages walking or mountainbiking among its brood of wild animals and feathered friends, and its Nyala camp gets guests eye to eye with the grand white-striped antelope it's named after. Quadbikes offer a noisy, dusty, bumpy alternative to the quiet charms of Nature. **Vaalkop dam** shares its loyalty among anglers, boating fraternity and naturalists come to spot bushveld game in the reserve. A bird sanctuary is open only to those who book ahead.

PILANESBERG NP
NEAREST TOWN (ALL PARKS)
Rustenburg

NEAREST AIRPORT (ALL PARKS)
Pilanesberg

SIZE
55 000ha

FAUNA
1 African Elephant
2 Black & White Rhino
3 Lion
4 Leopard
5 Hippopotamus

MAIN CONTACT DETAILS
014 555 5351/5/6/7
www.parksnorthwest.co.za

ACCOMMODATION INSIDE PARK
Kwa Maritane, Tshukudu, Bakubung, Manyane, Bakgatla
🛏 🏕 ⛽ 🅧

ACCOMMODATION OUTSIDE PARK
(ALL PARKS)
Tourist Info, Rustenburg
014 597 0904

METANI GAME RANCH
SIZE
1000ha

FAUNA
1 Gemsbok
2 Kudu
3 Small Antelope sp.

MAIN CONTACT DETAILS
014 573 3133

ACCOMMODATION INSIDE PARK
Metani Tented Lodge
🏕 🅧

VAALKOP DAM NR
SIZE
3996ha

FAUNA
1 White Rhino
2 Buffalo
3 Giraffe

MAIN CONTACT DETAILS
083 991 0028, 018 397 1500

ACCOMMODATION INSIDE PARK
Campsite
🏕 ⛽

SEASONAL INFORMATION

Gate opening times
Pilanesberg NP:
06:00 – 18:30 (Mar & Apr)
06:30 – 18:00 (May to Sept)
06:00 – 18:30 (Sept & Oct)
05:30 – 19:00 (Nov to Feb)
Metani Game Ranch:
Sunrise to sunset
Vaalkop Dam NR:
05:30 – 18:30

Mafikeng

Magaliesberg Nature Area
(Kgaswane Mountain Reserve, Mountain Sanctuary Park) & Hartbeespoort Dam Nature Reserve

The **Magaliesberg** mountain range, dating back 2400 million years, is listed as one of the oldest in the world. Nature sanctuaries abound in and around its chaotic jumble of shattered quartzite boulders softened by refreshingly green wooded ravines. **Kgaswane Mountain Reserve** is dominated by the Magaliesberg's largest vlei, a catchment area at the headwaters of the Hex River. Hiking trails, one with natural pools to splash about in, traverse a mix of Sour Bushveld, rocky plateau and broad valley basin. In the **Mountain Sanctuary Park**, hikers stick to trails or wander off at whim into the wilderness. There are balancing boulder formations to clamber over, wriggle through or shelter under and crystal-watered mountain hollows beside tinkling streams. The change of pace at **Hartbeespoort Dam Nature Reserve** hurtles you into the midst of parasailers, windsurfers and jet-skiers. Animal life is more of the "canned variety" – aquarium, zoo or snake park. You can take your pick.

KGASWANE MOUNTAIN RESERVE
NEAREST TOWN
(ALSO MOUNTAIN SANCTUARY PARK)
Rustenburg

NEAREST AIRPORT (ALL PARKS)
Johannesburg International

SIZE
4257ha

FAUNA
1 Kudu
2 Klipspringer
3 Duiker

MAIN CONTACT DETAILS
014 533 2050, 018 397 1500

ACCOMMODATION INSIDE PARK
Campsite, trail huts
🛏 🏕 ⛽ 🅧

ACCOMMODATION OUTSIDE PARK
(ALSO MOUNTAIN SANCTUARY PARK)
Tourist Info, Rustenburg
014 597 0904

MOUNTAIN SANCTUARY PARK
SIZE
1200ha

FAUNA
1 Zebra
2 Klipspringer
3 Duiker

MAIN CONTACT DETAILS
014 534 0114

ACCOMMODATION INSIDE PARK
Campsite, chalets, log cabins
🛏 🏕 ⛽ 🅧

HARTBEESPOORT DAM NR
NEAREST TOWN
Pretoria

SIZE
1620ha

AVIFAUNA
1 Cape Vulture

MAIN CONTACT DETAILS
012 253 1567, 012 318 9559

ACCOMMODATION INSIDE PARK
Campsite, chalets, cottages, guesthouses, lodges, hotels
🛏 🏕 ⛽ 🅧

ACCOMMODATION OUTSIDE PARK
012 337 4430
www.tshwane.gov.za

SEASONAL INFORMATION

Gate opening times
Kgaswane Mountain Reserve:
05:30 – 19:00 (summer)
06:00 – 18:30 (winter)
Mountain Sanctuary Park:
08:00 – 18:30 (1 Nov to 30 Apr)
08:00 – 17:30 (1 May to 31 Oct)
Hartbeespoort Dam NR:
06:00 – 18:00 (controlled areas)
Open 24 hours elsewhere

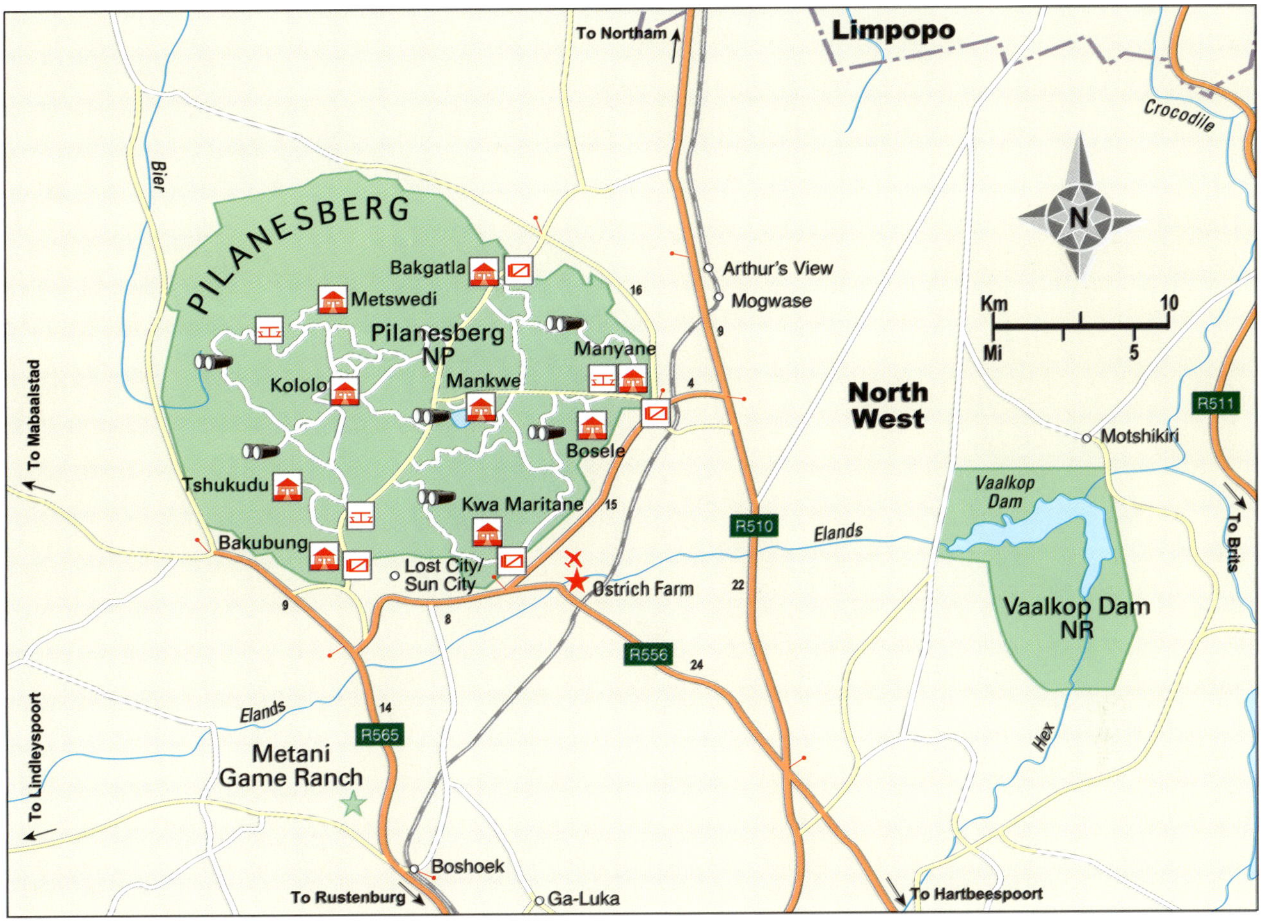

Map 1 (Pilanesberg / North West)

To Northam

Limpopo

Crocodile

PILANESBERG

Bakgatla
Metswedi
Pilanesberg NP
Manyane
Kololo
Mankwe
Bosele
Tshukudu
Kwa Maritane
Bakubung
Lost City/Sun City
Ostrich Farm

Arthur's View
Mogwase

North West

Motshikiri

Km 10
Mi 5

N

R511

To Brits

Vaalkop Dam

Vaalkop Dam NR

Elands
R510
R556

Hex

To Mabaalstad
To Lindleysport

Bier

Elands
R565

Metani Game Ranch

Boshoek
Ga-Luka
To Rustenburg
To Hartbeespoort

16
9
4
15
22
24
14
9
8

Map 2 (Rustenburg / Magaliesberg / Gauteng)

To Beestekraal

Boshoek
Kedar Lodge
Ga-Luka
Phokeng
Boekenhoutfontein 1873
Kgalestad
North West
Ananda
Rustenburg
Tabak
Norite
Marikana
Maroelakop
Sonop
Brits
De Wildt Cheetah Research Centre
Vredesboom
Ga-Rankuwa
Morula Sun
Werkmetlus
Pansdrif
Mamagoleskraal
Bethanie

Roodekopjes Dam
Hex
R510
Rooiwal
Bospoort Dam
R556
R511

Kgaswane Mountain Reserve
Bush Willows
Bergheim
Westwinds
ATKV
Barnardsvlei
Magaliesberg Nature Area
Magaliespark
Cable Way
Aquarium
MAGALIES TOLL ROAD
Hartbeespoort Dam
Hartbeespoort Dam NR
Wigwam Hotel
Aasvoëlkraans
Heldina
Mountain Sanctuary Park
Plumari Africa Reserve
Hekpoort
Hartebeeshoek Tracking Station
Cradle of Humankind (World Heritage Site)
Diepsloot NR
Sekelele
Maanhaarrand
Thorndale
De Hoek
Old Fort
Gauteng
Middelaagte
Boons
Bergbries
Wind in The Willows
Magaliesberg
Greensleeves
Sterkfontein Caves
Old Kromdraai Gold Mine
Randburg
Krugersdorp GR
Krugersdorp
Battery
Roodepoort

N4
R52
R30
R24
R509
R500
R24
R563
R560
R511
R552
R566
R513
R514
N4
N14

Mooi

To Swartruggens
To Derby
To Ventersdorp
To Sandton
To Centurion
To Atteridgeville

Km 10
Mi 5

N

Madikwe Game Reserve

What was once a great expanse of overgrazed farmland is today one of South Africa's top five largest wildlife reserves. The transformation started with what's credited as the largest ever translocation of game, when Operation Phoenix successfully transferred 10,000 animals (27 different species) to Madikwe. The land has since been restored to its natural wild state, and visitors are cosseted by skilled game rangers who make every attempt at bringing them within close proximity to not only the Big Five, but also Wild Dog, Sable Antelope and (if you're lucky) Cheetah. Among the plethora of luxury lodges, Jaci's Safari Lodge gets a great thumbs up. The open-plan main complex, on the banks of the Marico River, curves around a giant anthill, while eight stone-and-thatch rooms with cool canvas walls feature their own wooden viewing decks. Best of all in every room is the hand-hewn rock bath to wallow in!

MADIKWE GAME RESERVE
NEAREST TOWN
Zeerust

NEAREST AIRPORT
Johannesburg International

SIZE
75 000ha

FAUNA
1   African Elephant
2   Black & White Rhino
3   Buffalo
4   Lion
5   Cheetah
6   Sable Antelope
7   Spotted Hyena
8   Wild Dog

MAIN CONTACT DETAILS
018 3672 ask for 2411
083 629 8282
madikweadmin@wol.co.za
www.parksnorthwest.co.za

ACCOMMODATION INSIDE PARK
Tau Game Lodge: 018 385 9027
Mosetlha Bush Camp: 011 444 9345
Madikwe River Lodge: 014 778 9000
Kukama Lodge: 011 805 4888
Madikwe Hills: 083 658 8763
Royal Madikwe Lodge: 082 568 8867
Jaci's Safari Lodge: 083 700 2071

ACCOMMODATION OUTSIDE PARK
Tourist Info, Zeerust
018 642 1081 ext 215

SEASONAL INFORMATION

Gate opening times
Sunrise to sunset
Day visitors not allowed

Bloemhof Dam & SA Lombard Nature Reserves

The freshwater fishing is so good on the endless blue expanse of the **Bloemhof dam** fed by the Vaal River that it plays host every year to prestigious international and national angling championships. The nature reserve about its shores is thornveld country, rolling out wide, open plains of Kalahari scrub that make the viewing of browsers and grazers a cinch. Quirky ostriches are also here, throwing lazy long-lashed looks your way as you pass by. The **SA Lombard Nature Reserve**, distinctive in its small sector of open Kalahari grassland unfolding across a flood plain, claims to be one of the earliest wildlife conservation research centres in South Africa. A recovery programme here, using a small game stock of Black Wildebeest, apparently has saved this animal from extinction in its natural habitat. Black Wildebeest have since been translocated to reserves throughout South Africa.

BLOEMHOF DAM NR
NEAREST TOWN (BOTH PARKS)
Bloemhof

NEAREST AIRPORT (BOTH PARKS)
Kimberley

SIZE
7800ha (reserve)
25 000ha (dam area)

FAUNA
1   Black Wildebeest
2   Eland
3   Gemsbok
4   Zebra
5   Black-backed Jackal
6   Springbok
7   Rare Waterbird sp.
8   Ostrich

MAIN CONTACT DETAILS
053 433 1706
bloemhofdam@cybertrade.co.za
www.tourismnorthwest.co.za

ACCOMMODATION INSIDE PARK
Group Camp Complex, thatched safari camp, chalets, campsite, hunting camp

ACCOMMODATION OUTSIDE PARK
(BOTH PARKS)
Tourist Info, Bloemhof
053 433 1017
www.bloemhofonline.co.za

SA LOMBARD NR
SIZE
3663ha

FAUNA
1   Black Wildebeest
2   Red Hartebeest
3   Burchell's Zebra
4   Springbok

MAIN CONTACT DETAILS
053 433 1953

ACCOMMODATION INSIDE PARK
None

SEASONAL INFORMATION

Bloemhof Dam NR:
08:00 – 18:00
Day visitors allowed
SA Lombard NR:
No entry at present

Map 1 (Top)

Kgatleng

Medipane

To Mochudi

BOTSWANA

D316

Sikwane

Marico

Derdepoort

To Sentrum

GABORONE

18

Kopfontein Gate

15

Limpopo

R49

Tau Game Lodge

Madikwe Game Reserve

Madikwe River Lodge

Kaya se put

35

23

Sesobe Mission

1378m

Chonuane 1846-1847

1300m

Zwingli

1229m

1157m

Molatedi Dam

North West

18

Brakfontein

1035m

R49

SOUTH AFRICA

N

Km

20

Mi

10

Nietverdiend

To Zeerust

Silkaatskop Monument

Silkaatskop

Map 2 (Bottom)

To Wolmaransstad

To Makwassie

R502

15

Makwassie

Koosfontein

To Schweizer-Reneke

North West

N12

Boskuil

Makwassie

R505

Bamboes

43

Kingswood

46

Vaal

R34

Bloemhof Dam Nature Reserve

SA Lombard Nature Reserve

Bloemhof Dam

Beyers Pieterse Memorial

To Christiana

Bloemhof

R59

To Bothaville

N12

Vaal

Middeldeel

To Wesselsbron

Sandveld Nature Reserve

38

Free State

35

N

Km

20

Mi

10

Groenvlei

R34

Hoopstad

R59

R700

Vet

To Hertzogville

To Bultfontein

Marico Bosveld Nature Reserve & Botsalano Game Reserve

The focus of the **Marico Bosveld Nature Reserve** is its dam on the Groot Marico River, which, nature-viewing aside, makes for great rosy-hued sunset cruises. The setting is bushveld savannah interspersed with dolomite rock and Magaliesberg quartzite. Quite intriguing – and of great conservation significance due to its uniqueness – is the fact that the Marico River's source is a dolomitic "eye", a spring fed from groundwater that wells up through fractures in the underlying dolomite. **Botsalano Game Reserve**'s Kalahari thornveld of acacia and karee has made it a formidably successful breeding territory for White Rhino and antelope species, which go to the stocking of reserves throughout the province. Similar vegetation prevailing along the flood plain and along the riverbanks of the Pienaarsriver yields exciting birdlife, some in explosions of colour – try Blue Waxbill, Violet-eared Waxbill, Jameson's Firefinch and Greenwinged Pytilia for size. . .er. . .hue.

MARICO BOSVELD NR
NEAREST TOWN
Zeerust
NEAREST AIRPORT (BOTH PARKS)
Mafikeng
SIZE
2072ha
FAUNA
1 Bushbuck
2 Waterbird sp.
MAIN CONTACT DETAILS
083 2722 958
info@marico.co.za
www.marico.co.za
ACCOMMODATION INSIDE PARK
Campsite
🛖 📷
ACCOMMODATION OUTSIDE PARK
Tourist Info, Zeerust
018 642 1081 ext 215

BOTSALANO GAME RESERVE
NEAREST TOWN
Groot-Marico
SIZE
5800ha
FAUNA/FLORA
1 White Rhino
2 Giraffe
3 Gemsbok
4 Kudu

5 Eland
6 Red Hartebeest
7 Waterbuck
8 Springbok
9 Warthog
10 Acacia sp.
MAIN CONTACT DETAILS
018 386 2433, 018 397 1500
www.tourismnorthwest.co.za
ACCOMMODATION INSIDE PARK
Mogobi Tented Camp, safari bush camps, campsite
🛖 📷
ACCOMMODATION OUTSIDE PARK
Tourist Info, Groot-Marico
014 503 0085, 083 272 2958
info@marico.co.za

SEASONAL INFORMATION
Gate opening times
Marico Bosveld NR:
Sunrise to sunset
Botsalano GR:
07:30 – 17:00 (Mon to Fri)
06:30 – 18:30 (Sat to Sun)
Day visitors allowed

Lichtenburg Game Breeding Centre

This breeding centre is a project the National Zoological Gardens of South Africa (with headquarters in Pretoria) has tucked firmly under its belt. Its main aim – to strengthen the National Zoo's breeding of endangered species and to support its own animal populations. At the entrance area's dams, marshes and reedbeds, visitors are able to marvel at the collection of exotic mammals in reasonably natural surrounds. Some of the more unusual are the rare Pygmy Hippopotamus, seen in the wetland area, Arabian Oryx in breeding enclosures, North African Addax (say, what?!), Przewalski's Wild Horse from Mongolia and romantic-looking antlered deer from India and Southeast Asia. Talking indigenous species, you can see the rare and extremely elegant Black-faced Impala, today limited only to the northern parts of Namibia and south-western Angola. An experienced guide will take visitors on a night drive through the breeding centre.

LICHTENBURG GAME BREEDING CENTRE
NEAREST TOWN
Lichtenburg
NEAREST AIRPORT
Mafikeng
SIZE
4500ha
FAUNA
1 Axis Deer
2 Red Forest Buffalo
3 Pygmy Hippopotamus
4 Arabian Oryx
5 Gemsbok
6 Aardvark
7 Aardwolf
8 Springbok
9 Black-faced Impala
10 Wild Horse
11 Suricate
12 Warthog
MAIN CONTACT DETAILS
018 632 2818
www.ltxgamebreedingcentre.co.za
ACCOMMODATION INSIDE PARK
Guesthouse, 2 self-contained units, campsite
🛏 🛖 📷
ACCOMMODATION OUTSIDE PARK
Tourist Info, Mafikeng
018 381 3155/6

SEASONAL INFORMATION
08:00 – 16:00 (Mon to Fri)
08:00 – 18:00 (weekends/holidays)

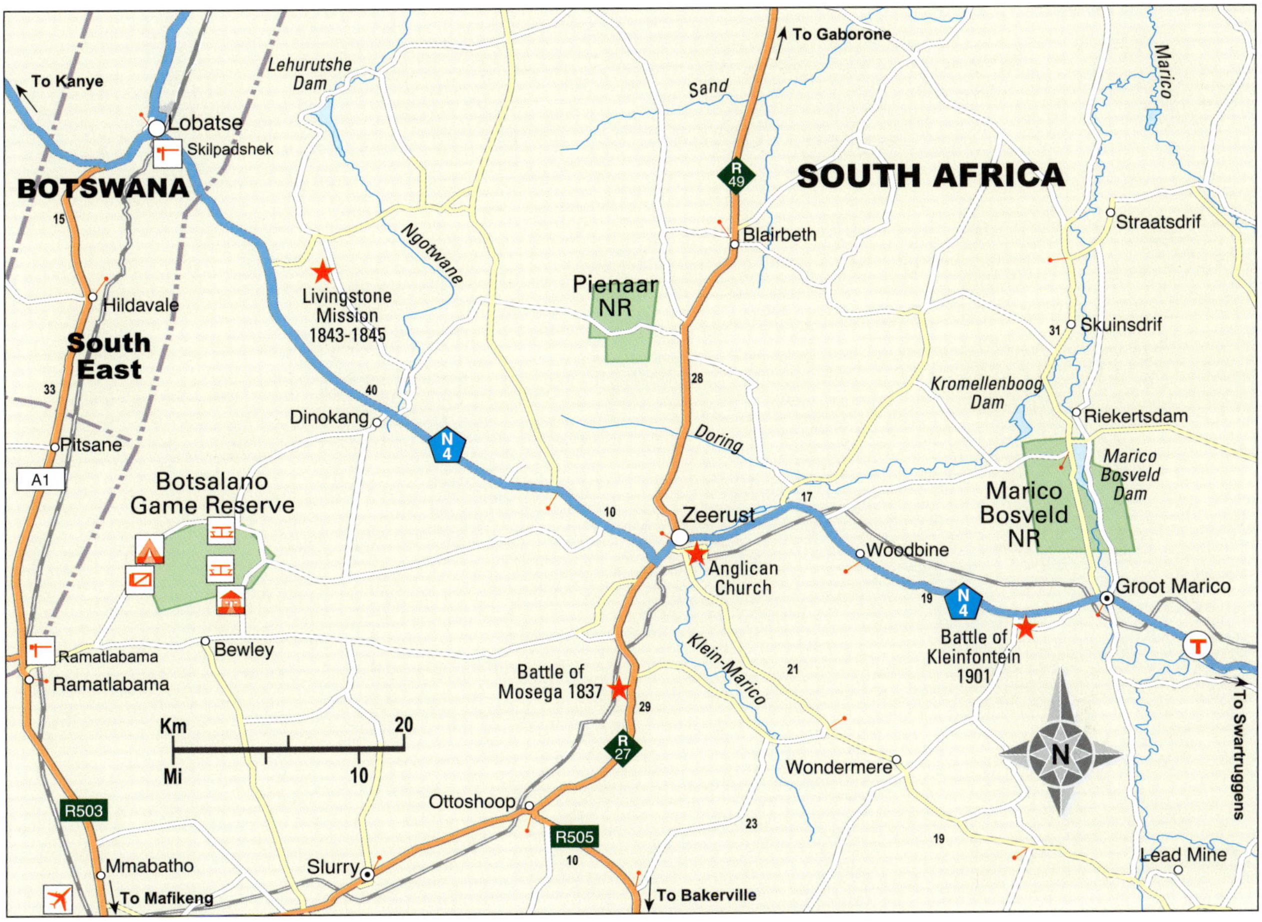

Map 1 — Botswana / South Africa border region

To Kanye

BOTSWANA

Lobatse
Skilpadshek

Lehurutshe Dam

Sand

To Gaborone

SOUTH AFRICA

R49

Marico

Straatsdrif

15

Hildavale

Ngotwane

Livingstone Mission 1843-1845

Blairbeth

Pienaar NR

Skuinsdrif

31

South East

33

40

Dinokang

N4

Kromellenboog Dam

Riekertsdam

Pitsane

A1

Botsalano Game Reserve

Doring

28

Marico Bosveld Dam

Marico Bosveld NR

Zeerust

17

10

Woodbine

Bewley

Anglican Church

Klein-Marico

19

N4

Groot Marico

Ramatlabama

Battle of Kleinfontein 1901

Ramatlabama

Battle of Mosega 1837

29

21

To Swartruggens

Km 20

R27

Mi 10

Wondermere

N

R503

Ottoshoop

23

19

Lead Mine

Mmabatho

Slurry

R505

10

To Mafikeng

To Bakerville

Map 2 — Lichtenburg Game Breeding Centre

To Bakerville

Km 5

Mi 2.5

Breeding Camps

Lichtenburg Game Breeding Centre

R505

Delwers Road

No Entry

Drinking Hole

Vulture Restaurant

Springbok Lane

Meerkat Road

To Mafikeng

N

Wildebeest Dr.

Cheetah Camp

To Koster

R52

R503

8

Lichtenburg

R505

To Gerdau

Barberspan Bird Sanctuary

This great flat expanse of pans, fed intermittently by the Harts River, acts as a crucial refuge for huge numbers of waterbirds that descend during the rain-free dry season. As one of the largest waterfowl and migratory bird sanctuaries in Southern Africa (365 species, they say!), it's no surprise then that it's also a Ramsar wetland. The surrounding undulating grassland and cultivated fields ensure the pans are largely undisturbed, so birders have a field day, hunkered down in the bird hides or gliding across the mirror surface of the pans in their rowboats or canoes (southern sector only). It appears that Barberspan is the only spot in South Africa where the Pintail Duck has been recorded.

Faan Meintjies Nature Reserve

When 12 Voortrekker families settled on the banks of the Schoonspruit in 1837, J de Clerq became the first magistrate – and the fledgling town of Klerksdorp inherited its name. Later, the Johan Neser dam was built on the Schoonspruit River, and today its nature reserve offers a calming diversion from humdrum urban life, while its waters entice boatsmen and fishermen to come out and play. Outside Klerksdorp, the acacia-thorn and koppie-dotted grassveld of the Faan Meintjies Nature Reserve is inhabited by no less than White Rhino, and seldom-seen but fascinating Aardwolf and Aardvark. Birdwatchers will comfortably crisscross the reserve in a day, and if they stay over, they could be rewarded with the magical call of a Barn or Giant Eagle Owl.

Borakalalo National Park

The Moretele River runs through an unusually beautiful sector of Kalahari thornveld and woodland in this national park, its riverine-forested banks brought to a halt by the Klipvoor dam. Angling on both dam and river is considered to be amongst the finest in the country with promises of carp, bream, tilapia and barbel; wilier fishermen could land a *Makriel* or yellowfish. Alluring to day visitors are the shady picnic nooks along the waterside and an established road network for tracking down wildlife (on wheels, that is). For those who prefer not to get too comfortable, there are also walking trails along which visitors can stalk their game. Birdlife is flamboyant – Lilacbreasted Roller, Crimsonbreasted Shrike and Redbilled Buffalo Weaver, for starters.

Molopo Nature Reserve

The arid savannah character of this remote reserve, with its undulating Kalahari grasslands and thornveld dunes, allows visitors to relish true wilderness. Of foremost interest is the reserve's role as part of a one-million-hectare interprovincial raptor conservancy. Breeding pairs of Bateleur, Tawny and Marshall Eagles exude a majestic presence; Whitebacked and Lappetfaced Vultures, the latter clearly recognisable by their gaudy crimson-purple heads, are prolific – often congregating on the ground in sociable clusters. And bird-lovers who adore the scholarly visage of owls and the mystical aura they project will hold their breath for the African Scops, Whitefaced and Giant Eagle Owls. Within the park, too, is the fossilised Phepane riverbed which, many millions of years ago, carried huge volumes of water.

BARBERSPAN BIRD SANCTUARY

NEAREST TOWN
Delareyville

NEAREST AIRPORT
Mafikeng

SIZE
2000ha

FAUNA/AVIFAUNA
1 Red Hartebeest
2 Zebra
3 Blesbok
4 Springbok
5 Greater & Lesser Flamingo
6 Pintail Duck
7 Egret sp.
8 Ibis sp.

MAIN CONTACT DETAILS
053 948 1854
barbersp@lantic.net

ACCOMMODATION INSIDE PARK
Weaver's Nest Guesthouse, campsite

ACCOMMODATION OUTSIDE PARK
Tourist Info, Delareyville
053 948 0900

SEASONAL INFORMATION

Gate opening times
06:00 – 21:00
Day visitors allowed

FAAN MEINTJIES NR

NEAREST TOWN
Klerksdorp

NEAREST AIRPORT
Johannesburg International

SIZE
1000ha

FAUNA
1 White Rhino
2 Giraffe
3 Sable Antelope
4 Eland
5 Aardvark
6 Aardwolf
7 Barn & Giant Eagle Owl
8 Mountain Chat
9 Cape Robin
10 Acacia sp.

MAIN CONTACT DETAILS
018 464 1386, 018 462 2211

ACCOMMODATION INSIDE PARK
Chalets, campsite

ACCOMMODATION OUTSIDE PARK
Tourist Info, Klerksdorp
018 464 2229

SEASONAL INFORMATION

Gate opening times
08:00 – 18:00
Day visitors allowed

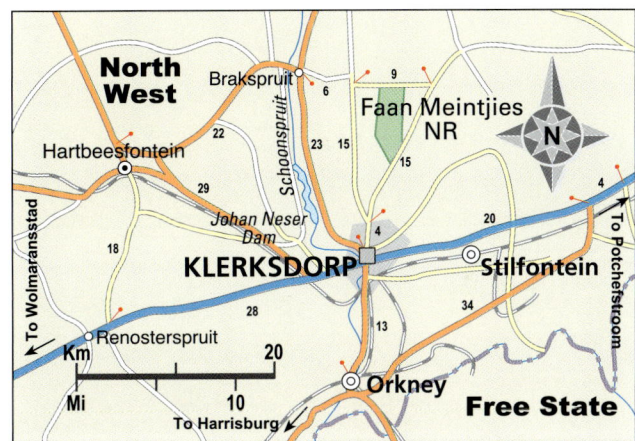

BORAKALALO NP

NEAREST TOWN
Brits

NEAREST AIRPORT
Pilanesberg

SIZE
13 000ha

FAUNA/AVIFAUNA
1 White Rhino
2 Giraffe
3 Leopard
4 Antelope sp.
5 Eagle sp.
6 Lilacbreasted Roller
7 Crimsonbreasted Shrike
8 Redbilled Buffalo Weaver

MAIN CONTACT DETAILS
012 729 1008

ACCOMMODATION INSIDE PARK
Moretele & Phudufudu Camps,
Pitjane Fishing Camp, campsite

SEASONAL INFORMATION

Gate opening times
07:00 – 16:30 (Mon to Thurs)
07:30 – 19:00 (Fri to Sat)
07:30 – 15:30 (Sun)
Day visitors allowed

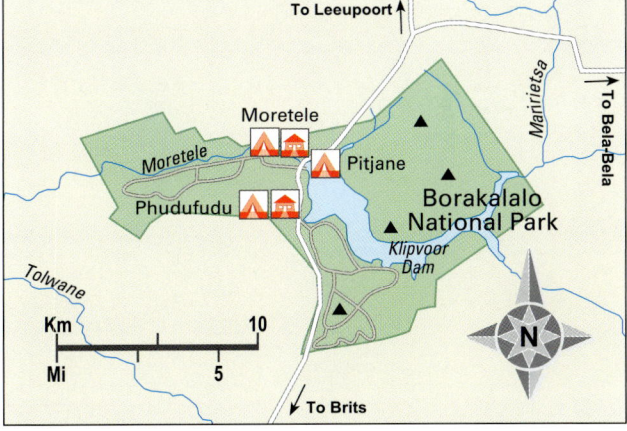

MOLOPO NR

NEAREST TOWN
Vryburg

NEAREST AIRPORT
Mafikeng

SIZE
24 000ha

FAUNA
1 Blue Wildebeest
2 Cheetah
3 Gemsbok
4 Red Hartebeest
5 Kudu
6 Eland
7 Burchell's Zebra
8 Impala
9 Springbok
10 Bateleur, Tawny & Marshal Eagle
11 Whitebacked & Lappedfaced Vulture
12 African Scops & Giant Eagle Owl

MAIN CONTACT DETAILS
072 172 1688, 082 925 7246

ACCOMMODATION INSIDE PARK
Motopi & Phiri Camps, campsite

ACCOMMODATION OUTSIDE PARK
Tourist Info, Vryburg
053 927 0681

SEASONAL INFORMATION

Gate opening times
Sunrise to sunset
Day visitors allowed

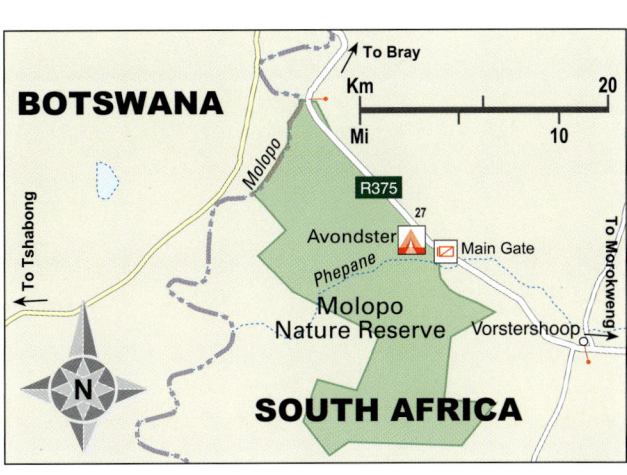

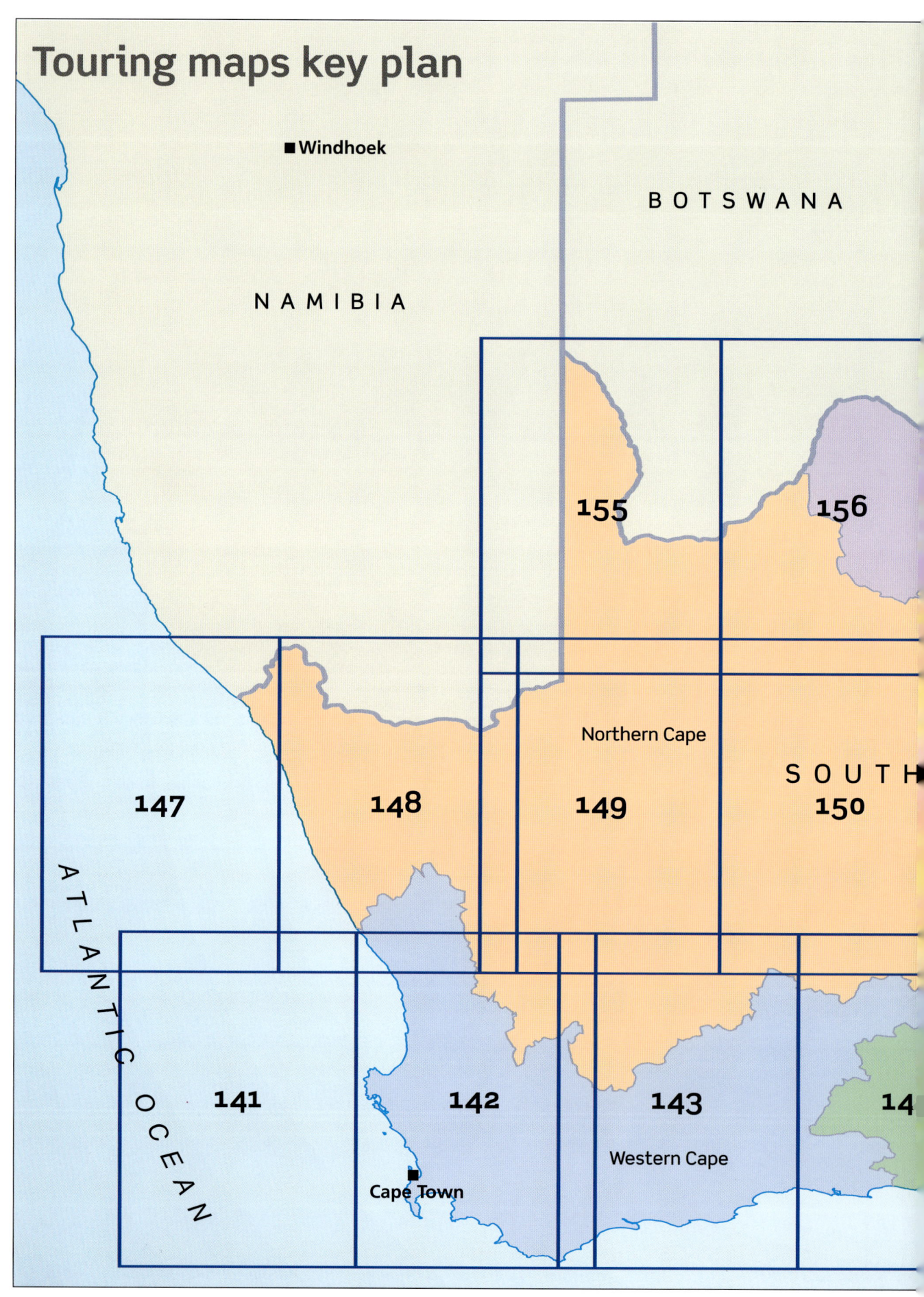

Touring maps key plan

■ Windhoek

BOTSWANA

NAMIBIA

155

156

Northern Cape

147

148

149

SOUTH

150

ATLANTIC OCEAN

141

142

143

14

Western Cape

Cape Town

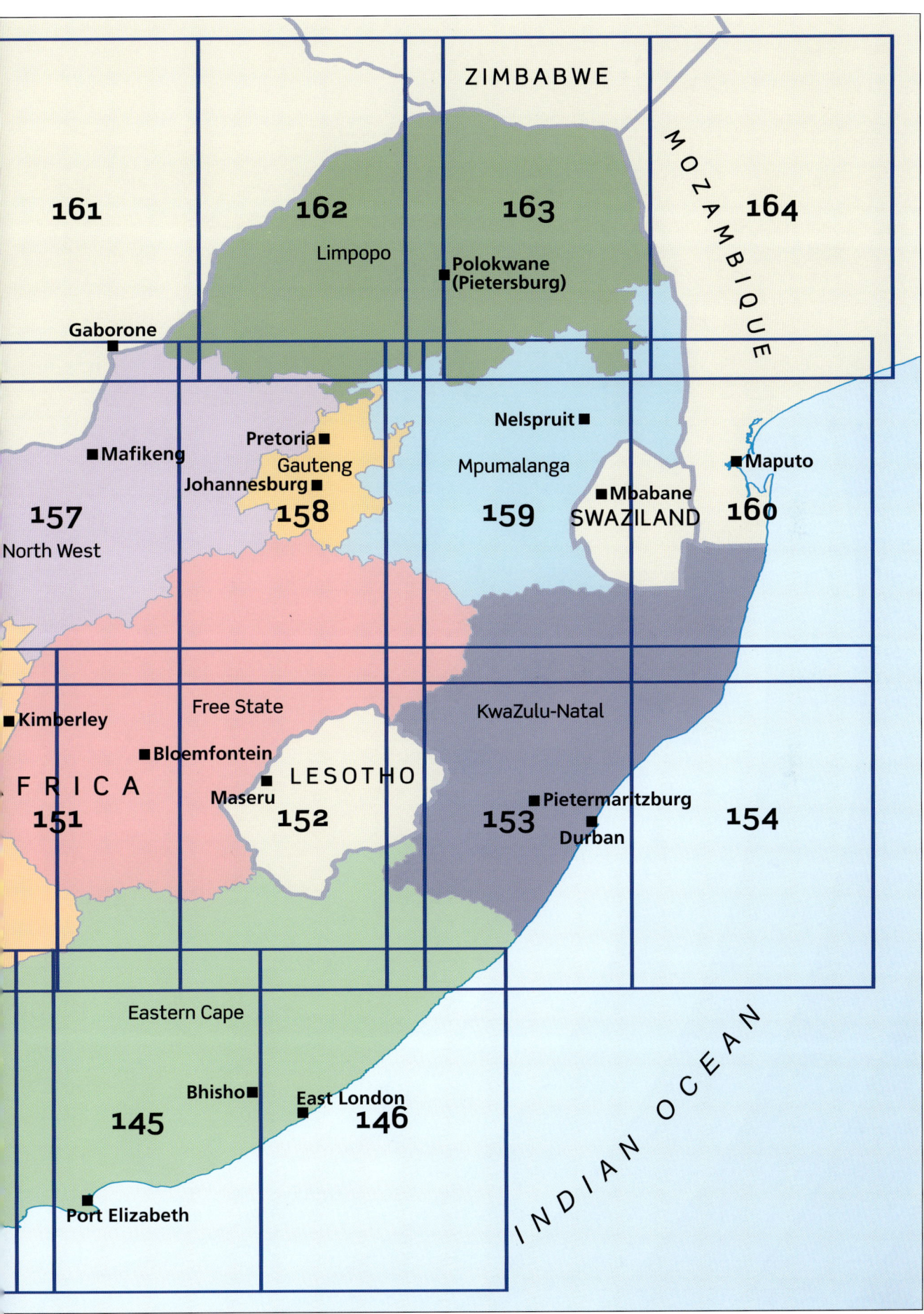

ZIMBABWE

MOZAMBIQUE

161

162
Limpopo

163
■ Polokwane
(Pietersburg)

164

Gaborone ■

■Mafikeng

Pretoria■
Gauteng
Johannesburg■

Nelspruit ■

Mpumalanga

Maputo■

157
North West

158

159

■Mbabane
SWAZILAND

160

■Kimberley

Free State

KwaZulu-Natal

■Bloemfontein

F R I C A

LESOTHO

■Pietermaritzburg
Durban■

151

Maseru

152

153

154

Eastern Cape

Bhisho■
East London
■

145

146

Port Elizabeth■

INDIAN OCEAN

Touring maps legend & distance chart

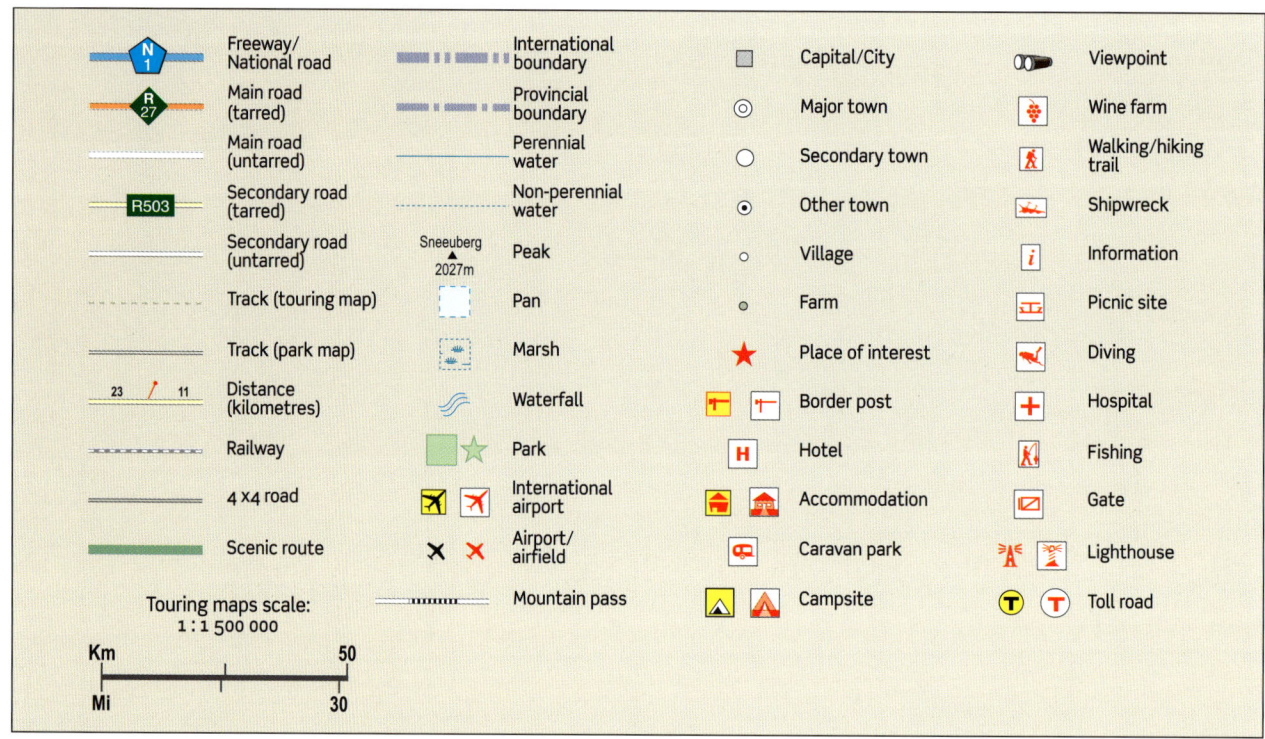

APPROXIMATE DISTANCES IN KILOMETRES	Bloemfontein	Cape Town	Durban	East London	Gaborone	Johannesburg	Kimberley	Mafikeng	Maputo	Maseru	Mbabane	Mthatha	Port Elizabeth	Pretoria
Bloemfontein	★	1004	634	584	622	398	177	464	862	157	677	570	681	455
Cape Town	1004	★	1753	1079	1501	1402	969	1343	1865	1160	1680	1314	769	1460
Colesberg	266	778	860	488	848	624	292	672	1085	383	903	517	451	682
Durban	634	1753	★	674	979	557	811	821	620	590	562	439	984	636
East London	584	1079	674	★	1206	982	780	1048	1301	630	1238	235	310	1040
Gaborone	622	1501	979	1206	★	358	538	158	919	702	719	1192	1299	350
George	773	438	1319	654	1361	1171	762	1203	1670	913	1450	880	335	1229
Graaff-Reinet	424	787	942	395	1012	822	490	854	1283	599	1101	503	291	880
Grahamstown	601	899	854	180	1223	999	667	1065	1478	692	1418	415	130	1057
Johannesburg	398	1402	557	982	358	★	476	287	555	438	361	869	1075	58
Keetmanshoop	1074	995	1708	1468	1230	1296	897	1072	1851	1283	1657	1547	1429	1354
Kimberley	177	969	811	780	538	476	★	380	1033	334	833	747	743	530
Ladysmith	410	1413	248	752	755	356	587	597	529	366	386	517	1062	414
Mafikeng	464	1343	821	1048	158	287	380	★	848	544	648	1034	1141	294
Maputo	862	1865	620	1301	919	555	1033	848	★	815	223	1064	1609	545
Maseru	157	1160	590	630	702	438	334	544	815	★	633	616	822	488
Mbabane	677	1680	562	1238	719	361	833	648	223	633	★	1003	1548	372
Mthatha	570	1314	439	235	1192	869	747	1034	1064	616	1003	★	545	928
Musina	928	1921	1107	1501	696	505	991	680	687	949	797	1392	1594	447
Nelspruit	757	1762	707	1226	672	355	827	635	206	713	173	976	1434	322
Pietermaritzburg	555	1674	79	595	900	499	732	742	706	511	640	360	905	557
Polokwane	706	1710	886	1290	485	297	780	569	567	738	504	1181	1383	250
Port Elizabeth	681	769	984	310	1299	1075	743	1141	1609	822	1548	545	★	1133
Pretoria	455	1460	636	1040	350	58	530	294	545	488	372	928	1133	★
Upington	574	894	1208	968	730	796	397	572	1357	731	1157	1047	933	854
Welkom	153	1156	564	737	479	258	294	321	775	249	451	718	830	316

INDIAN
OCEAN

Rosh
Pinah

JAKKALSBERGE

Lüderitz

Wor

Border
crossing only
with permit

Oranjemund ⊙ 14   57
Discovery of diamonds 1928 ★ ✕
Alexander Bay ⊙ ✕

82

Holgatpunt

Cl
Po

Port Ne
McDo
E

ATLANTIC
OCEAN

159

INDIAN
OCEAN

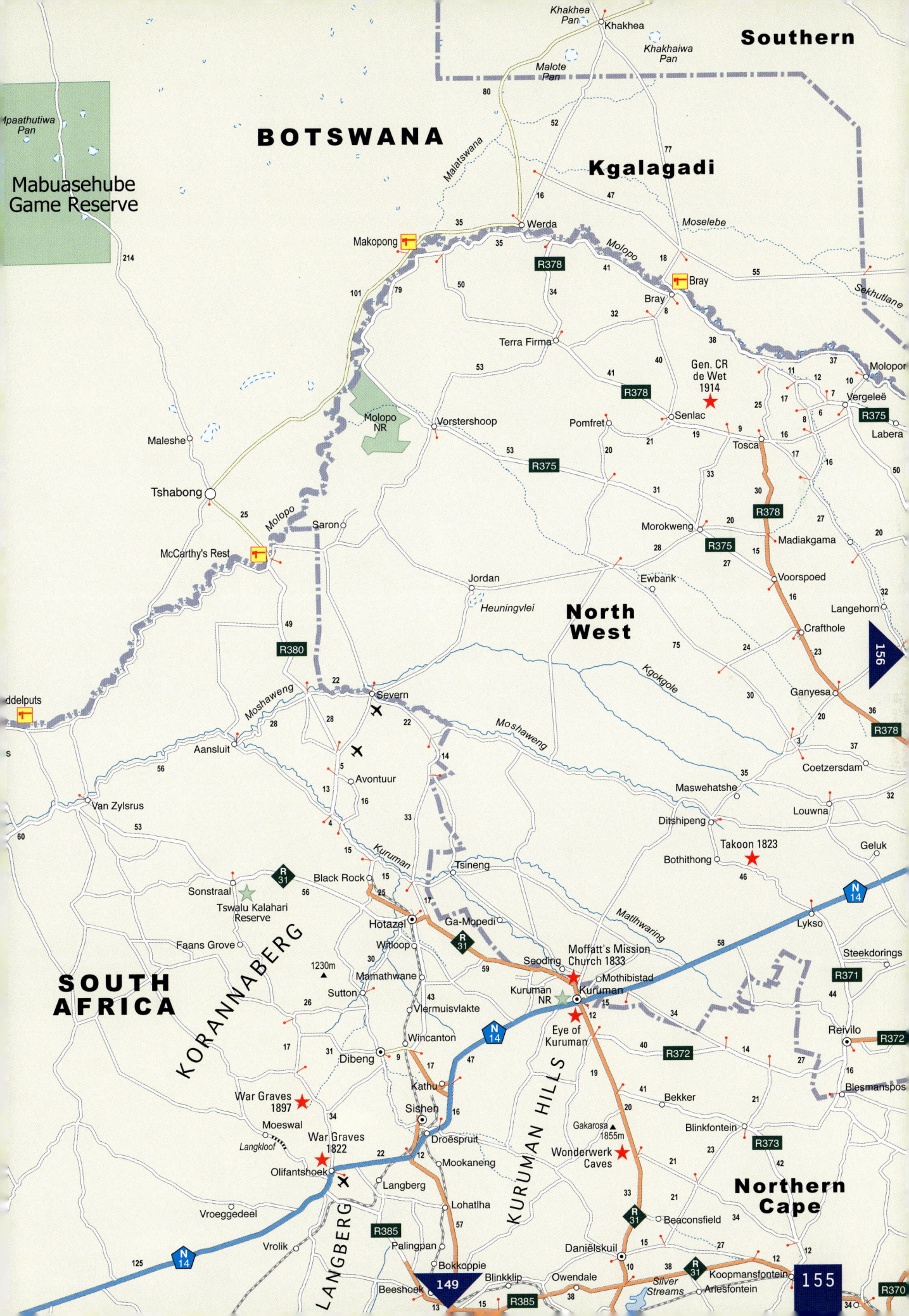

Street maps legend
& key plan

══════	Major road	[L]	Library	★ Museum		Point of interest
══════	Main road	[P]	Parking	✉		Post Office
──────	Minor road	[i]	Information	●		Police station
∙∙∙∙∙∙	Pedestrian mall	✝	Church	[U] Wits University		University
[M6] [R101] [N4]	Route number	[C]	Mosque			Park
→	One-way road	✡	Synagogue			Lake/dam
KING WILLIAM'S TOWN ↑	Directional	[H]	Hospital	Apies		Perennial river
Sunnyside	Area/suburb name	✈	Airport			Non-perennial river

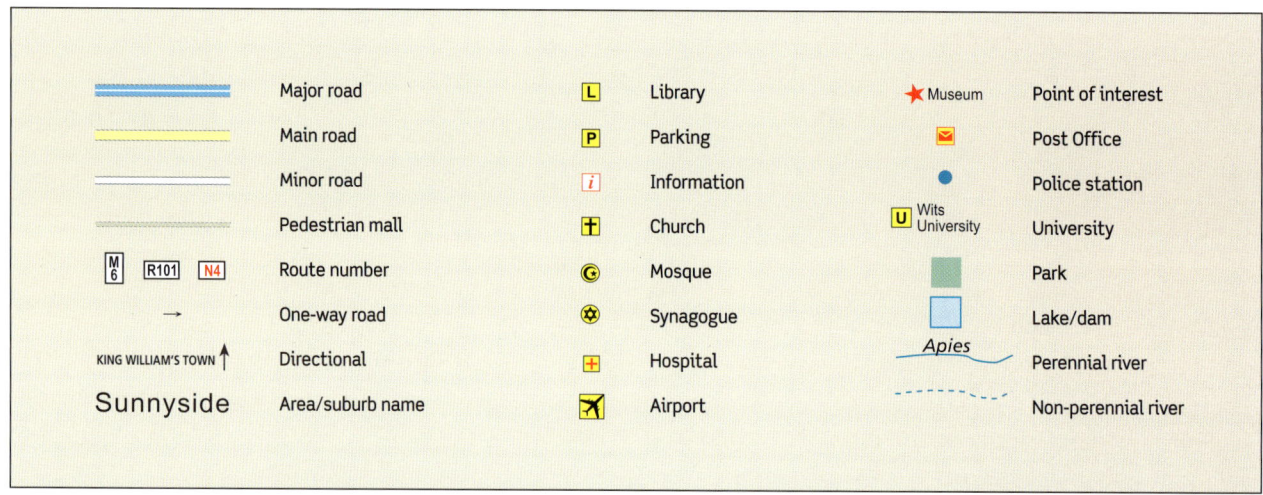

Limpopo

Polokwane
p171

Pretoria
p165

Nelspruit
p170

Mafikeng
p171

Gauteng   Mpumalanga

North West

Johannesburg
p167

Free State

KwaZulu-Natal

Upington
p171

Kimberley
p170

Bloemfontein
p168

Pietermaritzburg
p170

Northern Cape

Durban
p168

Eastern Cape

Bhisho
p170

East London
p169

Western Cape

Cape Town
p166

Knysna
p171

Port Elizabeth
p169

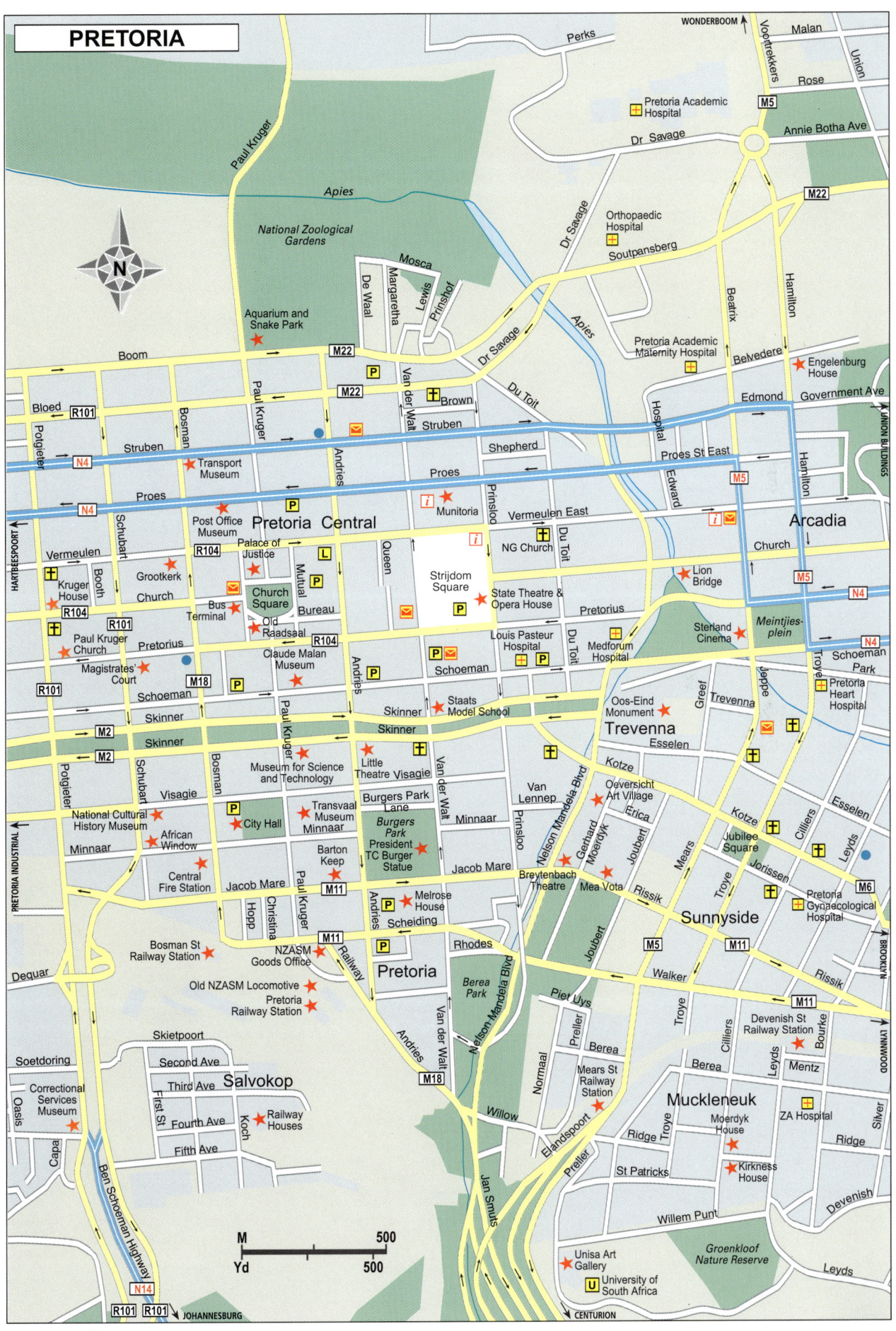

PRETORIA

CAPE TOWN

Table Bay

M ────── 500
Yd ────── 500

N

Mouille Point

5km Walkway

Viewpoint
Mouille Point Lighthouse
Bay
Mouille Point
Beach
Metropolitan Golf Course
Granger Bay
Helicopter Flights
Breakwater

Breakwater Blvd
Victoria Wharf
East Pier
Cruise Ship Berths

Stephan Way
Fort Wynyard
Kings Warehouse
VICTORIA & ALFRED WATERFRONT
Victoria Basin

Green Point Common
Green Point Vlei
Fritz Sonnenberg
Green Point
Somerset
Alfred Mall
Nelson Mandela Gateway to Robben Island
South Arm
B   A

Beach
Putt Putt Course
Bill Peters Dr.
Green Point Stadium
Green Point Track
Portswood
SA Maritime Museum
Art & Craft Market
Dock
C

M6
Western Boulevard
Green Point Market
Two Oceans Aquarium
V&A Marina
D

Town Hall
Main
M61
M6
Western Blvd
Waterfront Theatre School
Duncan Dock
E

St Brede's
Antrim
Sydney
Pine
Clyde
Wigtown
York
Boundary
Dock
Port
Alfred
Dock
F

Glengariff
Hill
High Level
Vesperdene
Main
Design Museum
M61
M6
Duncan
G

Ocean View Dr.
Springbok
Merriman
De Waterkant
De Smit
Napier
Dixon
Strand
Prestwich
Somerset
Hospital
Cape Town International Convention Centre
Foreshore
H
I
J

Noon Gun
Schotsche Kloof
Chiappini
Loop
Bree
Hans Strijdom
Coen Steytler
Dias Statue
DF Malan
Table Bay Blvd
N1

Viewpoint
Viewpoint
Signal Hill
Lion's Rump
Yusuf
Church
Castle
Rose
Buitengracht
Martin Melck House
Lutheran Church Koopmans-De Wet House
Waterkant
Longl
Riebeeck
Van Riebeeck Statue
Hertzog Boulevard
Artscape
Jan Smuts
Oswald Pirow
N1
N2
STELLENBOSCH

Pentz
Upper Bloem
St Stephen's
Shortmarket
Trout
St Georges
Airways Terminal
Civic Centre
M60

Walking Trail
Signal Hill
Bo-Kaap Museum
Auwal Mosque
Chris Barnard Memorial
Bree
Wale
Burg
Adderley Mall
Cape Town Railway Station
Bus Terminus
City Centre

Leeukloof
Devonport
Queens
Brownlow
Lion
Military
Buitengracht
Loop
Long
Greenmarket Square
Golden Acre
The Grand Parade
Strand

Tamboerskloof
Leeuwenvoet
Milner
Labia Gallery
Blue Lodge
St George's Cathedral
SA Library
Groote Kerk
Cultural History Museum
City Hall
Castle of Good Hope
Good Hope Centre
N2

Albert
Warren
Leeuwenhof
Tamboerskloof
Upr Buitengracht
New Church
Park
Long Street Baths
Queen Victoria
Houses of Parliament
De Tuynhuys
St Mary's Cathedral
Plein
Barrack
Caledon
District Six Museum
Canterbury
M4
Oriental Plaza

St Michael's
Bay View
Varsity
St
Kloof Nek
Nicol
Eaton
Kloof St
Company's Garden
Planetarium
SA Museum
Roeland
Constitution
Caledon
Tennant
Keizersgracht
N2
CAPE TOWN INTERNATIONAL AIRPORT

De Hoop
Leeukop
Hastings
Bath
Derwent
Camp
Vine
M3
Hatfield
Annandale
Little Theatre
Labia Cinema
Cape Town Holocaust Centre
Bertram House Museum
Great Synagogue
SA National Art Gallery
SA Jewish Museum
Rust en Vreugd
Glynn
Wesley
State Archives
De Villiers
M60
Cape Technikon
Zonnebloem (District Six)

De Lorentz
Gardens
Hof
Firdale
M62
Stephen
Hofmeyr
Lingen
Upper Orange
Breda
Upr Buitenkant
Buitenkant
Mill
Map Studio
Cape Town Fire Station
Justisie
De Waal Drive
M3

Higgo Cres.
Kloof Nek
Bellevue
Rosmead
Leeuwenhof & Bo-Tuin
Cape Town Medi-Clinic
De Waal Park
Molteno Reservoir
Booth Memorial
Old Pump House
Vredehoek Ave
Ludlow
Nazareth House
Derry
Lambert
Derry
Devil's Peak Estate

Higgo Rd
Glen Ave
Buxton Ave
Molteno
Alexandra Ave
Upper Orange
Yeoville
Wexford

Rosmead Ave
Montrose Ave
Oranjezicht
Davenport
Upper Buitenkant
Vredehoek

ATLAS OF NATIONAL PARKS AND RESERVES OF SOUTH AFRICA

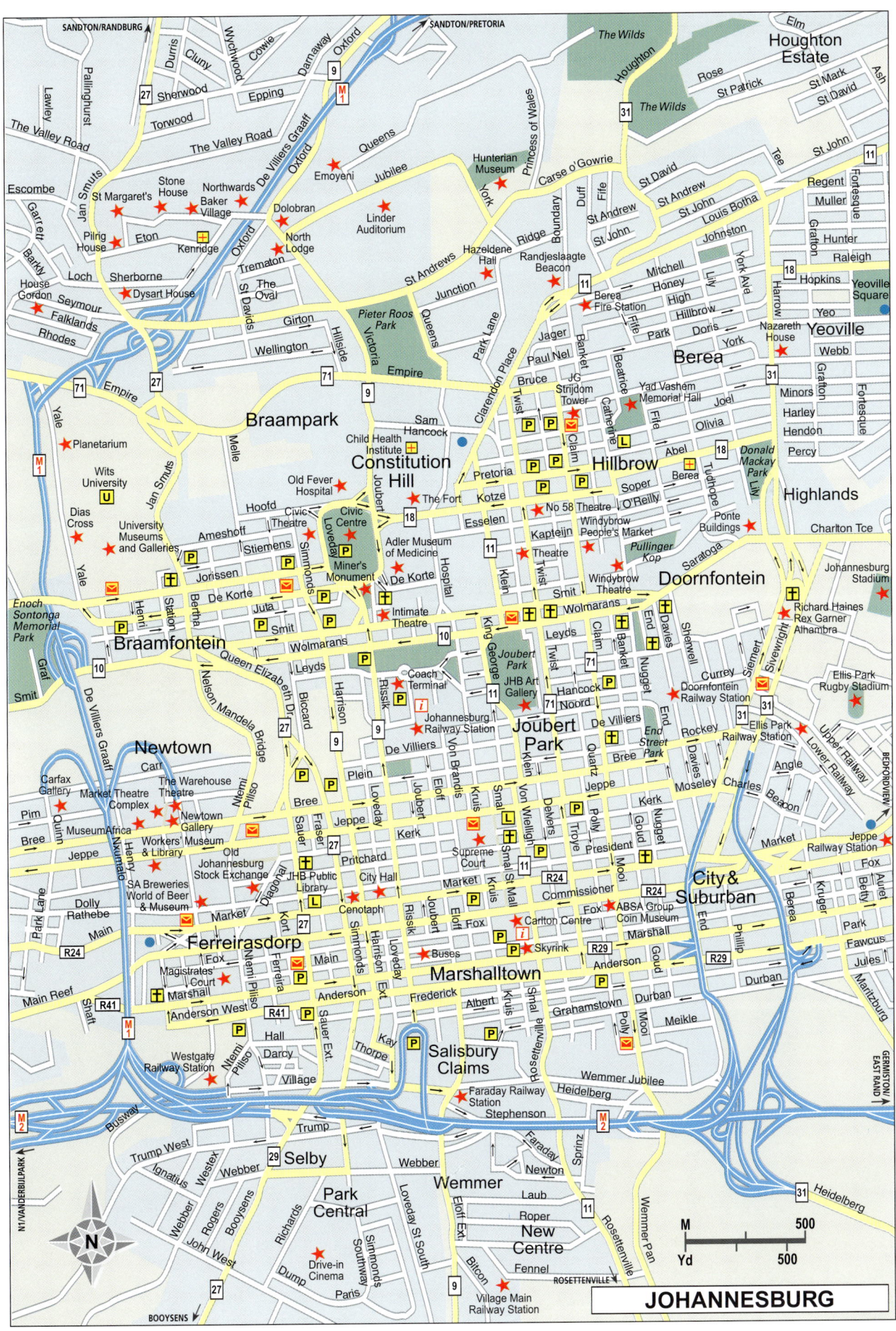

JOHANNESBURG

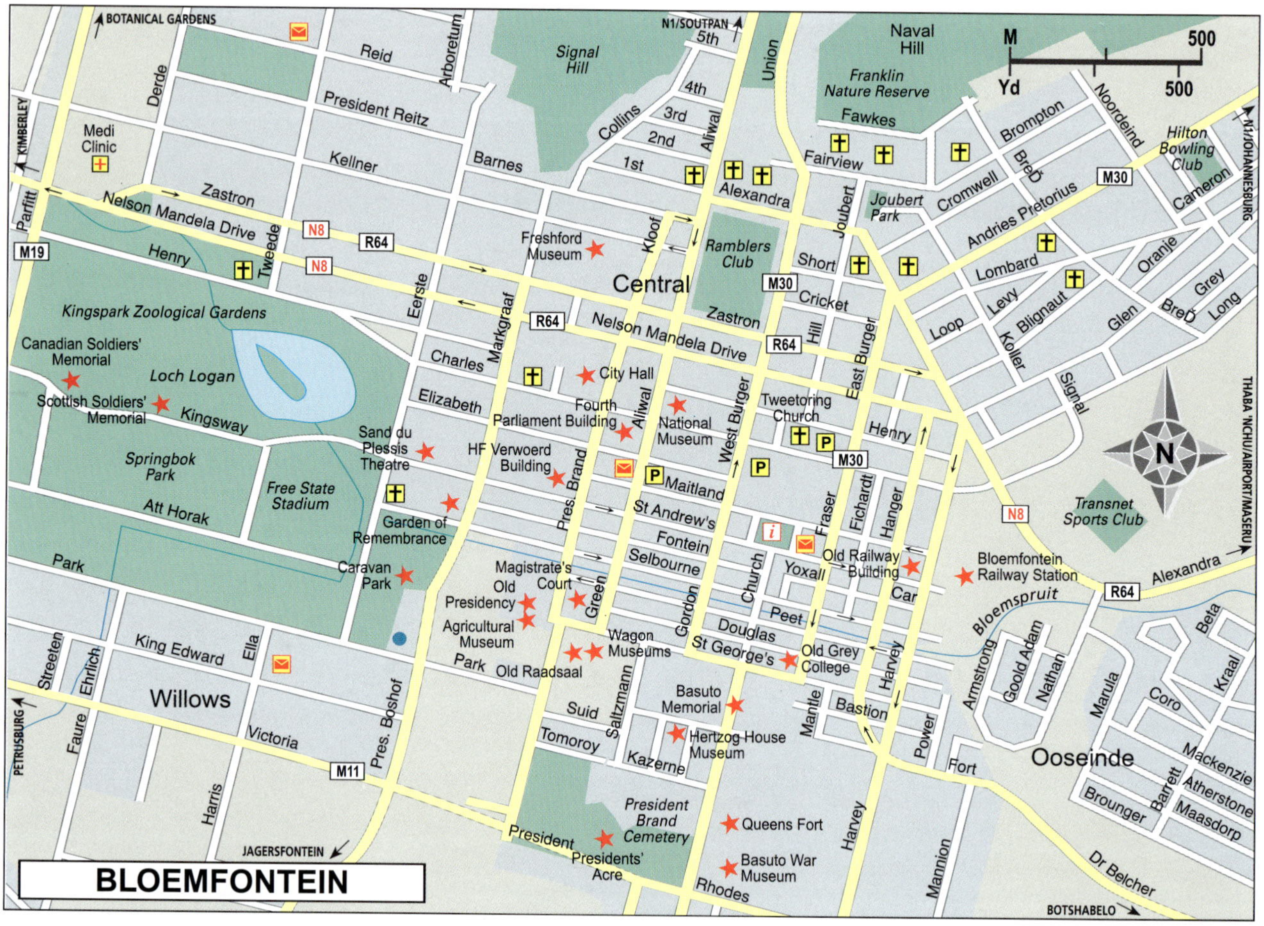

BLOEMFONTEIN

BOTANICAL GARDENS
N1/SOUTPAN
Naval Hill
M 500
Yd 500
KIMBERLEY
Medi Clinic
Reid
Derde
President Reitz
Arboretum
Signal Hill
Union
5th
4th
3rd
2nd
1st
Collins
Aliwal
Franklin Nature Reserve
Fawkes
Brompton
Noordeind
M1/JOHANNESBURG
Hilton Bowling Club
Cameron
M30
Kellner
Barnes
Alexandra
Fairview
Cromwell
Andries Pretorius
Joubert Park
Bred
Oranie
Grey
Parfitt
Zastron
Kloof
Ramblers Club
Joubert
Short
Lombard
Levy
Blignaut
Glen
Bred
Long
THABA 'NCHU/AIRPORT/MASERU
Nelson Mandela Drive
N8
R64
Freshford Museum
Central
M30
Cricket
Henry
Loop
Koller
Signal
M19
Henry
Tweede
N8
Eerste
R64
Nelson Mandela Drive
Zastron
East Burger
Kingspark Zoological Gardens
Charles
Markgraaf
City Hall
Tweetoring Church
Henry
N8
Transnet Sports Club
Canadian Soldiers' Memorial
Loch Logan
Elizabeth
Fourth
Parliament Building
National Museum
West Burger
P
M30
Fichardt
Scottish Soldiers' Memorial
Kingsway
HF Verwoerd Building
Pres. Brand
St Andrew's
Maitland
P
Fraser
Hanger
Bloemfontein Railway Station
R64
Alexandra
Beta
Springbok Park
Sand du Plessis Theatre
Fontein
Selbourne
i
Yoxall
Old Railway Building
Car
Bloemspruit
Att Horak
Free State Stadium
Garden of Remembrance
Magistrate's Old Presidency
Green
Gordon
Douglas
Church
Peet
Old Grey College
Harvey
Armstrong
Good Adam
Nathan
Marula
Coro
Kraal
Park
Caravan Park
Agricultural Museum
St George's
Wagon Museums
Mantle
Bastion
Ooseinde
Mackenzie
King Edward
Ella
Old Raadsaal
Suid
Basuto Memorial
Hertzog House Museum
Power
Fort
Brounger
Barrett
Atherstone
Maasdorp
Streeten
Ehrlich
Faure
Willows
Victoria
Pres. Boshof
Tomoroy
Kazerne
Mamion
PETRUSBURG
Harris
M11
President
President Brand Cemetery
Queens Fort
Dr Belcher
JAGERSFONTEIN
Presidents' Acre
Rhodes
Basuto War Museum
BOTSHABELO

BLOEMFONTEIN

DURBAN

WINDERMERE
NORTH COAST
Battery Beach I
M 600
Yd 600
N
Greyville Race Course
Stamford Hill Rd
R102
Durban Bowls Club
Queen's Tavern (Heritage Site)
M4
Durban Drive-In
Sol Harris Cres
Snell Parade
Snake Park Beach
Somtseu Rd Pier
Royal Durban Golf Course
Mitchell Rd
Brickhill Rd
M17
Bay of Plenty
Sydenham Rd
DLI Avenue
M12
Ocean City
FitzSimons Snake Park
INDIAN OCEAN
Greyville Race Course
Greyville
1st Ave
Umgeni Rd
Durban Fire Station
Somtseu Rd
Minitown
Stanger St
Amphitheatre Museum
Golden Mile
DLI Hall
Ascot Rd
Durban Railway Station
MMI
Playfair Rd
Old Fort Rd
Curries Fountain Sports Ground
Dartnell Cres
Derby St
Hoy Park
Prince Alfred St
Beaumann Rd
Durban Tourism
North Beach
Cane Cutters Hall
Cross St
Grey St
Albert St
Kingsmead Cricket Ground
Brickhill Rd
Marine Parade
Swimming Pool
St Aiden's Hospital
M15
Alice St
Old Fort and Warrior's Gate
Ordnance Rd
John Milne St
Victoria Park
L
Funworld
Dairy Beach
Swimming Pool
PIETERMARITZBURG
M13
Centenary Rd
Stable Theatre
Prince Edward St
Soldier's Way
Old Fort Rd
M4
Kwa Muhle Museum
Durban International Conference Centre
Morrison Rd
i
Wedge Beach
N3
M4
Russell St
Victoria St
Victoria St
Durban Central
Exhibition Centre
Aliwal St
Walnut Rd
Conservation Centre
Pine St
Whyalls Camera Museum
West St Mall
Berea Rd Railway Station
R102
Eliat Viaduct
Victoria St Market
Juma Musjid (Grey St) Mosque
Africa Art Centre
The Workshop
Commercial Rd
Tourist Junction
West St
Stanger St
Cato St
Smith St
Palmer St
i
South Beach
Trampolines
Warwick Pl
M4
Emmanuel Cathedral
Theatre La.
G
Pine St
St Paul's
City Hall
Jonsson St
Da Gama Clock
The Wheel
Little Top
City Market
West St
Smith St
The Playhouse
Napac
Winder St
Dutch Reformed Church (Heritage Site)
Bay Tce
Addington Beach
Botha Gardens
Cinema
Durdoc
GA Riches Building
Field St
Gardiner St
Dick King Statue
BAT Centre
Point Rd
Addington Hospital
Moore Rd
Smith St
Park St
Broad St
Quadrant House
Pleasure Cruises
Natal Maritime Museum
Shepstone Pl
Gillespie St
South Beach Ave
R102
St Andrews St
Russell St
Old House Museum
Royal Natal Yacht Club
Point Yacht Club
Bay of Natal
Natal
Quayside Rd
Hospital Rd
Prince St
Erskine Tce
Addington Children's Hospital
M11
Albert Park
Victoria Embankment
T Jetty
uShaka Marine World
M4
SOUTH COAST
Point

ATLAS OF NATIONAL PARKS AND RESERVES OF SOUTH AFRICA

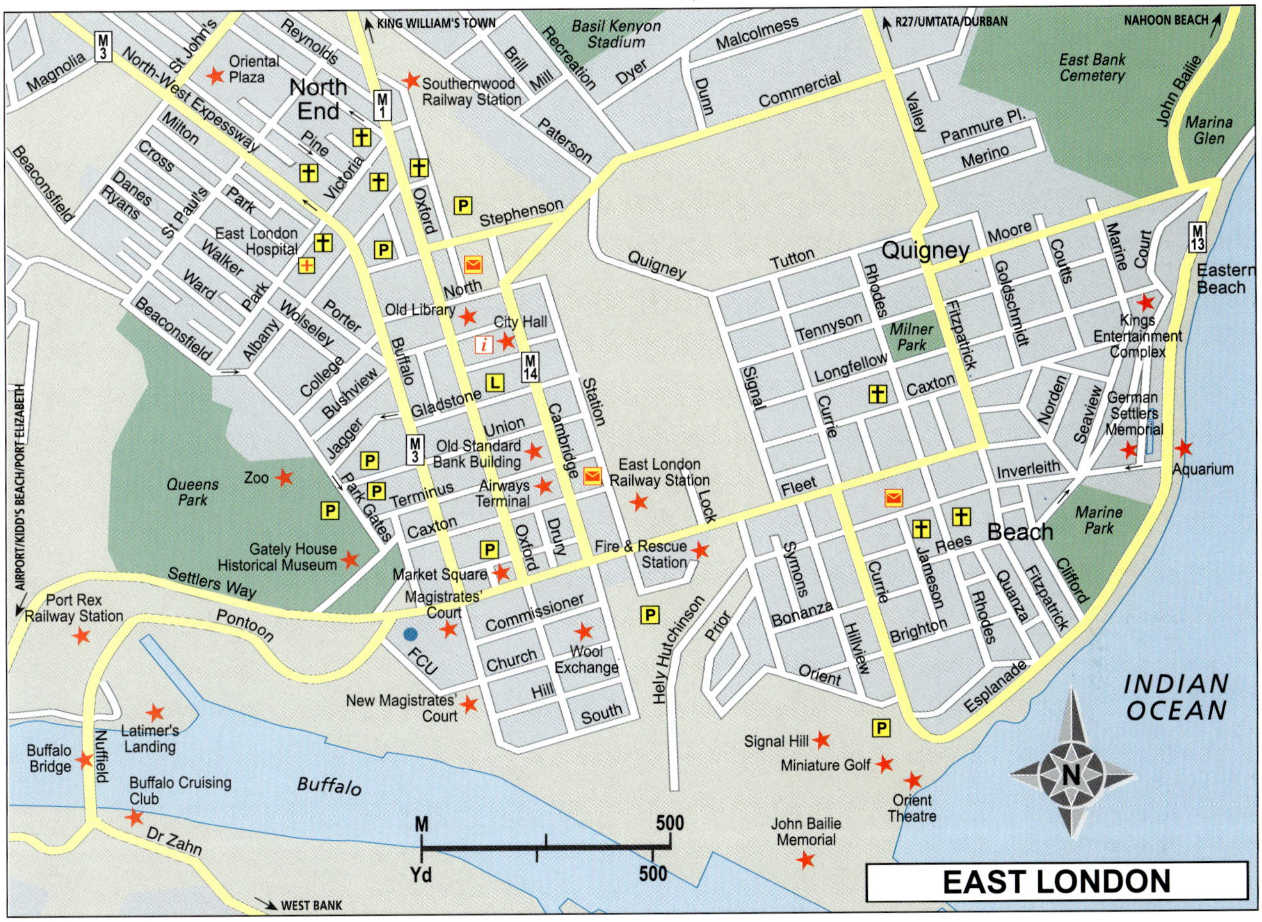

EAST LONDON

North End
Quigney
Beach
Queens Park
Marine Park
Milner Park
East Bank Cemetery
Marina Glen
Eastern Beach

INDIAN OCEAN

Magnolia
Beaconsfield
North-West Expressway
St John's
Reynolds
Oriental Plaza
Southernwood Railway Station
King William's Town
Basil Kenyon Stadium
Recreation
Brill
Mill
Paterson
Dyer
Dunn
Malcolmess
Commercial
R27/UMTATA/DURBAN
NAHOON BEACH
John Baillie

Cross
Ryans
Danes
Milton
St Paul's
Walker
Ward
Park
Albany
Wolseley
Bushview
College
Jagger
Beaconsfield
Pine
Victoria
Oxford
Stephenson
Quigney
Tutton
Panmure Pl.
Merino
Moore
Couts
Marine
Court

East London Hospital
Porter
Buffalo
North
Old Library
City Hall
Gladstone
Union
Cambridge
Station
Quigney
Signal
Tennyson
Longfellow
Currie
Caxton
Rhodes
Fitzpatrick
Goldschmidt
Norden
Seaview

Kings Entertainment Complex
German Settlers Memorial
Aquarium

Zoo
Queens Park
Park Gates
Terminus
Old Standard Bank Building
Airways Terminal
East London Railway Station
Lock
Fleet
Inverleith

Gately House Historical Museum
Settlers Way
Caxton
Oxford
Drury
Fire & Rescue Station
Rees
Currie
Jameson
Quanza
Clifford
Fitzpatrick

Port Rex Railway Station
Pontoon
Market Square
Magistrates' Court
Commissioner
Church
Wool Exchange
Hill
South
Hely Hutchinson
Prior
Symons
Bonanza
Hillview
Brighton
Rhodes
Orient
Esplanade

FCU
New Magistrates' Court

Buffalo Bridge
Nuffield
Latimer's Landing
Buffalo Cruising Club
Dr Zahn
WEST BANK
Buffalo

Signal Hill
Miniature Golf
Orient Theatre
John Bailie Memorial

M 500
Yd 500

N

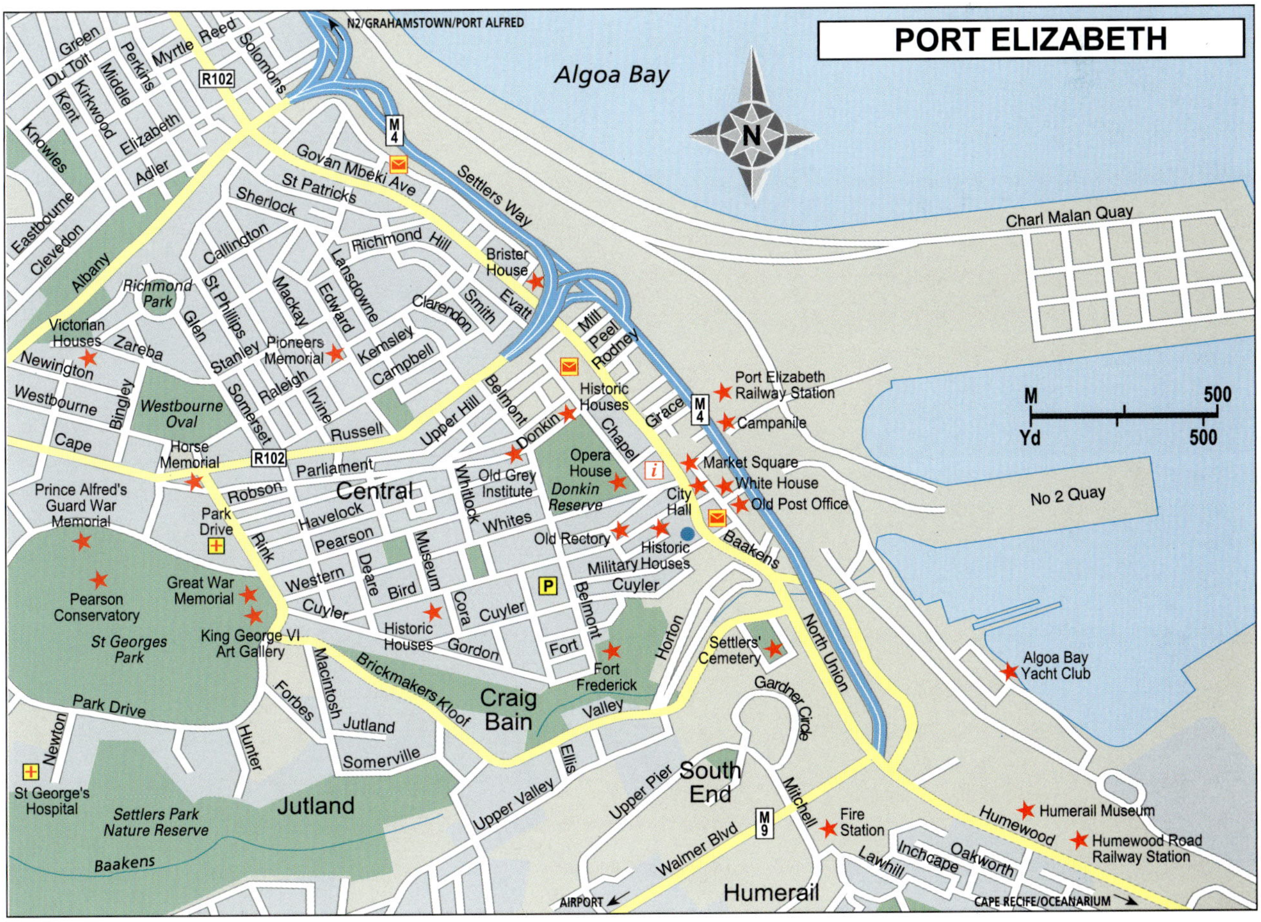

PORT ELIZABETH

N2/GRAHAMSTOWN/PORT ALFRED
Algoa Bay

N

Green
Du Toit
Myrtle
Reed
Solomons
R102
Perkins
Middle
Kirkwood
Elizabeth
Kent
Adler
Knowles
Eastbourne
Clevedon
Albany
Glen
Govan Mbeki Ave
St Patricks
Sherlock
Callington
Richmond Hill
Brister House
Evatt
Smith
Clarendon
M4
Settlers Way

Charl Malan Quay

Richmond Park
Victorian Houses
Zareba
Newington
Westbourne
Cape
Bingley
Westbourne Oval
Horse Memorial
St Phillips
Mackay
Stanley
Pioneers Memorial
Raleigh
Irvine
Russell
Edward
Kemsley
Campbell
Lansdowne
Upper Hill
Belmont
Donkin
Chapel
Grace
Mill
Peel
Rodney
Historic Houses
M4

Port Elizabeth Railway Station
Campanile

Prince Alfred's Guard War Memorial
Park Drive
Robson
Parliament
Havelock
Pearson
Whitlock
Whites
Museum
Deare
Old Grey Institute
Opera House
Donkin Reserve
Old Rectory
Historic Military Houses
Cuyler
Market Square
White House
Old Post Office
City Hall

No 2 Quay

Pearson Conservatory
Great War Memorial
St Georges Park
King George VI Art Gallery
Western
Cuyler
Cora
Gordon
Bird
Historic Houses
Fort
Brickmakers Kloof
Fort Frederick
Settlers' Cemetery
Baakens
North Union

Algoa Bay Yacht Club

Central
Craig Bain
Newton
Park Drive
St George's Hospital
Settlers Park Nature Reserve
Baakens
Jutland
Hunter
Macintosh
Forbes
Somerville
Jutland
Upper Valley
Upper Pier
Valley
Ellis
Horton
South End
Gardner Circle
Mitchell
Humewood

Fire Station
Humerail Museum
Humewood Road Railway Station
M9
Lawhill
Inchcape
Oakworth
Walmer Blvd
AIRPORT
Humerail
CAPE RECIFE/OCEANARIUM

M 500
Yd 500

169

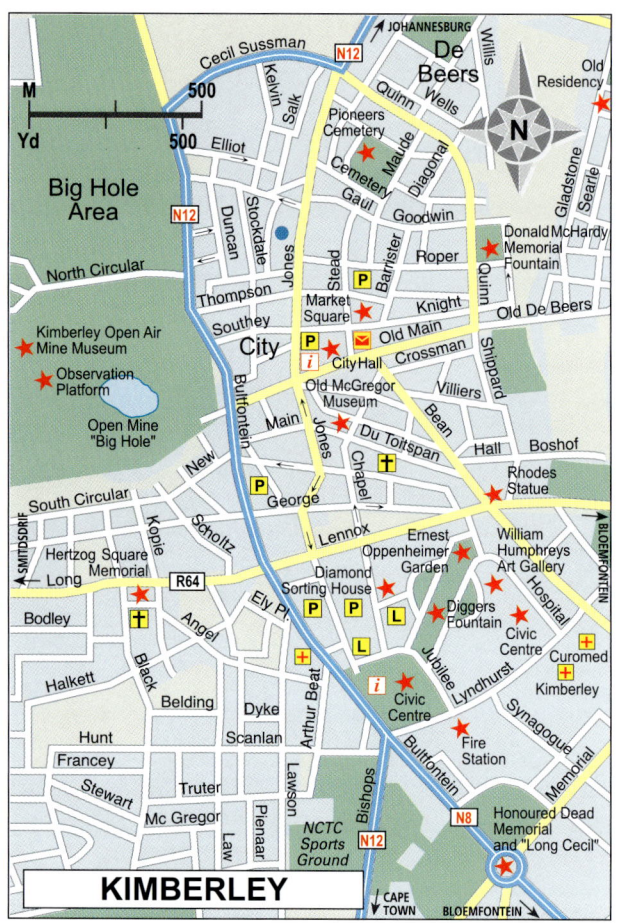

KIMBERLEY

BHISHO

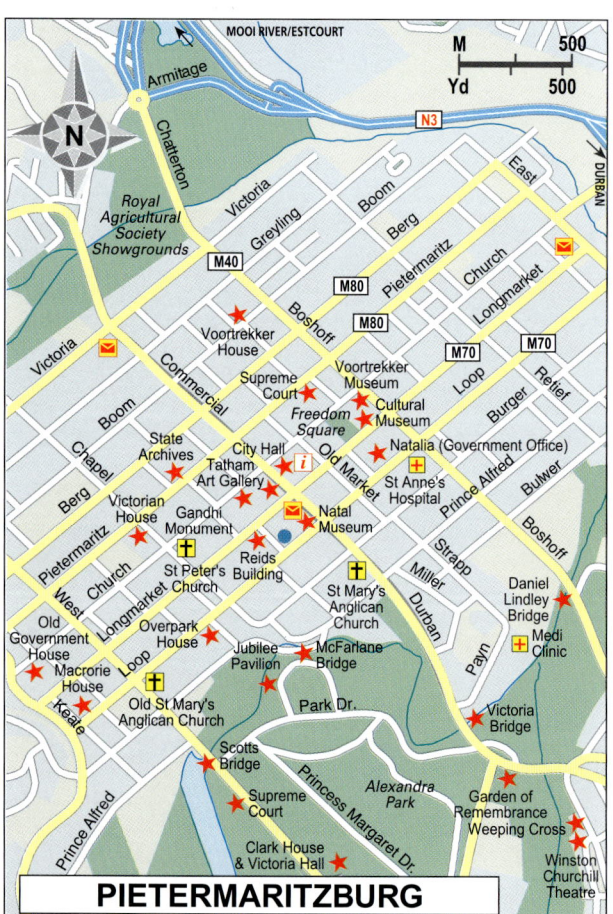

PIETERMARITZBURG

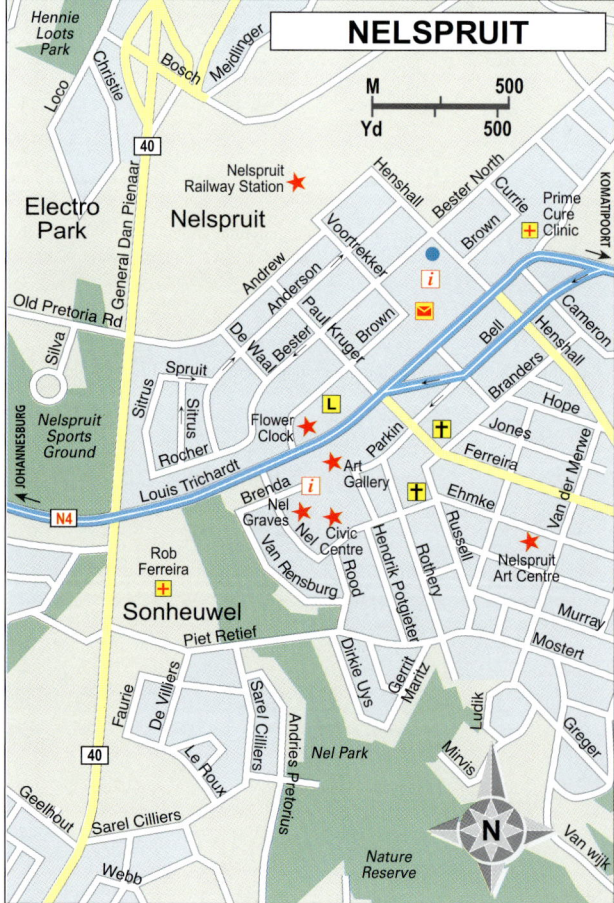

NELSPRUIT

ATLAS OF NATIONAL PARKS AND RESERVES OF SOUTH AFRICA

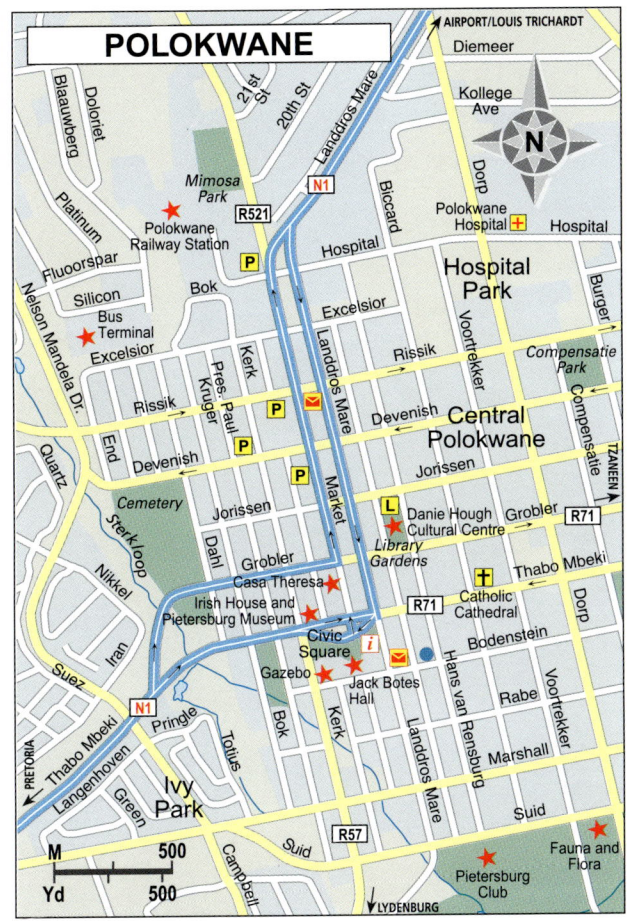

POLOKWANE

MAFIKENG

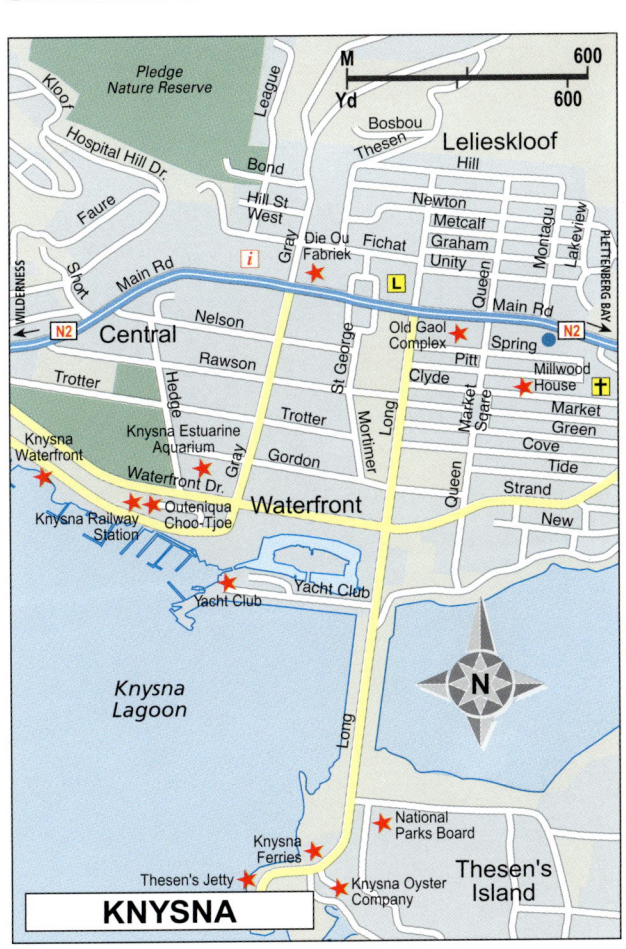

KNYSNA

UPINGTON

Overview:
Surrounding countries

Park

Transfrontier
Park

Luanda■
Quiçama
National
Park

Cuango

Luando
Integral
NR

L

Kam
NP

Lobito•

A N G O L A

•**Huambo**

**Cuito
Cuanavale**

Bikua
NP

Iona
NP

Mupa
NP

Kunene

Kavango

Capri
Game P

Khaudum
GP

Etosha NP

Skeleton
Coast
Park

N A M I B I A

Swakopmund•
Walvis Bay•

■**Windhoek**

Namib-
Naukluft
Park

Mal
seh
G

Namib Rand
NR

Kgalagadi
Transfrontier
Park

Keetmanshoop

Lüderitz•

Ai-Ais/Richtersveld
Transfrontier Park

Orange/Gariep

Upingto

Springbok•

S O U T

Cape Town■

ATLANTIC OCEAN

N

| Km | | 500 |
| Mi | | 300 |

DEMOCRATIC
REPUBLIC OF
THE CONGO

Upemba
NP

Lake Mweru

TANZANIA

Selous
Game
Reserve

Lubumbashi

Kitwe

South
Luangwa
NP

Nyika NP

Lake Malawi

Lake Malawi/
Nyasa/Niassa
Transfrontier Area

Niassa
Game
Reserve

ZAMBIA

MALAWI

Lilongwe

Lusaka

Kafue
National
Park

Cahora Bassa
Dam

Liwonde NP

Mana
Pools
NP

Doma
Safari
Area

Zambezi

Lake
Kariba

Matusadona
NP

MOZAMBIQUE

Gili
Reserve

Zambezi

bwata
NP

Chobe
Forest
Reserve

Zambezi
NP

Chizarira
NP

Harare

Nyanga
NP

Gorongosa
NP

Marromeu
GR

udumu
NP

remi
GR

Chobe
NP

Hwange
NP

Hartley
Safari Area

Mutare

Beira

Maun

Nxai
Pan NP

ZIMBABWE

Chimanimani
NP

Bulawayo

Makgadikgadi
Pans NR

Gonarezhou
NP

Bazaruto
NP

OTSWANA

Tuli Safari
Area

Malapati Safari
Area

Zinave
NP

ntral Kalahari
me Reserve

Limpopo/Shashe
Transfrontier Area

Great Limpopo
Transfrontier Park

Banhine
NP

Khutse
GR

Limpopo
Park

Inhambane

Kruger
NP

Gaborone

Pretoria

Nelspruit

Maputo

Mbabane

Maputo Elephant Reserve

SWAZILAND

Lubombo
Transfrontier Area

Bloemfontein

Hluhluwe-
iMfolozi Park

LESOTHO

Maseru

Durban

FRICA

Port Edward

INDIAN OCEAN

ufort West

Addo
Elephant NP

East London

ysna

Port Elizabeth

ATLANTIC OCEAN

Kunene
Ruacana Falls
Ruacana
*Otijijandjasemo Hot Spring
Opuwo
KAOKOLAND
*Dorsland Trekkers Monument
Seal Colony*
Karos Cons. Area
Etosha National Park
Etosha Pan
Kamanjab
Terrace Bay
Petrified Forest
*Burnt Mountain
White Lady Painting*
Messum Crater*
National West Coast Tourist Recreational Area
Diego Cão Cross
Henties Bay
Goanikontes
Swakopmund
Walvis Bay
Dune 7
Namib-Naukluft Park
Conception Bay
Kuiseb
Kuiseb Canyon
Solitaire
Sesriem Canyon*
Sossusvlei
St Francis Bay
Namib Rand Nature Reserve
Spencer Bay
Koichab Pan
Aus
Lüderitz
Kolmanskop Ghost Mining Town*
Elizabeth Bay Ghost Mining Town
Oranjemund
Noordoewer

Oshikango
B1
Oshakati
Ondangwa
Ovambo
Nkurenkuru
Rundu
Divu
Mahan Game P
Kavango
Khaudum
Khaudum Game Park
Giant Baobab Tree*
B8
Omatako
Dorslandtrek Baobab*
Tsumkwe
Tsumeb
Hoba Meteorite
Okaukuejo
Gamkarab Cave
Otavi
Grootfontein
Outjo
B1
Waterberg Plateau Park
Otjiwarongo
Ugab
Dinosaur's Footprints*
Omatako
Otjinene
Uis
SPITZKOPPE
Omaruru
Von Bach Rec. Resort
Rietfontein
Usakos
B2
Okahandja
Steinhausen
Tsaobis Leopard Nature Park
Windhoek
Charles' Hill
B6
Gobabis
Daan Viljoen Game Park
Arnhem Cave
Rehoboth
Hot Spring
Leonardville
Nossob
Zaris
Fish
Hardap Recreation Resort
Aranos
Maltahöhe
Mariental
Auob
Duwisib Castle*
Helmeringhausen
B1
Welverdiend
Extinct Volcano*
Keetmanshoop
Giant's Playground*
B4
Naute Recreation Area
Aroab
Konkiep
Fish River Canyon NP
Fish River Canyon
Grünau
Karasburg
Rosh Pinah
B1
B3
Ai-Ais/ Richtersveld Transfrontier Park
Orange (Gariep)
Velloorsdrif

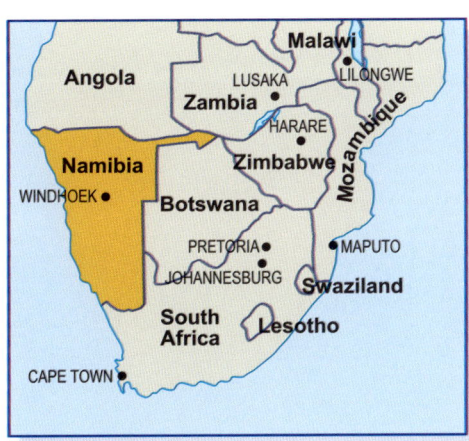

Km 200

Mi 100

Namibia

Ignored by the colonial powers (until diamonds were discovered) owing to its harsh and desolate terrain, Namibia is a land of great contrasts and stupendous natural features, including age-old rock art, the ominous Spitzkoppe hills, Sossusvlei's dramatic dunescapes as well as an amazing collection of flora and fauna. Its plantlife includes the ageless Welwitschia and Baobab, as well as dramatic collections of Quiver Trees and the iconic petrified forest.

Top Town

Windhoek is the capital city and the nation's tourist and economic hub. Despite its small and undeveloped nature, it is a lively, colourful and relatively modern city that caters well for international travellers.

Five Big Attractions

• The dramatic landscape of the Fish River Canyon, reputed to be third in size to America's Grand Canyon, draws geologists, sight-seers and adventurers.
• The Orange River (aka Gariep) originates in South Africa's Drakensberg mountains and cuts across South Africa to create the natural border with Namibia before emptying into the Atlantic Ocean – after flowing through the Fish River Canyon.
• The Etosha National Park is one of the finest game reserves in Southern Africa and is a vital visitor drawcard for Namibia.
• The Namib-Naukluft Park is larger than Switzerland, and its 50,000km^2 of pristine desert landscape is a testament to the country's conservation efforts in preserving the Namib Desert's dunes.
• Kolmanskop Ghost Town is a popular stop for travellers. It's a haunting reminder of what happens to a diamond-rush town when the diamonds run out.

Five Big Facts

• The Skeleton Coast's treacherous shores have earned this stretch its reputation as the world's largest shipping graveyard; over 100 vessels have run aground here.
• The wild and unpredictable wilderness of the Kaokoland consists of 50,000km^2 of rough roads and mountain terrain … and the locals have different names for most of the places you find on the maps.
• The mighty Kunene River in the north of Namibia forms part of the 325km border with Angola and is home to fearsome crocodiles, thundering waterfalls, raging whitewater rapids – and believe it or not – tranquil streams, making it a premier rafting destination.
• Lüderitz serves up charming German architecture, characterful buildings dating from the 1900s and houses painted in a kaleidoscope of clashing colours.
• The famous Desert Elephants of the Kaokoland spend days searching for water, and can trudge more than 60km for a single drink.

FACTS AND FIGURES
Area:
824,290 km^2 / 318,260mi^2
Population:
1.8 million
Main ethnic groups:
Ovambo (50%), Kavango (9%)
Herero (7%), Damara (7%), White (6%)
Main languages:
English
Afrikaans
Ovambo
Kavango
German
Main religion:
Christian and Lutheran (90%)
Currency:
Namibian dollar (100 cents)

TEN GREAT ADVENTURES
1 Sandboarding
2 Horse riding / camel riding
3 Shark spotting
4 Quadbiking
5 4x4 trails
6 Hiking
7 Climbing
8 Sea kayaking
9 Skydiving
10 Canoeing/whitewater rafting

FAUNA/FLORA
1 African Elephant
2 Black & White Rhino
3 Giraffe
4 Buffalo
5 Lion
6 Cheetah
7 Black-faced Impala
8 Oribi
9 Eland
10 Damara Dik Dik
11 Honey Badger
12 Herero Chat
13 Rockrunner
14 Monteiro's Hornbill
15 Damara Tern
16 African Fish Eagle
17 *Welwitschia mirabilis*
18 *Kokerboom* (Quiver Tree)
19 Elephant Foot
20 *Halfmens*

MAIN CONTACT DETAILS
Namibia Wildlife Resorts & Reservations:
061 285 7000/200
reservations@nmr.com.na
www.nmr.com.na
Namibian Tourism Board:
061 290 6000
info@namibiamtourism.com.na
www.namibiatourism.com.na

Botswana

Botswana is famed for its wildlife and the outstanding wetlands of the Okavango Delta, while Tsodilo Hills are a window into the past with their fascinating collection of rock art created by the San people who have occupied this land for centuries.

Top Town
Gaborone, the capital of Botswana, is a relatively small, compact city with few conventional tourist sites, yet it has an ever-improving infrastructure for locals and foreign visitors.

Five Big Attractions
• The Kalahari Desert is the largest continuous stretch of sand in the world – flat, dry and empty, it covers more than 80 per cent of Botswana.
• The Makgadikgadi Pans are the world's largest natural salt pans, covering 12,000km² and providing a magnificent quadbiking experience.
• Chobe National Park has a varied habitat, alternating between swamp and grassland, flood plain and bushveld. It is bordered by the Chobe River, Botswana's only perennial river.
• The Tuli Block of reserves and concession areas offers legendary horse-riding safaris that provide a unique viewing experience of local flora and fauna.
• The bird-rich Khutse Game Reserve is a small sanctuary located fairly close to Gaborone that is made up largely of undulating savannah within typical pan countryside, making it a no-questions-asked four-wheel-drive terrain.

Five Big Facts
• The Okavango Delta is the world's largest inland delta, spreading over 15,000km² during the dry season and, during times of high rainfall, over a massive 22,000km².
• Drotsky's Cave (aka Gcwihaba Cave, which means 'hyena's lair' in the Bushman tongue) dates back two million years and offers an amazing display of stalactites, stalagmites and flowstones.
• The Moremi Game Reserve is a vast, 2000km² expanse of contrasting terrain and is roamed by big game species such as Lion, Leopard, Cheetah, Elephant, Buffalo and Botswana's ubiquitous Lechwe.
• The Aha Hills date back 700 million years; set in a fascinating landscape, they are one of Botswana's most remote and difficult places to reach.
• Botswana's interior is dotted with Baobab trees (aka 'upside down trees'), of which the most prominent are the Seven Sisters. They are also referred to as Baines' Baobabs, after the famous painter who immortalised them.

FACTS AND FIGURES
Area:
   600,372km² / 231,805mi²
Population:
   1.6 million
Main ethnic groups:
   Tswana (75%), Shona (12%)
   San (3%), White (1%)
Main languages:
   English, Tswana, Shona
   San, Ndebele
Main religions:
   Traditional beliefs (50%)
   Christian (mostly Anglican) (50%)
Currency:
   Pula (100 thebe)

TEN GREAT ADVENTURES
1 Game-viewing
2 Canoeing (*mekoro*)
3 Caving
4 Horseback safaris
5 Hot-air ballooning
6 Scenic flights
7 Bird-watching
8 Quadbiking
9 Elephant-back safaris
10 Walks with the San

FAUNA/FLORA
1 Lion
2 Leopard
3 Cheetah
4 Burchell's Zebra
5 White Rhino
6 Warthog
7 Giraffe
8 Springbok
9 Steenbok
10 Impala
11 Blue Wildebeest
12 Tsessebe
13 Sable Antelope
14 Lechwe
15 Kudu
16 Eland
17 Buffalo
18 Hippopotamus
19 African Elephant
20 Chacma Baboon
21 Black-backed Jackal
22 Hyena sp.
23 Cormorant sp.
24 Cape Vulture
25 African Fish Eagle
26 African Jacana
27 Mopane Tree sp.
28 Marula Tree
29 Baobab
30 Tsamma Melon

MAIN CONTACT DETAILS
Department of Tourism:
   09267 395 3024
   botswanatourism@gov.bw
   www.botswanatourism.org
Department of Wildlife, National Parks
   and Reservations:
   09267 318 0774
   dwnp@gov.bw

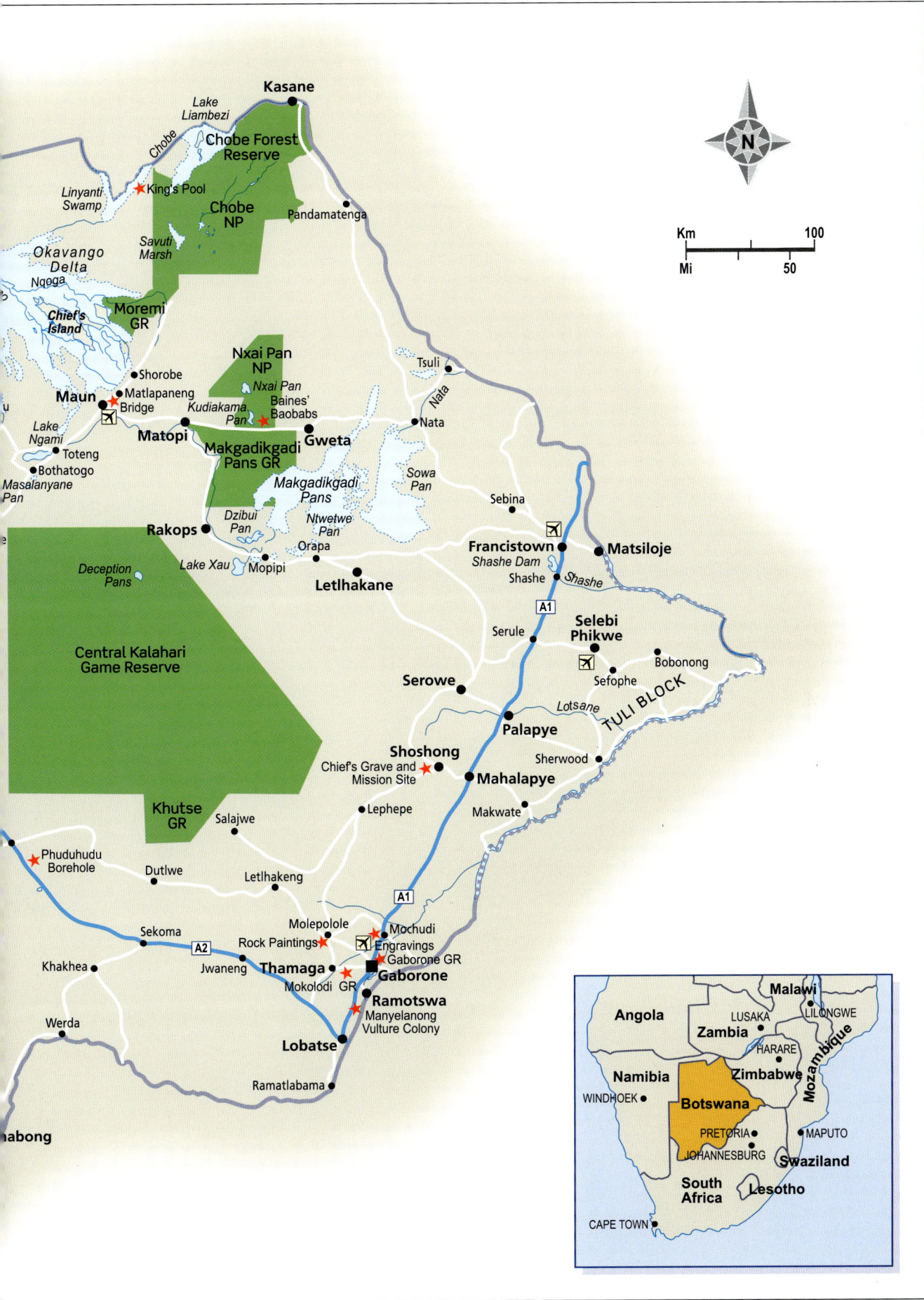

Kasane

Lake
Liambezi

Chobe Forest
Reserve

Chobe

Linyanti
Swamp

King's Pool

Chobe
NP

Pandamatenga

Okavango
Delta

Nqoga

Savuti
Marsh

Chief's
Island

Moremi
GR

Nxai Pan
NP

Tsuli

Nata

Shorobe

Matlapaneng
Bridge

Nxai Pan

Baines'
Baobabs

Nata

Maun

Kudiakama
Pan

Lake
Ngami

Matopi

Gweta

Toteng

Makgadikgadi
Pans GR

Sowa
Pan

Bothatogo

Masalanyane
Pan

Makgadikgadi
Pans

Sebina

Rakops

Dzibui
Pan

Ntwetwe
Pan

Deception
Pans

Lake Xau

Mopipi

Orapa

Letlhakane

Francistown

Matsiloje

Shashe Dam

Shashe

Shashe

A1

Serule

Selebi
Phikwe

Central Kalahari
Game Reserve

Serowe

Bobonong

Sefophe

TULI BLOCK

Lotsane

Palapye

Shoshong

Sherwood

Chief's Grave and
Mission Site

Mahalapye

Makwate

Khutse
GR

Salajwe

Lephepe

Phuduhudu
Borehole

Dutlwe

Letlhakeng

A1

Molepolole

Mochudi

Sekoma

Rock Paintings

Engravings

A2

Gaborone GR

Khakhea

Jwaneng

Thamaga

Gaborone

Werda

Mokolodi GR

Ramotswa

Manyelanong
Vulture Colony

Lobatse

Ramatlabama

abong

Km   100
Mi   50

N

Angola

Malawi

LUSAKA

LILONGWE

Zambia

HARARE

Namibia

Zimbabwe

WINDHOEK

Botswana

Mozambique

PRETORIA

MAPUTO

JOHANNESBURG

Swaziland

South
Africa

Lesotho

CAPE TOWN

179

Zimbabwe

Zimbabwe is best known for its great ruins (which date back to the 11th century) and the thunderous Victoria Falls, but it also has its fair share of adventure activities, national parks and wildlife areas.

Top Town

Once known as the most 'African' of the continent's principal cities, Harare has gone through a number of years of desperate social and economic turmoil. It still serves as the centre for the country's once-acclaimed arts and crafts industry.

Five Big Attractions

• The Zimbabwe Ruins are this country's most significant legacy, their majestic stone-walled enclosures making the medieval site one of the most impressive in Africa south of the Sahara.
• Zambezi National Park extends over 56,000ha and offers abundant wildlife.
• Victoria Falls (aka Mosi-oa-Tunya, 'the smoke that thunders') is one of Africa's great natural wonders and a source of numerous thrilling adventure activities.
• Hwange National Park is conveniently situated near to Victoria Falls; its 10-Mile Drive is a dependable and popular two-hour trip that should yield good wildlife-viewing.
• Mana Pools National Park is a World Heritage Site that is popular with fishing enthusiasts as well as wildlife spotters; it offers a wide range of accommodation options.

Five Big Facts

• The Matobo Hills is the final resting place of mining pioneer Cecil John Rhodes (at a spot known as View of the World), and the area is home to one of the most astounding collections of indigenous rock art in the world.
• The Zambezi River's waters are not always easy to navigate when the river is either extremely high or low. Its most popular trip is the three-day 65km whitewater trail from Kazungula to Victoria Falls' Big Tree.
• Chimanimani National Park is Zimbabwe's most popular hiking destination, with the Chimanimani mountain range towering up to heights of around 2200m; the highest peak at Mount Binga tops out at 2436m.
• Lake Kariba is Africa's third largest artificial body of water; its massive dam wall spans a perimeter of 579m and is 24m thick at the base and 128m high.
• The Zambezi River gorge bungee jump is an awesome 110m high, one of Africa's highest bridge leaps.

FACTS AND FIGURES
Area:
  390,580km² / 150,800mi²
Population:
  12.3 million
Main ethnic groups:
  Shona (71%), Ndebele (16%)
  White (1.5%), Asian (0.5%)
Main languages:
  English, Shona
  Ndebele
Main religions:
  Syncretic (combination Christian/
  traditional beliefs) (50%)
  Christian (26%)
  Traditional beliefs (24%)
Currency:
  Zimbabwean dollar (100 cents)

TEN GREAT ADVENTURES
1 Whitewater rafting
2 Bungee jumping
3 Fishing
4 Game-viewing
5 Houseboating
6 Hiking
7 Horse riding
8 Elephant-back safaris
9 Scenic flights
10 Canoeing

FAUNA/AVIFAUNA
1 Eland
2 Sable Antelope
3 Roan Antelope
4 Klipspringer
5 African Elephant
6 Black Rhino
7 Buffalo
8 Kudu
9 Sharpe's Grysbok
10 Tsessebe
11 Warthog
12 Lichtenstein's Hartebeest
13 Zebra
14 Giraffe
15 Nyala
16 Leopard
17 Otter
18 Waterbuck
19 Wildebeest
20 Rock Dassie
21 Gurney's Sugarbird
22 Malachite Sunbird
23 Rare Hooded Vulture
24 Pel's Fishing Owl
25 Silverycheeked Hornbill
26 Mashona Hyliota
27 Yellowbellied Sunbird
28 Verreaux's (Black) Eagle

MAIN CONTACT DETAILS
Zimbabwe Tourism:
  09263 4 758 730/4
  info@ztazim.co.zw
  www.zimbabwetourism.co.zw
Parks and Wildlife Management Authority:
  09263 4 706 077/8
  natprks@africaonline.co.zw
  www.zimbabwetourism.co.zw

Zambezi

Sapi
Safari Area

Kanyemba

Dande
Safari Area

Mana Pools
NP

Chirundu

Hurungwe
Safari Area

Chewore
Safari Area

Hunyani

Mukumbura

Makuti

Charara
Safari Area

Doma Safari
Area

Muzarabani

Kariba

Lake Kariba
Recreational Park

Angwa

A1

Karoi

Centenary

Mt Darwin

Mazowe

Portuguese
Forts

Lake
Kariba

Matusadona
NP

Magunje

Mhangura

Unfurudzi
Safari Area

Nyamapanda

Chete
afari Area

Chinhoyi Caves
National Park

Bindura

Katiyo

ke Kariba
creational
Park

Sanyati

Chinhoyi

Mazowe

Paradise
Pools

A2

Ruenya

izarira
NP

Ume

Umfuli
Recreational
Park

Lake Manyame
Recreational
Park

Murewa

Regina Coeli

Chirisa Safari
Area

Hartley
Safari Area

Harare

Chitungwiza

Lake Chivero
Recreational
Park

Fossil
Sites

Umsweswe

Chegutu

Marondera

A3

Nyanga
NP

Lutope

Kadoma

Juliasdale

Ngezi Dam
Recreational
Park

A4

Odzani
Falls

A5

Kwekwe

Sebakwe Dam
Recreational Park

Chivhu

Mutare

Bunga Forest
Botanical Reserve

Fort
Ingwenya

A8

Vungu

A17

Mvuma

Muchuchu
Ruins

Save

A9

Gweru

Shurugwi

A4

Muzhwi
Dam

Odzi Gorge

Chimanimani

A5

Robert Moffat's
Mission

Nalatale
Ruins

Nyika

Chimanimani
NP

Kame
Ruins

Dhlo Dhlo
Ruins

Mushandike
Sanctuary

Masvingo

A9

Chibvumani
Ruins

Chipinge
Safari Area

Chipinge

Bulawayo

Umzingwane
Recreational Park

Lake Cunningham
Recreational Park

Mutirikwi
Recreational Park

White Rhino
Shelter

umtree

A7

Zvishavane

A9

Great Zimbabwe
National Monument

Chirinda Forest
Botanical Reserve

Cecil Rhodes
Grave

Matobo
NP

Manjirenji
Recreational Park

Gwanda

Ngundu

Bangala Dam
Recreational Park

Insiza

Mchela
Cave

Bubiana

Manyuchi
Dam

Runde

Chiredzi

Simukwe

A6

Mzingwane

Shashe

Mwenezi

A4

Mwenezi

Bengi
Spring

Chilojo
Cliffs

mley

Tuli
Safari
Area

Pioneer
Memorial

Giraffe
Petroglyph

Bubye

Chipise
Hot Spring

Gonarezhou
NP

Malapati
Safari
Area

Beitbridge

Limpopo

Mozambique

Larger than France and Great Britain combined, Mozambique is a relatively flat land with an altitude average of around 350m high, but as a tourist destination, its star shines brightly – particularly along its 2500km coastline. The country is crossed by a multitude of rivers and mountains, fostering varied vegetation that encourages hiking, walking, canoeing and rafting.

Top Town

Formerly known as Lourenço Marques, Maputo is a lively port city criss-crossed by palm-fringed avenues that also bristle with Jacarandas and Flame Trees. The city nurtures a vibrant nightlife, along with evening markets and a brightly-lit seafront. It has a number of historic Portuguese forts as well as the fascinating Museum of the Revolution.

Five Big Attractions

• Mozambique Island – stretching just 2500m in length and at its widest point measuring just 600m – has a rich seafaring history and architectural heritage, having served Portuguese and Arab fleets for centuries.
• Recovering Gorongosa National Park fosters its wildlife in a setting of grassland, woodland, dense palmveld and fever tree forests lining seasonal pans.
• Inhaca Island lies around 24km away from the mainland; beautiful beaches lined with brightly coloured offshore reefs are fringed with stands of Mango Trees.
• The Maputo Game Reserve (aka Maputo Elephant Reserve) has good elephant numbers and a wealth of bird and marine life. It is an important breeding ground for the Leatherback Turtles that weigh in at 646kg and come to lay 1000 eggs each season.
• The Bazaruto Archipelago is a chain of tiny islands that lie 20km off the Mozambique Coast and offer a unique and isolated ecosystem with near-pristine warm-water diving conditions.

Five Big Facts

• The 3000km long Zambezi River empties into the Indian Ocean at the Zambezi Delta, which spans 100km and is home to big game such as Elephant, Buffalo, Rhino and Roan Antelope.
• The Dona Ana Bridge is Africa's longest railway bridge, spanning 3.7km over the Zambezi River.
• Mount Binga in the Chimanimani mountain range is the highest point in Mozambique, rising to a height of 2436m.
• The Inhambane area is home to two million Coconut Palms; the town, characterised by its hundreds of dhows, offers a fascinating glimpse back in time.
• The Cahora Bassa dam is one of Africa's largest civil engineering projects – and one of the largest dams on earth, shoring the waters of Lake Cahora Bassa, a monstrous 270km in length.

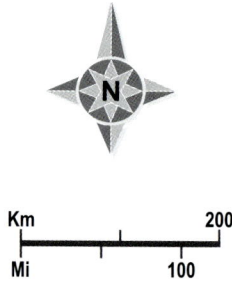

Km   200
Mi   100

FACTS AND FIGURES
Capital:
  Maputo
Area:
  799,380km² / 308,642mi²
Population:
  19.6 million
Main ethnic groups:
  Makua-Lomwe (47%)
  Tsonga (23%)
  Malawi (12%)
Main language:
  Portuguese
Main religions:
  Traditional beliefs (60%)
  Christian (30%)
  Muslim (10%)
Currency:
  Metical (100 centavos)

TEN GREAT ADVENTURES
1 Scuba diving
2 Dolphin safaris
3 Sailing
4 Game fishing
5 4x4 territory
6 Horse riding
7 Quadbiking
8 Microlighting
9 Water-skiing
10 Sea kayaking

FAUNA/FLORA
1 African Elephant
2 Lion
3 Leopard
4 Cheetah
5 Hippopotamus
6 Buffalo
7 Antelope sp.
8 Blue Niassa Wildebeest
9 Burchell's Zebra
10 Nile Crocodile
11 Leatherback Turtle
12 Dugong
13 Dolphin sp.
14 Whale sp.
15 Cashew Nut Tree
16 Mango Tree
17 Coconut Palm

MAIN CONTACT DETAILS
Ministry of Tourism, Mozambique:
  09258 1 307 320/3
  info@futur.org.com
  www.futur.org.mz

Namuiranga

Rovuma

Mocímboa da Praia

Negomane

Manda
Wilderness

**Niassa
GR**

Mecula

Mueda

Cóbuè

Sanga Community
Wildlife Project

Lake Malawi

Messalo

Sunate

Pemba

Quinta Capricórnio
Permaculture Farm

Marrupa

Montepuez

Baia de Memba

Lichinga

Lugenda

Lúrio

Fernão Veloso

Cassacatiza

Mualádzi

Mandimba

*Lagoa
Amaramba*

Ribáué

Namialo

*Mozambique
Island*
Mozambique

Lisula

Cuamba

Rock Paintings

Nampula

Fingoé

*Cahora
Bassa Dam*

Zóbuè

Alto Molócuè

Miruro

Boroma
Mission

103

Milange

**Gili
Reserve**

Angoche

Magoé

Tete

Ruins of Massangano
Citadel (1730-1870)

Chiramba

Mocuba

Changara

Zambezi

Mont
Morrumbala

Pebane

102

Canxixe

Dona Ana
Bridge

Grave of Mary
Moffat Livingstone

Quelimane

Inhamitanga

Gorongosa

**Gorongosa
NP**

**Marromeu
GR**

Chimoio

EN6

Dondo

Mount Binga

Beira

Espungabera

Ruins of
Fortress (1501)

I N D I A N   O C E A N

EN1

Ancient Dhow
Anchorage

Save

**Bazaruto
NP**

*Bazaruto
Island*

**Zinave
NP**

Pambarra

Chicualacuala

**Banhine
NP**

Mapai

**Great Limpopo
Transfrontier
Reserve**

Homoíne

**Limpopo
Park**

Inharrime

Lagoa Dongane

*Massingir
Dam*

Jantigué

Lagoa Poelela

Macarretane

Lagoa Quissico

Limpopo Flats

Lagoa Nhanzume

Ressano
Garcia

EN1

EN4

Baia de Maputo

Maputo

Namaacha

Inhaca Island

**Maputo
Elephant
Reserve**

Migrating
Elephants

Ponta do Ouro

Photographic credits

www.imagesofafrica.co.za

IMAGES OF AFRICA
PHOTO LIBRARY

All photography courtesy of Images of Africa (IOA), with the exception of those supplied by the following photographers and/or their agencies as listed below:

Cover
- MARTIN HARVEY

1
- SHAEN ADEY / IOA

2/3
- HEIN VON HÖRSTEN / IOA

8/9
- HEIN VON HÖRSTEN / IOA

12
- SHAEN ADEY / IOA
- CHANAN WEISS / IOA

14
- LEONARD HOFFMANN / IOA
- LANZ VON HÖRSTEN / IOA

16
- LEONARD HOFFMANN / IOA
- HEIN VON HÖRSTEN / IOA

18
- GERHARD DREYER / IOA
- COLOUR LIBRARY / IOA

20
- HEIN VON HÖRSTEN / IOA
- HEIN VON HÖRSTEN / IOA

22
- GERHARD DREYER / IOA
- SHAEN ADEY / IOA

24
- LANZ VON HÖRSTEN / IOA
- LANZ VON HÖRSTEN / IOA

26
- ROGER DE LA HARPE / IOA
- WALTER KNIRR / IOA

28
- WALTER KNIRR / IOA
- LANZ VON HÖRSTEN / IOA

30
- SHAEN ADEY / IOA
- CHANAN WEISS / IOA

32
- SHAEN ADEY / IOA
- GERHARD DREYER / IOA

34
- PETER PICKFORD / IOA
- NIGEL J DENNIS / IOA

36
- GERHARD DREYER / IOA
- SHAEN ADEY / IOA

38
- SHAEN ADEY / IOA
- LANZ VON HÖRSTEN / IOA
- PETER PICKFORD / IOA

40
- MARTIN HARVEY / IOA
- CHANAN WEISS / IOA

42
- MARTIN HARVEY / IOA
- NIGEL J DENNIS / IOA

44
- COLOUR LIBRARY / IOA
- RITA MEYER / IOA

46
- ANDREW BANNISTER / IOA
- HEIN VON HÖRSTEN / IOA

48
- LEONARD HOFFMANN / IOA
- PHILIP PERRY / IOA
- ARIADNE VAN ZANDBERGEN / IOA

50
- HEIN VON HÖRSTEN / IOA
- ARIADNE VAN ZANDBERGEN / IOA

52
- HEIN VON HÖRSTEN / IOA
- WALTER KNIRR / IOA

54
- SHAEN ADEY / IOA
- ALBERT FRONEMAN / IOA

56
- GERALD CUBITT
- WALTER KNIRR / IOA

58
- HEIN VON HÖRSTEN / IOA
- SAM J BASCH / IOA

60
- NIGEL J DENNIS / IOA
- HEIN VON HÖRSTEN / IOA

62
- HEIN VON HÖRSTEN / IOA
- DARYL & SHARNA BALFOUR / IOA
- KRISTO PIENAAR / IOA

64
- WALTER KNIRR / IOA
- SHAEN ADEY / IOA

66
- NIGEL J DENNIS / IOA
- ROGER DE LA HARPE / IOA

68
- WENDY DENNIS / IOA
- WALTER KNIRR / IOA

70
- COLOUR LIBRARY / IOA
- ANDREW WOODBURN / IOA
  www.woodburnphoto.co.za

72
- SHAEN ADEY / IOA
- HEIN VON HÖRSTEN / IOA
74
- WALTER KNIRR / IOA
- WALTER KNIRR / IOA

76
- SHAEN ADEY / IOA
- SHAEN ADEY / IOA

78
- KARL BEATH / IOA
- WALTER KNIRR / IOA

82
- SHAEN ADEY / IOA
- SHAEN ADEY / IOA

84
- PETER PICKFORD / IOA
- ARIADNE VAN ZANDBERGEN / IOA

86
- WALTER KNIRR / IOA
- NIGEL J DENNIS / IOA

88
- ROGER DE LA HARPE / IOA
- PETER PICKFORD / IOA
- MARTIN HARVEY / IOA
- PETER PICKFORD / IOA

90
- WALTER KNIRR / IOA
- NIGEL J DENNIS / IOA

92
- HEIN VON HÖRSTEN / IOA
- HEIN VON HÖRSTEN / IOA

94
- SAM J BASCH / IOA
- ROGER DE LA HARPE / IOA

96
- NIGEL J DENNIS / IOA
- NIGEL J DENNIS / IOA
- NIGEL J DENNIS / IOA
- NIGEL J DENNIS / IOA

98
- NIGEL J DENNIS / IOA

100
- ARIADNE VAN ZANDBERGEN / IOA
- ARIADNE VAN ZANDBERGEN / IOA

102
- MARTIN HARVEY / IOA
- ROGER DE LA HARPE / AFRICAIMAGERY

104
- WENDY DENNIS / AFRICAIMAGERY
- GERALD CUBITT

106
- PETER & BEVERLY PICKFORD / IOA
- KARL BEATH / IOA
- NIGEL J DENNIS / IOA

108
- PHILIP VAN DEN BERG / AFRICAIMAGERY
- ROGER DE LA HARPE / AFRICAIMAGERY

110
- PETER & BEVERLY PICKFORD / IOA
- SHAEN ADEY / IOA

112
- PETER PICKFORD / IOA
- NIGEL J DENNIS / IOA
- SAM J BASCH / IOA
- ARIADNE VAN ZANDBERGEN / IOA

114
- NIGEL J DENNIS / IOA
- KEITH BEGG / IOA
- GERHARD DREYER / IOA
- NIGEL J DENNIS / IOA

116
- NIGEL J DENNIS / IOA

118
- ROGER DE LA HARPE / AFRICAIMAGERY
- WALTER KNIRR / IOA

120
- WALTER KNIRR / IOA
- WALTER KNIRR / IOA

122
- STEVE WOODHALL / IOA
- WALTER KNIRR / IOA

124
- SAM J BASCH / IOA
- FRIEDRICH VON HORSTEN / IOA

126
- WALTER KNIRR / IOA
- ARIADNE VAN ZANDBERGEN / IOA
- PETER & BEVERLY PICKFORD / IOA

128
- NIGEL J DENNIS / IOA
- SHAEN ADEY / IOA

130
- MARTIN HARVEY / IOA
- NIGEL J DENNIS / IOA

132
- MAGGIE WESTROP / IOA
- MARTIN HARVEY / IOA

134
- ALBERT FRONEMAN / IOA
- DARYL & SHARNA BALFOUR / IOA
- NIGEL J DENNIS / IOA
- NIGEL J DENNIS / IOA

Atlas of National Parks and Reserves of South Africa

ISBN (10 digit) 1-86809-842-7
ISBN (13 digit) 978-1-86809-842-2

Map Studio
(a division of New Holland Publishing (South Africa) (Pty) Ltd)

New Holland Publishing is a member of Johnnic Communications Ltd

Visit us at www.mapstudio.co.za
Sharecall in South Africa on 0860-10-50-50

Visit our sales offices and showrooms in Johannesburg
7 Wessel Road, Rivonia, Telephone (011) 807-2292

CAPE TOWN
Unit 7, M5 Freeway Park (Off Black River Parkway), Maitland, Telephone (021) 510-4311

DURBAN
Suite 3, Sinembe Business Park, 8 Sinembe Crescent, La Lucia Ridge, Telephone (031) 566-2448

This edition first published in 2006 by Map Studio

80 McKenzie Street, Cape Town
PO Box 1144, Cape Town, 8000
Telephone (021) 462-4360

Author - Mariëlle Renssen
Designer - Peter Bosman
'Other countries' text - Simon Lewis, simon@theball.co.za

Production Manager - John Loubser
Project Manager - Elaine Fick
Senior Cartographer - Ryan Africa
Junior Cartographer - Randall Watson
Researcher - Deniellé Lategan

Photography © 2006 as credited opposite
Maps and map database © 2006 Map Studio
Text © 2006 Map Studio
Illustrations © 2006 Struik Publishers

Special thanks to
www.imagesofafrica.co.za for use of photographs

Reproduction by - Resolution Colours (Pty) Ltd, Cape Town
Printed and bound by - SNP Leefung Printers Limited, China

Ook in Afrikaans beskikbaar
Atlas van Nationale Parke en Reservate van Suid-Afrika
ISBN (10 digit) 1-86809-873-7
ISBN (13 digit) 978-1-89809-873-6

Index

This index refers to the entries that appear in the Touring map section (pp140 – 163). Park names appear in **bold**. Towns appearing in the Street map section (pp164 – 171) appear in *italic*. Refer to the Contents and Quickfinder (pp4 – 5) for further information regarding the individual parks.

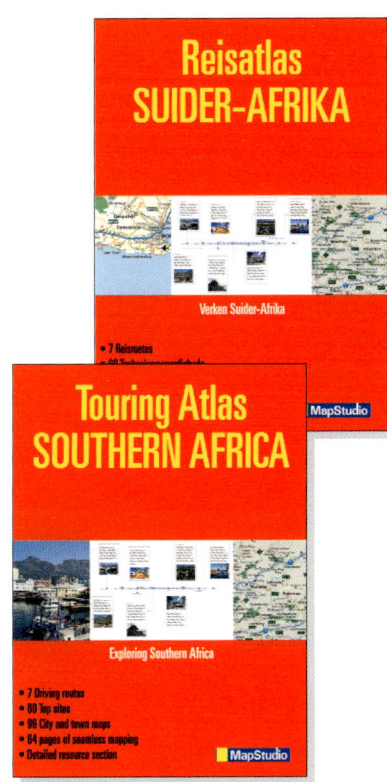

Other products in the series

Touring Atlas of Southern Africa
Reisatlas Suider-Afrika

Edition: 1st
Format: Softcover
Pages: 208
Size: 195 x 275mm
English ISBN: 1 86809 807 9
Afrikaans ISBN: 1 86809 814 1

Coverage:
South Africa (including Swaziland & Lesotho), Namibia, Botswana, Zimbabwe and Mozambique

This pictorial journey of Southern Africa divides the region into 7 major driving routes. Each driving route opens with a pictorial spread containing a strip map showing distances and places along the route. Beautiful images show the reader the visual journey they are about to drive. Following this, the route is split into smaller, more detailed sections covering areas of interest along the route. 20 sites of special interest are highlighted in more detail with images or maps.

The Town Plans section has over 100 city and town maps, covering all the capital cities and important towns along the route.

The Main Map section has 64 pages of seamless mapping covering the entire Southern African Region at a scale of 1,5 million.

The Resources section has 11 pages of contact details and listings of tour operators and tourist authorities.

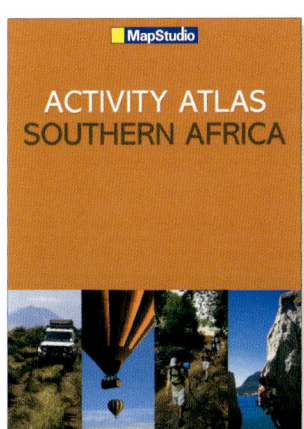

Activity Atlas Southern Africa

Edition: 1st
Format: Softcover
Pages: 208
Size: 195 x 275mm
ISBN: 1 86809 758 7

Coverage:
South Africa (including Swaziland & Lesotho), Namibia, Botswana, Zimbabwe and Mozambique

An informative reference atlas to Southern African activities of all kinds. Includes history, cities, natural wonders, wildlife and activities of the region. A selection of 20 city plans and detailed mapping of the region, specific sites and countries covered.

Other MapStudio Atlases

Southern Africa Road Atlas
South Africa Road Atlas
South Africa Road Atlas Glovebox Edition
South Africa Pocket Road Atlas
Eastern Cape Tourist Atlas
KwaZulu-Natal Tourist Atlas
Mpumalanga Tourist Atlas
Namibia Tourist Atlas
Touristenatlas Namibia (German)
Western Cape Tourist Atlas
Garden Route Visitors Guide
Cape Peninsula Visitors Guide
Kruger National Park Visitors Guide
World Atlas
Compact World Atlas
Pocket Atlas of Flags of the World
For full details visit www.mapstudio.co.za